Quiet Revolution in Welfare Economics

Quiet Revolution in Welfare Economics

Robin Hahnel
Michael Albert

Princeton University Press
Princeton, New Jersey

Copyright © 1990 by Princeton University Press
Published by Princeton University Press,
41 William Street, Princeton, New Jersey
In the United Kingdom: Princeton University Press, Oxford

All Rights Reserved

Library of Congress Cataloging-in-Publication Data

Hahnel, Robin.
Quiet revolution in welfare economics / Robin Hahnel and Michael Albert
p. cm.
ISBN 0-691-04252-7
1. Welfare economics.   I. Albert, Michael, 1947- . II. Title.
HB846.H34 1989   89-10995 CIP

This book has been composed in Times Roman

Princeton University Press books are printed on acid-free paper, and meet the
guidelines for permanence and durability of the Committee on Production Guidelines
for Book Longevity of the Council on Library Resources

Printed in the United States of America
by Princeton University Press, Princeton, New Jersey

10 9 8 7 6 5 4 3 2 1

Excerpts from the following were printed by permission: Samuel Bowles, "The
Production Process in a Competitive Economy: Walrasian, Neo-Hobbesian, and Marx-
ian Models," *American Economic Review*, March 1985, Vol. 75, No. 1; Arthur
DiQuattro, "Alienation and Justice in the Market," *The American Political Science
Review*, Vol. 72; E. K. Hunt, "A Radical Critique of Welfare Economics," in *Growth,
Profits, and Property*, edited by Edward Nell, copyright © 1980, reprinted by permis-
sion of Cambridge University Press; Robert Pollack, "Habit Formation and Long-Run
Utility Functions," *Journal of Economic Theory*, 1976, No. 13; Robert Pollack,
"Changes in Consumer Preferences: Endogenous Tastes in Demand and Welfare
Analysis," *American Economic Review*, May 1978, Vol. 68., No. 2; John Rawls, *A
Theory of Justice*, copyright © 1971 by the President and Fellows of Harvard College,
published by Belknap Press of Harvard University, reprinted by permission of the
Harvard University Press; Carl Christian von Weizsacker, "Notes on Endogenous
Change of Tastes," *Journal of Economic Theory*, 1971, No. 3.

CONTENTS

PART ONE
Limits of Traditional Welfare Theory

PART TWO
A New Welfare Theory

PART THREE
New Results

CONTENTS

THEOREMS

FIGURES

ACKNOWLEDGMENTS

There is no way to acknowledge all the "webs of connection" that morally bind our efforts in writing this book to the labors of countless others. We take this opportunity to thank only a few whose "strands" are impossible to detect by reading the book itself.

Virginia Barker's diligence and speed in copy editing were deeply appreciated, as were the efforts of our editor Jack Repcheck to ease the publishing process. These members of Princeton University Press made what could have been an onerous relationship delightful.

A decade of graduate students at The American University provided an invaluable sounding board for many of the ideas expressed, but in particular Shi Zhengfu, Joseph Rozansky, and Gao Hong detected numerous errors and provided detailed suggestions.

Years of experience at South End Press, with *Z Magazine*, and in diverse projects seeking to understand society in order to improve it have been fundamental to developing the ideas in this book.

The long-suffering patience of Ivy Hahnel and the four young Hahnels, Jesse, Ilana, Sara, and Tanya, as well as the flexible structure of South End Press and *Z Magazine* were critical to finding the time and energy needed to finish a book like this.

Quiet Revolution in Welfare Economics

INTRODUCTION

> Was it not only the timidity of an age which had lost all confidence in ultimate values which led us to attempt to claim scientific justification for attitudes which in the nature of things could not be justified (or refuted) by appeal to laboratory methods?
>
> —Lionel Robbins, *An Essay on the Nature and Significance of Economic Science*

ESTABLISHED ORDERS, be they social or intellectual, often acquire an aura of permanence beyond what is warranted by the facts. All too often incongruities go unnoticed longer than is reasonable, and what is obvious in retrospect eludes inhabitants of crumbling orders. Hence the logic of heeding the cries of heretics, even though most tremors they report are due to faulty seismographic equipment. But as John Stuart Mill remarked, what harm can come to a self-confident majority from granting an audience to heretical prophesies in hopes of uncovering a rare truth?[1]

0.1 The Unnoticed Crisis

We admit to heresy. In this book we argue that traditional welfare theory has little more to teach us, that the traditional welfare paradigm has become an obstacle to progress on most important frontiers of welfare economics, and that a new welfare paradigm is ready to yield substantive new results. In other words, we argue that traditional welfare theory is in crisis, and a "quiet revolution" in welfare economics is already under way. Refinement of the relationship between competitive equilibria and Pareto efficient allocations has entered the region of diminishing returns.

Traditional theorists have every reason to be proud of their work to isolate the minimal assumptions necessary to justify Adam Smith's two-hundred-year-old vision that it is as if competitive markets are guided by an "invisible hand" to yield social efficiency even though economic actors neither conceive nor pursue this goal. But this task is largely accomplished, and there is no need to quibble over when diminishing returns set in. The important point is that one of the few remaining frontiers of welfare economics which proves tractable to traditional approaches is the extension of familiar conclusions to situations involving uncertainty. Without demeaning important recent work in this area, we believe the final touches are already foreseeable, and few "surprises" remain to be uncovered.[2]

In other areas of ongoing research in welfare economics, the traditional paradigm no longer helps researchers define problems and uncover solutions. In many respects the traditional paradigm impedes progress. As we will see in part 1, the traditional paradigm has thwarted, rather than facilitated, advances in analyses of the labor process, externalities, public goods, preference development, and institutional structures. The traditional misconception of labor as an input indistinguishable from other production inputs yields questionable analyses of the efficiency of private enterprise production and hinders investigations in the economics of discrimination. The traditional presumption of "external effect exceptionality" not only biases evaluation of market institutions, but hinders development of "incentive compatible" mechanisms for solving the "free rider problem." And the traditional injunction not to question the origins of preference orderings frustrates a coherent analysis of the logic of preference development as well as an understanding of the relation between economic institutions and patterns of preference development.

Yet a different paradigm can facilitate progress along many of these frontiers that have proved intractable to traditional methods. By elaborating a conception of people as conscious, social beings who develop capacities and needs based on innate potentials as a result of the activities they engage in, we are able to clarify and consolidate important recent advances of others as well as derive new results of our own. In part 2 we develop the new paradigm and the "New Welfare Theory" based on it, and in part 3 we present "New Results" derived with the new theory. We show how the "conflict theory of the firm" and previous analyses of externalities and endogenous preferences can be fortified by using the new welfare theory. And we present substantive new critiques of markets, private enterprise, and central planning that challenge traditional conclusions. We also contribute to the theory of comparative economic systems by revealing fundamental properties of private enterprise market economies, public enterprise market economies, and public enterprise centrally planned economies ignored in traditional analyses.

Why has the current "crisis" in welfare economics gone largely unnoted? And why do we feel the situation is ripe for change?

Much work on the frontiers of welfare theory that casts doubt on the further usefulness of the traditional paradigm is highly technical and inaccessible even to professional economists. Not so long ago differential calculus was sufficient for perusing journal articles on welfare theory. By the early 1970s familiarity with convex set theory and fixed point theorems was necessary to follow critical developments in welfare theory. But a glance at the literature on endogenous preferences in the *Journal of Economic Theory*, iterative planning mechanisms in *Econometrica*, or incentive compatible mechanisms in the *Review of Economic Studies* reveals that the investment in mathematical tools necessary to follow recent developments in welfare theory has been raised another notch.

The relationship between welfare theory and the rest of economics has also become increasingly schizophrenic. Those results that refine and bolster the traditional economic paradigm relating competitive equilibria and Pareto allocations have, for the most part, been effectively communicated by welfare theorists through survey articles[3] in the *American Economic Review* and *Journal of Economic Literature*, and in mathematical economic texts.[4] And these refinements have been absorbed by the rest of the profession in graduate microeconomics curricula. But to a great extent the unsettling work on the frontiers of welfare theory has not been effectively brought to the attention of those outside the tiny elite of practicing theorists. And when work in areas such as endogenous preferences and incentive compatible mechanisms has been presented to the profession at large, the discussions have frequently emphasized only aspects that can be readily interpreted within the traditional paradigm.[5]

Those working on different frontiers of welfare theory have communicated little. Separate pieces of work remain isolated gems, unrelated to one another or to an overall critique of the traditional welfare paradigm. This is partly because of the incredible division of labor that exists even within this single area of economic theory and partly because most contributors do not see their work in a critical light and are not looking for critical connections.

Finally, political divisions have delayed a comprehensive reappraisal of traditional welfare theory. Although most of the unsettling work has been done by highly respected economists well within the mainstream of the profession, some innovations have been developed by "radical" economists. Since the profession falls far short of achieving the optimal degree of cross-fertilization between its mainstream and radical components, radical and mainstream theorists alike have remained ignorant of important work by those in different political quarters.

Beyond detecting an "unnoticed crisis," we are optimistic that a change in paradigm can break the log jam. Much current work on the frontiers of welfare theory requires a new view of people and society adequate to formulate problems it addresses and envision directions to proceed. This "pressure from within" is very different from "pressure from without." After all, the traditional welfare paradigm has not gone unchallenged. William Morris, Peter Kropotkin, Karl Marx, and Thorstein Veblen each presented a plausible case that the traditional conception of "economic man" inherited from Adam Smith precluded addressing important issues they wished to examine. Likewise, most modern psychologists and sociologists reject the view of human behavior envisioned in the traditional economic paradigm as ill-suited to defining and addressing the problems that concern them.

These challenges were not compelling for traditional welfare theorists because they were premised on different priorities and concerns than those operative in the economic mainstream. The traditional paradigm might have lost its appeal to outsiders, but its primary users were content because their model of "economic man" was invaluable for their purpose: studying the logic of individual rational choice in a particular social context. Challenges were not compelling as long as economists saw many remaining solvable problems in the theory of individual rational choice in the traditional social context and no means for solving problems of individual rational choice in more complex, albeit realistic, contexts.

These conditions that sustained the traditional paradigm no longer pertain. Not only is the work of unraveling the nonintuitive logic of rational choice in the traditional context largely complete, welfare theory "puzzle-solving" has led to a growing list of "anomalies" and "dead ends" that cannot be productively addressed within the traditional framework. Many remaining problems in welfare theory, such as preference development, incentive compatible mechanisms, the labor process, externalities, public goods, and social choice, fail to yield to familiar welfare assumptions and approaches. Moreover, in some cases conceptualizing new settings and reformulating questions is nearly impossible under the spell of the old paradigm. It is as if the traditional paradigm were a fence that once served the useful purpose of keeping welfare theorists from wandering outside a zone of rich oil reserves exploitable with existing technology. But now, instead of turning theorists away from barren rock and back toward high-expectation drillings, the fence is keeping welfare theorists drilling in an area already pumped dry and preventing them from exploiting solar energy with newly available technology.[6]

0.2 Our Argument

In chapter 1 we review traditional welfare theory. We trace its evolution from classical utilitarianism to modern neoclassical welfare theory and discuss recent contractarian interpretations. But while we distinguish between utilitarian, neoclassical, and contractarian formulations and compare their advantages and disadvantages, our major purpose is to understand the essential features of traditional welfare theory as a whole and identify the paradigm it seeks to represent.

In chapters 2, 3, and 4 we discuss specific failures of traditional welfare theory. Our criticism is not that a particular formulation of traditional welfare theory imperfectly represents the traditional paradigm. We argue that the traditional welfare paradigm itself is incapable of posing important questions and defining the concepts necessary for answering them and has become an obstacle to progress.

In chapter 2 we show how the traditional concept of the production function has obfuscated important effects of private enterprise on the labor process. We review challenges from the "conflict school" and "segmented labor market" traditions to standard conclusions that profit maximization in competitive environments promotes social efficiency and ameliorates economic discrimination. We conclude that despite much confusion and inconsistency the thrust of these challenges is sound.

In chapter 3 we review criticism of the traditional treatment of externalities and public goods and the exciting literature on "incentive compatible mechanisms" for solving the "free rider problem." We conclude that the unwarranted presumption of "external effect exceptionality" that is buried in the traditional paradigm must bear part of the blame for retarding theoretical progress in the field of public finance as well as for inducing fundamental misconceptions regarding the efficiency of markets.

In chapter 4 we evaluate the work of those few economists who dared to ignore the traditional taboo against inquiring into the origins of preferences and evaluate the decision of traditional theorists to ignore the effect of economic institutions on preference development. We reveal considerable disagreement among previous analysts about the ultimate significance of treating preferences as endogenous and discover that institutionalist economists have had virtually no influence on welfare theorists regarding the impact of institutions on preferences. In this chapter we complete our case that progress in pursuing important tasks facing welfare theory today has been hampered rather than aided by the traditional paradigm and lay the groundwork for our own major innovation: clarification of the welfare significance of the relation between economic institutions and preference development.

In chapter 5 we begin to replace the traditional paradigm with a new one that emphasizes human development, human sociality, and the structuring of individual choice by economic institutions.

In chapter 6 we present a new welfare theory based on the alternative paradigm. Using an original model of human development and endogenous preferences, we present a set of theorems that reveal an important mechanism whereby individual rationality proves counterproductive to social rationality. But while these striking new results do not hinge on any specific assumptions about preferences other than their endogeneity, we also elaborate a qualitative welfare theory that addresses fundamental philosophical issues.

In chapter 7 we use the new welfare theory to reevaluate markets. Adam Smith's vision of markets as cybernetic/incentive miracles is not sustained by our new welfare paradigm and theory. Instead new analysis suggests that "market failure" is likely to be far more pervasive than usually admitted and the cybernetic and incentive properties of markets compound the problem. Moreover, the argument in this chapter proves that once it is recognized that preferences are endogenous, the extent of the damage from "market failures" is greater than traditional theory leads one to suspect.

In chapter 8 we reanalyze the institution of private enterprise. The new theory sustains a careful reformulation of the "conflict theory of the firm" yielding the conclusion that individual employers have an incentive to engage in discriminatory practices, regardless of how competitive labor markets may be. We argue that conflict theory need not reduce to an implicit "conspiracy theory" whose conclusions obtain only under highly restrictive, unrealistic assumptions. Rather it is the traditional conclusion that profit maximization under competitive conditions acts to ameliorate economic discrimination that hinges on unrealistic assumptions. In this chapter we defend the charge that private enterprise generates inefficiency, even when "disciplined" by competitive market structures, from well-reasoned objections to previous formulations. And again we show how the discrepancy between employer rationality and social rationality will yield an increasingly inefficient use of productive capabilities in private enterprise economies to the extent preferences are endogenous. The result in chapters 7 and 8 imply two independent sources of increasing inefficiency in private enterprise, market economies, no matter how competitive their market structures or how fully informed their participants.

In chapter 9 we reexamine the principal alternative to market allocations—central planning. We demonstrate that traditional claims that central planning cannot calculate a socially efficient plan, even in theory, are overstated. While information and incentive problems certainly exist, these "practical" problems of central planning are not unlike "practical" problems in market economies that traditional theorists are willing to "abstract from." But while we argue that an evenhanded application of traditional welfare theory should grant public enterprise, centrally planned economies as much claim to efficiency as private and public enterprise market economies, our new welfare theory reveals an intrinsic flaw in central planning that no generous assumptions can disguise. We show that regardless of how democratic a process it adopts for determining society's social welfare function, central planning is inherently biased against self-managed labor. Consequently, no centrally planned economy can provide a socially optimal menu of job roles. When preferences are recognized as endogenous, we prove this deficiency leads centrally planned economies to increasingly inefficient allocations of society's laboring capabilities as well as to growing apathy among workers. This concludes our reexamination of the welfare properties of the major economic institutions and systems of our time.

In our conclusion we point out that traditional theory is increasingly unable to distinguish between the welfare properties of different economic systems except on "practical" grounds. Under equally generous assumptions, all the major economic systems appear equally efficient and flexible according to traditional theory. But our new results demonstrate that this conclusion is misleading because different economic systems will develop along very different trajectories. We offer new insights about why different kinds of economies will predictably have different distributional trajectories, despite theoretical flexibility. But more surprisingly, we show that the human development and resource allocation trajectories of different kinds of economies will differ precisely to the extent inhabitants make individually rational choices. Moreover, we show why the allocative trajectories of each traditional economic system will be increasingly inefficient.

Not too long ago, Leonid Hurwicz issued a challenge to welfare theorists to embrace the exciting research program of devising "new economic mechanisms" that improve upon traditional models.[7] The deficiencies we demonstrate in markets, central planning, and private enterprise institutions testify to the importance of accepting his challenge.

PART ONE

LIMITS OF TRADITIONAL WELFARE THEORY

1

TRADITIONAL
WELFARE THEORY

OUR SUMMARY of traditional welfare theory is guided by three purposes:

1. To uncover the paradigm that lies behind traditional welfare theory to evaluate the further usefulness of that paradigm

2. To assess undercurrents within traditional welfare theory showing how they elucidate essential features of the underlying paradigm

3. To criticize the traditional paradigm and theory in *all* its forms rather than only one or another

With these goals in mind, we present classical utilitarianism, neoclassical welfare theory, and a modern contractarian formulation of welfare theory and analyze the "debate" between these competing formulations.

1.1 Classical Utilitarianism

By utilitarianism is here meant the ethical theory that the conduct which, under any given circumstances, is objectively right, is that which will produce the greatest amount of happiness of the whole; that is, taking into account all whose happiness is affected by the conduct.[1]

This is Sidgwick's classic statement of the utilitarian criterion for judging social actions and institutions, a criterion prominently associated with the names of Jeremy Bentham, James Mill, and F. Y. Edgeworth.

As Sidgwick points out, the principle of the greatest sum of happiness logically presumes that pleasures (or utilities) are measurable and additive. Hence classical utilitarianism was committed by its "first principle" to the view that different pleasures suffered by the same individual are quantitatively comparable and additive as are different pleasures suffered by different individuals even of different generations.

Here as before, the assumption is involved that all pleasures included in our calculation are capable of being compared quantitatively with one another and with all pains; that every such feeling has a certain intensive quantity...in respect of its desirableness, and that this quantity may be to some extent known: so that each may be at least roughly weighed in ideal scales against any other. This assumption is involved in the very notion of maximum happiness; as the attempt to make "as great as possible" a sum of elements not quantitatively commensurable would be a mathematical absurdity.[2]

Uutilitarians and their critics have been quick to note that the "greatest happiness" criterion must subsume all other notions of social "good."

The utilitarian must, in the first place, endeavor to show that the principles of truth, justice, etc. have only dependent and subordinate validity: arguing either that the principle is really only affirmed by common sense as a general rule admitting of exceptions and qualifications, as in the case of truth, and that we require some further principle for systematizing these exceptions and qualifications; or that the fundamental notion is vague and needs further determination, as in the case of justice; and further, that the different rules are liable to conflict with each other, and that we require some higher principle to decide the issue thus raised.[3]

Finally, the classical utilitarians rejected any notion of a hierarchy of pleasures, or preferences, that were qualitatively superior or inferior to others. Bentham "thought it an insolent piece of dogmatism in one person to praise or condemn another in a matter of taste."[4] And, "Quantum of pleasure being equal, pushpin is as good as poetry."[5] While few today pay much attention to classical utilitarianism, we review it because

1. It is the historical antecedent to neoclassical welfare theory, and as we shall see, most "advances" in neoclassical welfare theory are represented by neoclassical theorists as weakenings of what they describe as the more dubious assumptions of classical utilitarian theory

2. It seems to us that the best explanation of the paradox that neoclassical welfare theory retains a utilitarian framework, even though the essence of traditional welfare theory is inimical to a teleological theory of utilitarian form, lies in the particular historical evolution that occurred

3. Classical utilitarianism is the clearest example of a complete theory of social choice

1.2 Neoclassical Welfare Theory

The essence of neoclassical welfare theory is that the performance of economic institutions can and should be judged according to whether they provide economic goods in quantities that accord with people's relative desires for those goods. High marks are given to economic systems that display a close "fit" between the relative terms on which economic goods are made available and people's relative preferences for those goods. As I.M.D. Little put it, "It is a good thing that individuals should have what they want, and they themselves know best what they want."[6]

1.2.1 Manifest Preference and the Robbins Principle

As Little's statement indicates, economists in their evaluative efforts are to take the individuals' preferences as their fundamental tool. Lionel Robbins provided the strongest defense for this procedure:

Economics is not concerned with ends as such. It assumes that human beings have ends in the same sense that they have tendencies to conduct which can be defined and understood, and it asks how their progress towards their objectives is conditioned by the scarcity of means....The ends may be noble or they may be base.....Economics takes all ends for granted.[7]

Herb Gintis dubbed this fundamental neoclassical welfare postulate the Robbins Principle and rephrased it:

The Robbins judgment might be more precisely stated as follows: the economist is instructed, other things being equal, to move the individual to a position chosen on the basis of his manifest preference ordering. In other words, we act as if it is a good thing that individuals have what they want, and as if they know best what they want.[8]

In sum, according to neoclassical welfare theory, the individual's manifest preferences are not data because they are assumed to be knowable, psychological, verifiable "truths" concerning an aspect of reality that we refer to as human happiness. Rather, the strongest statement of the justification can be phrased in negative form typical of the classical liberalism that is its source: If the individual is not to be accepted as the best judge of his or her own needs and desires, who is? What other person, group of people, or omniscient entity would you rather trust than yourself to define your preferences?

15

1.2.2 *Fundamental Theorems of Neoclassical Welfare Theory*

Armed with the individual's manifest preference ordering as the determinant of whether or not the individual is "better off," neoclassical economists proceeded to their second basic welfare premise, usually referred to as the principle of Pareto optimality: "The community becomes better off if one individual becomes better off and none worse off."[9]

In the neoclassical theorist's view the great advantage of the principle of Pareto optimality is that it is uncontroversial, whereas its disadvantage is that it does not provide a complete theory of social choice. Although neoclassicists were comfortable in their conclusion that Pareto optimality was a necessary condition for a social welfare maximum, it was clear that it could not be a sufficient condition because there are an infinity of Pareto optimal allocations. But with remarkable ingenuity neoclassicists used convex set theory and fixed point theorems to refine the relationship between Pareto optimality and the equilibria of competitive private enterprise market economies in ways transcending untidy treatments of local versus global maxima, corner solutions in which not all agents utilize positive amounts of all goods, and endogenous determinations of which goods would become "economic" rather than "free."[10]

Having eliminated the social welfare function explicit in classical utilitarianism, all that could be claimed for the theorem that under "traditional assumptions" any general equilibrium of a competitive private enterprise market economy was a Pareto optimum was that it kept such economies "in the running" for ideal economic system "after the trial heats."[11] More precisely, competitive private enterprise market economies satisfied one necessary condition for a social optimum.

However, the proof of a second theorem, that under "traditional assumptions" any Pareto optimum could be achieved as the equilibrium of some competitive private enterprise market economy with an appropriate set of initial endowments, seemed to provide a solution to the lack of closure in the Pareto principle as a welfare theory. This second theorem appeared to have refined the relationship between the equilibria of competitive private enterprise market economies and Pareto optima to a state of functional equivalence. That any Pareto optimum desired could be achieved as the equilibrium of a competitive private enterprise market economy with the appropriate initial endowments meant it was possible for neoclassical welfare theorists to conclude that we could cease our search for desirable economic institutions with private enterprise market systems. It appeared, in theory, such systems could deliver any result we might desire.

Of course, this was not the same as being able to declare which set of initial distributions economists recommended for achieving social bliss. But that was probably of lesser concern than the "cease search" announcement anyway. Koopmans spelled out the approach as follows:

To duplicate any imagined Pareto optimum through a competitive equilibrium will therefore require some particular distribution of rights to the income from ownership of resources and from profitable production—or some redistribution of such income flowing from given ownership and participation arrangements—through quite possibly discriminating head taxes and subsidies.[12]

And Arrow drove the point home:

Any complaints about its [competitive private enterprise market economy's] operation can be reduced to complaints about the distribution of income, which should then be rectified by lump sum transfers.[13]

The conclusion implied by the fundamental theorems seemed perfectly clear to most neoclassical theorists. Although various real world problems might prevent realization of a perfectly competitive, private enterprise market economy, such a system is, nonetheless, the ideal economic arrangement. It always delivers Pareto optimal outcomes, and by proper manipulation of initial conditions, it can deliver any particular Pareto optimum we might prefer on equity grounds.

1.2.3 *The Unspecified Bergsonian Social Welfare Function*

Since the late 1950s when they abandoned efforts to blaze a trail from the set of all Pareto optimal allocations to the bliss point using only the "hatchet" of efficiency in the form of compensation tests, neoclassical economists have had to content themselves with an unspecified "Bergsonian" social welfare function of all individuals' utilities, $W(U(1), U(2), \ldots U(N))$, or, of a weighted sum of individual utilities.

$$\sum_{i=1}^{N} k(i)U(i)$$

with the weights, $k(i)$, unspecified. However, neoclassicists point out that specification of the function, or weights, is sufficient to make neoclassical welfare theory a complete theory of social choice, as was its predecessor, classical utilitarianism. We are also assured that for any specification the optimum result can be achieved by an appropriate private enterprise, competitive market economy.

1.3 The New Contractarian Approach

The resurgence of contractarianism has only recently spread from social philosophers to economists. The tradition, of course, dates back to Kant, Rousseau, and Locke and was largely concerned with defining the rights of the governed by considering a transition from the "state of nature" to "civil society." Whether this transition from a nonsocial arrangement without duties, obligations, or rights, to a society in which individuals have contractual obligations was viewed as an historical or hypothetical process was often unclear. The principal concerns of modern contractarians have been to clarify: (1) the explicitly hypothetical interpretation, (2) the nature of the justificatory power of the contractual view, and (3) the kind of major social institutions that would conform to the principles that would be agreed to in a hypothetical, contractual situation. We confine our attention to John Rawls, the most important figure in the resurgence, and Robert Nozick, a leading exponent of a kind of libertarianism that has gained popularity in certain economic circles.[14]

Rawls identifies three fundamental differences between the contractarian and utilitarian approaches:

> It has seemed to many philosophers, and it appears to be supported by the conviction of common sense, that we distinguish as a matter of principle between the claims of liberty and right on the one hand and the desirability of increasing aggregate social welfare on the other; and that we give a certain priority, if not absolute weight, to the former....While the contract doctrine accepts our convictions about the priority of justice as on the whole sound, utilitarianism seeks to account for them as a socially useful illusion...[because] even the excessive zeal with which we are apt to affirm these precepts and to appeal to these rights is itself granted a certain usefulness, since it counterbalances a natural human tendency to violate them in ways not sanctioned by utility.

> A second contrast is that whereas the utilitarian extends to society the principle of choice for one man...a contract view assumes that the principles of social choice, and so the principles of justice, are themselves the object of an original agreement. There is no reason to suppose that the principles which should regulate an association of men are simply an extension of the principle of choice for one man. On the contrary: if we assume that the correct regulative principle for anything depends on the nature of that thing, and that the plurality of distinct persons with separate systems of ends is an essential feature of human societies, we should not expect the principles of social choice to be utilitarian.

> The last contrast...is that utilitarianism is a teleological theory whereas justice as fairness is not....Justice as fairness is a deontological theory [that]...does not interpret the right as maximizing the good....For if it is assumed that the persons in the original position would choose a principle of equal liberty and restrict economic and social inequalities

to those in everyone's interests, there is no reason to think that just institutions would maximize the good....The question of attaining the greatest net balance of satisfaction never arises in justice as fairness; this maximum principle is not used at all....This priority of the right over the good in justice as fairness turns out to be a central feature of the conception.[15]

Nozick points out that contractarian approaches to social philosophy reflect Kant's imperative: "Act in such a way that you always treat humanity, whether in your own person or in the person of any other, never simply as a means, but always at the same time as an end."[16] In Nozick's interpretation this means "there are only individual people, different individual people, with their own individual lives," and "using one of these people for the benefit of others...does not sufficiently respect and take account of the fact that he is a separate person."[17]

1.3.1 First Principles

Rawls refined the social contract through the concept of unanimous choice in an explicitly hypothetical "original position" behind a "veil of ignorance" designed to filter out all information that would allow the discussants to know what their personal positions would be in the actual society agreed on. The content of the discussion is then divided into (1) what principles would be agreed to by individuals in this situation, which is designed to embody the notion of fairness, and (2) what major social and economic institutions would conform to these principles.

Rawls argued that "rational" individuals in the original position would agree to a liberty principle of maximum individual liberty consistent with equal liberty for all and a distributive principle referred to as the "maximin" or "difference" principle, whereby inequalities in the distribution of "basic economic goods" are acceptable only if they serve to increase the value of basic economic goods available to the worst-off member of society.

Nozick disagreed vehemently with Rawls' second principle, arguing that the difference principle is unfair to the more "productive" members in the social cooperative process. Whereas Rawls extends the veil of ignorance to exclude knowledge concerning one's own "productivity," Nozick would permit individuals in the original position to know what he terms their "entitlements." The debate hinges on what information would be "fair" for people to have in the "original position," since Nozick argues convincingly that the "difference principle" would hardly be agreed to unanimously if people knew what their productivities were going to be.[18]

Rawls argued further—and in this regard Nozick would no doubt agree—that the liberty principle would be given absolute priority over the maximin principle by inhabitants of the original position.

1.3.2 *Major Social and Economic Institutions*

The major political institutions Rawls considered compatible with the two principles are a constitutional democracy and Bill of Rights similar to those of the United States. The economic institutions Rawls favored are private property and markets.[19] These institutions are judged to be compatible with the two principles provided (1) Markets are sufficiently competitive to generate the social efficiency necessary to satisfy the difference principle, and (2) lump-sum transfers of initial endowments conform to the distributional exigencies of the difference principle. Essentially, the new contractarian approach has supported private enterprise, competitive market economies, and political liberalism.

The important point for our purposes is that the form of the justification is quite different from that of neoclassical welfare theory. Whereas neoclassical welfare theory has retained a utilitarian form and justifies competitive private enterprise market economies on the grounds that any social welfare function could be maximized by an appropriate version of such an economy, the new contractarian approach justifies private enterprise market economies on the grounds that these institutions are compatible with individual liberty and are capable of yielding results that satisfy the distributive principle agreed to by those in the original position.

In either major version, the new contractarian approach is a complete theory of social choice. In Rawls' interpretation the initial endowments that should be established by lump-sum "redistributive" transfers are those that will achieve a final distribution of economic goods that maximizes the value of the bundle of the worst-off group. In Nozick's view redistributive transfers violate individual "entitlements" and cannot be justified. But in either case "closure" is achieved as one Pareto optimum is selected above all others.

The essence of the new contractarian approach is that each individual has a distinct conception of "the good," and the task of social institutions is not to maximize "the good," but to allow individuals maximum freedom to pursue their own concepts of the good without interference. So according to the new contractarian approach the institutions of private enterprise and competitive markets are justified because they respect individual liberty and are capable of yielding distributive justice, not because they maximize some concept of social welfare. As a separate issue, disagreements between Rawls and Nozick over whether or not the veil of ignorance should be permeable to information about "entitlements," and consequently, whether lump-sum redistributions should be made at all, much less according to the difference principle, will be of interest when we discuss "distributive maxims" in chapter 8.

20

1.4 Neoclassical Objections to Classical Utilitarianism

According to the protagonists, the evolution of the modern neoclassical approach from classical utilitarianism was marked not only by great successes, but by major disappointments as well. The step-by-step transition from cardinal utility to the choice theoretic framework, along with the perfection of the fundamental theorems relating the equilibria of private enterprise, competitive market economies with Pareto optima were accomplishments of great pride to modern neoclassical theorists. However, attempts to specify a social welfare function or even establish the possibility of a reasonably desirable social welfare function have ended in frustration. All attempts to date to make neoclassical welfare theory a complete theory of social choice have failed to do so despite painstaking work and, in some cases, brilliant insight. We discuss the successes first and the disappointments second.

1.4.1 From Cardinal Utility to Choice Theoretic Framework

Starting from the classical notion of knowable, additive, interpersonally comparable, "cardinal" utilities, neoclassical welfare theorists have finally arrived at the resting grounds of the choice theoretic framework. The pilgrimage was difficult, passing through ordinal utilities, indifference curves, revealed preferences, and finally the axioms of "rational choice." Each of these stations of the cross have been portrayed as a significant advance for what seem to us a frequently confused combination of reasons.

First, it was argued that the "hedonistic calculus" was an outdated theory of actual human behavior and, therefore, an unsound foundation for welfare theory. But this was no reason to reject cardinal utility as the basis of welfare theory. Some classical utilitarians staked a triple claim:

1. Social arrangements should be made in accord with the principle of the greatest happiness for all

2. People do, in fact, behave in accord with the dictates of the hedonistic calculus of maximizing their own individual happiness

3. Private property and market institutions are such that when individuals behave in accord with the hedonistic calculus in the context of these institutions the greatest happiness for all is in fact achieved, provided certain lump-sum transfers (of a generally egalitarian nature) are made

However, the first claim is logically independent of the truth of the latter two, so that a demonstration of the falseness of either of the latter propositions need not compel one to abandon the first.

Rejection of the second proposition might be good reason not to base an analytic theory of consumer demand on the hedonistic calculus.

Likewise, a rejection of the third proposition might lead us to abandon private property market institutions and search for other ways of organizing economic activity that generate more utility. But the truth of the latter two propositions has no bearing on whether the classical utilitarian principle is the most appropriate evaluative criterion.

A second reason given for abandoning cardinal utility for the choice theoretic framework was the principle of Occam's razor. It was the supreme accomplishment of neoclassical theorists to discover that the fundamental theorems of welfare theory did not require the assumption of cardinal utilities. In the choice theoretic framework it was discovered sufficient to assume that the set of consumption bundles at least equally preferred to a given bundle was convex in order to establish the fundamental theorems of welfare economics.[20]

Of course, the principle of Occam's razor could not be used to replace the assumption of cardinal utilities with the assumption of "rational choice" with regards to the problem of selecting one Pareto optimum from the infinity of Pareto optima as the "bliss point."[21] But since neoclassical theorists concerned themselves less and less with this problem, the gain from whittling down the assumptions necessary for equating competitive equilibria with Pareto optima was considered to outweigh the loss of a complete theory of social choice.

1.4.2 Sanctity of the Individual Unprotected

Neoclassicists have pointed out that the principle that the right course of action is to maximize the total sum happiness of all not only permits but requires blanket interference in the affairs of individuals whenever total happiness can be increased by doing so. For example, an individual's opinion regarding his or her happiness would have to be rejected if a reasonable argument could be made that a "scientific test," or more knowledgeable person had a higher probability of estimating the individual's welfare correctly. And changes that yield an increase in sum total happiness would have to be implemented even if they resulted in individual sacrifices deemed grossly unfair and undesirable by many systems of ethical standards. Examples mentioned include further immiserization of destitute peasants from an early generation to provide the primitive accumulation necessary for the affluence of succeeding generations and redistribution from poorer "uncultured" members of society to wealthy epicureans.

The objection is that classical utilitarianism might sanction not only totalitarian tendencies that prohibit individuals' freedom to make their own mistakes but gross violations of elementary justice as well. Neoclassical welfare theorists have claimed that the Robbins Principle prevents neoclassical welfare theory from making the first kind of mistake, and their extreme reluctance to consider interpersonal comparisons of utility prevents instances of the latter.

Of course, the early utilitarians, Bentham in particular, were anxious to employ their theory to just the opposite ends. They were dedicated social reformers. By combining the principle of the greatest happiness with the not implausible postulate of declining marginal utility of income and a firm rejection of elitist conceptions of pleasure, they thought they had forged a powerful argument for radical egalitarian programs. Bentham would no doubt find it ironic that his theory is assailed by modern neoclassicists for failure to adequately protect the rights of the disadvantaged, as in the hypothetical examples above. But it is undeniable that classical utilitarianism is open to the criticism of leaving individual liberties and elementary justice protected by the, at least questionable, factual proposition that observance of such liberties and justice will always coincide with maximization of sum total happiness. Although Rawls is, of course, not an adherent of neoclassical welfare theory, in the following quotation he provides an insightful interpretation of classical utilitarianism and an unsurpassed formulation of the objection that it does not reflect the sanctity of the individual. Neoclassical theorists would be fortunate to state the problem so eloquently. Whether or not their own theory is as fully insulated against this problem as they believe, we shall see presently.

> We may note first that there is indeed a way of thinking of society which makes it easy to suppose that the most rational conception of justice is utilitarian. For consider: each man in realizing his own interests is certainly free to balance his own losses against his own gains....Now why should not a society act on precisely the same principle applied to the group and therefore regard that which is rational for one man as right for an association of men? Since the principle for an individual is to advance as far as possible his own welfare, his own system of desires, the principle for society is to advance as far as possible the welfare of the group....The principle of choice for an association of men is interpreted as an extension of the principle of choice for one man. Social justice is the principle of rational prudence applied to an aggregate conception of the welfare of the group....On this conception of society separate individuals are thought of as so many different lines along which rights and duties are to be assigned and scarce means of satisfaction allocated in accordance with rules so as to give the greatest fulfillment of wants....Here we may note a curious anomaly. It is customary to think of utilitarianism as individualistic, and certainly there are good reasons for this. The utilitarians were strong defenders of liberty and freedom of thought, and they held that the good of society is constituted

by the advantages enjoyed by individuals. Yet utilitarianism is not individualistic, at least when arrived at by the more natural course of reflection, in that, by conflating all systems of desires, it applies to society the principle of choice for one man....It is this conflation, and the principle based on it, which subjects the rights secured by justice to the calculus of social interests.[22]

1.5 Neoclassical Incompleteness

Neoclassical theorists admit to disappointments as well as proclaim successes in the evolution from classical utilitarianism to modern welfare theory. In their view the main problem still plaguing them is their inability to close their system and make it a complete theory of social choice. First attempts at closure took the form of "compensation tests," while later work followed paths pioneered by Arrow's famous impossibility theorem.

1.5.1 Compensation Tests: A Cavalier Critique

The compensation tests turned out to be a vain search for a path from the set of all Pareto optimal outcomes to the bliss point of maximum social welfare eschewing interpersonal utility comparisons and using only the tool of efficiency.

> The compensation tests all spring from a desire to see what can be said about social welfare...without making interpersonal comparisons of well-being....They have a common origin in Pareto's definition of an increase in social welfare—that at least one man must be better off and no one worse off—but they are extended to situations in which some people are made worse off. It is here that the possibility of compensation tests becomes relevant.[23]

The search for an appropriate compensation test that would allow the ranking of certain Pareto optima above others on the basis that the gainers from movements from one Pareto optimum to another would be able to compensate the losers and still retain net positive benefits began with Kaldor in 1939 and extended through Hicks, Scitovsky, Samuelson, and Little.[24] But while the debate raged around whether or not different compensation criteria were equivalent, and if not, which was more compelling, the real problem lay elsewhere. When someone finally noticed the difference between compensation actually paid and compensation that was discussed but never handed over, it was apparent the compensation tests did not really leave the profession any "better off" than the Pareto principle we had begun with. In fact, we were not left any "better off" than the medieval Japanese townspeople of Titipu in their efforts to justify who should be favored:

24

See how the fates their gifts allot,
For A is happy, B is not.
Yet B is worthy, I dare say,
Of more prosperity than A.

B more worthy?
I should say,
He's worth a great deal more than A.
Yet A is happy! Oh, so happy!

Laughing, Ha! Ha! Chaffing, Ha! Ha!
Nectar quaffing, Ha! ha! ha!
Ever joyous, ever gay,
Happy, undeserving A!

If I were fortune—which I'm not—
B should enjoy A's happy lot
And A should die in misery—
That is assuming I am B.

But should A perish?
That should he
(Of course assuming I am B.)
B should be happy! Oh, so happy!

Laughing, Ha! Ha! Chaffing, Ha! ha!
Nectar quaffing, Ha! ha! ha!
But condemned to die is he,
Wretched, meritorious B!

But condemned to die is he,
Wretched, meritorious B!

—W. S. Gilbert and Arthur Sullivan, *The Mikado*

1.5.2 *Impossibility Theorems*

Just as a detailed examination of compensation tests was unnecessary to our argument, we need not delve into the intricacies of investigations parting from Arrow's impossibility theorem. Arrow's results, as well as those of Sen, Pattanaik, and others who followed, demonstrate that in context of a traditional conception of preferences even a small number of intuitively appealing characteristics cannot be incorporated into a minimally satisfactory social choice rule without contradicting one another. While the impact of this "negative" conclusion has been weakened by subsequent demonstrations that particular social choice rules can comply with something less than Arrow deemed "minimally acceptable conditions," the fact remains, no "positive" conclusion has emerged from that permits tradition-al welfare theory to elevate one Pareto optimum above all others. On the contrary, developments in the theory of social choice clarify that traditional welfare theory is farther from "closure" than had been assumed.

1.5.3 Minimizing the Significance of Incompleteness

In sum, neoclassical welfare theory admits to incompleteness. Yet, all in all, we believe it fair to characterize neoclassicists' attitude toward the problem of selecting from different Pareto optima as "indifference."

Some neoclassicists argue that in the modern world of specialization economists are only responsible for clarifying concepts related to efficien-cy anyway. In this view arguments concerning the relative merits of different efficient allocations should be left to moral philosophers who are, presumably, experts in such matters.

Other neoclassicists, with a more technocratic self-image, observe that the choice between different Pareto optima is a strictly distributional matter that will be settled on the battlefield of power politics rather than in the ivory towers of moral philosophy or welfare economics. These self-styled pragmatists console themselves (if not their victims) with the thought that if economists contribute to making Pareto improvements at least nobody is made any worse-off by their interventions.

A more virulent strain of neoclassicists centered around the "Chicago School" combine a strict interpretation of individual liberty, a religious devotion to the marginal productivity theory of entitlements, and a defini-tion of the individual that encompasses his or her entire line of ancestors so that "just" initial endowments become identical with historical distribu-tions. Or, "just" endowments would be identical with historical endow-ments had these never been tampered with by "meddling" governments who unwittingly confirm they are little more than expressions of "mob-tyranny" by implementing progressive taxes.[25] Obviously once "just" initial endowments have been located, Pareto optimality becomes a suffi-cient as well as necessary condition for maximizing social welfare. But this justification already takes us across the bridge between utilitarian and contractarian philosophical frameworks, whether self-styled neoclassical economists of this ilk realize it or not. While only some of these economists who persist in labeling themselves neoclassicists seem aware of their contractarian status, we must classify them properly as genus, traditional welfare theory; species, contractarian; age, modern.

Regardless which rationalization one prefers, all can rejoice that the "cease search" sign planted in front of the private enterprise, competitive market economy exhibit at the "Great Economic Institution Fair" can substitute for closure for neoclassical welfare theory.

1.6 <u>Contractarian Objections to Neoclassical Theory</u>

Contractarians' objections to neoclassical welfare theory are simple and to the point. Neoclassical welfare theory remains a utilitarian theory subject to weaknesses that plague any evaluative theory of utilitarian form; it "does not take seriously the distinction between persons."[26]

No matter how much more successfully neoclassical welfare theory has managed to protect the sanctity of the individual than classical utilitarian theory, as a utilitarian theory neoclassical theory itself continues to depart from the view that "the principles which should regulate an association of men is simply an extension of the principle of choice for one man."[27]

Neoclassical welfare theory remains a teleological theory committed to the view that the right social institutions or actions are those that maximize the good defined as a weighted sum of individual welfares. As such, the basic design of neoclassical theory cannot express the view that "individuals are ends and not merely means; they may not be sacrificed or used for the achieving of other ends without their consent; individuals are inviolable."[28]

Put differently, if we believe that "as a matter of principle each member of society is thought to have inviolability founded on justice which even the welfare of everyone else cannot override, [and] that a loss of freedom for some is [not] made right by a greater good share by others,"[29] we shall have to look beyond a utilitarian theory, which neoclassical theory remains, for an account of the principles of justice. The new contractarians admit that neoclassical welfare theory protects the sanctity of the individual in ways that classical utilitarian theory did not, just as they have nothing but praise for neoclassical efforts toward elevating the sanctity of the individual. But new contractarians point out that the protection afforded by neoclassical theory is inadequate because it fails to discard a philosophical form expressive of the principle of rational choice for one person for a form expressive of the inviolability of each individual.

That the Robbins Principle of neoclassical welfare theory guarantees the individual's right to define his or her own conception of "the good" against any benevolent (or otherwise) political or scientific dictatorship is recognized by contractarians. And it is recognized that an almost fanatical commitment to eschew "interpersonal welfare comparisons" creates an environment where "blanket interference in the affairs of individuals" is less likely than in an environment where different individual's utilities are presumed to be not only comparable but additive. But contractarians point out that no matter how much more protective of the sanctity of the individual these features of neoclassical welfare theory are than classical utilitarianism, the Bergsonian social welfare function continues to hang ominously over the individual's head.

The unquestioning acceptance of "manifest" preferences and an extreme aversion to "interpersonal utility comparisons" establishes an environment more respectful of the sanctity of the individual, but this notion of inviolability remains unincorporated into the basic framework of neoclassical welfare theory because the theory retains a social welfare function as the final arbiter. The specification of social welfare, W, as a function of individual utilities, $W(U(1),U(2),...U(N))$, not only permits, but insists on, interpersonal utility trade-offs whenever they would increase the value of W. Contractarians rightfully point out that an unspecified Bergsonian welfare function is potentially as dangerous to the sanctity of the individual as the classical utilitarian principle. But while contractarians may be sympathetic to neoclassicists' desire to protect the sanctity of the individual—just as neoclassicists were sympathetic to classical utilitarians' goal of establishing individual well-being as the yardstick of social worth—contractarians remain critical of the failure of neoclassical theory to recognize "that the plurality of distinct persons with separate systems of ends is an essential feature of human societies."[30]

1.7 Comparing the Three Approaches

As Rawls points out, classical utilitarian theory is a complete theory of social choice totally consistent with a "conception of society [where] separate individuals are thought of as so many different lines along which rights and duties are to be assigned and scarce means of satisfaction allocated in accordance with rules so as to give the greatest fulfillment of wants."[31] And according to this conception, just as "each man in realizing his own interests is certainly free to balance his own losses against his own gains...why should not a society act on precisely the same principle applied to the group?...The principle for an individual is to advance as far as possible his own welfare, his own system of desires, the principle for a society is to advance as far as possible the welfare of the group."[32]

In sum, classical utilitarian theory expresses the concept of social rationality as an extension of individual rationality and, ironically, provides the ideal justification for public enterprise, centrally planned economies rather than private enterprise, market economies—a matter we will return to in chapter 9.

Neoclassical welfare theory, on the other hand, is neither a complete theory of social choice nor a consistent reflection of a particular view of society. Neoclassicists, impressed by their ability to deduce fundamental theorems relating the equilibria of competitive, private enterprise market economies with Pareto optimal outcomes without assuming cardinal or interpersonally comparable utilities, jettisoned the classical utilitarian principle. As a result, neoclassicists drifted into the uncharted sea of incomplete evaluative methodologies, which proved far more difficult to cross than they had supposed.

The incompleteness of neoclassical welfare theory appeared to be alleviated when the two fundamental welfare theorems relating the equilibria of competitive, private enterprise market economies and Pareto optima were interpreted as reason to post a "cease search" sign. But as we shall see in part 3, under similarly generous assumptions, equally compelling proofs establish the ability of a number of other "ideal" economic systems to achieve whatever Pareto optimal outcome may be desired.[33] As a result, the placement of the "cease search" sign becomes arbitrary. Which exhibit in the Great Economic Institution Fair will display the prize depends only on which booth the judges visit first. In this light, not only is there no alleviating the liability of incompleteness, but neoclassical welfare theory may have very little to tell us about the relative advantages of different economic systems.

While abandoning cardinal utilities for the choice theoretic approach and eschewing interpersonal welfare comparisons appeared to more accurately reflect the notion of the sanctity of the individual, as we saw previously, in the end neoclassical welfare theory also fails to adequately express the view "that the plurality of distinct persons with separate systems of ends is an essential feature of human societies,"[34] due to its retention of a utilitarian form in general and the Bergsonian social welfare function in particular.

Although it might seem harsh, we are forced to conclude that neoclassical welfare theory is a philosophically unsophisticated halfway ground that retained a utilitarian format while attempting to express a notion of individual sanctity inimical to teleological theories of utilitarian form. Moreover, neoclassicists jettisoned the completeness contained in classical utilitarianism in the name of Occam's razor—a principle that applies only to jettisoning unnecessary equipment at embarkation, not cargo at disembarkation.

In contrast, the new contractarian approach is both a complete theory of social choice and a consistent reflection of a particular view of society. When combined with either lump-sum, redistributive transfers cum Rawls' difference principle, or "stand-pat" historical distributions cum Nozick's theory of entitlements, the institutions of private enterprise and competitive markets provide a complete answer to the economic problem for new contractarians. Furthermore, the justification is not that these institutions maximize some notion of social welfare, but that individuals with independent conceptions of "the good" would freely consent to these economic arrangements in a situation characterized by fairness.

In our opinion, the claim that only a contractarian doctrine fully expresses the view "that the plurality of distinct persons with separate systems of ends is an essential feature of human societies"[35] must be taken seriously. In sum, contractarianism seems a more appropriate expression of the sanctity of the individual so critical to the traditional welfare theory research project.

1.8 Strengths of Traditional Welfare Theory

Although we have taken great pains to distinguish between the different versions of traditional welfare theory as they evolved, we now return to the primary task of this chapter: formulating the essence and principle strengths of traditional welfare theory when viewed as a whole.[36]

1.8.1 *Sanctity of the Individual*

It seems to us the most powerful statement of the desire to defend the sanctity of the individual lies in its implicit challenge to alternative views: If the individual is not to be accepted as the best judge of his or her own needs and desires, then who is? Or, as John Stuart Mill put it:

> [The individual's] own good, either physical or moral, is not a sufficient warrant [to interfere with preferences]. He cannot rightfully be compelled to do or forbear because it will be better for him to do so, because it will make him happier, because in the opinions of others, to do so would be wise, or even right. These are good reasons for remonstrating with him, or entreating him, but not for compelling him or visiting him with any evil in case he do otherwise.[37]

Classical utilitarians tried to express this notion by denying that there was any hierarchy of pleasures, their intuition being that the greatest threat to the sanctity of the individual came from a paternalistic view that the "masses" were ill-equipped, through lack of education and cultural exposure, to enjoy "higher" pleasures.

As we have seen, neoclassical welfare theory's main bulwark for protecting the sanctity of the individual is the Robbins Principle, sometimes approvingly referred to as the principle of ethical neutrality. This principle directs economists to accept the individual's manifest preferences as part of the fundamental data for judging economic systems and policies and to leave unexplored and unquestioned the origins and merits of these preferences themselves.

The new contractarians insist that adequate protection of the sanctity of the individual must not only recognize the individual's inalienable right to define his or her own conception of "the good," but also guarantee the individual's freedom to pursue that conception without being overruled in the interests of society-at-large, unless the individual would have consented to do so in a fair situation. Contractarians argue further that all forms

30

of utilitarian theories are incapable of protecting the sanctity of the individual—whether the danger be from classical utilitarians' first principle in the form of individual pleasure machines, primitive accumulation, or wise rulers, or from neoclassicists' unspecified Bergsonian social welfare function—and insist that only contractarian theories are suited to this task.[38]

1.8.2 Welfare as Individual Well-being

> There is no social entity...that undergoes some sacrifice for its own good. There are only individual people, different individual people, with their own individual lives.[39]

This view is common to all three variants of traditional welfare theory. As Rawls points out, classical utilitarians "held that the good of society is constituted by the advantages enjoyed by individuals,"[40] even if they are willing to permit the welfare of some to be sacrificed to the greater welfare of others. Neoclassical theorists are equally insistent that only individuals can experience welfare and are much more hesitant than classical utilitarians to discuss the merits of particular trade-offs between individuals' welfare.

Stated in negative form, all three variants of traditional welfare theory adamantly eschew the concept of "collective values" or "a social good" that is not derived from individual well-being.

1.8.3 Distinguishing Evaluative Theories

The evolution of traditional welfare theory has helped sharpen the distinctions between different forms of evaluative theories. Rawls enumerates four disjoint and exhaustive categories of evaluative theories: utilitarian, contractarian, perfectionist, and intuitionist.

Utilitarian theories justify choices according to whether they maximize "the good," or in our case, some aggregation of individual welfares. Contractarian theories justify on grounds that choices would have been freely agreed to under circumstances characterized by fairness. Perfectionist theories judge social institutions and decisions according to whether or not they achieve some particular form of human or societal "excellence" without reference to the consequent well-being of individuals or whether or not individuals would have freely consented to abide by their rules. Intuitionist theories refuse to commit to any single form of justification and reserve the right to apply different forms of justification in different circumstances as determined by their "intuition."

Traditional welfare theorists are unanimous in rejecting all forms of perfectionist theories. Examples of perfectionist theories that express some form of "individual" excellence as their goal can be found in Aristotle and

Nietzsche. A variety of fundamentalist Moslem, Christian, and Jewish sects are examples of "modern" perfectionist theories. Marxism has been characterized as "socially" perfectionist as well. And the label is apt for Marxists who make evaluative judgments based simply on the efficiency of policies in achieving the social "goal" of "communism" without justifying such an achievement in terms of the well-being of individuals, or on grounds that such a society would be chosen by fully informed individuals in a fair situation.

In any case, clarification of the nature of different justificatory procedures brought to traditional welfare theory principally by new contractarians is a positive contribution. And the unanimous rejection of perfectionist forms of justification is one of the strengths of traditional welfare theory as a whole.

1.8.4 Summary

The problem for traditional welfare theorists has been how best to secure a particular view of the sanctity of the individual while generating a complete theory of social choice. We have examined all three variants of traditional welfare theory to elucidate this problem. In the process we discovered that both classical utilitarian theory and neoclassical welfare theory fail to solve the problem.

While the new contractarian approach solves the problem posed by traditional welfare theory better than its predecessors—thereby better expressing the traditional welfare paradigm—it is just as incapable as its predecessors of resolving the remaining problems of welfare theory. We are now ready to demonstrate this point, which will be our task for the remainder of part 1. The reason is simple to state: the traditional paradigm itself is wanting as a vehicle for addressing the remaining issues.

The problem is no longer with the means of expressing the traditional paradigm. Neoclassical theorists honed the meaning of social efficiency and its relation to competitive equilibria. Then the philosophical incongruities of the inherited utilitarian format were corrected by a new generation of contractarians. The result is a technically and philosophically refined theory that fully expresses the traditional welfare paradigm. If traditional welfare theory has reached the end of the problems it can solve, it is not due to lack of refinement but to inadequacies of the underlying paradigm itself.

2

THE LABOR
PROCESS

The QUESTION we pose in this and the following three chapters is whether the traditional welfare paradigm in any representation is suited to a number of tasks that stand before it. In this chapter we review the work of diverse economists who dispute traditional conclusions about the labor process under private enterprise. We show that while useful for some purposes, the traditional concepts of production functions and production possibility sets impede analysis of issues posed by adherents of the "conflict theory of the firm" and the theory of "segmented labor markets." In the process we show how erecting a "black box" around the labor process blinded traditional theorists to ways in which competition for profit can lead to inefficient technologies and economic discrimination.

Traditional welfare theory has employed the production function[1] or production possibility set[2] as its central concept for analyzing "the production process." Production is visualized as an instantaneous transformation of one set of material "inputs" into a different set of material "outputs" through the mediation of specific "quantities" of human labor, interestingly enough, measured in units of time. The production possibility set, or the less general production function, are treated as exogenous data describing all possible transformations available at the moment of analysis to production units of an economy. It is a matter of choosing from the set of possible transformations according to some criterion.

In this conception the production process itself disappears inside what has been critically referred to as the "black box" of the production possibility set. For every combination of "inputs" entering the black box a determinate combination of "outputs" emerges. The whys and wherefores

33

are left to other disciplines to consider. The traditional welfare theorist takes the "mappings" as exogenous.[3]

Outside the economic mainstream a dramatically different conception of production that stresses the social aspects of the "labor process" has long existed. In this conception the social coordination and direction of human labor occurring in the production processes of any economy is a critical subject for economic analysis. And the logic of these social activities, that is, the dynamics within the neoclassical "black box," cannot be ignored without debilitating consequences.

Marxist economists have long argued that the distinction between "labor" (the work actually performed), and "labor power" (the capacity to do work) is critical to an understanding of different economies. Institutional economists have developed an analysis of segmented labor markets, internal labor markets, and labor-management relations by viewing the firm as an elaborate social organization. Recently, neoclassical theorists have begun to treat the information and incentive complexities of production relations in the theory of contracts and principal agent models.

Adherents of the view that production must be analyzed within a particular social organization of the labor process have argued:

1. Labor inputs should not be treated as conceptually indistinguishable from nonhuman inputs

2. The production possibility set is not independent of the "social relations of production" or means chosen for coordinating production

3. The "outputs" that will result from a particular combination of "inputs" remain indeterminate until a host of factors, not included in the concept of a production possibility set, but critical to the functioning of the labor process, are specified

4. In capitalism the labor exchange, whereby workers formally accede disposition over their laboring capacities for a specified time in return for an agreed wage, is not symmetrical with other exchanges in markets for raw materials, intermediate products, or capital goods

5. No automatically enforceable quid pro quo guarantees the "integrity" of the labor exchange in private enterprise economies. Instead, the actual outcome of an incompletely specifiable agreement remains to be settled, in large part, by the functioning of the labor process itself and all that goes into its determination.

But what is relatively new is the idea that the nontraditional conceptualization has important welfare-theoretic implications—that one or more of the above points implies the traditional conclusion that profit-maximizing behavior of owners will coincide with socially efficient production decisions holds only under highly restrictive and unrealistic assumptions. A host of modern, radical economists have contributed to developing a theory that has come to be known as the "conflict theory of the firm." Harry Braverman, Stephen Marglin, William Lazonick, Kathy Stone, Herb Gintis, Richard Edwards, David Gordon, Michael Reich, James Devine, Michael Burawoy, Andy Zimbalist, David Noble, Michelle Naples, and Sam Bowles,[4] among others, have played variations on Marx's theme that there is a fundamental difference between the capacity to work, which the employer pays for, and the actual work that is done. They have greatly refined the argument that the implications of neglecting the conditions under which the former is transformed into the latter are far from trivial.

Besides criticism inspired by a rereading of Marx's analysis of "alienated labor," a body of work referred to as "dual or segmented labor market theory" has emerged from empirical work by institutionalist and labor economists challenging the traditional notion of competitive labor markets. Building on the work of J. R. Commons, Peter Doeringer and Michael Piore[5] sparked a new wave of interest pursued by others such as Barry Bluestone, Samuel Rosenberg, Paul Osterman, Martin Carnoy, Russell Rumberger, Robert Buchele, Francine Blau, and Lawrence Kahn. Closer to the mainstream, Armen Alchian and Harold Demsetz initiated a literature inspired by Ronald Coase's conception of the firm as a consequence of high market transaction costs.[6]

Finally, very recent efforts have attempted to apply the analytical tools of principal-agent theory to the firm. Since the principal-agent model was designed for situations in which "principals" contract with "agents" to engage in activities that have different utilities for "principals" and "agents" and about which "principals" and "agents" have different information, the potential for sharpening treatment of the employment relation is obvious. We review these different bodies of literature and leave the task of elaborating their weaknesses and building upon their insights to chapter 8 where we reconsider the institution of private enterprise in light of our new welfare paradigm and theory.

2.1 The Labor Exchange

2.1.1 Karl Marx

Marx himself considered recognition of the difference between "labor" and "labor power" his single most important contribution to economic theory because he believed it solved the mystery of the origins of capitalist profits. By distinguishing between "labor" and "labor power" Marx believed he had perfected the Labor Theory of Value inherited from David

Ricardo and had located the origins of profits "in the production process," thereby explaining how positive profits resulted in the context of "equal" (competitive) exchange. This is not the place to dwell on our conviction that by choosing to focus on a presumed "quantitative" difference between the "exchange value" of labor power and labor performed, Marx (and most of his economic disciples since) proceeded down one of the longest dead ends in the history of economic thought.[7] However, a number of radical economists have recently returned to exploration of the implications of the qualitative difference between labor and labor power that Marx originally emphasized in his treatment of alienated labor in the *1844 Philosophical Manuscripts*. It is the development and relevance of this qualitative distinction that we treat here.

In addition to pointing out the qualitative distinction between the capacity to work, or what he called "labor power," and actual work performed, which he called "labor," in the *1844 Philosophical Manuscripts* Marx criticized production as it is carried out under the conditions of private enterprise independently of its "quantitative" outcome, or what he called the degree of "exploitation." According to Marx, regardless of how poorly or well workers were paid, laborers were necessarily "alienated" from the work process, from the products of their work, from each other, and from their "species being" under a capitalist organization of production. The reason was that under capitalism workers do not conceptualize and organize their own laboring activities. The conceptualization and direction of workers' capacities is done by another, either their employer or a manager representing the employer. For this reason, Marx argued, workers under capitalism are inevitably "alienated" from the work process. He further concluded that if they are "alienated" from the work process they must be "alienated" from the "products" of that process as well. Moreover, if they do not control their work efforts individually, they are certainly in no position to coordinate collaborative efforts with other workers, which "alienates" them from their fellow workers. Most generally, Marx argued that the ability to conceive, evaluate, plan, and coordinate the effects of one's laboring capacities with others was the defining characteristic of the human species. Therefore, any economic system that denied people the opportunity to exercise this capacity necessarily "alienated" them from their "species being."

2.1.2 *Cornelius Castoriadis*

Cornelius Castoriadis was the first to effectively reemphasize the profound difference between what an employer hopes he will get and what he actually buys when he purchases the chance to try and direct someone's productive capabilities for an agreed period. Castoriadis argued not only that the outcome of the capitalist labor exchange remains to be determined by antagonistic struggle between employees and employer over who will direct the formers' productive activities toward what ends, but that, ironically, the very reproduction of the capitalist economic system hinges on neither protagonist in this fundamental contest emerging totally victorious.

Obviously if employees directed their efforts only toward their own ends after receiving their wages—doing whatever suits their inclinations and preferences without regard to orders levied by capitalists—there would be no more buyers of "labor power" because "owning" labor power would give capitalists no advantages. Capitalism would cease to exist.

Less obviously, Castoriadis pointed out that "in real life, capitalism is obliged to base itself on people's capacity for self-organization, on the individual and collective creativity of the producers without which it could not survive a day even though the whole 'official organization' of modern society ignores and seeks to suppress these abilities to the utmost."[8]

Certainly this observation provides a poignant reminder that much of what occurs during the capitalist labor process does not result from explicit directives from owners and their managerial personnel, but emanates instead from employees' initiatives and responses to unforeseen eventualities arising during the labor process within the context of a specific system of organizational control and motivation. Put differently, for Castoriadis the assumption that employers will get exactly what they hoped they had purchased in the labor market is at odds with an implicit assumption of any analysis of a capitalist economy that the basic institutions of private enterprise market economies will be reproduced.

Regrettably, Castoriadis' work in this area was largely unavailable to English-speaking audiences until 1988. As a result, rekindling interest in the qualitative distinction between "labor" and "labor power" among U.S. radical economists fell to Stephen Marglin, who, in an unpublished essay in 1969 titled "What Do Bosses Do?,"[9] stimulated a veritable flood of research about the historical transformation of the labor process.

2.1.3 *Stephen Marglin*

Stephen Marglin observed that (1) capitalist production defeated noncapitalist artisan and putting-out production in the rise of English capitalism, and (2) capitalist production utilized a hierarchical system of control. Yet Marglin denied these facts necessarily implied that hierarchical systems of control were technically more efficient than nonhierarchical systems—a conclusion that had long gone unchallenged even by most who argued against hierarchical organization of production on other grounds.

After observing the logical possibility that some other difference between early capitalist and noncapitalist producers' methods determined the victor in their competitive struggle in markets where they all sold the same goods, Marglin went on to cite (sketchy) historical evidence that (1) early capitalist producers often used the same techniques of production as their noncapitalist competitors, and (2) the decisive phase in the competitive struggle between capitalist and precapitalist "modes of production" occurred before the development of new technology and the increasing division of labor within the enterprise so much celebrated in Adam Smith's description of a pin factory.

Even should Marglin's historical hypothesis eventually prove insubstantial, it served the important function of undermining the long unchallenged assumption that "the weight of history" had closed the door on any rational questioning of the technological superiority of hierarchical systems of control of the labor process.

If hierarchical control was not (or might not have been) initiated because it permitted an increasing division of labor and greater technological efficiency and thereby allowed capitalists to lower costs and out-compete noncapitalist producers, why was it implemented? Marglin offered a twofold answer: (1) hierarchical control was instituted to increase the intensity and length of the workday beyond the intensity and length of the average workday in artisan and putting-out systems, and (2) control, not profit, was the ultimate objective for capitalists in any case.

Without discussing either the validity of Marglin's historical evidence, the weight of contrary historical evidence he did not consider at the time of his article, or the logical consistency of the arguments as he presented them, it is sufficient for us to note that Marglin reopened a debate that had long been closed for a new generation of radical economists by (1) challenging the conclusion that history proved that new technology made possible by hierarchical control of production explained the victory of early capitalist producers over their noncapitalist rivals, and (2) suggesting that hierarchical control served other functions besides promoting increased technological efficiency in a capitalist production process

Not surprisingly, members of the new generation of radical economic historians quickly emerged to examine the validity of Marglin's hypothesis in other historical contexts. Kathy Stone studied the transformation of the post-Civil War American steel industry,[10] and a number of other contributors to the journal *Radical America* examined the function of changing job structures in different historical contexts in a debate that came to be referred to (unfortunately) as "profit versus control."

2.1.4 *Harry Braverman*

In 1974 the field was restimulated by publication of Harry Braverman's major work, *Labor and Monopoly Capital*. Unlike Marglin's essay, which was suggestive and highly provisional, Braverman's work was the culmination of a lifetime of research applying Marx's theory of the capitalist labor process to the economic transformations undergone during the era of "monopoly capitalism" in the U.S. In addition to reiterating the qualitative uniqueness of human labor power and the inherent struggle over the division of "conception" and "execution" that the capitalist form of production implies, which Marx and, more recently, Castoriadis had elaborated, Braverman argued that the system of Taylorism was developed not only to increase the accountability of workers, thereby permitting extraction of a greater quantity of "labor" from the "labor power" purchased, but also to "de-skill" employees, thereby permitting capitalists to negotiate lower wage bills for the labor power they purchased.

Moreover, to his great credit Braverman traced recognition of the phenomenon of "de-skilling" back to the eighteenth-century British economist Charles Babbage after whom Braverman dubbed the employer's motivation to de-skill the "Babbage Principle."

In addition to Braverman's own application of this theoretical framework to highlight the contradictory interests of employers and employees over the effects of new technology and organizational systems on both the level and dispersal of skills and on the ability of employers to extract work in a number of industries in the twentieth-century U.S. economy, Braverman's book stimulated others including Michael Burawoy to explore similar matters.[11]

The important question for welfare theory is whether application of the Babbage Principle serves the social interest as fully as the private interest of the employer. We can assume Adam Smith's invisible hand of competition compels employers to adopt any technological possibilities that minimize the use of expensive skills. But Braverman argued that if these expensive (and, therefore, presumably productive) skills already exist in the labor force to some extent, underemploying them serves no social purpose. As we shall see in chapter 8, the extent to which private and public interest converge or diverge here must be treated more carefully in a dynamic model that includes education and training of the labor force. Even if Braverman misformulated parts of his critique of capitalist efficiency, he certainly deserves credit for raising the possibility of a divergence between public and private interests in "de-skilling."

2.1.5 *Herb Gintis*

Herb Gintis most clearly formulated radicals' alternative view of the labor process as a direct challenge to conclusions of traditional welfare theory. In his early work,[12] Gintis outlined the logic of traditional welfare theory's analysis of the capitalist firm and cataloged a series of empirical anomalies. Gintis pointed out that precisely by modeling the production process as a black box and treating labor as conceptually indistinguishable from nonhuman inputs, traditional welfare theory was able to deduce that profit maximizing production decisions would be Pareto optimal; wage differentials would reflect differences in the marginal productivity of workers; and job structures would reflect the trade-off in workers' desires for wages and job satisfaction. But contrary to these expectations Gintis cited: numerous experimental and policy-oriented attempts to introduce varying degrees of worker control in production that tended to exhibit increases in both productivity and worker satisfaction; strong evidence that wage differentials within firms correlate weakly with skill differentials among workers and conditions of market supply; and the empirical importance of nontechnical considerations such as sex, race, and demeanor in determining wages.

While one could try to explain these anomalies as results of imperfect information and special circumstances, Gintis argued that a faulty analysis of the labor exchange on the part of traditional welfare theory was responsible for the divergence between theoretical predictions and reality. Because the employer must be concerned with guaranteeing the "integrity" of the labor exchange during production since the exchange cannot be taken as a simple quid pro quo, Gintis reasoned that choice of technology and organization of work would be influenced by concerns other than choosing the technology and organization of work that would maximize output if employees could always be counted on to perform according to employers' desires. Specifically employers would have to take into account to what degree a particular technology would elicit the performance from workers they hoped they had purchased, not just how much output and how agreeable work roles (and, therefore, how little wages) a technology would yield if workers could always be counted on to perform as desired. He summarized the problem as follows:

> The defining character of neoclassical economics lies in the restriction of its investigation to the sphere of exchange relations....But the way in which exchange relations affect the choice of a productive technique cannot be understood by treating the firm as a "black box" of exogenously given material and organizational technical opportunities.[13]

In later work Gintis and Donald Katzner[14] constructed a formal model of internal decision making in the firm. As a special case, their model included a treatment of the firm originally envisioned by Coase[15] and Simon.[16] Both Coase and Simon recognized authoritative rather than market allocation as the hallmark of the firm as an economic organization. As Coase pointed out as early as 1937:

If a workman moves from department Y to department X, he does not go because of a change in relative prices, but because he is ordered to do so....Outside the firm, price movements direct production, which is coordinated through a series of exchange transactions on the market....Within the firm...is substituted the entrepreneur-coordinator, who directs production.[17]

However, Coase and Simon argued that the existence of these "authoritative allocations" within the firm was no reason to fear that private enterprise, market economies would make socially inefficient decisions. Coase argued that certain allocations are more efficiently executed by authoritative decree than by market transaction. And precisely because the profit-maximizing entrepreneur can be relied on to determine which these are, Coase reasoned that the combination of private enterprise and competitive market institutions generate socially efficient allocations.

Simon, in turn, contributed to a sophisticated defense of the neoclassical treatment of the production process as a black box by making the assumptions of authoritative allocation totally explicit.[18] He argued that if every worker is capable of performing a set of activities, A, then "work" or "production" can occur in either of two ways. If the worker contracts to perform a specific activity, from A for a price, then he or she is working as an independent agent and the "problem" of authoritative allocation disappears. But the worker may instead contract a fixed wage, w, in return for which he or she turns over to the employer the right to choose any b in B equal to some subset of A defined as part of the labor contract. Simon concluded that utility-maximizing employees and profit-maximizing employers facing each other in competitive labor markets could be relied on to fix w and B so that the structure of work would be characterized by "producer sovereignty," and the selection of b from B would maximize output for a given set of inputs.

Coase and Simon essentially assumed that "once the contract between entrepreneur and worker, $[w,B]$, is settled, the former tells the latter exactly what to do, [and] the worker either does it or finds another job."[19] In contrast, Gintis and Katzner argued "contracts are not explicit enough, nor are capitalists' powers sufficiently encompassing to dictate a worker's attitudes, values, relations with superiors, subordinates and co-workers, the manner in which he or she discharges his or her responsibilities, and so on."[20] In other words, Gintis and Katzner claimed it cannot be assumed that the capitalist will be able to choose any b in B. "The worker may allow the capitalist to do this, or the capitalist may somehow induce the worker to perform b, but this is certainly not guaranteed by the contract."[21]

Therefore, Gintis and Katzner propose a model of the enterprise as an institution in which not only is the employer maximizing profits, but workers are maximizing their own objective functions after signing their contracts subject to indirect constraints employers can place on them in the form of rule, incentive, and information/guidance structures. In their own words, what emerges from a more rigorous treatment than traditional neoclassical analysis is the "fundamental observation...that except under highly restrictive conditions, the pursuit of profit maximization by the firm may not allocate internal human activity Pareto optimally."[22]

More specifically, Gintis and Katzner rigorously establish a series of theorems stipulating sufficient conditions for profit-maximizing decisions by employers to yield Pareto optimal outcomes. Although a number of technical complications must be guaranteed as well, any of the following conditions is essentially sufficient:

1. If the employer can choose each worker's act, b, from among the set of actions, B, which the employee makes available to the employer in return for wage, w, profit-maximizing decisions by the employer will be Pareto optimal as well (the Coase/Simon conclusion)

2. If workers' preferences are such that of their own free will they make decisions that conform perfectly to the needs of the director; profit maximization yields Pareto optimality

3. If workers are exclusively influenced by immediate superior's goals and premises, profit-maximizing decisions will be Pareto optimal

4. If workers have no preferences concerning what action from B they perform, but are exclusively motivated by monetary incentives; profit-maximizing decisions will be Pareto optimal

It is worth noting that Gintis and Katzner do not establish necessary conditions for the equivalence of profit-maximizing decisions with decisions that generate a Pareto optimal organization of the workplace, whose restrictiveness could then be explicitly evaluated. On the other hand, the highly restrictive sufficient conditions they do establish is certainly suggestive. If one must assume complete employer control over worker behavior, or worker preferences that coincide with employer preferences concerning what workers do for their wages, or workers whose only on-the-job desire is to please the immediate supervisor, or workers who will do anything their employer asks for the tiniest monetary bonus, in order for profit maximization to yield Pareto optimal organization of production, how likely is this to occur?

2.1.6 Samuel Bowles

In 1985, the *American Economic Review* ended more than ten years of "benign neglect" of the radical "conflict school" when it published an article by Samuel Bowles that succinctly explained the logic of many conflict theorists.[23] Bowles presented the argument in terms familiar to traditional theorists. He demonstrated that if an employee's "objective function includes some positively valued on-the-job activities (or inactivity) that are associated with a positive opportunity cost in terms of working,"[24] individual employer profit-maximizing behavior sometimes requires (1) employing supervisory workers even though they produce nothing themselves, and (2) rejecting technologies that generate more output for ones that produce less.

The logic is quite simple, profit-maximizing employers must hire supervisory staff who produce nothing, as long as their wages are less than the revenues gained from the additional output the supervisors extract from other employees. When choosing between alternative technologies, profit maximizers must forgo technologies yielding greater output in favor of technologies that require smaller supervisory staffs and thereby reduce supervisory costs by more than the loss in revenues. Bowles argued that his simple model demonstrated the essential logic of the conflict theory as he made clear that the conclusions were independent of asymmetric knowledge on the part of employer and employee.

However, these conclusions should come as no surprise to traditional theorists who cannot have been unaware that capitalists employ and pay supervisors who produce nothing themselves. Once it is conceded that employing supervisors capable of producing something, but who, in fact, produce nothing is necessary for profit maximization, all of Bowles' formal modeling and the first two-thirds of his argument become unnecessary because the conclusion of social inefficiency is immediate.

To his credit, Bowles recognizes that before private enterprise is blamed for this social inefficiency one must point out how the inefficiency could be avoided. In other words, one must point out why the problem of "malfeasance" would be greater in private enterprise systems than under some alternative organization of production. In this vein Bowles distinguishes between what he terms the "Neo-Hobbesian" concept of malfeasance and the "Marxian" concept of class conflict. He states:

> If the organization of the work process and the principles determining the distribution of net revenues rising therefrom influence workers' attitudes toward work and hence are among the determinants of the extraction function, the Neo-Hobbesian conclusions [that the social costs of combating malfeasance are unavoidable] are considerably altered.[25]

> If it could be shown that in an environment which workers perceived to be more fair, or more consistent with their self-respect, for example, they would choose to expend more effort for any given employer strategy, then it is a simple matter to demonstrate that the initial outputs could be

produced with unchanged levels of labor effort in production and using less surveillance labor.[26]

And Bowles makes explicit the challenge of the conflict school:

Class conflict in the labor process of a capitalist economy is the result of a specific and mutable set of social institutions; the conflict over work intensity being at least in part the consequence of the particular organization of work and the resulting alienated nature of labor.[27]

In the end, the entire issue is remarkably simple, if there is an alternative social organization of production in which workers have less impulse to shirk, or in which that impulse can be checked at less social cost, private enterprise is demonstrably inefficient. The waste might take the form of employing people who could have been producing output to merely watch over others or using technologies that produce less but reduce surveillance costs. In either case, more waste occurs under conditions of private enterprise production than under some alternative arrangement in which work effort is more readily forthcoming or coerced at lower social cost.

Regrettably, Bowles does not explain further in his *American Economic Review* article exactly what alternative social organizations of production might reduce the problem of malfeasance or why we should expect them to do so. But from this and other writings it is clear he believes more participatory and egalitarian arrangements would be likely to induce greater work effort at less social cost,[28] and we certainly agree. However, as we explain in chapter 8, a "hard boiled" Neo-Hobbesian might feel uncompelled to accept Bowles' conclusion without further elaboration.

2.1.7 Gil Skillman

The task of applying principal-agent theory to the conflict theory of the firm has only recently begun. In 1985, Gil Skillman[29] reviewed previous contributions and paved the way for further applications. In the principal-agent relationship agents are contracted by a principal to perform actions that affect the utility of the latter under conditions where (1) the principal and agents have different preferences regarding decisions such as effort, compensation, or risk; and, (2) the principal and agents have nonidentical information sets concerning agents' potentials or actions.

The central thrust of this literature has analyzed the implications for allocative efficiency and choice of contracts of moral hazard, in which the agents' unseen action affects the probability distribution of the outcome, and adverse selection, in which the agents' actions can be observed, but not evaluated properly.[30] But if we relax traditional assumptions of perfect knowledge of the production possibility set by employers and employees alike, potential for using the theory to gaze inside the "black box" erected by traditional welfare theory around the production process is obvious.

In just the past few years "principal-agent theory" has been used to increase the theoretical rigor of both "radical/conflict" and "institutionalist/malfeasance" analyses of the firm. Sappington analyzed contracts under the condition that agents cannot be forced to work "too hard" in debilitating conditions, exploring implications of the "limited liability condition" for employment contracts.[31] Stiglitz analyzed the trade-off between piece rates and wages in a principal-agent relationship.[32] Holmstrom, Sappington, Harris, Raviv, Christensen, and Skillman have analyzed the implications of assuming agents are better informed than the principal about productive parameters.[33] There have been numerous applications with multiple agents, and Radner and Skillman have initiated models in which the principal-agent relation is analyzed over time.[34]

2.2 Economic Discrimination

The question is not whether economic discrimination exists in the U.S., because empirical evidence is overwhelming.[35] The question is not even what the *causes* may be, since there are clearly various reasons why individuals of different races and sexes, but with comparable initial potentials, receive disparate forms of employment. The question is whether private employment, under competitive conditions, can be expected to ameliorate or aggravate economic discrimination, or if there are reasons to believe it may do both.

Adherents of the "radical/conflict" school of the labor process have argued that recognizing the qualitatively unique aspects of human labor in the production process, and specifically the importance to employers of limiting workers' ability to resist managerial initiatives collectively, are crucial to understanding the economics of discrimination. Such explanations have come to be known as "divide and conquer" theories of economic discrimination. In a major empirical treatment of black/white income and wage differentials in the U.S., Michael Reich presented a simple theoretical model of the "divide and conquer" theory in which profit maximization under competitive conditions requires discriminatory behavior by employers.[36] Obviously this explanation of economic discrimination runs directly contrary to the conclusions of traditional welfare theory which hold that

1. Competitive labor, goods, and financial markets tend to mitigate discriminatory behavior on the part of employers

2. "Divide and conquer" theories amount to "conspiracy theories" that lack an explanation of why the employers' "cartel" does not break down under competitive conditions

Once again, the debate—or more accurately, the lack of productive debate—between mainstream and nonmainstream theories of economic discrimination is highly instructive about the influence of the traditional paradigm. First we review traditional neoclassical treatment and then "divide and conquer" theory.

2.2.1 Kenneth Arrow

Kenneth Arrow has provided a beautiful presentation of the logic and coherence of the neoclassical view, and since he goes to considerable lengths to consciously consider the methodological biases of the approach, his treatment is of particular interest.[37]

Arrow begins by warning that his discussion is "a programmatic and methodological rather than a confident analysis,"[38] and that his "intention is to present the deficiencies of neoclassical analysis" as well as its strengths. He continues:

> To avoid misunderstanding, let me make clear my general attitude toward the fruitfulness and value of marginal analysis. On the one hand, I believe its clarifying value in social thought is great....So long as scarcity is an issue and social organizations for coping with it are complex, these principles and their logical elaboration and empirical implementation will be important....On the other hand, everyone knows that neoclassical economics is seriously deficient in two directions: (1) its implications, though often exemplified in the real world, are also often falsified;...and (2) the implications of neoclassical economics are frequently very weak. Consequently, neoclassical economics says nothing about important economic phenomena.

But after noting that income differentials are obviously linked with other social dimensions, and there is no reason to impose the burden of a full explanation upon economic theory, Arrow elaborates upon the traditional neoclassical theory of economic discrimination. While Arrow accepts the fact that only about half the 35 percent differential that persists between black and white mean earnings in the U.S. can be explained by differences in unemployment rates and supply-side factors, he argues that economic discrimination can still best be explained by the neoclassical theory in which white employees' "taste for discrimination" plays the critical role. His own contribution is to elaborate the concepts of "personnel investment" and "employer information costs" to eliminate important anomalies in previous versions of this neoclassical model.

In the process, Arrow specifically exonerates employers from the list of suspects who might be responsible for economic discrimination. According to Arrow the forces of competition both eliminate employers who would discriminate out of a personal "taste" to do so, and prevent employers from colluding to enhance profits through a "divide and conquer" strategy. We quote Arrow at great length to illustrate how the blind spot in the traditional paradigm for the production process can affect even the most critically self-conscious and brilliant theoretician.

Arrow reasons: "Since it appears that supply considerations can explain only part of the black-white income differential, it is advisable to turn to the demand side." "If we assume away productivity differences between black and white employees, the simplest explanation of the existence of wage differences is the taste of the employer." He then recapitulates the results of modeling an "employer taste for discrimination" hypothesis. If all employers discriminate equally, and if employers' utility depends only on the ratio of the two kinds of workers, it can be shown that black workers lose, white workers gain an equal amount of wages, and employers neither gain nor lose as compared with a nondiscriminatory situation.

At this point Arrow observes, "We have a coherent and by no means implausible account of the economic implications of racial discrimination. In the grossest sense, it accounts for the known facts." Yet he concludes, "Still, I do not find this is satisfactory."

He explains it is not "the excessive generality of utility hypotheses about economic behavior" that troubles him, since this "seems intrinsic in the nature of the case." Nor is the charge that "we have offered no explanation of racial discrimination but simply referred the problem to an unanalyzed realm—like Moliere's intellectual who explained that opium produces sleep because it contains a great deal of the dormitive principle"—what leads him to reject "tastes for discrimination" explanations. To this charge he answers, "In a sense, all scientific explanation involves the same process of musical chairs; all we ask is that the explanatory principles have some degree of generality and parsimony."

Instead, Arrow rejects "employer taste" explanations of persistent wage differentials unrelated to productivity differentials because they neglect the influence of "those vast forces of greed and aggressiveness that we are assured and assure students are the mainsprings of economic activity in a private enterprise economy; not the best but the strongest motives of humanity, as Marshall had said." Assuming the trade-off between discrimination and profits is less for some employers than others, "presumably they will take advantage of the gap between black and white wages by demanding the black labor. In the long run, the less discriminatory will either drive the more discriminatory out of business or, if not, will cause the wage difference to fall. If we suppose that there are some actual or potential employers who do not discriminate at all, then the wage difference should, in the long run, fall to zero." In other words, if employer tastes for discrimination were the cause of wage discrimination, competition for profits and investment funds in goods and capital markets should erode these differentials in the long run.

Arrow qualifies this conclusion by observing that even with forces of competition in the capital market to make up for whatever degree of lack of competition might exist in goods markets providing "leeway" for the survival of discriminating employers, it is not necessary to assume that "they are driven out as sharply as might be supposed." It is more that "the price they have to pay for their tastes will depend on the tastes of others in the market" as well as the degree of indeterminacy permitted by the incompleteness of competitive forces. But regardless of their degree of success, Arrow reiterates the key conclusion of neoclassical theory concerning discrimination:

> *The fundamental point is that the competitive pressures*, to the extent that they are decisive, *work toward the elimination of racial differences* in income, under the usual assumptions of economic theory [emphasis added].

Having concluded that "employer taste" explanations are unpersuasive, Arrow proceeds to apply the same utility analysis to "other members of the productive team." If white workers in higher ranks in the firm dislike working with blacks under them, and if it is assumed that these discriminatory tastes "are determined by the ratio of blacks to whites under them rather than the amounts, it can be shown that in equilibrium the black workers lose, the white workers in lower ranks gain an equal amount, and neither the white higher ranking workers nor the employers gain or lose money income." Similarly, if white workers in lower ranks dislike working with blacks above them, "neutral" employer behavior will yield a black/white wage disparity in the higher echelons.

Moreover Arrow points out: "Even if the wage compensation needed to work with blacks is the same in the two situations, lower working with higher and vice versa, the cost to the employer is much greater in one case than the other simply because there are so many more lower level employees...[which is] especially interesting, because it explains why more highly educated blacks are more heavily discriminated against."

But the critical reason Arrow finds "employee taste" explanations of discrimination more plausible than "employer taste" models is that he finds competitive pressures more restrictive of employer tastes than white worker tastes.

> A model in which white employers and employees were motivated by a dislike of association with blacks as well as more narrowly economic motives would give a satisfactory qualitative account of observed racial discrimination in wages but, *at least as far as employers are concerned,*

it is hard to understand how discriminatory behavior could persist in the long run in the face of competitive pressures [emphasis added].

Seeing no disciplining forces of competition to render "employee taste" explanations implausible, Arrow discusses two such models in detail: the first due to Gary Becker with white and black employees perfect substitutes, and the second an extension of Becker's model to the case of "complementary" kinds of labor.

Suppose for a simple model that there is only one kind of utility function [of the white employees] expressing a tradeoff between wages and the proportion of white workers in the labor force of the firm. Any employer can purchase black labor at a fixed price, but for white labor he must choose some point on an indifference curve between wages and the white proportion....If the wages required by whites for an all-white labor force are lower than black wages, total segregation for whites is optimum for the firm, while in the contrary case an all-black labor force is cheapest....At a general equilibrium with full employment of both types of labor, some firms must be segregated in one direction and some in the other. It would never pay a firm to have a mixed labor force, since they would have to raise the wages of their white workers above the level for the all-white option. The firms would also have to find the two types of segregation equally profitable; otherwise, they would all switch to one or the other. This requires that...there would be no wage differentials.

The analysis of discriminatory feelings by perfect substitutes has lessons for discrimination by complementary types of labor too. If we suppose that there are black workers available at both higher and lower levels the employer can exploit any racial wage differentials by hiring a labor force that is black at all levels. If the proportions of the different skills in the black labor force are different from those desired, the resulting equilibrium will not equate wages at each level, but there will be a tendency to equate wages on the average.

However, Arrow quickly admits obvious problems with these models. While they "explain" the significantly improbable degree of segregation we find in individual firms, they also predict (1) in the long run discriminatory wage differentials should disappear; and (2) slight variations in black/white wage differentials should stampede firms from one kind of segregation to another.

Arrow agrees that neither of these "predictions" correspond to reality. These were the "anomalies" that plagued the traditional neoclassical explanation of economic discrimination.

Here we can do no better than let Arrow speak for himself:

One might search for other and more stable explanatory structures, but I know of none that have been proposed or that seem at all credible. I propose that we look more closely at the long run adjustment process.

> In particular, as I have already suggested, when dealing with nonconvexities [the fact that firms prefer extreme alternatives to compromises is technically a "failure of convexity"], the adjustment process may have to be very rapid indeed. You must recall that in these circumstances marginal adjustments are punished, not rewarded. If the firm is to gain by a change, it has to go all the way. Intuitively, we are not surprised that a firm will hesitate to scrap its entire labor force and replace it with another. The problem is to give an acceptable formalization of this intuition.

While we seldom find Arrow engaged in such practices, this appears to be attaching an epicycle to an old theory to rationalize an anomaly that would otherwise fester like an open sore. Arrow argues:

> We have only to assume that the employer makes an investment, let us call it a personnel investment, every time a worker is hired...to explain why the adjustments that would wipe out racial wage differentials do not occur or at least are greatly retarded....If the firm starts with an all-white labor force, it will not find it profitable to fire that force, in which its personnel capital has already been sunk, and hire an all-black force in which a new investment has to be made simply because black wages are now slightly less than white wages.

This concludes the argument, but the full rescue of neoclassical theory is spelled out as follows:

> Suppose that initially the labor force is devoid of blacks and then some enter; at the same time an additional entry of whites occurs, and some new equilibrium emerges. Under the kinds of assumptions we have been making, a change, if it occurs at all, must be an extreme change, but three kinds of extremes, or corner maxima now exist. The typical firm may remain segregated white though possibly adding more white workers, it may switch entirely to a segregated black state, or it may find it best to keep its present white working force while adding black workers. In the last case, of course, it will have to increase the wages of the white workers to compensate for their feelings of dislike, but may still find it profitable to do so because replacing the existing white workers by blacks means a personnel investment. If we stick closely to the model...we note that only the all-white firms are absorbing the additional supply of white workers, so there must be some of those in the new equilibrium situation. On the other hand, there must be some firms that

are all black or else some integrated firms whose new workers are black in order to absorb the new black workers. It can be concluded in either case, however, that a wage difference between black and white workers will always remain in this model.[39] Furthermore, there will be some segregated white firms. Whether the remaining firms will be segregated black or integrated will depend on the degree of discriminatory feeling by white workers against mixing with blacks.

The generalization that may be hazarded on the basis of the discussion thus far can be stated as follows: if we start from a position where black workers enter an essentially all-white world, the social feelings of racialism by employers and by employees, both of the same and of complementary types, will lead to a difference in wages. The forces of competition and the tendency to profit-maximization operate to mitigate these differences [in employers' racism]. The basic fact of a personnel investment, however, prevents these counteracting tendencies from working with full force [on employees' racism]. In the end, we remain with wage differences coupled with tendencies to segregation.[40]

Having gone to these great lengths to rescue the traditional explanation of economic discrimination as deriving essentially from the prejudices of white employees, Arrow finally explains why he finds a theory based on the "proximate determinant of the demand for labor, the [profit-maximizing] employer's decisions," unacceptable. Again we offer extensive citation to illustrate the pervasive effects of the traditional paradigm.

Finally, a comment on the question of group interests. It is certainly a common view that in some sense racial discrimination is a device by which the whites in the aggregate gain at the expense of the blacks....On purely methodological grounds, I do not think such a view can be denied, provided it works, though it is contrary to the tradition of economics. Economic explanations for discrimination or other phenomena tend to run in individualistic terms, and the models presented earlier [the neoclassical models Arrow reviews and finally modifies to his satisfaction] are no exception. Economists ask what motivates an employer or an individual worker. They tend not to accept as an explanation a statement that employers as a class would gain by discrimination, for they ask what would prevent an individual employer from refusing to discriminate if he prefers and thereby profit. Economists do indeed recognize group interests if they appear in legal form, as in tariffs, or licensing.

I think something can be said for views of this kind, but their mechanism needs careful exploration. We must really ask who benefits, and how are

51

the exploitative agreements carried out? In particular, how are the competitive pressures that would undermine them held in check? The exploitation of the blacks can work only if the tendency of individual employers to buy the cheapest labor is somehow suppressed.[41] Recall the great difficulty that producers of rubber and of coffee have had in their efforts to create a mutually beneficial monopoly.

It seems very difficult to construct a model in which employers gain in any obvious way; the gains to the whites appear to accrue to white workers primarily. This fact, if it is one, already creates difficulties for the group interest hypothesis; after all, the employers are the most direct possible agents of exploitation, and it would be better for the theory if they were beneficiaries. In any case, we are not to imagine conspiracies in which 170 million white Americans put their heads together.

Thus Arrow rejects what he admits at first appears a more reasonable form of explanation, one in which the perpetrators of the discriminatory acts do so because it is in their own interest.

Our purpose in dwelling at such length on the neoclassical treatment of economic discrimination was to illustrate the detrimental impact of the traditional welfare paradigm on where and how one looks for explanations. In this particular case we find a peerless theorist, far more sensitive than most to the limitations and biases of his chosen approach, struggling to make his theory fit the facts. Our point is not that he does not, in the end, succeed in explaining the anomalies. Ironically our point is precisely that he does succeed!

Arrow provides the best treatment of economic discrimination possible within the traditional paradigm.[42] With a black box surrounding the production process it is literally impossible to make competitive employer behavior consistent with purposeful economic discrimination on the part of employers. Hence the necessity of what we find a far-fetched, convoluted explanation. Indeed, it appears Arrow finds it so as well.

It would be difficult to find a better example of a brilliant theorist at disadvantage precisely because of his knowledge. As Arrow states with justified confidence, "Especially when dealing with problems central to economics, the difference in approach between trained economists and others, however able, is enormous." But not only does mastery of theory make possible clarification of truly insightful intuitions, it "selects" what intuitions will receive attention and "channels" their development. For this reason it is possible from time to time for noneconomists to see an economic problem more clearly than "trained economists." Who but "trained economists," for instance, would have believed in the validity of Say's Law, which asserts the theoretical impossibility of "a general glut" during the century between the writings of David Ricardo and J. M. Keynes? And who but "trained economists" would find their explanation of racial discrimination in a rationalization of what long-run adjustment really means to permit nonconvexities imposed by discriminating tastes of employees to coincide with the observed fact that profit-maximizing employers continue to find it profitable to pay blacks less than whites?

Our argument is not with Kenneth Arrow, who is constantly at pains to avoid the pitfalls of his theoretical training (read, "traditional paradigm"), and who almost always explicitly warns of the dangers of hidden neoclassical presumptions, and to whom we owe much. Our argument is with the paradigm itself, which in this case prevents analysts from dropping the abstractions that create a black box around the production process, for inserting a small quantity of "realism" (read, "one ray of light") inside the black box permits formulation of a direct explanation of continuing discrimination on the grounds that it is profitable for employers even in competitive conditions, that is, an explanation that avoids the pitfalls of assuming a successful conspiracy. It is only the traditional paradigm, with its blind spot inside the black box, that makes the far more "natural starting point, the proximate determinant of the demand for labor, [profit-maximizing] employer's decisions," in Arrow's words, impossible to accept because it is impossible to reconcile with the traditional framework.

2.2.2 *Michael Reich*

While Michael Reich is not the only one to present a "divide and conquer" explanation of economic discrimination in terms of the "conflict theory of the firm,"[43] his is the easiest analysis for us to build upon.

Reich presents a theoretical model[44] in which output depends only on "labor done," and in which black and white labor are technically perfect substitutes. However, Reich stipulates that "labor done" is a function not only of the quantity of "labor power" hired, but of the "bargaining power" of employees within the firm after they have signed the labor contract. He further stipulates that the "bargaining power" of employees is a function of the white/black wage ratio and the white/black employment ratio within the firm. In particular, since black and white labor are perfect substitutes and all labor is homogeneous, Reich reasons that by paying whites more than blacks, employers can aggravate racial antagonisms among the work force, thereby weakening workers' bargaining power and enhancing employers' ability to extract "labor done" from "labor power hired." Reich also stipulates that by raising the white/black employment ratio within the firm above the white/black ratio in the work force as a whole, employers can aggravate racial antagonisms, thereby weakening their employees' solidarity.

The employer must choose how many whites and how many blacks to hire and what to pay employees of each race. Assuming that the black wage rate is set in the marketplace, but that individual employers can raise white employees' wage rate above the market rate for blacks, the employer's choice variables can be modeled as: how many blacks to hire, what white/black employment ratio to establish, and what white/black wage ratio to set.

Reich demonstrates that in this model necessary conditions for profit maximization are that individual employers make the white/black wage ratio in their firms greater than one and the white/black employment ratio greater than the white/black ratio in the labor force at large. In other words, Reich demonstrates that under his assumptions employers who are competitors in both input and output markets must engage in wage and employment discrimination precisely in order to maximize profits.

In this very simple but elegant "conflict" model of the firm we arrive at exactly the opposite conclusions from Arrow regarding who benefits from discrimination and the relationship of competitive pressures to maximize profits and economic discrimination. For while white employees do better than blacks in Reich's model as well, the competitive employer is a direct beneficiary of his discriminatory actions, and it is impossible to say whether or not white employees would have a lower or higher real wage in the absence of discrimination. The reasons for these results are obvious:

1. It would be profit reducing for employers in Reich's model not to aggravate racial antagonisms as long as doing so raises revenues by increasing the actual labor they extract from the labor power they hire more than it raises costs from the differential paid their white workers.

2. Whether or not white employees receive a lower or higher real wage due to employer discrimination depends on whether the differential money wage they receive is outweighed by the greater amount of work they must perform because of lower bargaining power.

The model abstracts from all extraneous matters: Homogeneous labor is the only input. Black and white labor are perfect technical substitutes. The model stipulates competitive conditions; no collusion or cartel is necessary to explain how employers benefit from discrimination. Consequently, there is no need to explain, in turn, how the cartel is preserved from competitive pressures to cheat. The only racial condition assumed is the historical legacy of racial mistrust and antagonism between whites and blacks; there is no presumption of "tastes" for discrimination on the parts of employers nor even any assumption that white workers prefer not to work under or over blacks. The model fulfills all of Arrow's wishes for a more direct explanation, based on the self-interest of those who make decisions as those interests are defined by forces of competition for profits.

But to be accepted, the model also requires analysts to treat labor as a qualitatively distinct input. It requires analysts to distinguish between what is paid for in the labor market and the actual result in the labor process. It requires looking inside the black box of the production possibility set and seeing at least the rudimentary forms of a labor process carried out under the social organization of private enterprise. In sum, it requires analysts to do the one thing that is most difficult for them—to step outside the traditional welfare paradigm.

2.3 Segmented Labor Markets

In the late 1960s and early 1970s interest and empirical research rekindled along institutional lines originally pioneered by J. R. Commons concerning the structure of internal and external labor markets. What is most interesting from our perspective was the new light this work shed on possible reasons for the appearance of "segmented labor markets." Joan Robinson had developed a coherent analysis of segmented labor markets in terms of differential elasticities of supply of different laboring groups as early as the 1930s.[45] But the work of a new generation of institutionalists investigating segmented labor markets implied an alternative explanation: development of internal job ladders (or what was confusingly termed internal labor markets) within large firms might contribute to segmentation of external markets for labor. On the one hand, an explanation was sought on the supply side, and the traditional paradigm was no obstacle to developing the analysis. On the other hand, analysts looked to the demand side, and a detailed vision of the dynamics of the production process inside the traditional black box was required.

2.3.1 Peter Doeringer and Michael Piore

Doeringer and Piore were credited for sparking a body of work that came to be known as the "dual" or "segmented" labor market school.[46] Inherent in their approach was the idea that segmented labor markets were due more to employers' behavior than objective conditions of labor supply. Difficulty in even conceiving the demand-side explanation within the traditional paradigm is sufficient to demonstrate our point. But it is worth pointing out empirical anomalies of the supply-side explanation. If empirical evidence were totally consistent with a supply-side explanation of segmented labor markets, the theoretical failure of the traditional paradigm would, perhaps, be of little practical consequence. But explanation in terms of differential supply elasticities of workers implies that the group with the smaller elasticity of supply would receive the lower wage. While there may be reason to think that econometric studies have misspecified what are, in fact, demand-side influences as differential supply elasticities of black and female labor, the case remains that a wide variety of careful empirical studies conclude that the labor supply of blacks and women is more, not less, elastic than that of white men.[47]

In any case, the logic of the demand-side explanation that was invisible to those immersed in the traditional paradigm is as follows: Employers have an incentive to develop internal job ladders with pay rates that vary from marginal revenue products and pay rates for equivalent labor categories in external markets. The incentive derives from the internal ladder's usefulness in extracting effort and diminishing employee solidarity—nonproblems for the traditional paradigm but very real problems for employers. This entails two consequences.

1. If much worker mobility occurs within the job ladders of large firms rather than between firms,[48] employers can create a degree of monopsony power for themselves with internal job ladders even if external labor markets are competitive.

2. If participation in the economy of large firms with internal job ladders is significant, over time internal structures will necessarily shape demand structures of external labor markets since the latter are ultimately nothing more than aggregates of the internal structures of all firms. Hence arises a demand-side explanation of segmented external labor markets.

We will use our new welfare theory to further explore the logic of such a demand-side explanation of segmented external labor markets and their relation to internal job ladders, more carefully specifying the conditions under which such phenomenon would presumably exist, in chapter 8.

2.4 Influence of the Traditional Paradigm

Without doing them too great an injustice, we can organize nontraditional treatments of the labor process into "schools" that variously combine four types of insight or "themes":

1. The first theme emphasizes that in private enterprise economies the right to conceptualize, organize, and direct the laboring capacities of workers lies with their employers. And independent of how just or generous the terms of compensation may, or may not, be, this situation implies a necessary loss of potential well-being as a fundamental human need—the need to conceive and direct one's own activities—goes unmet. Moreover, in all likelihood a loss of efficiency occurs as well because important human productive capacities go unutilized.

2. The second theme highlights the formal difference between hiring specific labor services and employing people with particular capacities for a period of time. It notes that signing the labor contract

does not automatically preserve the "integrity" of the labor exchange from the employer's view point, and observes that the employer must consider the choice of technology and reward structure in this light.

3. The third theme emphasizes that aggravating employees' social antagonisms can serve to diminish workers' ability to resist employers' efforts to extract more "labor done" from "labor power hired."

4. The fourth theme stresses that employees may well know things about their own capabilities and the production process that employers do not so that the information sets of employers and employees regarding the production process may be asymmetric.

Different previous treatments of the labor process emphasize different combinations of these themes. And certainly all four themes have important consequences that deserve to be explored. However, as we will explain in chapter 8, traditional theory can pose appealing rebuttal to these criticisms as they have been presented. On the other hand, we believe the criticisms we have reviewed in this chapter are well taken and apply even in the most competitive conditions.

We will find the implications of the four themes taken alone are limited, whereas the criticisms can be better defended, and the consequences are more far reaching when presented within the new welfare paradigm and theory we develop in part 2. Specifically, combining the above themes in a multiperiod model with a fifth theme that has been little emphasized in nontraditional treatments to date yields a more theoretically solid critique of private enterprise production. The fifth theme, which emerges directly from the alternative paradigm we develop in chapter 5, can be stated as follows:

5. Employees' capacities, personalities, attitudes, and relations with one another are all potentially affected by the production process. Moreover, there is every reason to believe employers and employees will have very different preferences for what kind of transformations of employees' human characteristics they would prefer to take place. Whereas the traditional paradigm and theory either ignores these changes in human characteristics or presumes they are only of concern to the employees in whom they reside, we will discover that for reasons such as those reviewed in this chapter there is every reason to believe these "human" effects should be of great concern to the employer as well.

While the full argument must await future chapters, it is important to note here the debilitating influence of the traditional paradigm on a careful analysis of the production process under private enterprise. The traditional paradigm ignores the problem of getting employees to "honor" the wage contract, offers no vision of human development, defines no concepts identifying "human characteristics" and "human outputs" of production, and offers no treatment of social relations among people in different and similar roles in production. All these omissions blind traditional theorists to important aspects of the production process necessary for advancing our understanding of discrimination, labor market structure, and the efficiency of private enterprise. Instead of a welfare theoretic analysis of the production process we have had a vacuous production possibility set, that is, a nontheory of production.[49]

As Abba Lerner once said, "An economic transaction is a solved political problem. Economics has gained the title of queen of the social sciences by choosing solved political problems as its domain."[50] Which is perfectly fine if we are analyzing an economic arena in which all the political problems have truly been solved. But after signing the labor contract, important "political" problems still remain. And particularly in a multiperiod analysis of production, among the important remaining problems is determination of what individual and group characteristics employees will have when they face their employer in future negotiations over the wage rate and over how much "integrity" the labor contract will have.

3

EXTERNALITIES
AND PUBLIC GOODS

I<small>T WAS ONCE</small> a commonplace among economists that market institutions could not be relied on to generate Pareto optimal outcomes in the presence of externalities and public goods. Richard Musgrave referred to externalities as among those conditions "where the forces of the market cannot secure optimal results," and to public goods as a condition "where the market mechanism fails altogether."[1]

For most neoclassical theorists the conclusion was obvious: While markets are ideal institutions for allocating resources in the case of "normal" goods, some "political" mechanism must be sought for determining allocation of resources in "abnormal" cases of externalities and public goods. Musgrave put it succinctly:

> Since the market mechanism fails to reveal consumer preferences in social wants, it may be asked what mechanism there is by which the government can determine the extent to which resources should be released for the satisfaction of such wants....A political process must be substituted for the market mechanism.[2]

The purpose of this chapter is to

1. Summarize the state of public finance theory as of 1970

2. Call attention to the work of the most noteworthy previous critic of the neoclassical view and treatment of externalities and public goods, E. K. Hunt, which has been, regrettably, almost totally ignored

3. Situate recent work on "incentive compatible mechanisms" in the context of the traditional theory of public finance

4. Explain how, in our view, the traditional paradigm served to delay rather than facilitate progress in this area

3.1 Theory of Public Finance as of 1970

Public finance theory could have been summarized in 1970 as follows:

1. In the presence of externalities and public goods competitive market equilibria could not be expected to yield socially efficient resource allocations. This was due to "special" characteristics of externalities and public goods called "nonexcludability" and "market thinness," or what was more commonly called the "free rider problem."

2. This was not to say that in the presence of externalities and public goods Pareto optimal allocations did not exist. Indeed, as Samuelson showed, if one knew the preferences and technological capabilities of all agents in an economy, Pareto optimal allocations could be calculated even in the presence of externalities and public goods.[3]

3. Though there was disagreement regarding the best course of action to be taken concerning externalities and public goods, there was a general consensus that no known mechanism that might be substituted for the market could be relied on to generate efficient allocations. Not only were markets combined with "voluntary associations" judged predictably inefficient, all proposed alternatives to the market mechanism and "voluntary" initiatives were also considered demonstrably imperfect. Sentiment was strong that a procedure that "solved" the "free rider problem" was theoretically impossible, and the best that could ever be hoped for was maximum amelioration.

4. The preceding conclusions were not regarded as particularly disheartening because most goods were viewed as private goods. Externalities and public goods, while troublesome, were exceptions to the rule.

We quote Richard Musgrave, a senior spokesperson in the field, to demonstrate that these are not our conclusions alone. Regarding the inefficiency of markets and "voluntary" initiatives, Musgrave said, "social wants are those wants satisfied by services that must be consumed in equal amounts by all. People who do not pay for the services cannot be excluded from the benefits that result; and since they cannot be excluded from the benefits, they will not engage in voluntary payments. Hence, the market cannot satisfy such wants."[4]

While sympathetic to "solutions" according to benefit received, Musgrave admitted, "the benefit approach has the advantage of tying the expenditure and tax sides of the budget together and relating both to individual preferences. Yet it fails in that it provides no way of ascertaining the true benefits."[5] But according to Musgrave, "the ability-to-pay approach to the theory of taxation proves even less satisfactory. It gives no clear-cut principles of tax distribution and fails altogether to answer the problem of expenditure determination. Later versions, categorizing the budget as a welfare plan, introduced the expenditure side of the budget and have the merit of emphasizing the planning aspects. However, these versions do not show how to determine the social preferences, without which determination the requirements of the welfare approach are an empty shell."[6]

Musgrave spelled out the common wisdom regarding problems with various voting systems in detail. "In evaluating various voting systems, we must ask ourselves whether they will give a solution that comes close to the utility frontier, and what principles underlie the choice between various points on the frontier. In comparing the rationale of various systems, we can hardly avoid reasoning as if interpersonal utility comparisons can be made, the difference between the old and the new welfare economics of this type being less than is frequently supposed. Disregarding considerations of strategy, much is to be said in favor of the more sensitive ordering resulting from a system of point or plurality voting. Allowing for considerations of strategy, results of the cruder system of majority voting may be the better choice...[But] a voting mechanism, together with a compulsory application of the budget plan thus decided upon...[and the] necessity for compulsory application of a general tax formula means that the resulting solution will not be optimal."[7] And regarding the solution proposed by Tiebout[8] of having people "vote with their feet," Musgrave aptly observed, "the possibility of moving to other communities establishes something equivalent to a market mechanism in local finance, [but] the determination of social wants within any one community remains a problem in social wants."[9] In other words, Tiebout's scheme avoided rather than addressed the fundamental problems of public finance.

All of which led Musgrave, and many others to conclude that while "there is a wide array of situations where the market mechanism involves varying degrees of inefficiency in resource allocation—inefficiencies that arise collateral to the satisfaction of private wants—nevertheless, the satisfaction of such wants in most cases is best left to the market."[10]

3.2 Previous Treatments

3.2.1 E. K. Hunt

No criticism of neoclassical welfare theory is more direct than E. K. Hunt's. Yet no criticism is so little known or has fewer echoing voices.[11]

The Achilles heel of welfare economics is its treatment of externalities....When reference is made to externalities, one usually takes as
a typical example an upwind factory that emits large quantities of sulfur
oxides and particulate matter inducing rising probabilities of em-
physema, lung cancer, and other respiratory diseases to residents
downwind, or a strip-mining operation that leaves an irreparable aesthetic scar on the countryside. The fact is, however, that most of the
millions of acts of production and consumption in which we daily
engage involve externalities. In a market economy any action of one
individual or enterprise which induces pleasure or pain to any other
individual or enterprise and is under priced by a market constitutes an
externality. Since the vast majority of productive and consumptive acts
are social, i.e., to some degree they involve more than one person, it
follows that they will involve externalities. Our table manners in a
restaurant, the general appearance of our house, our yard or our person,
our personal hygiene, the route we pick for a joy ride, the time of day
we mow our lawn, or nearly any one of the thousands of ordinary daily
acts, all affect, to some degree, the pleasures or happiness of others. *The
fact is...externalities are totally pervasive....*Only the most extreme
bourgeois individualism could have resulted in an economic theory that
assumed otherwise [emphasis added].[12]

From which Hunt concludes "the theory's absolute inability to handle
pervasive externalities should more than suffice to convince any
reasonable person of its utter irrelevance."[13]

Hunt's argument is frighteningly direct. The implicit assumption underlying traditional welfare theory that "private goods" are the rule and
"public goods" the exception is exactly backward. The presumption should
be that a good has "social" aspects until proven otherwise. But the neoclassical assumption is seldom made explicit. And it rarely occurs to anyone
to try to test it empirically, which only makes it more difficult to challenge.
Hunt is brushed off as a Don Quixote tilting at windmills largely because
the assumption is well hidden in the traditional paradigm. Accepting the
"external effect exceptionality assumption" is part of the ideological leap
of faith underlying acceptance of the whole traditional paradigm.

Hunt's first point concerning the relative prevalence of social aspects of
economic actions is as simple as it is significant. His second observation
is equally important but more subtle. Traditional welfare theory "simply
takes the externalities, for which property rights and markets are to be
established, as somehow metaphysically given and fixed. In ignoring the
relational aspects of social life their theory ignores the fact that individuals
can create externalities almost at will."[14] Hunt's explanation is as eloquent
as it is penetrating and begs to be quoted in full:

If we assume the maximizing economic man of bourgeois economics, and if we assume the government establishes property rights and markets for these rights whenever an external diseconomy is discovered [the preferred "solution" of the conservative and increasingly dominant trend within the field of public finance], then each man will soon discover that through contrivance he can impose external diseconomies on other men, knowing that the bargaining within the new market that will be established will surely make him better off. The more significant the social cost imposed upon his neighbor, the greater will be his reward in the bargaining process. It follows from the orthodox assumption of maximizing man that each man will create a maximum of social costs which he can impose on others. D'Arge and I have labeled this process "the invisible foot" of the laissez faire...market place. The "invisible foot" ensures us that in a free-market...economy each person pursuing only his own good will automatically, and most efficiently, do his part in maximizing the general public misery.

To see why this principle has some validity, note that a self-oriented individual will maximize the value, to him, of participating in organized markets and creating nonmarket transactions. Taking this production possibility set for creating external diseconomies, he will select only those with a higher return than he could earn by engaging in market transactions. But by so doing, he will maximize the cost to others in that his gain is someone else's loss. All individuals acting independently to maximize the cost imposed on others will yield a maximum of these costs or payments to society, that is, by selecting only highly productive external effects. The recipient of contrived or inadvertent external diseconomies will undertake defensive expenditures or pay bribes until the usual marginal conditions of efficiency are fulfilled. Thus, the recipient's cost will be minimized for each external diseconomy, and an efficient pattern of external effects will emerge.

But if external diseconomies, in terms of value to the generator, are maximized in the society and if they are efficiently contended with by recipients, then we have a mirror image of consumption theory and Pareto efficiency. That is, instead of allocation of a good to its highest value use with its production costs minimized, we have allocation of a bad (external diseconomy) to its most costly impact, with the impact being minimized in terms of recipient cost as well as production costs. The economy, of course, is efficient but efficient only in providing misery.

To paraphrase a well-known precursor of this theory: every individual necessarily labors to render the annual external costs of the society as great as he can. He generally, indeed, neither intends to promote the public misery nor knows how much he is promoting it. He intends only his own gain, and he is in this, as in many other cases, led by an invisible foot to promote an end which was no part of his intention. Nor is it any better for society that it was no part of it. By pursuing his own interest he frequently promotes social misery more effectually than when he really intends to promote it.[15]

We will pursue Hunt's lead regarding external effects in building our alternative paradigm in chapter 5 and analyzing markets in chapter 7. But in some respects we find his criticisms of traditional welfare theory overdrawn or wide of the mark. Since he is not so lonely in areas where, in our opinion, he errs, as in areas where he hits the mark, these points are worth mentioning.

We find no fault with the concept of Pareto optimality as a formalization of the intuitive notion of social efficiency. Therefore, we reject Hunt's charge that "the neoclassical notion of market efficiency encountered in every branch of applied economics, as well as the bourgeois notion of rational prices encountered in so many discussions of the role of the market in socialist society, have absolutely no meaning whatsoever other than the belief that a free competitive market will tend toward a Pareto optimal situation in which by definition, resources are said to be efficiently allocated and prices are said to be rational. There is no further criterion or justification for using the words efficient and rational than the assertion that the particular resource allocation and price structure obtaining in a free competitive market will have some connection with that envisioned in the analysis of Pareto optimality."[16]

In our view no further justification is needed for deeming an outcome "efficient" than that it is Pareto optimal since the concept of Pareto optimality captures the useful aspects of the notion of social efficiency very well.[17] We have already stipulated that the concept of Pareto optimality has proved exceptionally helpful in formulating difficult propositions and conclusions concerning efficiency with greater precision and rigor. And if a set of prices accurately summarized the relative social costs and benefits of different goods, we would not hesitate to call those prices "rational."[18]

Hunt also voices another claim not uncommon among radical economists. "It is...obvious that this theory is applicable only where individual preferences or tastes do not change over time."[19] We certainly must dissociate ourselves from this view since in chapter 6 we reformulate the three fundamental theorems of welfare economics in a formal model in which individuals' preferences are endogenous and change over time and thereby lay this intuitively appealing criticism to rest. We also find the derivative criticism that traditional welfare theory is inherently static overdrawn as well.

What maximizes welfare in a growing economy is not clear. Is it maximizing the rate of growth, maximizing profit, maximizing consumption, maximizing consumption per head? And with each of these questions comes the issue of the nature and significance of a social rate of time discount to appropriately weight the welfare of unborn generations which is being decisively affected by current consumption and investment decisions. The various criteria of welfare in a growing economy have no necessary consistency. The neoclassical Pareto criterion simply cannot handle such problems. It is by its very nature a static theory which cannot be extended to describe a growing or changing economy.[20]

In the practical world of development policy all the problems Hunt catalogs above do exist, and it is critical to recognize these ambiguities. But in theory, and we emphasize "in theory," it is perfectly clear what is to be maximized for any individual and how "new" individuals must be treated. What is to be maximized for any individual is total utility over his or her entire life. This of course requires an individual well-being function that evaluates the relative contributions to well-being of utility in different time periods. But this is analytically no different from requiring individual preference orderings that evaluate the relative contributions to an individual's well-being of different consumption activities during the same time period. "New" individuals can appear on the scene at any time, as long as they are similarly equipped. Viewed in this way, the problem of "interpersonal" trade-offs in well-being between present and future generations is analytically no different than the problem of "interpersonal comparisons" and trade-offs between individuals living at the same time. In neither case does the concept of Pareto optimality have anything to tell us. But this is not a new, or different, problem, as Hunt implies.

Hunt is also wrong in thinking that the so-called "Cambridge Controversy" has implications for neoclassical welfare theory as applied to "Debreuvian" type models. Among conditions Hunt lists as necessary to guarantee Pareto optimality in private enterprise market economies are: "(c) homogeneous inputs and outputs each divisible into units of any desired size," and "(f) production functions being of smooth curvature, not having increasing returns to scale, and having diminishing marginal rates of substitution along any isoquant curve."[21] He then argues that "assumption (c) on homogeneity of inputs (particularly capital) and (f) about properly behaved production functions, have both been definitively shown to be untenable by the recent Cambridge capital controversy."[22]

This is a misinterpretation of the so-called "Cambridge Controversy." In fact, the Cambridge, England, side of the Cambridge debate successfully challenges the theoretical coherence of the neoclassical concept of "capital" as a homogeneous input that can be used as an argument along with homogeneous "labor" in an "aggregate" production function that is subsequently used to derive the rate of profit in the economy. But homogeneous "capital" is not the kind of homogeneous input relevant to welfare theory. In Debreuvian models the inputs that must be "homogeneous" are particular types of machinery. If two machines thought to be "homogeneous" turned out not to be, a Debreuvian model simply defines two inputs (and two prices) instead of one. Put differently, there are no aggregate variables in Debreuvian models, so any difficulties in defining the aggregate variable, "capital," are of no consequence.

Similarly, in Debreuvian models production functions are individual production functions, or more general yet, production possibility sets. The theoretical coherence and properties of an aggregate production function are irrelevant to a Debreuvian model because no such concept ever appears. In any case, the properties of production functions to which Hunt refers in (f) are relevant to the existence of general equilibria in private enterprise competitive market economies, not to whether or not any equilibria that do exist would be Pareto optimal in any case. The smoothness property of production functions (by which we assume Hunt means infinite input substitutability) is not even necessary for existence of equilibria once one substitutes convex production possibility sets for production functions.

Finally, Hunt and many other critics make much of what is called "the theory of the second best." We in no way dispute the theory as it was admirably demonstrated by Lipsey and Lancaster,[23] but we believe it is often misinterpreted and misapplied.

In Hunt's interpretation "according to the theory of the second best, policies designed to remedy only some and not all of the defects (since simultaneously remedying all would obviously be impossible) will often result in effects diametrically opposed to those envisioned by the authors of these policies."[24] In our view, a more careful interpretation would be: In a context of multidefects, there is no reason to suppose that implementing corrective policies in a random order will not move the economy farther away from optimality rather than closer at each step, up to the last. Before comparing these interpretations, two points need clarifying:

1. The theory of the second best cannot be a direct criticism of neoclassical welfare theory. A welfare theory is a system for ranking outcomes. The theory of the second best says nothing about the particular (incomplete) system of ranking outcomes that we call neoclassical welfare theory except by using it to implicitly accept it. Instead the theory of the second best warns that in a market economy a policy that would move us from a state neoclassical theory it ranks lower to a state it ranks higher if there were only one defect, might instead

move us from a higher to a lower ranked state, if other defects the policy does not address are also present.

2. Nor can the theory of the second best be seen as relevant to only market economies. In a centrally planned economy, if two or more goods were misvalued, correcting the evaluation of one and not the others might well move the economy farther away from Pareto optimality. We might say a "general 'general theory of the second best'" applies to economies that are highly integrated technologically (indecomposable) irrespective of the economic institutions chosen for administering them.

To summarize, while Lipsey and Lancaster demonstrate that piecemeal policy correctives might be counterproductive according to the particular system of ranking we call neoclassical welfare theory in the particular kind of economy called competitive capitalism, their result is most often not sensitive to what system of ranking and what economic institutions one chooses.[25] Instead, the "problem" the theory warns against is the result of technological and social possibilities that are highly integrated.

With all this said, what is the point of the theory of the second best, and how does our interpretation differ from that of Hunt and others? Hunt interprets the theory to mean that the numerous inefficiencies of market economies are hopelessly insensitive to policy correctives as calculated by a partial equilibrium application of neoclassical welfare theory. In short, Hunt feels that the neoclassical claim that market imperfections and failures are correctable via tax, subsidy, and antitrust policies is, in fact, a delusion in a world of multidefects and piecemeal policy making. Interestingly enough, conservatives interpret the theory of the second best as proving there is no point in trying to implement policy correctives at all for what they see as the few demonstrable cases of market inefficiency.

Like Hunt, we do not expect policy correctives to fix most inefficiencies of market economies that, we agree, are totally pervasive. We also see this as good reason to look for an alternative to market allocations. But we draw this conclusion because of the pervasiveness of market failures, the ever present incentives to create more, and the lack of political means and will to correct all but the most egregious. For us the conclusion of incorrectability does not derive from a supposed difficulty with piecemeal policy approaches. And for us the theory of the second best, while indicating that caution is warranted, in no way can be used to defend a policy of inaction in the face of deficiencies.

The key to piecemeal policy correctives is selecting the order of implementation with a little common sense. Imagine an economy that produces two intermediate products and one final good. Suppose the final good is produced by a single firm and sold to hundreds of millions of consumers, one intermediate good is produced by millions of enterprises and the other is produced by fifty firms, and all intermediate goods are purchased as inputs by the firm making the final good. If the corrective policy is antitrust, two industries need to be busted to create competitive conditions everywhere. If we bust piecemeal and select where to begin by flipping a coin, we are obviously as likely to make matters worse as better after step one. This is what the theory of the second best tells us.

But the theory does not say we cannot break up the monopoly/monopsony first and take care of the mildly noncompetitive intermediate industry second. It does not say there is not a second best that falls short of the "best" option of implementing both antitrust policies, but improves upon doing nothing at all. It just cautions that there may be a fourth best that is worse than the third best of standing pat, and that moving without any caution whatsoever is as likely to move us from third to fourth as third to second.

Once this is understood, the practical question becomes: How obvious is the order in which piecemeal corrective policies should be implemented likely to be if we want to achieve the practical goal of improving matters at each step? Our answer is: Frequently, fairly obvious, although technical and social interrelatedness can complicate matters. But we repeat, in any case, these are primarily practical matters equally problematical for all reasonable welfare theories and all highly integrated economies.[26]

3.2.2 *Theodore Groves and Company*

"Incentive compatible mechanisms" have revolutionized the theory of public finance by offering nonmarket mechanisms for allocating resources to public goods with reasonable claims to social efficiency. If the innovators have had to decrease the vacuity of the assumptions concerning preferences or weaken the notion of strategy equilibrium to solve critical social problems others had given up on, what will be remembered eventually is their wisdom in so doing as opposed to the sterile stubbornness of those who crossed their arms and refused to change assumptions long after theirs had no further conclusions to yield.

As late as 1972, Milleron devoted only two of fifty-eight dense pages in his excellent article, "Theory of Value with Public Goods: A Survey Article," to proposed "solutions." After fifty-six pages reviewing work on the meaning of Pareto optimality, core, and equilibrium in an economy with public goods, Milleron needed only two pages to review mechanisms claiming optimality properties and conclude that none were satisfactory. He proved quite prophetic, however, in remarking, "One must remember that the investigations in this field are just beginning and that many new developments are to be expected in the next few years."[27]

Seven years later the *Review of Economic Studies* sponsored a symposium on "incentive compatibility" devoted to "solution" mechanisms to the "free rider problem." The ten new papers published as part of the symposium, together with the path-breaking papers of the previous few years, required an entire essay by Peter Hammond to introduce them. There was suddenly a torrent of sound where before there had been silence. As Hammond explained:

> The only minor exception to the general avoidance of...the important question of how the information from individual agents needed...is to be elicited...[prior to the revolution of "incentive compatible mechanisms"] came in brief discussions by Dreze and de la Vallee Poussin [1971] and by Malinvaud [1972], but their discussions were not thorough since the papers were more concerned with other matters. In recent years, however, particularly since the publication of Hurwicz's fundamental papers [1972 and 1973], much work has been done on identifying "incentive compatible" planning mechanisms. These mechanisms, even if they do not necessarily encourage agents to reveal truthfully and directly the information a planner needs, at least lead to desirable outcomes even when agents do try to manipulate them.[28]

In other words, suddenly a number of "mechanisms" with claims of "solving" what had been considered the "irresolvable" problem of efficient provision of public goods appeared on the scene. In his contribution to the symposium one of those most responsible for the intellectual breakthrough, Theodore Groves, gave the following interpretation:

> [While a planner could easily] pick efficient outcomes when all agents are "telling the truth," it may not be in any agent's self-interest to "tell the truth." ...By reporting falsely his valuations of the choices an agent may be able to secure a larger transfer than necessary to compensate him for any change in y [the vector of public goods] his false reporting causes. For example, by professing little interest in the public good, an agent may reduce his cost share sufficiently to compensate for the otherwise lower quantity of the public good provided, thereby being a "free rider" on the amounts provided by others.

> But whether or not such misrepresentation would benefit an agent depends on the transfer rules specified by the mechanism. Conventional wisdom has long maintained that no transfer rules exist which remove any incentive for dissembling. However, this view has recently been challenged by the discovery of Demand Revealing Mechanisms.[29]

While Vickrey had described examples of demand revealing mechanisms in a paper published in 1961,[30] the idea languished until Groves[31] and Clarke[32] independently picked up the theme in the early 1970s. We attribute the fact that nobody recognized the importance of Vickrey's discovery for so long partly to the influence of the traditional welfare paradigm we have been criticizing. That many continue in ignorance of the significance of incentive compatible mechanisms today is a further effect of a traditional paradigm that minimizes the importance of the problem and steers one away from solutions. It is of particular interest that the full flurry of creative activity that succeeded by the close of the decade in substantially elaborating the set of incentive compatible mechanisms only occurred after Hurwicz had taken a long step toward redefining critical parts of the traditional paradigm in papers published in 1972 and 1973.[33]

The search for "demand-revealing" or "incentive-compatible" mechanisms departed from the assumption that efficient provision of public goods would be possible if only consumers could be induced to reveal their true preferences for public goods; but the problem was that rational consumers would presumably consider how their "messages" about the desirability of public goods affected not only the quantity of public goods the government would end up supplying, but the taxes they would be assessed to pay for them. If reporting high benefits could be expected to raise one's assessment, false reporting and "free riding" would make sense. The key idea was to sever the link between reporting high preferences and receiving high assessments in order to eliminate the incentive to report untruthfully.

Dreze and de la Vallee Poussin[34] drastically weakened the link by distinguishing between assessments to finance the cost of producing the total quantity of a public good and assessments to finance the cost of producing a marginal unit of a public good. If I am asked my willingness to pay for another unit of a public good, and my assessment for the entire amount of the public good that is provided is a positive function of my response, I have a strong incentive to disclaim interest. But if all that is at stake when I report my willingness to pay for another unit of a public good is how much I will be assessed for provision of an additional unit, the incentive to underreport is drastically reduced. Effectively, my answer can have a significant impact on my budget in the first case but not in the second. In the authors' own words:

> For those who would find...that consumers have an incentive to reveal their preferences correctly...surprising, we...remark that it is only natural, since (i) the adjustments in the output of public goods are governed by the revealed preferences of the consumers, and (ii) the revealed preferences of the consumers are used to determine their contributions towards financing these adjustments; they thus apply to the marginal units produced, but not to the intra-marginal units. This second property is crucial in providing the correct incentives.[35]

70

Groves and others rediscovered Vickrey's idea and refined ways to sever the link between an individual's reported willingness to pay and his or her assessment even more completely. The crucial idea behind "demand-revealing mechanisms" is to base one individual's assessment on the reported marginal willingness to pay of others.

Clark[36] incorporated this idea into what has come to be called the pivot mechanism, which Groves and Loeb[37] generalized. The pivot mechanism charges each agent for the sum reported willingness of all others to pay for substituting the public good supply that would have resulted had the agent reported complete indifference to all supplies of public goods for the public good supply resulting from the preferences the agent actually reported. In other words, if by expressing a preference for public goods an individual changes what others have to live with, the individual is assessed the sum inconvenience others claim.

The formulation that most directly revolutionized the field is due to Groves and Ledyard. In Groves and Ledyard's demand-revealing mechanism, "consumer i is simply assessed his proportional cost share of y [the package of public goods provided] minus the reported consumers' surplus of the others plus possibly some lump sum transfer that is independent of his message."[38]

Under the incentive system established by this mechanism, when we ask, How can I reduce my tax bill? the answer is, To all intents and purposes, not at all.[39] And when we ask, How can I best affect the quantities of different public goods I (along with all others) will consume? the answer is, By reporting my willingness to pay truthfully.[40]

Once consumers report their preferences truthfully the government has only to produce the quantity of each public good at which the total marginal willingness to pay, or marginal social benefit, equals marginal cost.

Lest our justifiable enthusiasm be interpreted to imply all problems in the field have been solved, we should note that several sobering "impossibility" theorems have already been demonstrated. A "dominant strategy equilibrium" is said to exist in a game if each player has a strategy that is best regardless of the strategy chosen by any other player. Gibbard and Satterthwaith[41] have proven that no nondictatorial mechanisms exist to yield dominant strategy equilibria for all conceivable preference profiles. Green, Laffont, and Hurwicz[42] have demonstrated that no mechanism exists for all quasi-linear preference profiles (roughly preferences in which collective choices can be compared quantitatively in terms of a "money" equivalent that displays no "income effects") that yields an efficient dominant strategy equilibrium. Moreover, Groves and Ledyard in 1977 acknowledged that demand-revealing mechanisms fail to generate totally efficient allocations because they cannot guarantee a balanced government budget and compliance with Walras' Law.

All this is not to say that what appeared a promising breakthrough on closer inspection is turning sour. By usefully restricting preferences, by usefully weakening our notion of equilibria, and by constructing modifying devices that guarantee budgetary equilibrium,[43] the suggestive power of the initial idea behind the revolution in incentive-compatible mechanisms is being more than adequately defended.

3.3 Influence of the Traditional Paradigm

At the risk of being judged overly harsh, we could say public finance theorists did not seriously get down to work on the central problem of public finance until 1970. The traditional welfare paradigm cannot avoid all responsibility for this delay.

1. The traditional paradigm minimized the importance of the problem by fostering the illusion that external effects were infrequent pieces of flotsam bobbing in a vast, rolling sea of private goods.

2. The concepts of the traditional paradigm were useless, if not debilitating, for thinking about the problems of social rather than individual choice.

The key concept—ordinal preferences that are not interpersonally comparable over commodity space—is very useful for individual commodity spaces that are separate and exclusive. In the private good context no less vague (more restrictive) conception of evaluations proved necessary. But thinking with the concept of ordinal preference orderings that are not interpersonally comparable retarded thinking about efficient ways of allocating resources when all individuals have the same commodity space and nothing is, therefore, separate and exclusive. Instead, a less vague (more restrictive) conception of evaluation was necessary, namely, that individuals have preferences over "public goods commodity space" and for a moneylike good that could be used for "compensatory transfers." But over one hundred years of "progress" in refining conceptions of preference orderings over "individual commodity space" and as "interpersonally comparable," in other words, in the opposite direction, stood in the way.

3. The traditional paradigm failed to define concepts necessary for thinking about social choice.

It proved necessary to define concepts that permitted talking about communication of values (information sets and message spaces); concepts that permitted thinking about negotiation and back scratching (iterative mechanisms and assessments based on how others are affected by one's choices); concepts that saw rational individual behavior as system defined and therefore malleable; and concepts that recognized incentives are defined by the rules of the game people are forced to play. But none of these concepts were forthcoming from the traditional paradigm, and all this was necessary before the welfare theorists' "game" could be recognized for what it should be: "Find the rules that create the incentive to speak truly."

4. The traditional paradigm defined the search for solutions as outside economics proper by equating "market mechanism" with "economic mechanism," and labeling possible "nonmarket mechanisms" for provision of public goods "political," and, therefore, presumably non-economic.

This is hardly an incentive-compatible mechanism for eliciting maximum creative efforts from economic theorists in the publish or perish world of modern academia! The welfare establishment had to do a drastic turnabout before journal-page points and tenure could be earned by dreaming up "two, three, many new creative economic 'games.'"

In hindsight it is perfectly obvious: the solution set you would expect to get from the traditional paradigm is exactly what we got—policy prescriptions for resolving external effects by assigning additional property rights and creating new markets—which is to say, no solution at all. A paradigm was needed that would "analyze the social forces underlying the incentive structure" to encourage a mind set "to alter the incentive system itself…in order to move toward a better efficiency of the economy."[44]

4

ENDOGENOUS
PREFERENCES
AND INSTITUTIONS

Some...readers may have had the same childhood fantasy as myself: a walk in the landscape alone where from any point you could come to any other point without ever having to go uphill, because the landscape contours were changing all the time as a function of your path. A modified fantasy...might be the following. From any point in the landscape you may move effortlessly to any point situated at a lower level, regardless of any hills that might lie between. Also suppose that as you go from one point to a lower-level point, the landscape changes so that some of the points formerly situated at a higher level now become lower level points. An intriguing question would then be to ask *which* points are attainable...from a given initial point a_1. Obviously a point b would be accessible if and only if there is a sequence $a_1, a_2, \ldots a_n$, b such that a_2 is downhill from a_1, a_3 downhill from a_2, ..., and b downhill from a_n. This, however, is not very helpful unless we also specify how, as a result from the step from a_i to a_{i+1}, the set of points downhill from a_{i+1} and the set of points downhill from any other point as well, are changing....We have to specify how the possibly possible changes when we realize one of the possibles.... In our fantasy...possibilities are constantly appearing and disappearing: some may be lost forever, others may turn up again.

—John Elster, *Logic and Society*

THE ISSUE has never been whether or not tastes change. Rather the question is whether or not economists should concern themselves with such changes. Milton Friedman justifies traditional nonconcern as follows:

> Despite qualifications, economic theory proceeds largely to take wants as fixed. This is primarily a case of division of labor. The economist has little to say about the formation of wants; this is the province of the psychologist. The economist's task is to trace the consequences of any given set of wants. The legitimacy of any justification for this abstraction must rest ultimately, in this case as with any other abstraction, on the light that is shed and the power to predict that is yielded by the abstraction.[1]

While we agree with Friedman that "the proof is in the pudding," we believe economists should have much to say about preference formation and that our ability to compare the welfare properties of different economic systems hinges largely on our ability to do so.

4.1 Endogenous Preferences

Aristotle explained long ago: Our actions flow from our character and our character is formed by our actions. In the words of a modern-day economist: "Choice depends on tastes and tastes depend on past choices."[2] Or, as a former Chinese leader might have put it: Where do preferences come from? Do they come from the sky? Do they come from the sky filtered only through the clouds of social and cultural institutions? Put this way, our answer is no. They come from human nature filtered not only through the "clouds" of social and cultural institutions but also directly through the "thunderheads" of economic institutions, which profoundly influence other cloud formations as well.

The fact that "we are what we make ourselves through our daily activities" entails the view that human characteristics and consciousness, and thereby preferences as well, are "produced," in part, by our previous activities. And these previous activities certainly include our previous economic activities. Someone who "consumes" piano lessons as a youngster becomes more likely to "prefer" classical music concerts to rock concerts and to "manifest" preferences for an FM radio than an AM radio later in life. One who "consumes" erector sets in childhood is more likely to "choose" an engineering career; whereas someone who "consumes" dolls with all the appropriate props is more likely to "manifest" preferences for the work activity of a parent and housekeeper. One who played Little League baseball as a youth in the 1950s was more likely to spend an entertainment dollar attending professional baseball games than professional soccer matches as an adult in the 1970s. As Elster explains, "this

76

holds up a promise of improvement and a danger of inconsistency; a tool for self-education and manipulation alike. The crucial feature of this approach to human action is that it brings together two aspects often thought to be incompatible: intentionality and causality. Choice according to consistent preferences is an important part of what we mean by intentionality, whereas the laws governing the endogenous change of preferences are purely causal operating 'behind the back' of the actor concerned. The actor may, of course, try to anticipate the impact of present behavior upon future preferences and make his [or her] present choice in light of his [or her] evaluation of these consequences; indeed this is what Aristotle tells us to do."[3]

In chapter 2 we began to see how recognizing the "human characteristic transforming" effects of the production process can change our view of the welfare properties of production under conditions of private enterprise.[4] In this chapter we review others' treatments of the related issue of endogenous preferences and begin to explain the significance of the concept.

4.2 Previous Treatments

4.2.1 John Stuart Mill

John Stuart Mill found the Benthamite version of classical utilitarian theory wanting because it precluded discussing the phenomenon of preference development by insisting that "quantum of pleasure being equal, pushpin is as good as poetry." For Mill, human progress was practically synonymous with the development of ever-superior preference structures, hence his reluctance to forgo comparison between preferences themselves. So while Mill claimed to remain within the utilitarian tradition:

> I regard utility as the ultimate appeal on all ethical questions; but it must be utility in the largest sense, grounded on the permanent interests of man as a progressive being.[5]

He nonetheless insisted on broadening the Benthamite interpretation of "the largest sense" to conform with his own firmly held belief paraphrased by Bertrand Russell:

> As a matter of fact, we consider some tastes better than others: We do not merely hold that some tastes are ours and other tastes are other people's. We do not even always consider our own tastes the best: We may prefer bridge to poetry, but think it is better to prefer poetry to bridge.[6]

Mill attempted to do this by treating pleasure as having a qualitative as well as quantitative aspect.

It would be absurd that while, in estimating all other things, quality is considered as well as quantity, the estimation of pleasure should be supposed to depend on quantity alone....It is quite compatible with the principles of utility to recognize the fact that some kinds of pleasure are more desirable and more valuable than others...there is no known Epicurean [i.e., utilitarian] theory of life which does not assign to the pleasures of the intellect, of the feelings and imagination, and of the moral sentiments, a much higher value as pleasures than to those of mere sensation.[7]

Mill has been frequently ridiculed for inconsistency by the likes of Sidgwick for failing to understand that the classical utilitarian principle precludes noncomparable, qualitative distinctions between pleasures.[8] But we find it more productive to interpret Mill as arguing that certain preferences are qualitatively superior in the sense that they allow for the enjoyment of greater quantities of pleasure than do "less-cultured" preferences.

A cultivated mind finds sources of inexhaustible interest in all that surrounds it; in the objects of nature, in the achievements of art, the imaginations of poetry, the incidents of history, the ways of mankind, past and present, and their prospects in the future.[9]

In this interpretation, Mill felt no need to discard the utilitarian principle as the final arbiter, but felt increases in pleasure resulted not only from more complete fulfillment of existing desires but also through the development of new systems of desires that could be deemed superior in that they were capable of yielding greater quantities of pleasure through their fulfillment. In other words, instead of being "fuzzy headed," perhaps Mill recognized the importance of preference development as well as preference fulfillment to a valuative methodology and merely wished to insist on an adequate analysis of the factors affecting preference development as well as fulfillment for utilitarianism to be a useful valuative methodology. On the other hand, Mill concluded that however important preference development was in general, economic institutions had little effect in this regard. Mill focused his arguments on the importance of considering preference development when evaluating political and cultural institutions.

Mill's analysis of preference development and the reasoning process necessary to justify his conclusion that preferences could be treated as exogenous to the economic system is carefully explained by Gintis in his chapter on Mill. We merely offer Gintis' conclusions:

Mill resolves this problem...that welfare increases not only on the basis of fixed wants, but in the development of wants themselves...by postulating that the system of personality structures [upon which preferences depend] develops according to an internal social mechanism, logically as well as causally unaffected by the social [economic] mechanisms devoted to the satisfaction of manifest preferences at a particular point in time.[10]

Mill does not assert preferences are exogenous to political and cultural institutions. Indeed, Gintis argued convincingly that Mill's most noteworthy interpreters have committed a gross oversight in not viewing Mill's writings in social philosophy and recommendations concerning political institutions designed to preserve "individual liberty" as largely motivated by a concern that political and cultural institutions be appropriately fashioned to ensure optimal preference development. The relevance of political and cultural institutions for Mill stems from his belief that:

> the attributes of superior preference structures are sufficiently objective and identifiable [that]…if the individual is "unimpeded" in his activity toward preference development, the systems of preference structure will themselves develop in a proper manner.[11]

Mill sees repressive political and cultural institutions as the only possible impediments to the exercise of individuality and emulation that are the driving forces of his "internal mechanism" for the development of preferences. Gintis' critique of Mill goes straight to the point:

> In broadest perspective…the model must be operationally interpreted as saying there are no functionally supported socioeconomic institutions directly concerned with preference development.[12]

That is, once political and cultural institutions have been recognized as structures relevant to individual preference development, why are economic institutions excluded? Gintis' more general point is that there is a bias in evaluating economic institutions solely on the basis of their efficiency in providing material goods as judged by today's preferences. Once we have asserted preference development as a social goal, economic institutions must be judged from this point of view as well. Gintis drives the point home in the citation below by observing that were a specific kind of spiritual development the only social goal, highly "inefficient" precapitalist institutions would receive high marks, while presumably "efficient" capitalist institutions would receive low scores (not that Gintis means to champion this particular goal).

> This view [that economic institutions do not influence preference development] is especially curious in the case of the economist, who is more than willing to accept the position that social organization around issues of material development can further individual goals. But in what sense does an institution like "Alcoholics Anonymous," as an example of an institution directed toward a form of self-development that cannot

be achieved by individuals in isolation, differ from a steel plant, as a form of material development that cannot be achieved by individuals in isolation? In short, this asymmetrical treatment of material and developmental goals, and of the degree to which social organization can promote their advancement, leads to an inherent bias in favor of the Robbins judgment in any analysis.

We could in fact parody Mill's argument by reversing it. Suppose a society in which individual development goals, say "spiritual growth," held primacy. A social welfare analyst would then devote the major part of his time exhibiting the precise form social organization would take toward the end of individual spiritual growth, noting that while economic security is also of considerable importance, this could be achieved by allowing individuals the "liberty" of forming informal, functionally unsupported groupings to further their material ends. It should be no surprise that he arrives at a "traditional" nonindustrial society as an ideal type![13]

How a thinker as humanistic in his orientation and as broad in his views as Mill could recognize the crucial importance of preference development to valuative methodology as well as the influence of social and cultural institutions on preference development without recognizing that economic institutions influence preference development as well, might seem hard to explain. On the other hand, belief in the separability of functions, specifically regarding the economic institutions of competitive capitalism, appears elsewhere in Mill's thought. Just as Mill asserted that distribution could be separated from efficiency in private enterprise market economies, he assumed that preference development could be separated from efficiency in fulfilling preferences.

In chapter 5 we will argue for a more holistic paradigm. For many purposes labeling institutions "political," or "cultural," or "economic" is helpful, but for other purposes such labels obfuscate important relationships. While it might be the case that particular political, cultural, or economic institutions exert an influence only within "their spheres," this should not be presumed, much less taken for granted, as a consequence of their labeling. In some cases "economic" institutions might perform functions other than those traditionally thought of as economic functions. Mill believed this was not the case for the economic institutions of private enterprise and competitive markets regarding preference development. The traditional welfare paradigm presumes this is not the case for "economic" institutions in general with respect to the "cultural" function of preference development. While we will argue against the "separability" assumption in both the particular case of private enterprise market institutions and the case of economic institutions in general, for now we simply wish to thank John Stuart Mill for pointing out the importance of preference development for welfare theory.

4.2.2 *C. C. von Weizsacker and Robert Pollak*

While C. C. von Weizsacker and Robert Pollak are not the only modern-day neoclassical economists to treat endogenous preferences, they are among a very small group who have broken the taboo against questioning the origins of preferences. Trygve Haavelmo broached the subject in his doctoral dissertation in 1944.[14] Georgescu-Roegen, Strotz, and Hasanyi introduced the subject in the economic journals in the 1950s.[15] C. C. von Weizsacker called attention to the potential significance of the issue for modern neoclassical theory in an article in 1971.[16] Peter Hammond, C. Luch, and Marcel Boyer among others have written occasionally on the subject more recently.[17] But it was Robert Pollak who, almost single-handed, kept the subject alive in neoclassical journals during the 1970s.[18]

C. C. von Weizsacker posed the problem that had troubled few since J. S. Mill as follows:

> There are influences on tastes which may have little to do with those variables economists are usually concerned about. From the point of view of the economist we can call them exogenous influences. We may acknowledge their existence, but we need not investigate them very much further. But other influences on tastes may depend more or less directly on certain economic variables like, for instance, the tendency of firms to increase their profits through advertising, or the consumption patterns of other consumers, or the consumer's past experience with consumer goods. If these influences on tastes are not taken into account, we clearly would be in danger of making false predictions due to mis-specification of certain parameters in our model.[19]

In this book, we will not be concerned with advertising at all, and we treat interconsumer externalities as simply a subcategory of external effects in general. But the influence and implications of "consumer's past experience with consumer goods" on their present preferences directly concerns us. Von Weizsacker proceeds to pinpoint the relevant question for welfare theory even more precisely:

> The efficiency or Pareto optimality properties of general equilibrium models rest on the assumption of fixed tastes. Are these efficiency theorems relevant to a world with changing tastes? Surely, purely exogenous changes of tastes (from the point of view of the economist) will essentially not alter these theorems....But what about Pareto optimality if endogenous variables of the economic system influence tastes?[20]

Finally, von Weizsacker evaluates the status of traditional welfare theory regarding this subject in a way we wholeheartedly support:

> I think it is fair to say that this question has not yet been investigated in sufficient depth by economists. Yet it appears to be one of the important problems in the discussion about the social relevance of economic theory. Does the model with fixed tastes give insights into the problems of an economy with endogenously changing tastes? One of the reasons why economists did not very deeply discuss this question may be that their present concepts of Pareto optimality and efficiency possibly are not flexible enough to cope with endogenously changing tastes. It may become necessary to change the conceptual framework of our theory; we may be forced to ask almost philosophical questions about the concepts we use. In every discipline, there is always a reluctance to engage in this kind of activity.[21]

Or, since addressing the issue requires changing the traditional paradigm, it has been more convenient to pretend the subject is of little interest. Unfortunately, the manner in which von Weizsacker pursued the issue in his article permitted subsequent neoclassical treatments to effectively "bury" the welfare implications he sought to emphasize.

Von Weizsacker presents a model with only two goods, and assumes tastes are only influenced by consumption in the previous period. He conjectures "although the mathematics would become more complicated, I presume the relaxation of these two assumptions would not change the substance of the argument."[22] Ahmad El-Safty proves *this* conjecture correct.[23] But while von Weizsacker's conclusions are not sensitive to the number of goods or the length of the adaptive process, they are sensitive to his assumption that the adaptive process is myopic habit formation. El-Safty and Pollak both demonstrate that von Weizsacker's conclusions based on a myopic habit formation modeling of the adaptive process are not generalizable. In the words of El-Safty, "the long-run demand functions can be rationalized by a utility function if and only if the short-run utility function is such that any good that experiences learning or taste change is separable from all other goods."[24] And Pollak concludes, "Von Weizsacker's long-run utility function approach to the evaluation of welfare is technically possible only in a narrow class of cases.[25] Since El-Safty and Pollak's criticisms are technically correct, it is clear that a myopic habit formation conceptualization of endogenous preferences is of very limited relevance to welfare theory.

With hindsight, for two reasons choosing to model endogenous preferences as myopic habit formation appears to have been unfortunate, at least regarding uncovering the implications of endogenous preferences for welfare theory. First, "habit formation" is, more than anything else, relevant to convexity; it complicates matters concerning theorems that establish the existence of long-run demand functions and the existence of equilibria in market economies.

Especially Pollak, in subsequent treatments, has focused on these problems. But existence, and optimality of anything that might exist, are two separable concerns. We are inclined to agree with Pollak that "habit formation" is of little additional relevance to welfare theory, but this does not mean that other kinds of endogenous preferences are not of great relevance to welfare theory.[26] By concentrating on habit formation von Weizsacker also made more likely subsequent focus on the theory of empirical estimation of consumer demand rather than the welfare implications of endogenous preferences. In other words, von Weizsacker's choice of habit formation as the form of endogenous preferences to analyze leads to largely irrelevant technical complications and a focus on the positive rather than the normative implications of endogenous preferences, all quite contrary to his own desires.

Second, and more importantly, by focusing on *"myopic* adaptive behavior" rather than on what we might term "knowledgable" or "purposeful preference molding" von Weizsacker created a context in which the most significant welfare theoretic implications of adaptive behavior are absent by supposition and a situation in which the existence of long-run "meta" utility functions that rationalize long-run demand functions exist only under highly restrictive conditions. Creating myopic habits, an individual fails to recognize that consumption of a good now increases the desire for that same good later. Purposefully molding preferences, an individual recognizes that present choice of consumption will both fulfill present preferences (more or less efficiently) and change future preferences in a particular direction (that may be more or less convenient in light of expected conditions of future availability). In both cases previous consumption affects future preferences—making the latter "endogenous." But in the first case the individual only recognizes the "preference fulfillment effect," while in the second case he or she recognizes the "preference fulfillment effect" and the "preference development effect" as well. In the first case individuals are presumed oblivious to the causal laws of their adaptive behavior. In the second case, they are granted perfect foresight of all the implications of their choices.[27] It should cause little surprise that individual behavior that fails to recognize the preference-development effects of choices can be rationalized by a long-run utility function only under singular conditions. But there is no reason to suppose this problem will affect purposeful preference molding. As will become apparent from our own treatment in chapter 6, the dynamic of purposeful preference development poses far more significant welfare theoretic questions than myopic habit formation.

In any case, von Weizsacker draws the following generalization from his treatment of myopic habit formation:

> We therefore have to ask whether it is reasonable for a society to build its decisions on its present preferences or on some other criterion. If present preferences are strongly influenced by myopic thinking, by lack of imagination how a different world would look, we should not accept these preferences as the last word.[28]

While true, we would classify this conclusion as obvious. In essence it says: If individuals incorrectly estimate the effects of different choices on their well-being, leaving individuals to make their own choices in all likelihood will not maximize their well-being. The possibility of "myopic habit formation" simply points out another way this might happen. But von Weizsacker recognizes the importance of what we regard as the more interesting question of "purposeful preference molding" as well as the philosophical dilemma it poses in his conclusion:

> It will require another paper to discuss this problem of intertemporal decision making in view of anticipated and planned changes of tastes. Society...may have to opt for a metapreference in favor of challenging the prevailing preferences of its members and to ask if and how these preferences can perhaps be improved....This does not, of course, mean that there should be some person or group of persons who from their "superior" point of view dictate the values of society.[29]

In our view, he also foresees the only acceptable answer to the dilemma:

> Society's decisions must rest on the preferences of all its members. *But we have to acknowledge and make use of the fact that preferences are partly the product of people's environment* [emphasis added].[30]

Robert Pollak does not pursue von Weizsacker's plea for "another paper...to discuss...intertemporal decision making in view of anticipated and planned changes in tastes." As he explains:

> Those who favor incorporating taste formation and change into economic analysis fall into two groups whose intersection is almost empty. One is primarily interested in the welfare implications of changing tastes, the other in the analysis of household behavior....The recent impetus to incorporate taste formation and change into economic analysis has come primarily from those interested in household behavior rather than welfare, and the principle focus of this work has been empirical demand analysis.[31]

Pollak concentrates primarily on implications of myopic habit formation for the positive theory of demand estimation. Because this subject does not concern us, we ignore Pollak's important contributions in this area. But, as a secondary concern, Pollak also addresses welfare implications of endogenous preferences. Since his conclusions regarding welfare theory are so different from ours, it is important to review his results.

Pollak argues specifically that von Weizsacker's conclusions regarding endogenous preferences are both technically and substantially unsustainable. He specifically rejects the alternative approach that would avoid the objections he poses to von Weizsacker's treatment. He concludes that if preferences are endogenous, welfare conclusions are greatly complicated and we must be more cautious about drawing welfare conclusions. But for Pollak, nothing definitive can be concluded. If anything, endogenous preferences render the whole project of welfare theory obsolete. We will deal with these points one by one.

First, Pollak claims von Weizsacker's approach to welfare analysis is technically inadequate:

Von Weizsacker argues that the long-run utility function is the appropriate criterion by which to judge the welfare effects of changes in consumption. Since we have shown, contrary to his conjecture, that when there are more than two goods the long-run utility function exists only in special cases, it cannot serve as a general welfare criterion. Revealed preference arguments provide no help; the counterpart of the nonexistence of the long-run utility function is violation of the long-run version of the strong axiom of revealed preference. At most, then, the long-run utility function may be the appropriate welfare criterion only for a narrow class of cases in which it exists.[32]

Pollak is technically correct. But the "existence" problem he demonstrates is a direct consequence of modeling endogenous preferences as myopic habit formation. Since that is the form of endogenous preferences von Weizsacker treated, Pollak's objection is well taken as far as von Weizsaker's "conjectures" are concerned. But Pollak's "impossibility theorem" regarding nonexistence of long-run utility functions except for a narrow class of cases is not universally applicable to other formulations of endogenous preferences, and to our own formulation in particular.[33]

Pollak goes on to argue, however, that von Weizsacker's long-run utility function is not an appropriate criterion for judging the welfare effects of changes in consumption, even when it does exist. For von Weizsacker the long-run utility function defines an indifference map in which a consumption vector, $q(0)$, will be on a higher indifference surface than another consumption vector, $q(n)$, if and only if the consumer can move from $q(0)$ to $q(n)$ in a finite sequence of steps where she or he feels better off at each step along the way. Pollak explains why he rejects von Weizsacker's indifference map as a welfare criterion via the following example:

A nonsmoker might prefer to remain a nonsmoker rather than smoke three packs of cigarettes a day, but he might choose to smoke half a pack a day rather than abstain completely. After becoming accustomed to smoking half a pack a day, the individual might prefer to remain a light smoker rather than smoke three packs a day, but he might choose to smoke a pack a day rather than continue at half a pack a day. By this process, the myopic nonsmoker is led to become a heavy smoker. This scenario is entirely consistent with von Weizsacker's assumptions, yet I am loath to conclude that the individual is better off at $q(n)$ than $q(0)$.[34]

Pollak generalizes as follows:

I interpret the individual's willingness to move from $q(0)$ to $q(n)$ in a sequence of small steps when he is unwilling to do so in a single large step as indicative of his failure to understand the habit formation mechanism and not of the underlying superiority of $q(n)$.[35]

Once again, we agree with Pollak. Von Weizsacker's conception of a long-run utility function that is appropriate for welfare purposes is unacceptable—ironically, particularly in a myopic habit formation context. But this does not mean no other conception of a long-run utility function is appropriate for welfare purposes in context of a different conception of endogenous preferences.

Pollak finally considers such an alternative formulation of long-run utility functions:

Since von Weizsacker's long-run utility function approach to the evaluation of welfare is technically possible only in a narrow class of cases and is conceptually unsatisfactory even for those, it is desirable to consider alternative approaches. One such alternative, one which von Weizsacker suggests in his concluding paragraph, is to view the problem in an intertemporal framework. That is, instead of focusing on the one-period utility function, $U(q(t), q(t-1))$, assumed to be the same in every period, we could evaluate welfare in terms of the intertemporal utility function $V(q) = W[U(q(1), q(0)), ...U(q(t), q(t-1))]$. The proposed welfare test, in other words, is whether the individual—taking full account of the impact of his present consumption on his future tastes—would be willing to undertake a particular change.[36]

But rather than accept this alternative formulation, Pollak rejects it.

The principal difficulty with this approach is that it is schizophrenic. The habit formation model is tractable because the individual is assumed to be myopic—he fails to recognize the impact of his current consumption on his future tastes. If he could be persuaded to recognize the effects of habit formation, then it would certainly be appropriate to base welfare comparisons on the intertemporal utility function, but then his demand behavior would be far more complex than that predicted by the model of "myopic" habit formation. If an individual insists on being myopic, it is less clear that the intertemporal utility function is the appropriate welfare criterion, but it is tempting to take a paternalistic view and argue that it is. However, it is difficult to reconcile this approach to welfare with an approach to demand analysis based on myopic habit formation.[37]

Frankly, Pollak's double fixation on the phenomenon of myopic habit formation and demand analysis seem to have rendered him myopic regarding conscious or "purposeful preference molding" and welfare theory. A model with identical utility functions in all periods that evaluate consumption of a commodity more highly if more of it was consumed in the previous period is quite appropriate to analyzing the effects of changing initial consumption levels on demand under conditions of habit formation. Specialization of addiction is hardly a surprising result. But the model Pollak rejects appears to us obviously suited to analyzing the welfare effects of all manner of recognized preference development effects. What do his objections amount to?

Obviously, "myopic habit formation" and "purposeful preference molding" are different behavioral phenomena. While it does not appear unreasonable to consider the possibility that both occur in the economy as a whole and even in the behavior of a single individual who recognizes the "preference development effects" of some of his or her choices but not others, we need not debate the point. Pollak concedes all that is necessary by admitting "it would certainly be appropriate to base welfare comparisons on the intertemporal utility function" if people recognize what we call the "preference development effects" of their choices. We might point out that the tradition of welfare theory has always been to focus on the implications of rational behavior of economic actors. In this light to focus on purposeful preference molding appears quite logical if we are concerned with the implications of endogenous preferences for welfare theory.[38] After all, to find that myopic and rational behavior are "schizophrenic" is hardly surprising and in no case a reason to reject analyzing rational behavior, even if one wishes, as Pollak did, to analyze the effects of myopic behavior as well.

Pollak's second objection is that demand behavior would be "far more complex" in the case of conscious preference molding than myopic habit formation. We can only respond: So what? The additional complexity is only objectionable in the sense that we should not try to incorporate it in our formal analyses if it proves so intractable that it prevents drawing any conclusions. As the results of part 3 demonstrate, this is not the case. If we assume away nonconvexities and stipulate perfect foresight—time-honored traditions among welfare theorists—both the technical and substantive objections posed by Pollak to assuming long-run "meta" utility functions disappear. But even if the situation did prove so much more complex that it was intractable, if conscious preference molding exists and has important effects, welfare theorists should take great pains to qualify conclusions derived from formal models that are unable to incorporate the phenomenon. And developing ways to incorporate conscious preference molding into our formal models should rank high on the list of projects challenging welfare theorists if they wish to be taken seriously by those trying to evaluate economies and formulate appropriate policies.

Finally, Pollak believes it is difficult to reconcile a conscious preference molding approach to welfare theory with a myopic habit formation approach to demand analysis. We believe this reveals a misunderstanding of the welfare project. There are good reasons to believe that analyses of rational and actual behavior will differ—perhaps markedly.[39] In any case, even if there were a "conflict of interest," as welfare theorists we could hardly accept Pollak's priorities.

Having rejected von Weizsacker's conclusions and the alternative approach that appears so promising to us, what are Pollak's conclusions regarding the implication of endogenous preferences for welfare theory? Pollak draws an important distinction between the kinds of preferences appropriate for demand analysis and welfare analysis:

> In demand analysis the objects of choice are vectors of private decision variables, Q, and preferences over them depend on a vector of predetermined "state variables," Z; we call such a preference ordering "conditional."...Welfare analysis must compare the individual's well-being in alternative situations which differ with respect to the state variables as well as the private decision variables....Welfare analysis requires us to redefine the objects of choice to include not only the private decision variables but also the state variables which, from the standpoint of conditional preferences, are predetermined. We call an ordering over such an augmented set of alternatives an "unconditional preference ordering."... The additional information contained in the unconditional preference ordering is irrelevant to demand analysis, but for welfare evaluation it is indispensable.[40]

For Pollak the problem lies precisely in the fact that while "unconditional preferences are necessary for welfare analysis they cannot be inferred from market behavior or any other conditional choices."[41] In his view, this means very little can be said about "taste change and welfare analysis."[42]

To his credit Pollak recognizes a disturbing implication:

Taste formation...poses...difficult problems for welfare analysis. Variable tastes undermine the normative significance of the fundamental theorem of welfare economics which asserts (in a precise sense and under fairly stringent assumptions) that in competitive equilibrium everyone gets what he wants, subject to the constraints imposed by technology, resources, and the satisfaction of the wants of others. However if tastes are sufficiently malleable, then this may be no more than a corollary of the more general proposition that people come to want what they get.[43]

But Pollak's narrow interpretation of endogenous preferences as myopic habit formation leads him to mistakenly conclude that the sets of "private decision variables" and "state variables" are necessarily disjoint. Yet this is not the case for the kinds of endogenous preferences most relevant to welfare analysis. Pollak interprets state variables as follows:

State variables may be the individual's own past consumption (habit formation) or the consumption of others (interdependent preferences). They may be environmental variables...or goods or services provided by the government....Or they may be socioeconomic variables or demographic variables.[44]

Obviously, state variables influence the satisfaction an individual will attain from different "private decisions." And obviously, the values of state variables in the present cannot be affected by present choices. But, for Pollak, individuals do not believe themselves capable of affecting values of state variables at all. Pollak is correct that habits formed myopically are similar to the consumption of others, supplies of public goods, and values of demographic variables in that all exist beyond the conscious control of individual decision makers. But if preference development effects of consumption are recognized, one's own past consumption is still a "state variable" in that it is part of the "state" of affairs that cannot be willed away yet influences the satisfaction obtainable from different present choices. However, it is not a variable beyond the reach of "private decision making." This is precisely the interesting feature of endogenous preferences as far as the theory of rational choice and welfare analysis is concerned. Yet it seems to escape Pollak entirely. We must turn to Herb Gintis to find someone who

1. Accepts von Weizsacker's challenge to "write another paper" treating the "problem of intertemporal decision making in view of anticipated and planned changes of tastes"

2. Accepts the obviously relevant conception of long-run utility functions that Pollak rejected

3. Understands that the importance of endogenous preferences for welfare theory lies in their status as state variables that are not beyond the ability of individual decision makers to influence

4.2.3 Herb Gintis

Whereas Pollak pursued the positive implications of "myopic habit formation" and denied any serious normative implications, Gintis pursued the normative implications of "purposeful preference molding" and insisted that they dramatically affect traditional conclusions.[45] Gintis begins by exploring precisely what the modern conception of an individual's "manifest" preference structure is, formulating three useful conceptions of preference ordering along the way:

> The Incomplete Knowledge Preference Ordering (IKPO) is determined as follows: the individual is isolated at the beginning of time period t, presented with a price structure over commodities and factors, and directed to choose a bundle of commodities and factor supplies based on this precise structure, satisfying an income constraint. By varying the price structure presented to the individual, we arrive at the Incomplete Knowledge Preference Ordering, in the usual manner of revealed preference theory. The Complete Knowledge Preference Ordering (CKPO) is obtained by allowing the individual to "experience" each bundle compatible with a given price structure, asking him ex post which he actually preferred. In both cases, we shall ask the individual to assume, for the purposes of choice, that his preference structure cannot be altered over the time period in question. Thus we shall refer to the IKPO and the CKPO as instantaneous preference structures.

> Economic theory normally posits the stability of individual preference structures; this is a factually incorrect interpretation of the individual's own intentions...the individual not only possesses an IKPO and a CKPO at time t, but...has certain definite ideas about changing this structure during the time period in question, arriving at another preference structure at time $t+1$. In short, we assume the individual has at least a vague set of "preferences on preference structures" themselves. The source of these preferences may be briefly described. Some will be based on the individual's desire to change his skills, some on the desire to acquire new tastes, some to improve the moral or aesthetic character of his preference structure, and some perhaps to correct past mistakes in preference structure formation. Thus the individual may "prefer" an IKPO which values a certain commodity more highly than his present structure....For example, he might consider that an IKPO that values poetry more highly than his present IKPO desirable in that the "cost" of

90

poetry is small, and in that persons who do prefer poetry seem to feel the benefits are great....Clearly the activity involved in moving from one preference structure to another will involve the outlay of certain skills, and the foregoing of certain types of consumption, as well as certain other subjective costs and perhaps benefits. All in all, it is assumed the individual weighs all these factors in deciding a course of action for the period t; he will consume, produce, and alter his preference structure. Thus in a larger context, we can amalgamate the IKPO for period t with the above valuation in preference-on-preference structures into one grand preference ordering for period t. We shall call this the individual's Complete Preference Structure (CPS).[46]

The obvious question is where does the revealed preference structure of modern neoclassical welfare theory fit into this framework? Gintis replies:

It cannot be the CKPO, as revealed preference theory does not assume the individual has perfect knowledge. Nor is it the IKPO, as revealed preference theory, in recording individual choices, does not ask the individual to assume his preference structure cannot be altered over the time period. It would seem, rather, that the CPS coincides with the "revealed" preference structure of traditional theory, as both are determined merely by bidding the subject to exhibit his choices at time t.[47]

Next, Gintis concludes that "preference structures described in revealed preference theory must change over time, and in particular will tend to be intransitive."[48] We might add there is no longer reason to assume revealed preferences would display even the more fundamental property of simple consistency! The source of these undesirable properties is that preferences are now seen to depend on previous economic activities or the actual choices of previous consumption and work bundles. In acting upon the dictates of my present IKPO and income constraint, I consume different goods and engage in different work activities, thereby changing my IKPO in the future. It is as if I became a "new person," and just as neoclassical theory never expected to find different individuals' revealed preferences characterized by consistency or transitivity, there is no more reason to expect this of a single individual's revealed preferences.[49]

First we summarize the parts of Gintis' critique of neoclassical welfare theory we agree with and build upon. Then we present the parts we object to and improve upon.

Preferences depend on previous economic choices because preferences are now seen to be explicitly mediated (parameterized) by an individual's human characteristics where, in turn, these human characteristics are seen to be partially produced by (functions of) previous choices of all kinds, including economic choices traditionally conceived as choices of consumption bundles and work activities. A mathematical formalization of these relationships is presented as model 1 in chapter 6. It does no more than precisely express:

1. The relationship between individuals' previous work and consumption activity choices and their human characteristics. We envision these characteristics as various personality traits, talents or skills, knowledge, and values or attitudes toward what they understand is going on in the world.

2. The parametric relationship between these human characteristics and the enjoyment, pleasure, satisfaction, utility, or well-being individuals obtain from any consumption bundle or work activity in the present—that is, their instantaneous welfare function.

A further justification of these choices of human characteristics will be offered in chapter 5 as an important part of our own treatment. However, the above verbal formulation of these relations is sufficient to suggest a problem more damaging to traditional welfare theory than the previous observation that commonly presumed characteristics of revealed preferences are not justified. Gintis was the first to pose the question whether Pareto optimality in terms of "manifest preferences" has any "moral" significance if preferences are endogenous. The essence of traditional welfare theory was summarized previously as "high marks are to be given to economic systems that display a close 'fit' between the relative terms on which economic goods are made available and people's relative preferences for those goods." But theorists presumed the "close fit" had something to recommend it because they assumed the fit was achieved by an adjustment of the relative supplies of different goods to people's relative desires for those goods. The possibility that a "close fit" between desires and supplies is achieved by an adjustment of people's desires to conditions of relative supply undermines the worth of neoclassical welfare theory's principle criterion for judging the performance of economies. Gintis put it this way:

> To justify a set of economic institutions on the basis of the manifest preferences of individuals who were formed through their preparation for participation in these institutions involves making an arbitrary cut in a system of causal linkages. Not only are preference orderings formed on the basis of economic organization, but this organization clearly erects certain functional prerequisites, certain structural uniformities in patterns of preference orderings in the absence of which the system as a whole would fail to cohere. The apparent mutual determination of a social structure (and economic structure in particular) and individual personality systems thus presents severe problems for a purely atomistic welfare theory.[50]

The point is that Pareto optimality, judged according to manifest preferences, might signify stability rather than merit. If an economic system adjusts provisions to people's desires, a "close mesh" is meritorious. But if people get what they want because they adjust their desires to what is made available by the economic system, a "close mesh" may only indicate that the system is stable since people's desires and expectations are being fulfilled. Ironically, endogeneity of preferences seems to transform Pareto optimality from an evaluative concept into an analytic concept.

It is possible to demonstrate that rational individuals, who recognize their preferences are endogenous, will adjust to changes in the relative terms of supply of different goods not only by changing the relative amounts of those goods they consume, but by changing their preferences for those commodities as well. They will diminish their desires for commodities whose terms of availability they believe will become more difficult, and augment their desires for commodities whose terms of availability they believe will become easier by changing consumption and work activity choices in earlier time periods so as to change their future human characteristics and, thereby, their future preferences. This result is formulated and proved in chapter 6 as Theorem 6.2, and destroys an important "separability" result that is a cornerstone of at least the partial equilibrium version of traditional welfare theory. Gintis summarized the conclusion as follows:

> ...the movement of preference structures over time will in part depend on both commodity price structure and wage structure. As the individual moves from one IKPO to another on the basis of expectations as to the prices of commodities and remuneration for work skills that they accentuate to various degrees, the assumption of fixed preferences and the resulting implementation of Pareto optimality conditions in the determination of wages and prices in themselves alter the preference structures originally posited. This observation radically alters the interpretation and the validity of the axioms of welfare economics.[51]

Of course, if rational individuals take into account that present consumption and work activities not only fulfill present preferences but also change future preferences, whereas traditional welfare theory does not recognize this "preference development" effect, traditional theory will obviously misestimate the welfare effects of different actions. It follows that policy recommendations of traditional theory based on erroneous predictions of the overall welfare effects of different choices should not be given much weight. A proof of the proposition that in its present form traditional welfare theory consistently misestimates welfare effects of different economic choices if preferences are endogenous, originally derived by Gintis, is formulated and proved in chapter 6 as Theorem 6.1.

The phenomenon of rational adjustment of preferences, toward wanting what is presumed will be most readily available and away from wanting what is presumed will be difficult to obtain, should not be confused with another way that "utility" might be a function of price—namely the "snob effect," or "keeping up with the Joneses," or Veblen's concept of "conspicuous consumption."[52] The clear difference between the phenomena can be appreciated by noticing that the direction of the individual's adjustment is exactly opposite in the two cases. Whereas the phenomena we are discussing lead rational individuals to diminish their consumption of goods whose future prices are expected to be high, conspicuous consumption leads individuals to increase consumption of goods with high prices. One could conclude that both phenomena occur in the real world and that the effects of both are significant. On the other hand, whereas it has been relatively easy for neoclassical welfare theory to dismiss the "snob effect" as "irrational" behavior in which the individual "pays" for snobbery regardless of how prevalent the motivation might be, the phenomenon we refer to is characterized precisely by its rationality, and therefore, at least according to neoclassical tradition, by its prevalence if not universality.

Up to this point we are willing to follow Gintis in exploring the consequences of endogenous preferences. However, Gintis traveled down a path we find less interesting than a path branching in a different direction. Gintis' observations are not incorrect or devoid of interest, but in our opinion they do not reveal the fundamental deficiency of traditional welfare theory's treatment of preferences. We present Gintis' argument first and motivate the interpretation we will pursue throughout the book second.

Gintis proceeded by observing that a considerable amount of uncertainty is involved in the concept of the Complete Preference Structure (CPS).

> Firstly, it is based on the IKPO rather than the CKPO. Secondly, the process by which the new preference structure is achieved may lead to a new structure, differing more or less from that at which the individual originally aimed. Thirdly, the "costs" and "benefits" of undertaking the activity leading to the change in preference structure are only incompletely known to the individual, particularly in that he cannot experience beforehand the process of preference structure change....Lastly, and perhaps most importantly, he can know only indirectly and by inference how satisfied he might be with the new preference structure.[53]

But Gintis rejected moving toward "abstraction" from the problems of uncertainty on the following basis:

> It is tempting to postulate a "complete knowledge" counterpart to the individual's CPO. This would involve positing an individual with known CKPO and complete knowledge of his "capacities," moving him to

every possible CKPO for the next period, and registering his "preferred CKPO." In fact, this type of "gedanken experiment" abstracts from the human situation to such an extent as to be useless in understanding the dynamics of preference systems development.[54]

We agree with Gintis that this type of "gedanken experiment" abstracts mightily from the human situation. To assume that all individuals can know how their preferences depend on their various human characteristics, and how the development of those characteristics is influenced by consumption and work choices, and also the conditions of future availabilities of all economic goods, violates two important aspects of our human condition. First, as much as we might try to estimate from others' verbal and nonverbal behavior what it would be like to be different from what we are, it must always remain somewhat impossible for us to know such a thing. Our conception of the realm of human possibilities outside our own experience is inevitably influenced and limited by our own experience. Unfortunately, the postulation of a preordering of preferences—a complete, reflexive, and transitive ordering of preferences themselves—ignores this difficulty.

Second, there are good reasons to believe, particularly in light of endogenous preferences, that the future is not determinate. Granting that preferences themselves are moldable removes half of the "fixed data" of traditional general equilibrium models and makes even more likely the existence of more than one path that our economic world might take from any initial situation. It is the misfortune of the assumption of perfect knowledge of the future terms of availabilities of economic goods that it ignores this problem of many different possible futures.

However, in our opinion Gintis made a tactical error in formulating the essence of his critique of traditional welfare theory around the problems of uncertainty that endogenous preferences certainly do create.[55] In our view, emphasizing the additional problems of uncertainty posed by endogenous preferences ultimately limits one's critique of particular economic institutions to highly technical grounds. We may agree with the sentiments Gintis expressed in the passage just quoted, but we feel it is possible to grant traditional welfare theory all the perfect knowledge assumptions it requires, no matter how unreflective of the human situation they may be, and still formulate a critique of the traditional approach. Moreover, we feel that doing so gets us to the heart of the traditional paradigm, whereas focusing on additional problems of uncertainty does not.

Abstracting from the imperfect knowledge that is very much part of the human condition is entirely within the tradition of welfare theory, and, in our opinion, justified. To think otherwise is to misunderstand the nature of welfare theory and confuse the purpose of welfare theory with that of positive economic theory. The fact that the knowledge required by the perfect knowledge version of the CPO stretches credulity well beyond the breaking point is good reason to reject the concept as useful in explaining actual human behavior. But that is not the essential purpose of welfare theory. The major purpose of welfare theory is to analyze the implications of rational behavior, and the extent to which this informs aspects of actual human behavior is secondary. How interesting the question of what the welfare effects of perfectly informed rational behavior in different institutional environments would be, compared to many other interesting questions, is, of course, a matter of debate. But that is the question welfare theory has always chosen to address.

Gintis maintained, on the other hand, that "the attractiveness of modern welfare economics lies in the simplicity of its underlying normative assumptions."[56] By this he means that the Robbins Principle appears unobjectionable in not requiring elaborate ethical justification. Gintis asserted:

> The common argument against the inclusion of preference change in welfare theory relies on the inadvisability of the economist's "dabbling in value judgments." ...This, in fact, lies at the heart of the "revolution" in welfare economics, of which the Robbins judgment, the Hicks-Kaldor Scitovsky analysis, and the Bergsonian social welfare function mark the high points.[57]

Based on this belief, Gintis stated his purpose:

> I shall show that both the intuitive nature and irreducibility of welfare judgments are unwarranted in that they are derived from a simplistic and ultimately reductionist formulation of the individual choice situation and the nature of individual preference ordering.[58]

He proceeded by observing:

> We have seen that the statement, "individuals themselves know best what they want" cannot be taken to mean that they have complete knowledge—for the statement that the IKPO and the CKPO coincide is factual and not normative. Moreover, it is clearly false.[59]

Gintis then stated the obvious conclusion:

> Implicitly, the Robbins Principle exhorts us to assume the CPO as the final judge and arbiter for the individual in spite of the fact that it may not be the best instrument in some, or even most, cases.[60]

Unfortunately, Gintis then drew precisely the secondary conclusion that, in our opinion, welfare theorists should be most careful to studiously avoid:

It is conceivable, for instance, that the science of psychological testing be developed to the point where the character-development goals of the individual can in certain circumstances be better determined by this method than by naive preference on preference structures. Yet this occurrence would in no way affect the validity of this aspect of the Robbins Principle. For we are here faced with another "normative identification": we must treat the CPO as if it were the best guide and arbiter, independent of whether this is true in each particular case, or even in most cases. While the factual inaccuracy of this normative identification in no way invalidates the value judgment involved, it can by no stretch of the word be referred to as a "fundamental intuition" as is commonly asserted.[61]

But justifiable fear of the implications of this kind of reasoning is precisely what makes the neoclassical "value judgment" behind the Robbins Principle so appealing! It is the notion of the sanctity of the individual that is the chief appeal of traditional welfare theory, not its seeming simplicity, or ethical neutrality. And the main reason that this notion is so attractive is that it appeals to people's healthy antitotalitarian instinct that people have the right to choose for themselves what kind of people they want to become and what kind of preferences they wish to develop. And this is, indeed, a "fundamental intuition!" Gintis' reasoning might be misread by some to imply support for preference structure choice by expert testing rather than by people's own choice should the former appear more "accurate"—whatever that would mean in such a situation. We believe that to paint welfare theory into the kind of corner described in the previous quotation would place a new welfare paradigm on the worst possible ground.

But to conclude, Gintis summarized what he accomplished by focusing on the problem of uncertainty in preference development:

> I have emphasized that the seeming immediacy of neoclassical welfare economics results from a peculiarly simplistic representation of the individual choice situation and the relation of the individual to his social environment....The assumption of "tastes as data" in the formation of social policy is neither a tautology, nor is it a factual statement in light of the violability of preference structures; it is yet another value judgment couched in terms of an "as if" statement. The new definition states that an individual is "better off" in one period, provided he would have chosen to be in that position in the preceding period. Such an individual need not be happier, better off, more secure, more satisfied, or even alive—but as economists we are instructed to place him there, insofar as it is possible.

The importance of this presupposition cannot be overstated; without this premise, the theory of allocation efficiency becomes inoperative from the point of view of decision making. Indeed, Pareto optimality has no meaning in the absence of this judgment; unable to say that one individual should be in a preferred position, we could hardly generalize to all. One could yet analyze conditions of "efficiency," but there would remain no reason to prefer an efficient state to any other....We conclude that the methodological purity which in part accounts for the striking popularity of modern welfare economics is ephemeral. The premises are indeed simple in statement, but involve a number of separate judgments each by no means obviously true, and each wanting for justification. Doubtless none but the dogmatic could emerge from a genuine attempt at such justification without realizing the need to reintroduce a host of considerations not today considered a part of welfare economics proper....Having shown welfare axioms to involve complex and questionable value premises, rather than standing as simple intuitions, it becomes plausible to search for replacements.[62]

In Gintis' view, "few would be willing to leave the abstract and analytic treatment of Little and Samuelson"[63] unless already convinced that those waters were as ethically muddied as the ones they were headed for.

But according to Gintis, what are the implications of endogenous preferences for the conclusions of traditional welfare theory? It is one thing to argue that endogenous preferences signal the need for reconstruction of traditional welfare theory—for a different way of posing our valuative questions. It is another thing to argue that any of our conclusions regarding the welfare properties of different sets of economic institutions will be altered as a consequence of treating preferences as endogenous.

When Gintis finally ignored the difficulties he went to such pains to emphasize, and proceeded to "assess the ability of neoclassical analysis to come to terms with welfare problems in a situation where preferences change, but where there is complete knowledge on the part of the individuals as to the welfare effects of these changes,"[64] what did he conclude? Gintis stated an equilibrium price structure will yield a Pareto optimal outcome in a competitive market economy under the usual assumptions.[65] That is, if all the traditional assumptions are retained, except preferences are treated as endogenous rather than exogenous, any perfectly competitive capitalist economy will still have a general equilibrium that will be Pareto optimal. But Gintis argued this is of little benefit because "there is no reason to believe the solution to the multi-period problem to be unique."[66] And, therefore, "the only realistic recourse is to posit a collective economic instrument (e.g., a State Planning Board) to replace the Invisible Hand in the determination of expected prices"[67] in light of "multiple 'self-fulfilling' sets of price expectations compatible with maximization and market clearance."[68]

Presumably, Gintis meant multiple equilibria "compatible with individual maximization," since if he meant social maximization in the sense of Pareto optimal, a Central Planning Board to choose the "correct" price path from the many equilibrium price paths would not be needed to guide individual maximizing behavior toward achieving social optimality—any path would be fine. In other words, Gintis surmised that endogenous preferences implied a competitive private enterprise market economy could take many equilibrium paths, at least some of which would not be Pareto optimal. We see no other way to interpret his words consistent with the conclusion that some sort of State Planning Board would be required to replace the invisible hand to choose the socially desirable as distinct from socially undesirable equilibrium price vector(s).

If Gintis were correct that some of the multiple equilibria might not be Pareto optimal, we would agree with him that the logical necessity of inserting a State Planning Board to guarantee Pareto optimality would carry us far indeed from the original conception of a competitive market economy. Especially since the knowledge required by the Planning Board to carry out its appointed function in such a system would have to be the complete and perfect kind envisioned in some models of Centrally Planned Economies.[69] But we will prove in chapter 6 that all equilibria envisioned by Gintis in a purposeful preference molding vision of endogenous preferences under the assumption of perfect foresight must necessarily be Pareto optimal if they exist. And, therefore, if endogenous preferences are to play a role in a substantive criticism of the welfare properties of competitive market economies, the criticism must be of a different nature.

4.3 Evaluation of Previous Treatments

A major part of our work treats both human characteristics and preferences as endogenous. Therefore, it is useful to summarize and evaluate the contributions of previous treatments of preference development.

1. Preference development as well as preference fulfillment should be analyzed as part of a meaningful welfare theory.

2. Individual preferences are not only endogenous to the major cultural, political, and kinship institutions of society, but to previous economic choices made by the individual, and therefore, presumably to any aspect of the economic structure that influences those choices.

3. At least in a partial equilibrium setting, the "separability axiom" of neoclassical welfare theory that permits independent treatment of

supply and demand is untenable. As soon as individuals recognize their preferences are endogenous, it becomes irrational for them to ignore consideration of future expected prices when making decisions today that will have predictable effects on future preferences.

4. For welfare theorists to ignore the preference development effects of consumption and work choices and focus exclusively on the preference fulfillment effects leads to systematic misestimations of welfare effects of economic choice.

5. The Robbins judgment underlying traditional welfare theory, that economists should take tastes as givens, is by no means intuitively obvious, but requires a "number of separate judgments each by no means obviously true, and each wanting for justification."

How damaging is all this to traditional theory? Previous treatments make clear that taking preference development seriously raises difficulties that have long been ignored by most welfare theorists. To that extent, previous treatments of preference development are certainly "troublesome" for welfare theory as it has been practiced. But for any of us with a highly activated instinct for efficiency—which should be expected among economists as a product of our training rituals—the question arises whether taking preference development seriously will change any fundamental conclusions of welfare theory. If not, the task can be undertaken by those so inclined, at their leisure, while the rest continue with other tasks untroubled by doubts that the premises underlying their work are eroded.

The majority of those who have taken the time to treat preference development have concluded that doing so does not change any fundamental conclusions of welfare theory. The intuition of J. S. Mill was that private enterprise market institutions posed no difficulties for optimal preference development and efficient preference fulfillment. Modern neoclassical theorists such as von Weizsacker, Pollak, El Safty, and Hammond who have taken the trouble to extend the traditional welfare paradigm to incorporate endogenous preference development have not been primarily concerned with welfare implications but with implications for the analytical theory of demand. Reviewing their work one would conclude that while endogenous preferences pose a number of technical complications, they can be adequately treated through natural extensions of neoclassical theory. No neoclassicist writing in the 1970s and 1980s has exhibited any concern regarding the optimality properties of competitive, private enterprise market equilibria, only concern with the existence of various utility functions and the stability and interpretation of various demand relations when preferences are treated as endogenous. Certainly nothing in their writing suggests panic over the traditional welfare paradigm!

Herb Gintis, on the other hand, came to very different conclusions. His treatment of preference development led him to conclude that the logical/philosophical basis of the Robbins Principle is far more complicated than neoclassical welfare theory would have us believe. He also argued it is fundamentally unacceptable, requiring a reconstruction of welfare theory. Finally, he argued that treatment of preferences as endogenous casts considerable doubt on the welfare properties of private enterprise market institutions.

We will end in agreement with many of Gintis' conclusions, but often for reasons quite different than those he offers. In chapter 5 we will argue for a reconstruction of welfare theory based on a paradigm that emphasizes personal and, therefore, preference development, but not because we reject the Robbins judgment. In chapter 6 we will argue that an appropriate treatment of preferences as endogenous does play a critical role in altering some of the most fundamental conclusions of traditional welfare theory. But we will also demonstrate that this cannot be for the reason Gintis believed—that some of the multiple equilibria in a competitive economy with endogenous preferences may not be Pareto optimal. Nor is it, as Pollak suspected, because nothing can be concluded about the welfare properties of systems once we countenance purposeful preference development. Rather, we will show that endogenous preferences play a critical role in a substantive critique of the welfare properties of competitive market and other economies, but one that is quite different from what previous analysts of endogenous preferences have imagined. We will also show that endogenous preferences are critical to explaining an important mechanism by which the characteristics of institutional settings affect the characteristics and desires of those who live and make choices within those settings, all of which will allow us to distinguish important welfare properties of different economic systems that are indistinguishable from the perspective of traditional welfare theory.

4.4 **Institutions and the Neoclassical "Blind Spot"**

Traditional welfare theory cannot be faulted for failure to analyze the efficiency properties of different economic institutions—in particular the institutions of competitive markets and private enterprise. Whether one finds the conclusions illuminating, misleading, or both is another matter. But with the exception of inquiring about the distributional flexibility of economic systems, that is the extent of the traditional analysis of the properties and consequences of institutional structures. Specifically, traditional welfare theory fails to ask:

1. How do different institutional structures influence the pattern of preference development?

101

2. How do different economic institutions affect incentive structures, which in turn help define rational behavior itself?

Or, as Herb Gintis put it "does the set of approved institutionalized decision-making mechanisms itself bias the way the individual approaches the problem of personal development, and if so, does it do so in a 'desirable' direction? An acceptable welfare theory must satisfactorily deal with these central issues."[70] This critical "blind spot" in neoclassical theory is well illustrated in Roy Harrod's description of neoclassical methodology:

> The method of procedure is to take certain elements of the structure as given—namely the preference lists of individuals for goods and services, the terms on which they are willing to contribute their assistance to production, and the current state of technology....The object of this procedure would be to provide means of showing how changes in the fundamental data, desires, etc., will govern the course of events.[71]

But something is missing from Harrod's list of fundamental data: the institutional context in which technology and preferences are developed in the first place. It is hard to believe anyone would seriously argue that the development of technology or preferences is a random walk with respect to institutional environment. Yet the only alternative interpretations of the traditional view are that the specific institutions of private enterprise and competitive markets are (1) totally neutral, or (2) uniquely optimal with respect to effects on preference development and technological change. Before spelling out the objection, it is worth exploring each of these claims.

The most literal interpretation of the traditional approach is that, at most, economic institutions can influence preference development and/or technological change only minimally, and the impact can be ignored for practical purposes. In this case, changes in preference orderings and technology are taken to occur independently of economic institutions and should simply be "taken as givens" for economic analysis.

If this is not the view of traditional welfare theory, for example, if traditional theorists wish to argue that some undesirable economic institutions thwart or bias preference or technological development, then we must examine the reasons for believing that the particular institutions of private enterprise and competitive markets can be assumed not to influence Harrod's "fundamental data." It is conceivable that though many economic institutions distort preference and technological development, institutions of perfectly competitive capitalism can be ignored as neutral in this regard. Or, it could be that along with their supposed virtues of efficiency and equity flexibility, private enterprise and competitive market institutions optimally affect preference and technological developments as well.

While numerous theorists have argued that the combination of private enterprise and competitive market institutions is felicitous regarding technological progress,[72] very few traditional theorists have considered effects of these institutions on preference development.

The usual argument regarding technology has two parts: (1) private enterprise stimulates innovators by allowing them to reap the rewards of their cleverness, and, (2) competitive markets hasten the spread of clever ideas on pain of being driven out of business. We could make the point that there seems to be something of a contradiction here: If competitive markets maximize the spread of clever ideas, how is it that innovators capture the full rewards of their cleverness?[73] But we choose to highlight the fact that most neoclassical treatments of relations between private enterprise, competitive market institutions, and technological change have focused entirely on the degree of effort they are likely to stimulate without questioning the directions those efforts take. We have already seen that according to the conflict theory of the firm the most profitable technique may not coincide with the most efficient technique. While this reasoning applies to choice of techniques from the set of known technology, it certainly also suggests that under private enterprise we can expect to find a bias in the direction technological change takes. "Profitable" technological change should not necessarily be equated with "efficient" technological change no matter how rapid innovation may be.

4.5 Institutional Economics Fails to Come to the Rescue

As we have seen, traditional welfare theorists "abstract" from the institutional impact on the "fundamental data" of tastes, only to proceed to judge the efficiency of those same institutions in terms of the "fundamental data." John Stuart Mill was exceptional in providing at least a semiexplicit justification for this procedure, and Alfred Marshall expressed his opinion in passing that private enterprise market institutions have an optimal effect on preference development.[74] But most traditional theorists simply take the abstraction for granted.

Of course, the obvious place to look for treatment of this issue is among institutionalist economists. But surprisingly, while institutionalist economic theory has long proclaimed the importance of institutional structures in molding economic behavior, their insights have never been incorporated into welfare theory. A principal reason is that most institutionalist admonitions that institutionalized social pressures strongly influence economic behavior have been formulated as alternatives to explanations in terms of "rational choice." Institutionalist concepts such as "habit," "inertia," "peer pressure," and "invidious comparisons" are usually counterpoised to welfare theoretic concepts such as "individual rational choice" and "opportunity sets." Moreover, descendant from the writings of Thorstein Veblen, institutionalist economists have retained a strong methodological injunction to forswear what others call "normative" economic theory as little more than thinly disguised ideology in order to develop what they envision as truly "nonteleological," "evolutionary" analytical economics.

Regardless of reasons, economists with an institutionalist "bent" have been loath to transgress the preserves of welfare theory—particularly since welfare theory became ever more densely forested with advanced mathematical species. And welfare theorists have seldom considered institutionalist notions to be other than inconsistent with their own approach. We can only lament the consequences of an almost complete lack of cross-fertilization. Recognition that individual rational choice can only be institutionally defined remains far from universal. And construction of a careful analysis of the implications of different economic institutional structures for rational individual choice has long been delayed.

An excellent example of one of the infrequent attempts at cross-fertilization is an article by John Sawyer published in the *American Economic Review*.[75] Sawyer offered some important insights, but regrettably displayed just the kind of attitudes that have precluded incorporation of his insights into welfare theory.

Sawyer began by insisting that "the institutional context cannot be taken as constant or assumed away," and that "the ways in which the formal and informal social structure persistently shapes the behavior for all economic actors" is greatly underappreciated. Moreover, he rejected as totally insufficient the "formal bow to the importance of 'non-economic' factors...customary in opening chapters of economic textbooks and opening lectures of elementary economics courses."[76] He then observed:

> When forced back into sociocultural categories we rapidly discover how little we know...of how to incorporate such categories of explanation into the systematic analysis of economic processes....The newer social sciences, however, offer useful concepts....One of the most useful of these approaches—so-called "functional-structural" analysis, as developed in contemporary sociology—focuses attention on the extent to which social action tends to be "structured," both as to ends and means. Any society necessarily institutionalizes particular goals and values, patterns of social relationship, and ways of doing things requisite to the continued operation of that social system; in sociological language, it prescribes patterns of normative conduct in a system of structured roles....[77] It is evident that different institutional systems will be more or less encouraging or discouraging to particular patterns of economic activity.[78]

These are important insights indeed. Moreover, as Sawyer indicated, they are no longer avant-garde, or the exclusive property of social critics. These propositions have become fundamentals of mainstream sociology. Yet they continue to be almost totally ignored by traditional economic theory. Unfortunately, Sawyer minimized the potential impact of his observations on welfare theory.

First, he focused his insights on technological change rather than preference development. "Our interest here is in the economic drag, the rigidities and resistances to economic development."[79] Next, Sawyer applied his insights concerning the importance of institutional structures only to the noneconomic sphere. He argued for the importance of analyzing effects of social and cultural institutions on "productive" economic behavior, but it did not seem to occur to him that different economic institutions might have differential effects on development of preferences over economic opportunity sets. He certainly failed to extend his insights in this direction. Finally, he recommended that economists must borrow from modern theories of human motivation and behavior of sociologists and psychologists. But he warned that "since we do not yet have the social theory or understanding of the human personality adequate to demonstrate precise interrelationships," it must be recognized that we "clearly cannot offer quantitative solutions."[80] Leaving aside the "precisely" predictable psychological effects of such language on today's proud and highly mathematical economists, Sawyer's instincts distract from the most fundamental implications of his insights.

The problem for welfare theorists is not to explain and predict actual behavior but to explain what would be rational behavior under stipulated conditions. It is enough to recognize these are two very different tasks and point out that welfare theory has, for better or worse, concerned itself with the latter rather than the former, to explain why Sawyer's insights are so easy for welfare theorists to dismiss. But however clear most welfare theorists are about the difference between the two tasks, confusion is rampant within the profession at large. Clarification and motivation for the task pursued by welfare theorists is in order.

Many assume the sole scientific purpose of welfare theory—investigation of the implications of individual rationality—is to contribute to an understanding of actual economic behavior. In this view, the aesthetic quality of investigations of abstract rationality may appeal to those who engage in its intricacies and prove sufficiently alluring to guarantee its continuation as an art form. But unless the conclusions of welfare theory can be brought to bear on explanations of actual human behavior, they have no scientific legitimacy. For example, institutionalist economists, following in Veblen's wake, have preferred concepts such as "habit," "inertia," and "status" to the "hedonistic calculus" as explanations of actual human behavior. But institutionalists are not alone. Much in modern psychological and sociological literature suggests that a great deal of human behavior cannot be explained by appeals to rationality, hence, the conclusion that welfare theory has but a limited role to play in an analytic theory of human economic behavior.

We do not need to take a stand on this issue. While we believe welfare theory has a role to play in analytical theory because we believe elements of rationality frequently are displayed in individual economic choice, we are more than prepared to admit that role is limited. For us the undeniable importance of welfare economics is as an evaluative theory of economic institutions. If we wish to know what impact an economic institution has on human well-being, we must evaluate the kind of behavior that institution promotes. Does a particular economic institution promote behavior that is socially efficient? Does it promote outcomes in accord with some definition of equity? Does it promote human development that renders people capable of garnering greater satisfaction from the circumstances they will face in the future? And when we inquire how institutions "promote" one kind of behavior rather than another, we discover they do so by making some behavior individually rational and other behavior individually irrational.

The important distinction here is that while an economic institution may "promote" some kind of behavior by making it "individually rational," and while such behavior may be socially productive or counterproductive in ways welfare theory spells out with great care, we do not have to believe people always behave in accord with the behavior "promoted" in order to take great interest in the kind of behavior promoted. In a certain sense, the degree to which people follow the dictates of their institutional environment is irrelevant. To the extent that an economic institution has an impact on human welfare, its impact must be measured by the coincidence or discrepancy between the behavior it promotes as individually rational and socially rational behavior.[81] In other words, it is the task of welfare theory to define and compare individually rational and socially rational behavior, irrespective of the extent to which either pattern of behavior coincides with actual behavior. Only in this way can we evaluate the impact of different economic institutions. In this sense, welfare theorists are correct in viewing the details of more or less accurate sociological and psychological theories of actual human behavior as effectively irrelevant to their project. But this does not mean that a theory of rational individual choice from economic opportunity sets does not require a component that analyzes the effects of specifically economic institutions.

It is only because modern sociologists have taken human developmental effects of the institutions that concern them seriously that such analysis is labeled "sociological." In this sense, yes, welfare economics needs a "sociological" component. But by this we mean welfare theorists should "think" in one of the ways sociologists think. Economists should analyze developmental effects of the institutions in whose analysis they specialize. This is quite different from integrating the insights of sociologists concerning social but noneconomic institutions and the determinants of actual human behavior with the insights of economists concerning the efficiency properties of different economic institutions—which is our reading of the research program proposed by Sawyer and others from the "institutionalist" school of economics through the years.

Moreover, in the sense that modern welfare theory has always provided "quantitative" solutions, a welfare theory recognizing the influence of economic structures on choice and preference development can do so as well. In other words, the project we propose need not be any less "quantifiable" than traditional welfare theory. To the extent a theory of rational individual choice as defined by institutional context has anything to contribute to a theory of actual human behavior, sociologists and psychologists would be well advised to borrow from the theories of a new breed of welfare economists! How is that for an incentive compatible mechanism for welfare theorists?

In any case, we will make these issues a major focus of our welfare theory and analysis throughout the rest of this book. Without revealing all our results prematurely, we can outline the logic of why analyzing the effect of economic institutions on preference development is particularly important if welfare theory is to have anything further to say.

4.6 **What Is at Stake**

The influence of the traditional paradigm on the analysis of preference development can be summarized quite briefly. The most sacred methodological principle of traditional welfare theory is a categorical injunction to economists not to question where preferences come from. Following Gintis we dub this methodological injunction the Robbins Principle and simply note that in cultures considered less civilized it would be called a taboo. Whether we will be able to preserve the notion of the sanctity of the individual while recognizing the importance of preference development remains to be seen. But there is no doubt the traditional paradigm long discouraged analysis of preference development.

The effect of the traditional paradigm on exploring the effects of economic institutions on preference development has been no less damaging. Traditional welfare theory sensitizes us to the efficiency effects of institutional structures—that is, the effect of economic institutions on preference fulfillment. But a "blind spot" in the traditional paradigm has made it all but impossible for traditional theorists to even recognize the potential importance of the effects of economic institutions on preference development.

It is our major contention that exploring the relation between institutional structures and preference development is one of the most fertile fields welfare economists have yet to cultivate. It is also our contention that diminishing returns have set in from extensive cultivation using traditional tools of the relation between familiar institutions and preference fulfillment, and that traditional welfare theory is increasingly unable to distinguish between the major economic systems on welfare theoretic rather than practical grounds. Of course, we must substantiate both these claims as we do in parts 2 and 3 of this book. But assuming, for now, we succeed in arguing our case, the pernicious effect of the traditional paradigm is apparent. The Robbins judgment interpreted as "taboo" has long combined with the institutional "blind spot" to obstruct progress on what we find the most promising frontiers of welfare economics. We close with a brief explanation of what is at stake between the traditional and new welfare paradigms.

Until recently welfare theorists had seriously analyzed only a small number of abstract economies, or combinations of economic institutions. They combined competitive markets and private enterprise production to analyze what is commonly called Perfectly Competitive Capitalism (PCC). They combined public enterprise and central planning to analyze what many call Centrally Planned Socialism (CPS). And they combined competitive markets and employee-managed public enterprise to analyze what some call Workers' Self-managed Market Socialism (WSMS). Prior to the quiet revolution in welfare theory that has been recently unfolding in response to Hurwicz's call for theorists to think of themselves as economic mechanism designers, there were very few other well-defined, abstract, economic models. One exception was the model developed by Oskar Lange, Abba Lerner, and Frederick Taylor. By combining markets with a kind of public enterprise in which a state agency appoints managers and directs them to follow a few simple rules, Lange, Lerner, and Taylor developed a different model of what they called Market Socialism (LLTMS) in a conscious effort to refute the proposition that "socialist" economies could not be efficient.[82] But the work of Lange, Lerner, and Taylor was deemed only a footnote in the long debate about whether or not idealized models of the different major economies could achieve Pareto optimality.[83]

We will avoid use of the value-laden words "socialism" and "capitalism," and employ more specific and less "politicized" labels throughout the remainder of this book. We will refer to Private Enterprise Market Economies (PrEMEs), Public Enterprise Centrally Planned Economies (PuECPEs), and Public Enterprise Market Economies (PuEMEs) of two different kinds: Public Enterprise Employee-Managed Market Economies (PuEEMMEs) and Public Enterprise State-Managed Market Economies (PuESMMEs). Regardless of the comparative merits of different definitions of "socialism" and "capitalism," something, no doubt, can be said for "defusing" the discussion.

In sum, welfare theorists have spent considerable time analyzing efficiency properties of a small number of combinations of economic institutions. Though opinion has long been divided, and practical matters are to be considered, it is our belief this "old welfare debate" is essentially over. In later chapters we demonstrate that under similarly generous assumptions, from the perspective of traditional welfare theory, all of the above abstract models are equally capable of generating efficient social outcomes. Moreover, they are all equally "flexible" regarding equity.

While this may come as a surprise to many outside the field, and a few within, it is certainly not unknown to all welfare theorists. And while we save the demonstration for later chapters, we can usefully interpret the conclusion here.

If all the above abstract economies are equally efficient and flexible from the perspective of traditional welfare theory, and if traditional theory defines welfare entirely in terms of efficiency and income flexibility, traditional welfare theory cannot distinguish between these different fundamental economic models.[84] This is not to say traditional welfare theory cannot recognize that the systems are characterized by different economic institutions. But from the perspective of traditional welfare theory the institutional differences do not affect the welfare results.

We believe this is a rather awkward position for welfare theory. It seems to us a reasonable spectator of the welfare theory research project might fail to see the "efficiency" of complicated analyses that are technically taxing, but explain only how "practical" considerations might prevent real world approximations of major economic systems from achieving the equally beneficent results that all achieve in theory. One of the principal advantages of the paradigm and welfare theory we champion is that it can distinguish between welfare properties of these economic models by distinguishing the effects of different institutional "fundamental data" on preference and human development.

Anticipating the findings of parts 2 and 3:

1. Traditional welfare theory, if applied evenhandedly, is unable to distinguish between the performances of the different major economic systems except on the basis of "practical" criticisms.

2. Our new welfare theory, on the other hand, predicts very different results for different major economies and identifies different "welfare theoretic" as well as "practical" problems with each.

PART TWO

A NEW WELFARE THEORY

5

A NEW WELFARE
PARADIGM

IN PART 1 we examined numerous failings of traditional welfare theory, tracing the origins of many of those failings to the failure to view people as conscious agents who develop within particular institutional contexts. While it might seem that the task of creating a new welfare paradigm would be monumental, if modern welfare theorists are willing to borrow from alternative social paradigms, much can be accomplished quickly. After all, welfare theorists have seldom elaborated the paradigms they employed in the past. In this area we have always exploited the advantages of "late comers" by borrowing freely from others.

5.1 People and Society

Individual people try to fulfill their needs and desires as they perceive them, frequently in cooperation with others. We are a self-conscious, social species because we define and seek to fulfill so many needs in relations with others. Moreover, in seeking to meet needs we identify today, we choose to act in ways that may change needs we perceive tomorrow.

Historically, people have created elaborate social organizations to meet their most urgent needs and desires. To satisfy their economic needs people have generated a variety of social arrangements that define and mediate frequently complicated divisions of responsibilities and rewards among participants. But we have also created intricate kinship relations through which individuals seek to satisfy sexual needs and accomplish their child-rearing goals, as well as religious, cultural, and political organizations and institutions for meeting different needs. Of course, the particular social

113

arrangements and the relations among them all vary from society to society. But what is common to all human societies is the elaboration of social relationships for the identification and pursuit of individual need fulfillment.

To develop a paradigm expressive of this view of humans and society we first concentrate on concepts helpful in treating individual people and then on concepts helpful in discussing social organizations and institutions in general. After developing means to combine the two, we distinguish between different "spheres" of social life and the possible relations between them. We conclude chapter 5 by elaborating a qualitative model for conceptualizing economic activity.

By no means do we offer an exhaustive treatment of all issues we touch upon. Nor can we offer here a full argument in favor of the paradigm we present. The interested reader should consult other works.[1] Our goal in this chapter is limited to explaining the essentials of the paradigm sufficiently to use it throughout the rest of this book. As far as welfare theory is concerned, we are happy to judge the new paradigm on the basis of the economic results it proves capable of facilitating.[2]

5.2 The Human Center

We are matter and alive, so we are presumably subject to the laws of matter and the laws of evolution. We are also a particular animal species, so presumably some species characteristics distinguish us from other animals. Not many insights are to be gleaned from dwelling on how humans are subject to the laws of matter, but the subjects of evolutionary laws and human nature provide a useful starting point for welfare analysis.

5.2.1 Huxley versus Kropotkin

Except for "creationists," most analysts consider "the laws of evolution" fairly straightforward and noncontroversial. Unfortunately, the dominant interpretation sprinkles more ideology over the scientific basis of Darwin's theory than most "secularists" care to admit.

T. H. Huxley inaugurated ideological interpretations of Darwin's theory of natural selection as survival of the fittest individuals in mortal combat. Peter Kropotkin responded with an alternative interpretation of natural selection in which species specific social relations contour individual competition within any species. Moreover, Kropotkin argued both logically and empirically that species specific social relations most often differ greatly from relations fostering hostile competition between individual members because effective tendencies toward what he termed "mutual aid" among members of a species was often useful in preserving species survival.[3]

114

Whether there is any more reason to assume human evolution produced an innate tendency toward intraspecies aggression than an innate tendency toward mutual aid or solidarity is an important debate. But for our purposes it is not necessary to embrace the "mutualist" view. All that is required to lend credulity to our undertaking is recognition that the view of humans as inevitably doomed to a perpetual Hobbesian joust by the inexorable laws of evolution may be exaggerated. If readers merely allow that the interpretation of evolutionary laws begun by Huxley known as "Social Darwinism" is controversial and may be more ideology than science, our arguments should be of interest. We attempt to motivate this kind of open-mindedness in the following section.

5.2.2 *The Laws of Evolution Reconsidered*

Human nature as it now exists was formed in accord with laws of evolution under conditions pertaining well before recorded history. Certainly conditions have since changed drastically; so if "historic time" had already lasted a million years, these changed conditions might have significantly altered human nature. But historic time has only been an evolutionary instant, making it doubtful history's altered conditions could have selected genetic characteristics significantly different from those bequeathed by our prehistory.

The obvious conclusion is that one cannot reasonably argue that human wars and pervasive hostile relationships between and within human communities during the human history known to us have caused our natures to become Hobbesian. Throughout recorded history we have been genetically essentially what we were at the outset. To believe otherwise is to believe that a baby plucked from the arms of its mother, moments after birth, five thousand years ago, and time-traveled to the present would be genetically different from babies born today.[4]

Which is not to say that our history of war, oppression, and exploitation has had no impact. These aspects of our history have had important effects on our consciousness, culture, and social institutions that cannot be "willed away." But the point is that recorded history has left ideological and institutional residues, not genetic ones. Under changed institutional conditions it is possible our behavior—the combined product of our genetic inheritance and our institutional environment—need not be so Hobbesian.

This is not a conclusive case against the Hobbesian hypothesis. It merely establishes that it is unlikely the events of historic time made us innately aggressive. Of course, this only pushes the question farther back in time, and the Hobbesian hypothesis can still be formulated. But establishing the relevant time period can influence one's assessment of the plausibility of competing hypotheses. Human nature was not forged in the anvil of known human history but under the neolithic conditions of prehistory about which we know far less. Were these conditions more likely to "select" individually aggressive traits or traits that enhanced effective cooperative behavior?

If the answer to this question is not obvious, and if particular social institutions in recorded history would have elicited antisocial behavior even from people with sociable genetic dispositions, there is no more a priori reason to suppose that the "laws of evolution" have doomed us to be Hobbesian combatants than saints.

5.2.3 Human Nature

The simplest argument for the existence of a human nature is that if we are a unique species something must distinguish us from all other species. Bluntly, a human being is not a pigeon, and no conceivabely rearrangement of environments can change this. Pigeon nature is not human nature. Our genetically determined physical and mental characteristics and potentials are different. We have a human nature in the strong, genetic sense.[5] Attributes that distinguish us from all other living things as a species, and they include more than simply our physical appearance are "wired in."[6]

There is nothing mystical or idealistic in this. "Material" biological processes ensure that with human reproduction certain wired-in attributes remain essentially invariant over long periods of time. So we humans are not just what we eat. The human result is not merely an imprint upon a blank slate. If we were totally a product of our worldly situations, we would be perfectly and infinitely moldable. If this were the case, the effects of environmental differences would eventually mold infinitely flexible humans into shapes as different from one another as diverse patterns of clay subjected to different pressures. With no genetic structural similarities people subjected to different environments would presumably be incapable of communicating or understanding one another. If humans had unlimited behavioral flexibility, treated to "proper socialization" we would be as satisfied living in isolation as in community, repeating mindless tasks as employing creative intelligence, and hating and being hated as loving and being loved. The only cause for us to feel uncomfortable, "alienated," or "oppressed" would be a discrepancy between what we had been molded to desire and what we actually received. As long as we were socialized to expect what was coming and to desire and appreciate it, we would be as happy and fulfilled in one set of circumstances as any other.

This is the view of the behaviorist school of psychology that claims its origins in a specially chosen subset of the writings of B. F. Skinner. We are what we are "reinforced" to be; we want what we have been "programmed" to want.[7] Ironically, this is also the dominant Marxist view: "Marx wholly denied any abstract human nature," holding instead that "human beings are totally malleable and derive whatever nature they possess from their concrete sociohistorical environment," that we human beings "make our own nature."[8] But this is a sorry misuse of words. To present the fact that social environment influences how people develop as evidence that no such thing as "human nature" exists is a redefinition of the ordinary meaning of "human nature," not a refutation of its existence.

One might conceivably argue that "human nature" is unhelpful in studying and evaluating the functioning of human societies. But that is not the same as saying that there is no such thing as human nature. This claim could only be valid if constraints imposed by human nature rarely, if ever, played any role in important outcomes. The remainder of this chapter and the next present our picture of human nature and use it to construct a welfare paradigm whose application will refute the view that the results of human evolution can be ignored in analyzing human societies.

5.2.4 Natural, Species, and Derived Needs and Potentials

All people, simply by virtue of being human, have various needs, capacities, and powers. Some of these needs, like the needs for food and sex, or the abilities to eat and copulate, are shared with other living creatures. We call these our natural needs and potentials. Others, such as the needs for knowledge, creative activity, and love, and the powers to conceptualize, plan ahead, evaluate complex activities, and experience complex emotions, are more distinctly human. We call these our species needs and potentials. Finally, most of our needs and powers, like the needs for Bruce Springsteen albums, to share feelings with a particular loved one, or to know the rules of baseball, and the abilities to play the guitar, repair a roof, or solve differential equations, we develop over the course of our lives (though the underlying capabilities are natural or species traits). We call these our derived needs and potentials.

In short, every person has natural attributes similar to those of other animals and species attributes shared only by other humans, both of which can be thought of as genetically "wired-in." Based on these genetic potentials people develop particular derived needs and capacities as a result of their particular life experiences.

The first important point is that derived needs and capabilities must be developed within limits set by natural and species needs and potentials that are, in turn, innately fixed. We do not create our human nature alone, as individuals, or even together, as historically connected generations elaborating changing social environments. To all intents and purposes, wired-in results of past human evolution are not subject to modification by individual or social activity. Instead, our unchanging nature provides the foundation for everything we become in our lives.

This leads to the second important point: As individuals we create our derived attributes not only within limits set by our innate natural and species characteristics but also within limits set by our historically generated social environment. While all humans have certain innate needs and potentials, the forms in which these manifest themselves are always historically mediated, as are the interrelations between them.

The absence of any conception of species needs and powers in the traditional paradigm is a major weakness we wish to redress. The traditional paradigm lumps needs, desires, and whims under the umbrella concept "preference ordering." In its effort to protect the sanctity of the individual it eschews any restrictions on people's preferences other than what it portrays as "axioms of rationality." These minimal restrictions can be justified on the grounds that no theory can reasonably be expected to say much about totally erratic behavior, or on the grounds that regardless of how erratic people's actual behavior, it is of interest to know what rational behavior would be. But rational pursuit of totally unrestricted preference fulfillment is not the same as rational pursuit of preference fulfillment within the confines of an array of innately limited potential human preferences. In other words, traditional welfare theory is less a theory of rational human behavior and more a theory of rational behavior as it might be undertaken by infinitely programmable robots.

Admittedly, specifying restrictions on the potential development patterns of human preferences can be tricky. We do not wish to violate the sanctity of the individual. Nor do we wish to assert restrictions that may prove inaccurate. But we think there are ways around these problems that permit us to develop a theory of rational choice specifically appropriate to humans. The reason for our optimism is that we do not need to defend an inclusive list of species needs and powers to develop our theory and present our argument. Instead, a rather minimal, and we believe noncontroversial, list of restrictions on potential patterns of human development will suffice.

Human Consciousness. Human beings have intellectual tools that permit them to understand and situate themselves in their surroundings. This is not to say all humans attain an accurate understanding of their physical and social environment and their position in it. No doubt, most of us deceive ourselves greatly. But an incessant striving to develop some interpretation of our relationship to our surroundings, and to act in accord with that understanding seems endemic to normally functioning human beings. Put differently, human beings have the capacity to act purposefully and a need to exercise that capacity. We call this ability and associated need "human consciousness," which has a variety of attributes and is largely responsible for complicating human systems compared to nonhuman systems.

All animals engage in activities that both change the world and themselves, but only humans consciously choose activities in light of predicted effects on both their environment and themselves. In a sense, this adds a "third dimension" to human systems. In addition to human activity and the physical and social environments exists a third "mediating" dimension of consciousness. Marx explained this crucial species difference as follows:

> A spider conducts operations that resemble those of a weaver and a bee puts to shame many an architect in the construction of her cells. But what distinguishes the worst architect from the best of bees is this, that the architect raises his structure in imagination before he erects it in reality. At the end of every labor-process, we get a result that already existed in the imagination of the laborer at its commencement. He not only effects a change of form in the material on which he works but he also realizes a purpose of his own that gives the law to his modus operandi, and to which he must subordinate his will.[9]

In other words, consciousness allows humans to select activities in light of preconceived effects on both their environment and themselves. One kind of effect our activities have is to more or less completely fulfill our present needs and desires, but a second effect is to either reinforce or transform our needs and desires. The capacity to analyze and evaluate these latter effects is what makes endogenous preferences so much more interesting from a welfare theoretic point of view than simple habit formation, and why, along with "preference fulfillment," "preference development" must become a central concern of welfare theory. It is also in this sense that we humans, unlike all other species, are potentially the subjects as well as the objects of our histories and can be "self-reproductive."

The human capacity to act purposefully implies the need to exercise that capacity. Not only can we analyze and evaluate the effects of our actions, we need to exercise choice over alternatives, and we, therefore, need to be in positions to do so. While some call this the "need for freedom," it is important to note that our "need for freedom" goes considerably beyond the "need for freedom" of many animal species. There are animals that cannot be domesticated or will not reproduce in captivity, thereby exhibiting an innate "need for freedom." But the human need to employ our powers of consciousness requires "freedom" beyond the "physical freedom" other species require. People require "freedom" to choose and direct their own activities in accord with their understanding and evaluation of the effects of that activity. Later we will define the concept self-management to express this peculiarly human species need in a way that subsumes the better-known concept "individual freedom" as a special case.

Consciousness implies another species trait, which although not necessary for arguments concerning welfare theory proper, is very helpful to understanding how humans and societies function. Because we see ourselves as choosing among alternatives, we frequently need to interpret our choices in some positive light. If we saw our behavior as completely beyond our own control, there would be no need to justify it, even to ourselves. But to the extent that we see ourselves as choosing among options, it can be very uncomfortable if we are not able to "rationalize" our decisions. We need an interpretation of our involvement with the world that judges our activities to be effectively oriented toward achieving our purposes and our purposes to be in some sense worthwhile. In other words, we have the need for a positive self-image.

If we could not consciously assess and control our behavior, presumably we never would have developed a wired-in need to justify it, even to ourselves. But to the extent that we came to see ourselves as choosing among options, it apparently became serviceable to survival to develop "stories" that made sense of our decisions. Evolution, we hypothesize, took this apparently useful trend far enough so that we now have a wired-in need for a positive self-image. Again, this is not to say all humans succeed in justifying their actions, even to themselves, much less that many who succeed deserve to do so! Nor do all social circumstances make it equally easy to develop a positive self-image. The point is simply that a striving to minimize "cognitive dissonance" appears to be a common human trait related to our species power of consciousness.

Finally, few other critics of traditional welfare theory have emphasized that traditional concepts fail to reflect the intrinsic importance of how and by whom choices are made. Since this would not be a problem for a welfare theory concerned with agents who were not self-conscious, this is an appropriate time to consider the issue.

According to neoclassical theory my level of happiness is a function of the quantities of material commodities I consume and the number of hours and kind of work I perform since my preference ordering is defined on commodity/work space. What if some master chooses my commodity bundle? What if I choose the same bundle myself? Neoclassical welfare theory concludes that my level of happiness, or the ranking of those two experiences by my preference ordering, would be exactly the same. But this is most unlikely for human beings.

A similar problem arises with respect to social choice. In terms of the Bergsonian social welfare function, it doesn't matter how weights multiplying each individual's level of utility are determined. Suppose a dictator chooses particular weights. Suppose the same set of weights are determined by mutual negotiation among all members of society in a "fair" environment free from information distortion. Neoclassical welfare theory concludes that if the "correct" social welfare function as defined by a given set of weights is maximized, social bliss is achieved irrespective of how the weights were determined. The more contemporary theory of social choice adds only the ad hoc principle of nondictatorship, a rather limited improvement as far as taking the decision-making process seriously.

The above problems stem from the fact that a theory of well-being relevant to agents with consciousness must account for how things get decided. Whether we are concerned with commodity bundles consumed by individuals or weights signifying the relative importance of different individual's opinions, more than just the bundles and weights matter. The process by which bundles are selected and the process by which weights are chosen matter in societies of conscious agents. Who chooses under what circumstances matters as well as what gets chosen. It is because we are conscious agents that one cannot separate ends from means.[10]

Not all variants of traditional welfare theory are equally insensitive to this problem. The contractarian approach expresses the importance of how choices are made both through its concept of free consent in an "original position" characterized by "fairness," and in its first principle of liberty.[11] Later we will explain in what respects we find the contractarian solution to this problem deficient. But we hope by building on the positive parts of the contractarian attempt our paradigm can move us forward.

Human Sociability. Human beings are a social species in a number of important senses. First, the vast majority of our needs and potentials can only be satisfied and developed in conjunction with other humans. Needs for sexual and emotional gratification can only be pursued in relations with others. Intellectual and communicative potentials can only be developed in relations with others. Needs for camaraderie, community, and social esteem can only be satisfied in relation with others.

Second, needs and potentials that might, conceivably, be pursued independently seldom are. For example, people could try to satisfy their economic needs self-sufficiently, but they seldom have because establishing social relationships that define and mediate elaborate divisions of responsibilities and benefits has always proved so much more "efficient." And the same holds true for spiritual, cultural, and most other needs. Even when desires might be pursued individually, people have generally found it more fruitful to pursue them jointly.

Third, human consciousness contributes a special character to our sociability. Numerous other animal species are social in the sense that many of their needs can only be satisfied in conjunction with one another. But human beings have the ability to understand and plan their activity. And since we recognize this ability in others, we logically hold them accountable and expect them to do likewise. Our social ties, therefore, stem not only from mutual activity and dependence but also from mutual conscious understanding and expectation.

121

A more aesthetic expression of this social view of what it means to be human does not make it any less "scientific":

> Kant called the realm of connection the kingdom of ends. Erich Gutkind's name for it was the absolute collective. My own term for the same thing is the human harvest—by which I mean the webs of connection in which all human goods (in the doubled sense of value and product) are clearly the results of a collective labor that morally binds us irrevocably to distant others. Even the words we use, the gestures we make, and the ideas we have, come to us already worn smooth by the labor of others, and they confer upon us an immense debt we do not fully acknowledge....That is why Freud, trying to be as precise as possible, chose the word 'eros' to describe human vitality or energy. He meant by that to acknowledge the motion of all individual life toward the reality around it. We are the makers of value, all, and Eros, the force of life within the self, cannot ripen in the flesh until we find a place for it in the world.[12]

It is the individualistic rather than the social view of human beings that is seen to be absurd and unscientific when examined more closely:

> The individual cannot escape his dependence on society even when he acts on his own. A scientist who spends his lifetime in a laboratory may delude himself that he is a modern version of Robinson Crusoe, but the material of his activity and the apparatus and skills with which he operates are social products. They are indelible signs of the cooperation which binds men together. The very language in which a scientist thinks has been learned in a particular society. Social context also determines the career and other life goals that an individual adopts.... No one becomes a scientist or even wants to become one in a society which does not have any. In short, man's consciousness of himself and of his relations with others and with nature are that of a social being, since the manner in which he conceives of anything is a function of his society.[13]

In fact, not even Robinson Crusoe was intelligible apart from the society from which he had become separated:

> Production by isolated individuals outside of society—something which might happen as an exception to a civilized man who by accident got into the wilderness and already dynamically possessed within himself the forces of society—is as great an absurdity as the idea of the development of language without individuals living together and talking to one another.[14]

In sum, contrary to contractarians' "hypothetical history," there never was a "Hobbesian state of nature" where individuals roamed the wilds of European forests in a "natural" state of war. Human beings have always lived in social units—tribes preceding clans and nuclear families. The roots of our sociability—our "realm of connection," or "human harvest"—are both physical-emotional and mental-conceptual. The unique aspect of human sociability is that the "webs of connection" that connect all human beings are woven not just by a "resonance of the flesh" but by shared consciousness and mutual accountability. So it is especially true that humans do not exist in isolation from their species community. It is impossible to fulfill our needs and employ our powers independently of others. Not only have we never lived except in active interrelation with one another, we are meaningful only in this context; and no human with any sense would ever desire it to be otherwise! But before proceeding, to avoid misinterpretation we wish to clarify what we mean by human sociability.

The above argument claims that human beings are inevitably social and that this is true regardless of the particular form of society they inhabit. But we will later criticize the relative absence of sociability in both fact and consciousness in market economies. In chapter 7 we will argue that market institutions contribute to a loss of potential well-being described by Peter Marin in the following terms: "To lose touch with the social world is to lose a part of the self, and the fatigue now at work in our own lives is directly connected to its absence, for moral activity and a life in the larger world are necessary to our own well-being."[15] The question we wish to clarify is whether these two claims are contradictory. The answer is they are not, if one adopts the view we recommend in this book of the relationship between human characteristics and social institutions.

At times we treat human characteristics and social institutions as separate entities. Often there is nothing wrong with this. It can be convenient and introduces no serious distortions regarding some issues. But regarding other matters it is critical to focus on the "interplay" between human characteristics and social institutions. Once we recognize that people derive some of their characteristics, and that the availability of particular social roles (and unavailability of others) can influence developmental trajectories, the potential connection between role offerings and derived traits becomes clear.

The paradigm we are proposing entails a view of people and society in which each affects the characteristics of the other. It is in this way we can claim, without being contradictory, both that the human world is irrevocably social and that particular social institutions might inadequately reflect this essential human quality and thereby obstruct our ability to enjoy satisfactions that derive from development of our social potentials.

Human Character Structures. People are more than their constantly developing needs and powers. At any moment we have certain personality traits, skills, ideas, and attitudes. These structural characteristics play a crucial mediating role. On the one hand, they largely determine the activities we will select by defining the goals of these activities—our present needs, desires, or preferences. On the other hand, the structures themselves are merely the cumulative imprint of our past activities on our innate potentials. What is important regarding human characteristics is to neither underestimate nor overestimate their permanence. Although we have emphasized that people derive needs, powers, and characteristics over their lifetimes as the result of their activities, we are never completely "free" to do so at any point in time. Not only are people limited by the particular menu of role offerings of the social institutions that surround them, they are constrained at any moment by the personalities, skills, knowledge, and values they have accumulated as of that moment. But even though these character structures may persist over long periods of time, they are not totally invariant. Any change in the nature of our activities that persists long enough can lead to changes in our personalities, skills, ideas, and values. In this case, the new human structural characteristics can lead to new preferences as well.

We can illustrate using a metaphor from Ilya Prigogine's theory of dissipative systems applied originally in the field of thermodynamics. For Prigogine, energy and matter are continually flowing through "dissipative systems," but usually the system remains largely unchanged. That is, the manner in which energy and matter enter, leave, and affect the system does not change appreciably over time. Occasionally, however, the whole system is transformed—the manner in which energy and matter flow through the system is altered. Thinking of human beings as dissipative systems, we can imagine people constantly "consuming" material and information "inputs" and "producing" material and information "outputs." The usual result is to "reproduce" our human character structures intact. Or, put differently, the usual result leaves our relation to material and information flows unchanged. But sometimes the character structure is altered in some substantial way, and our reaction to material and information possibility sets is changed dramatically.

In any case, a full theory of human development would have to explain how personalities, skills, ideas, and values form, why they usually persist but occasionally change, and what relationship exists between these semi-permanent structures and people's needs and capacities. No such theory now exists, or is visible on the horizon. But fortunately for welfare theory, a few "low level" insights are sufficient for our purposes.

The Relation of Consciousness to Activity. The fact that our knowledge and values influence our choice of activities is easy to understand. The manner in which our activities influence our consciousness and the importance of this relation is less apparent. As discussed above, the ability and need to act "knowledgeably" implies a need to rationalize what we do. But the tendency to minimize "cognitive dissonance" can work in two directions, and creates a subtle duality to the relationship between thought and action in which each influences the other. On the one hand, we seek to choose activities harmonious with our consciousness. But we also form consciousness that put activities we find we must engage in, for whatever reason, in a good light. So when we fulfill needs through particular activities we are induced to mold our thoughts to rationalize both the logic and merit of those activities as well, thereby generating consciousness/personality structures that have a permanence beyond that of the activities that formed them.

The Possibility of Detrimental Character Structures. Individuals' needs and powers at any moment are defined and constrained by their previously developed personalities, skills, and consciousness. But these characteristics were not always "givens." They are the products of previously chosen activities in combination with "given" genetic potentials. So why would anyone choose to engage in activities that resulted in characteristics detrimental to future need fulfillment and the maximum development of future powers?

One possibility is that someone else, who does not hold our interests foremost, made the decision for us. Another possibility is that we failed to recognize important structure-producing effects of current activities chosen primarily to fulfill immediate needs.[16] But imposed choices and mistakes are not the most interesting possibilities for welfare theory.

A fully informed individual might consciously choose to develop characteristics that fail to maximize future fulfillment if the "cost" in terms of lost present fulfillment were high enough. In fact, rational choice would require such behavior. Once we recognize that the present choice of activities affects our future characteristics and that our future characteristics influence our future preference structures, what we will term "preference fulfillment" and "preference development" become competing ends, and there is every reason to expect a "trade-off" between them. In this case, people with pressing present needs may well forego opportunities to develop traits that permit greater future fulfillment, whereas people with less pressing present needs or greater overall opportunities will concentrate more on future preference development.[17]

On the other hand, people may develop detrimental characteristics precisely because they orient their preference development so as to increase the fulfillment they can obtain under future conditions of activity availability. If institutional structures establish conditions in which some activities are available on easy terms while other activities can only be engaged in with great difficulty, it is sensible for people to choose present activities that develop traits that enhance appreciation of the former and minimize needs for the latter. As we will see later, the conditions under which these traits can be meaningfully termed "detrimental" must be analyzed with great care, and we leave that task to chapter 6. To foreshadow the results of that discussion, if the future conditions of availability reflect nothing other than the scarcities of productive means, the limitations of known technologies, and the desires of others, it is not sensible to describe the characteristics people develop to "cope" with these conditions "detrimental." On the other hand, if institutional structures that organize social activities exert an additional influence, so that some activities are accessible only on terms that exceed their true opportunity costs while others are accessible on terms that understate their opportunity costs, traits developed to accommodate these biased conditions can be meaningfully described as "detrimental."[18]

In assessing the plausibility and extent of institutional biases of this kind we need to note the subtle but important difference between a conceptualization of choice among goods and choice among activities. We can plausibly imagine an infinite continuum of items and sizes when thinking of the supply of goods. It is problematic to envision an infinite continuum of activities to choose from when most activity is socially organized.

No society can offer an infinite spectrum of social activities. In large part what distinguishes different societies is precisely which activities appear on the "menu" citizens can choose from and which activities do not. In other words, most activities come in socially structured packages, and at least as far as individuals are concerned some packages are available and some are not.[19] So, if we think of the "objects" that impact on people's well-being as goods from which they choose, it is easier to ignore the possibility of biases in the conditions of availability. Whereas once we recognize that activities are what satisfy our needs to a greater or lesser extent and that a substantial portion of our activities are socially organized by important institutions, we are far more likely to consider the possibility of institutional biases seriously.

It seems the "problem of rational choice" has somehow been turned around. One view is people choosing goods from consumption possibility sets in light of given preference orderings. The other view is people choosing what preferences to develop in light of the terms of availability of different activities that are "given" by the institutions they face.[20]

Summary. People are self-creative within the limits defined by human nature, but this must be interpreted carefully. At any moment individuals are constrained by their previously developed personalities, skills, and consciousness. Moreover, individually we are powerless to change the social roles defined by society's major institutions within which most of our activity must take place. So as individuals we are largely powerless to affect the kind of behavior that will mold our future character traits. Hence, these traits and any preferences that may depend on them remain to some extent beyond our reach, and our power of self-generation is effectively constrained by the social situations in which we find ourselves. But in the sense that these social situations are ultimately human creations and individuals have maneuverability within given social situations the potential for self-creation is preserved. We humans are both the subjects and the objects of history—as we might have expected. We define the concept of the Human Center to incorporate these conclusions.

> THE HUMAN CENTER is the collection of people who live within a society including all their needs, powers, personalities, skills, and consciousness. This includes our natural and species needs and powers—the results of a human evolutionary process that we assume to be complete for purposes of studying known human history. It includes all the structural human characteristics that are givens for the individual at any moment, but are, in fact, the accumulated imprint of previous activity choices on innate potentials. And it includes our derived needs and powers, or preferences and capacities, which are determined by the interaction of our natural and species needs and powers with the structure of human characteristics existing at the time.

5.3 The Institutional Boundary

We have seen that people "create" themselves only in closely defined settings that limit their options beyond the limits of genetic human potential. In addition to the natural environment, and man-made objects or "artifacts," social institutions also "structure" people's "self-creative" efforts. We will refer to all three of these together as the "boundary" that "surrounds" the human center both defining and limiting its potentials. But we will also distinguish between our world's physical endowments (the natural environment), the physical transformations of the natural environment that take the form of both useful artifacts and environmental deterioration (the built environment), and social institutions that establish patterns of expectations that mediate activity (the institutional boundary), without implying a firm dividing line between them.[21]

Social institutions are conglomerations of interrelated roles. At the risk of belaboring points that are commonplace for generations of "institutionalist" economists and the subject matter of introductory sociology courses, we clarify these matters that most economists seldom consider.

A factory's buildings, assembly lines, raw materials, and material products are part of the "built" environment. Ruth, Joe, Helen, and Sam, the people who work in or own the factory, are people and part of society's human center. The factory as an institution, however, is the roles and the relationships between those roles: assembly-line worker, foreman, supervisor, plant manager, pay clerk, union steward, minority stockholder, majority stockholder, member of the board of directors, etc.

Similarly, the market as an institution comprises the roles of buyers and sellers. It is neither the place where buying and selling occurs nor the actual people who buy and sell. It is not even the actual behavior of buying and selling (or, in the case of the factory, riveting, accounting, managing, etc.). The actual behavior belongs in the sphere of human activity, or history itself, and is not the same as the social institution that produces that history in interaction with the human center. Precisely stated, the market institution is the commonly held expectation that the social activity of material exchange will take place through the patterned activities of "freely" agreed to buying and selling. Insofar as such expectations are codified in rules, these rules are also part of the institution. But nothing more.

Please note, we have defined roles and institutions apart from whether or not expectations that establish them are actually fulfilled or rules that define them are actually obeyed. To think of roles or conglomerations of roles as fulfilled expectations or obeyed rules lends them permanence they may not deserve. A social institution only achieves structural continuity if the commonly held expectation or codified rules concerning potential behavior are confirmed by repeated actual behavior. But if institutions are defined as fulfilled expectations or obeyed rules, it becomes difficult to understand how they might change.

In order not to presume stability, we define institutions as commonly held expectations or codified rules of behavior and leave open whether or not these expectations or rules are or will continue to be fulfilled or obeyed. That is, whether or not particular institutions will maintain their structural continuity or be transformed should not be prejudged.

But why do institutions exist? Why must we add to the sphere of activity and the sphere of consciousness, a sphere of commonly held expectations about the behavior patterns of others? Once again, specifically human potentials and limitations enter our paradigm where there is a void in the traditional "choice theoretic" approach.

If we were all mind readers, or had infinite consultative time, or if decision making were infinitely fast compared to acting, human societies might not require mediating institutions. But if there is a "division of labor," and if we are not blessed with infinite time to search out and consult with countless others, we must act on the basis of expectations about the behavior of others. If you make a pair of shoes to sell in order to pay a dentist to fill your daughter's cavities, you expect others to play the role of shoe buyer, and dentists to render their services for a fee. You neither read the shoe-buyers' and dentist's minds nor take the time to arrange and confirm all these coordinated activities before proceeding to make each pair of shoes; so you must act on the basis of expectations about others' behavior in a market economy.

Stated differently, institutions are the necessary consequence of human's lack of omniscience, and we might well have listed this limitation as a species characteristic of human nature. Consequently, the relevant question about institutions is not whether they should exist but, as we shall see, whether particular institutions foster our development and fulfillment or pose unnecessarily oppressive limits.[22] If one insists on asking the question "where can I find the institutional boundary," the answer is that beyond codified rules of behavior which may be written down, commonly held expectations about individual behavior patterns are mental phenomena. But because our definition of roles and institutions locates these features where we have also located consciousness does not mean the two are the same. Expectations are different from consciousness. Consciousness makes it possible to change expectations, roles, and thus society's institutions. Animals cannot change their institutions. They do not create or adapt them, but simply encounter their institutions as part of their "wired-in" genetic inheritance. In contrast, humans inherit only the necessity of creating some social institutions as well as potentials for and limits on our abilities to do so. Our sociability and lack of omniscience impose the need for institutions as a condition of survival and fulfillment. But the specific institutions are, within the limits of our potentials, ours to design.[23]

> THE INSTITUTIONAL BOUNDARY is any society's particular set of social institutions understood as conglomerations of interconnected roles or commonly held expectations about appropriate behavior patterns. These roles exist independently of whether or not the expectations they represent will continue to be fulfilled and apart from whatever incentives might or might not exist for individuals to choose to behave in their accord. The institutional boundary is a necessary sphere in any human society because we lack omniscience, but is distinct from both the sphere of consciousness and the sphere of activity. While the institutional boundary necessarily constrains individuals' behavior, the sphere of consciousness makes possible purposeful transformations of the institutional boundary through social activity.

5.4 Complementary Holism

We want a paradigm more appropriate to specifically human social conditions and more sensitive to the relations among institutional structures and between institutional structures and human characteristics than the paradigm economists have traditionally relied on. Therefore, it is sensible to pay close attention to the possible relations between different kinds of social institutions and between the whole institutional boundary and the human center. Elsewhere we have called our treatment of such issues "complementary holism."[24] Here we outline enough of this approach to inform a paradigm relevant for welfare theory.

5.4.1 Four Spheres of Social Life

The economy is not the only "sphere" of social activity. In addition to creating social institutions to organize their efforts to meet material needs and desires, people have organized complex relationships for addressing their cultural and spiritual needs, intricate "sex-gender systems" for satisfying their sexual needs and discharging their parental functions, and elaborate political arrangements for mediating social conflicts and enforcing social decisions. So in addition to the "economic sphere" of social life we have what we call a "community sphere," a "kinship sphere," and a "political sphere" as well. While we are concerned here with evaluating the performance of the economic sphere, the possible relationships between that sphere and other spheres of social life deserve consideration.

A "monist" paradigm presumes some form of dominance, or hierarchy of influence among the spheres, while a "pluralist" approach studies the dynamics of each sphere separately and then attempts to "sum" the results. We espouse a "complementary holist" approach that assumes any form of dominance (or lack of dominance) among spheres will be historically contingent and is a matter to be determined by studying particular situations. Since all four spheres are socially necessary and can take many different forms, any patterns of dominance that may (or may not) result in a particular society and time cannot be determined by theory alone. Instead of a priori presumptions of dominance, complementary holism holds that a number of possible kinds of relations can exist among spheres. The possibilities are somewhat limited, but which possibility pertains in a particular situation can only be determined by empirical investigation.

5.4.2 Relations between Center and Boundary and between Spheres

The human center and institutional boundary, and the four spheres of social life are fundamental conceptual building blocks of the complementary holist paradigm. The human center and institutional boundary concepts include all four kinds of social activity, but distinguish between people and institutions. The concepts of spheres of social activity encompass both the human and institutional aspects of social activity but distinguish between different primary functions of different activities. The

130

possible relations between center and boundary and between different spheres is obviously critical.

It is evident that if a society is to be stable people must generally "fit" the roles they are going to fill. Actual behavior must generally conform to the expected patterns of behavior defined by society's major social institutions. People must choose activities in accord with the finite number of role offerings available, and this requires that people's personalities, skills, and consciousness be such that they do so.

In our terms, there must be conformity between society's human center and institutional boundary for social stability. We must be capable and willing to do what is required of us. Suppose this were not the case. For example, suppose South African whites shed their racist consciousness overnight but all the institutions of apartheid remained intact. Unless the natures of the institutions were also changed, rationalization of continued participation in institutions guided by racist norms would eventually regenerate racist consciousness among South African whites. On a smaller scale, suppose one university professor eliminates grades, makes papers optional, and no longer dictates course curriculum or delivers monologues but instead awaits student initiatives. If students arrive conditioned to respond to grading incentives and wanting to be led and entertained by the instructor, elimination of authoritarianism in a single classroom in context of highly authoritarian expectations in the student body might well result in very little learning in the "participatory" classroom.

Whether the final result of any "discrepancy" between the human center and institutional boundary be remolding the center to conform with an unchanging boundary, or elimination of aspects of the boundary that prove incompatible with an unyielding human center, the point is stabilizing forces within societies usually act to bring the center and boundary into conformity, and lack of conformity is a sign of social instability.

But this is not to say that all societies' human centers and institutional boundaries are equally "stabilizable." While we are always being "socialized" by the institutions that confront us, this process can run into more or fewer obstacles depending on the extent to which particular institutional structures are compatible or incompatible with innate human potentials. In other words, just as "stabilizing" forces are always at work in societies, to date there have always been "destabilizing" forces as well resulting from institutional incompatibilities with fundamental human needs. For instance, no matter how "well oiled" the socialization processes of a slave society, a fundamental incompatibility remains between the social role of slave and aspects of innate human potential. That incompatibility is a constant source of potential instability in societies that seek to confine people to slave status.

131

The possible relations among spheres are somewhat analogous. It is possible that the organization of social activity in one sphere is highly compatible with the organization of social activity in another sphere. For example, it might be that the functioning of the nuclear family produces personality structures that are compatible with economic role requirements, and vice versa. On the other hand, it is possible for the activity in one sphere to be disruptive of the manner in which activity is organized in another sphere. For instance, the educational system in the kinship sphere might graduate more people seeking a particular kind of economic role than the economic sphere can provide under its current organization. This would produce "destabilizing" expectations and demands in the economic sphere and/or the kinship sphere. Some argued this was the case during the 1960s and 1970s when expansion of college education produced "too many" with higher level thinking skills for the number of positions permitting the exercise of such potentials in the U.S. economy, giving rise, in part, to student rebellion. In any case, at the broadest level, we might have conformity between spheres or destabilizing relations. But within the general category of conformity there are possibilities worth distinguishing further.

One kind of interaction between spheres consistent with stability is accommodation wherein critical features of one sphere accommodate to requirements of other spheres. For example, assignment of people to economic roles accommodates prevailing racial hierarchies in the community sphere if the income of minorities is less than whites and thereby consistent with their extraeconomic subordination. But it is also possible for the definition of roles in one sphere to reflect dynamics emanating from another sphere. For instance, if the economic role of secretary includes tending the coffee machine as well as typing, filing, and taking dictation, it is likely the role of secretary is defined not only by purely economic dynamics but by kinship dynamics as well. When compatibility is stronger than simple accommodation, we say the relationship between spheres is one of co-definition, and the activity of one sphere co-reproduces defining features of the organization of activity in another sphere. Thus, whereas social stability implies compatible relations between spheres as well as between human center and institutional boundary, the fact of stability does not tell us whether spheres merely accommodate or more actively co-reproduce one another's defining features.

Finally, we should also note that in any society "underlying" stabilizing and destabilizing forces that exist between center and boundary and among different spheres may, of course, be complemented by more conscious efforts of particular social groups who seek to maintain or transform the status quo in light of whether they feel benefited or prejudiced by existing institutional arrangements.

5.5 A Qualitative Model of the Economic Sphere

A paradigm provides an orienting vision of what we intend to study. So an economic paradigm must project an image of what an economy is, what its components are, and what basic rules guide their interactions. We propose thinking of the economy as groups of people engaging in economic activities thought of, in turn, as economic processes, where for any period of time, t, each economic process is usefully characterized by six aspects:

1. All material objects and human efforts that enter the process as inputs

2. All material objects and human fulfillments that emerge from the process as outputs

3. The initial state of the individual human and group characteristics of the people carrying out the process

4. The final state of the individual human and group characteristics of the people who engaged in the process

5. The initial state of the tools (plant and machinery) used

6. The final state of the tools used

5.5.1 Flow Variables Described

First, we can usefully distinguish between material outputs of other human economic processes and materials that are not humanly produced, or natural resources. The purpose here is to make our paradigm useful for studying ecological relations between the natural environment and the economic sphere of social life.[25] We wish to distinguish between steel produced by economic processes in the present and oil "produced" by natural processes long ago. The latter exist in some ultimately limited supply regardless of our changing skills.[26]

Second, when we refer to human inputs we are talking about mental and physical human efforts applied in carrying out particular tasks. Traditionally, such efforts are measured in terms of hours of different laboring activities expended. To account for intensity as well as duration, it is important to note that if effort is measured in hours, we implicitly assume average intensity and that above and below average intensity are possible. We also note that human inputs enter "consumption" processes as well as "production" processes, since consumption activity necessarily entails effort of a given intensity over a given time.[27]

Third, by our definition no material natural resources can be produced as outputs of human economic activities, but there certainly can be material outputs such as steel and shirts, or services such as nursing care and

133

research studies.[28] In the traditional conceptualization of "production" the primary focus is precisely on material outputs. In our conceptualization there are also human outputs of all economic activities in the form of needs that are met more or less satisfactorily. In other words, whether it be laboring or consuming activity, all economic activity either succeeds or fails to fulfill the preferences of those engaging in that activity to some particular extent. We conceptualize these levels of fulfillment as the human outputs of economic activity.[29]

5.5.2 State Variables Described

We find it useful to distinguish between inputs and outputs of "flows" that enter and leave an economic process and the initial and final values of "state" variables that characterize the human and physical center of the economic activity.

First, the physical state variables consist of the "tools" that the people who carry out the activity use, which in modern economies include buildings and various forms of frequently incredibly complicated machinery. Since the initial and final conditions of these physical state variables may differ as a result of the economic activity in which they are used, we identify initial and final values for their status.

Second, each of the individual people who participate in an economic activity have initial characteristics such as personality traits, talents, or skills, knowledge about technical and social aspects of the economic process they are presently engaged in as well as broader knowledge about how the world works in general, and attitudes or "values" toward what they understand to be going on in their proximity or farther away. As a result of carrying out their assignments, people's various individual characteristics may be transformed and the final values of these human state variables may differ from their initial values. This is a second human consequence of economic activity. In addition to generating well-being or preference fulfillment, economic activity can transform or reinforce any of a variety of human characteristics.[30]

Finally, some human state variables we do not define individually because they are more appropriately conceptualized as characteristics of the group of people carrying out the activity. For example, suppose the group carrying out the activity is characterized by a particular kind of relation between its male and female members, or between members of different races or religions, or between those who have and those who do not have certain kinds of knowledge and information concerning the activity they jointly carry out. One possible consequence of carrying out the activity according to a particular assignment of duties and respon-sibilities might be to erode or reinforce any of these possible group characteristics. Therefore, we include social characteristics of the group of people engaged in an activity as one of our human state variables whose initial and final values we chart in our alternative paradigm.

5.5.3 *Flow Variables Formalized*

Any group of people, i, in time period t, can be thought of as engaging in a particular (kth) economic activity, $A_k(i,t)$. A full description of any $A_k(i,t)$ includes all the material and human inputs and outputs that "flow" into and out of $A_k(i,t)$, as well as values for all the physical, human, and social state variables at the beginning and end of the period t.

If we can imagine a list of all available natural resources, then we can let $R^i = (r_1, \ldots r_R)^i$ represent the quantity of each resource "consumed" by the activity as an [i]nput.

Likewise, while its entries would all necessarily be zero, we can let $R^o = (r_1, \ldots r_R)^o$ represent natural resources "produced" by the activity as [o]utputs.

If we imagine a list of all producible materials (and services), we can let $X^i = (x_1, \ldots x_X)^i$ represent the quantity of each produced object or service "consumed" by the activity as an input, and $X^o = (x_1, \ldots x_X)^o$ represent the quantities "produced" as outputs.

We must be careful that the list of produced inputs includes all inputs "consumed" whether or not their "consumption" precludes their consumption by other activities and whether or not those who carry out the activity are in some sense held accountable for their "consumption." We must also be careful that the list of produced outputs includes all "bads" along with all "goods" irrespective of whether or not those who carry out the activity are held accountable for their production. With these provisos, our descriptive catalog of producible materials will be exhaustive.

If we imagine a list of all possible kinds of human economic efforts we can let $E^i = (e_1 [\%], \ldots e_E [\%])^i$ represent the quantity of each kind of human input measured in units of time applied and degree of effort expended.

For what are traditionally thought of as production processes, these effort inputs would be hours of different kinds of labor at specific intensities. For example, if those performing a particular operation in an assembly line involving the jth type of effort were working at average intensity, we would record their hours on the job as $e_j [100\%]$. If they were working at an intensity level 25 percent above average, their human input would be recorded as $e_j [125\%]$, while if working at 25 percent below average intensity we would record their input as $e_j [75\%]$.

But what if the kth activity of group i during time t refers to "consumption" rather than "production"? While it takes time to drink a six-pack

135

while consuming the Monday night football game, recording these two-plus hours of "effort" is unimportant. But in other cases "consumption" does require time and effort important to track. The time it takes to fill and check out your grocery cart can be as important as what objects are in it. The intensity of four hours of toy shopping the Friday after Thanksgiving as compared to four hours early in January matters to many with experience in such matters. A paradigm capable of approaching efforts of homemakers with the same seriousness as efforts of factory workers might prove useful in an area feminists have exposed as a theoretical cul de sac for others.[31]

Human outputs are degrees of fulfillment that individuals attain from carrying out their particular assignments in activities. Since there is a long tradition of treating different individual's satisfactions as incomparable, and since for many purposes there is no need to draw such comparisons, we need to track the fulfillment individuals obtain from participating in activity which in many cases is undertaken in concert with others. A long tradition in welfare theory treats individual fulfillment as a "ranking" of different possible activities according to whether they yield more or less overall satisfaction. This approach explicitly conflates different needs and the different degrees to which they are fulfilled under the traditional conception of individual preference orderings. We believe that much may be lost by such a conceptualization because individuals undoubtedly have different needs that are fulfilled to different extents by particular activities or bundles of activities—and tracking all this may be important for some purposes.[32] But with some misgivings we follow the traditional lead of conceptualizing need fulfillment in terms of overall preference orderings.

This said, we can represent human outputs of any particular activity, $A_k(i,t)$, by a vector each component of which represents overall satisfaction obtained by an individual member of group i. These are to be interpreted as self-judged, interpersonally incomparable, ordinal rankings under the assumption of a given set of assignments in all other activities in which the individual participates. We thus have $U^o = (u_1, \ldots u_I)^o$ as the vector of human outputs for activity $A_k(i,t)$, where the group i has I participants.

5.5.4 *State Variables Formalized*

Imagine a list of all the "machines" that might conceivably be utilized in any possible economic activity in our economy. We can let the vector $M^b = (m_1 [\%], \ldots m_M [\%])^b$ represent the "beginning" status of these machines in the locale of the economic activity.

The process begins with a stock of machine j in a given state of repair that will be recorded by $m_j [\%]_b$ where m_j is the number of machines of type j in the stock and percent is an "efficiency" rating for the machine ranging from 0 percent for a machine that has become completely useless to 100 percent for a new tool just successfully "broken in." Likewise, we can let the vector $\boldsymbol{M^f} = (\ m_1\ [\%]\ ,\ \dots\ m_M\ [\%]\ )^f$ represent the "final" status of all machines associated with the activity center. Additions, deletions, or changes in the stock of machine j will be indicated by a difference between $m_j\ [\%\ ]^b$ and $m_j\ [\%\ ]^f$.

We also want to treat individuals' human characteristics as state variables whose beginning and final status may differ. If we can list all the components of personality traits, skills, knowledge, and values toward what we understand to be going on, we can represent initial human characteristics of individuals participating in an economic activity with the vectors:

$$\boldsymbol{P^b} = (\ p_1,\ \dots\ p_P\ )^b$$

$$\boldsymbol{S^b} = (\ s_1,\ \dots\ s_S\ )^b$$

$$\boldsymbol{K^b} = (\ k_1,\ \dots\ k_K\ )^b$$

$$\boldsymbol{V^b} = (\ v_1,\ \dots\ v_V\ )^b$$

and his or her final characteristics with the vectors

$$\boldsymbol{P^f} = (\ p_1,\ \dots\ p_P\ )^f$$

$$\boldsymbol{S^f} = (\ s_1,\ \dots\ s_S\ )^f$$

$$\boldsymbol{K^f} = (\ k_1,\ \dots\ k_K\ )^f$$

$$\boldsymbol{V^f} = (\ v_1,\ \dots\ v_V\ )^f$$

Any additions, deletions, strengthening, or eroding of characteristic p_1 would be noted by a difference between $p_1{}^b$ and $p_1{}^f$ tracking the human development effects of participating in different economic activities. When combined with our above defined $\boldsymbol{U^o}$ we have both fulfillment and development human consequences of economic activities.

While tracking development effects for particular individuals is of primary concern for some welfare purposes, for other purposes it need not concern us precisely which members of group i undergo transformations. While our formal welfare theory will leave evaluation of development effects to individuals themselves and not treat them as interpersonally comparable, in less formal analyses we will "aggregate" these effects over all members of group i participating in $A_k(i,t)$. Since for human "state" variables the difference between the final and beginning values is qualitative and directional, summing the difference over all individuals in the group provides a rough indication of the number of people enhancing or reducing a particular human characteristic as a result of the activity carried out by the group.

Finally, the representation of group human characteristics presents no individualization or aggregation problems. If we imagine an exhaustive list of social characteristics pertaining to a group of humans rather than distinct individuals, then the vectors

$$G^b = (g_1, \ldots g_G)^b$$

$$G^f = (g_1, \ldots g_G)^f$$

list the beginning and final status of these characteristics for the group.

And our overall image of any economic activity, for any group of people i, carried out during period t, would be:

$$A_k(i,t) = \begin{matrix} i \\ R \\ X \\ E \end{matrix} \rightarrow \begin{matrix} b \\ M \\ P \\ S \\ K \\ V \\ G \end{matrix} \rightarrow \begin{matrix} f \\ M \\ P \\ S \\ K \\ V \\ G \end{matrix} \rightarrow \begin{matrix} o \\ R \\ X \\ U \end{matrix}$$

This way of looking at a particular economic activity or process for any period is easily extended to a view of the whole economy at any period or to a view of the development of the economy over time. At any time, t, what is actually happening in the economy consists of $A_k(i,t)$ with k running over all activities and i running over all groups carrying out activities. The development of the economy over time would be seen by observing $A_k(i,t)$ with k running over all activities, i running over all groups, and t running over all time periods.

5.5.5 Possibility Sets, Choice, Information, and Incentives

As incredibly cluttered as our symbolic representation already appears, we have yet to incorporate most of what we need to know about the economic sphere. No matter how many actual economic activities we may chart for groups and time periods, all we will note is what actually happens. Presumably, for every economic activity any particular group i undertakes in period t, there exists a much larger set of activities the group might have carried out with alternative sets of inputs.[33] And while not all activities that are individually possible are mutually compatible, there is presumably a set of all economic activities compatible with one another at a point in time that is considerably larger than the actual outcome in the economy for that period. And while not all outcomes for the economy in different periods are mutually compatible, there is presumably a set of all mutually compatible economic histories that is considerably larger than the single economic development trajectory that occurs historically. In other words, since what actually happens is only one element from the set of all possible economic histories that could conceivably have occurred, so far we have dealt with only the tip of the formal representational iceberg.

Let us represent the set of all possible activities i can carry out in period t by $\{A(i,t)\}$. Let us further represent the set of all possible mutually compatible activities for all groups in the economy at time t by $\{A(t)\}$. Finally, let us symbolize all the mutually compatible histories of economic activities for all groups in the economy over a span of time encompassing many periods by $\{A\}$. Since mutual compatibility requires that any vector of inputs to be used be available, clearly the set $\{A(t)\}$ is considerably smaller than the cartesian product of the individual possibility sets $\{A(i,t)\}$ for all i, and the set $\{A\}$ is considerably smaller than the cartesian product of the sets $\{A(t)\}$ for all t.

Nonetheless, the sets $\{A(i,t)\}$, $\{A(t)\}$, and $\{A\}$ are all multielement sets. And this poses the dilemma of how a specific element of $\{A(i,t)\}$ comes to be chosen for each group in each period; how a specific element of $\{A(t)\}$ gets chosen for the whole society for a single period; and how a specific element of $\{A\}$ gets chosen for the whole society for a sequence of many periods. Conceptualizing this "planning problem" finally brings us to grips with the real complexities of interconnected human economies in which a great variety of possible combinations of conscious human and institutional decision-making processes choose among multiple possibilities at every juncture. All of which brings us to the importance of viewing a human economy not only as realized human activity—as we have above—but as an elaborate decision-making system, mixing conscious choices of individuals and groups with unconscious institutional limitations, processing vast stores of information to settle on particular outcomes from an array of possibilities.

Thus a complete understanding of any economy requires more than knowing all inputs and outputs and changes in material and human state variables that occur. We also need to know how, and by whom, or by what institutionalized process some $A_k(i,t)$ was selected from $\{A(i,t)\}$, some $A(t)$ was selected from $\{A(t)\}$, and some A is selected from $\{A\}$. In some cases it might be relatively easy to identify a particular person or group who selected a particular option for the economy from a set of possible options. In other cases it might be clear that decisions were more or less "automatic" results of particular institutional requirements. But generally,

139

we should be prepared to find complicated and subtle combinations of institutional requirements and groups of interested people together determining what occurs.

In dealing with these complex decisions, sometimes we will focus on the selection of a single element from a set of possibilities. Other times we will find it more useful to envision the "choice" process as elimination of subsets of various $A_k(i,t)$'s from consideration. By seeing how certain possibilities are "whittled" away, as well as how final options are selected from remaining possibilities, we will better understand how institutions influence economic choice.

To the extent individuals and groups make conscious choices, they do so based on goals they conceptualize and information they possess. If economic institutions influence what goals people formulate and what information does or does not come into their hands, they influence choices indirectly as well as directly. One way to make sure we do not ignore such matters is to think of an economy not just as a conglomeration of actual activities, but as an incentive system and cybernetic system as well. Even if we conceptualize individuals' overall goals as maximizing fulfillment over their lives according to preference orderings they develop, the institutions that organize social economic activity can powerfully influence how this goal is translated into a more specific incentive system. And even if we frequently grant the same "perfect knowledge" assumptions so common to the traditional welfare paradigm, at times we will be at pains to track what information comes to whom far more carefully. We hope a welfare paradigm that insists that the economy be seen as an incentive system and an information system as well as a network of activities will yield new insights by forcing more explicit treatment of assumptions and issues long overlooked.

6

A NEW WELFARE
THEORY

OUR NEW evaluative theory is based on our new paradigm and specifically our theory of natural, species, and derived needs. Our most general statement of how to evaluate the performance of any set of economic institutions is to ask whether or not those institutions serve to maximize human fulfillment and development. We must obviously clarify what we mean by this and how we propose to "measure" welfare conceived in this way. But it is worth pointing out before beginning, that our approach obviously goes beyond the traditional notion of efficiency in satisfying peoples' manifest preferences by insisting on also evaluating the development of needs themselves.

In the previous chapter we explained how people have a variety of natural and species needs such as needs for food, shelter, sexual gratification, knowledge, affection, self-esteem, social recognition, and self-management. It is obviously a good thing to fulfill these needs to the greatest extent possible. But these needs never exist in a "pure form." They are always expressed through a host of derived needs like those for particular types of food, marriage to a particular person, a car of a certain make and model, etc. Under no circumstances do we call any of these derived needs "false needs," since once they exist they are no less urgent than our underlying natural and species needs, which are expressed through particular derived needs in any case. But, like John Stuart Mill before us, we cannot convince ourselves that maximum fulfillment of different sets of derived needs necessarily yields the same degree of satisfaction. As we explained in the previous chapter, it is perfectly possible to develop detrimental character traits that can take on a structural life of their own by defining derived needs whose fulfillment generates less well-being than would be experienced by the fulfillment of a different set of derived needs. Therefore, the development of derived needs is just as much the proper subject matter of evaluative theory as is the fulfillment of derived needs. In short, we will not take the "ostrich" approach to the admittedly difficult problem of need development.

In the first section we use concepts from the previous chapter to develop a formal model of a person with endogenous preferences. In the second section we use the model to derive a series of theorems that establish interesting welfare theoretic results. In some cases the results contradict traditional conclusions, and in other cases the results contradict the intuitions of other pioneers in the theory of endogenous preferences. As we will see, endogenous preferences raise issues traditional theory is blind to, pose fewer difficulties for fundamental welfare theorems than some pioneers believed, yet imply a far more disturbing interpretation of nonoptimalities and their consequences than hitherto recognized.

But while all this is demonstrated with a model that does not entail any explicit evaluation of different developmental trajectories, much in our welfare theory proceeds from an explicit evaluation of alternative human development patterns. We take up these critical matters in the final section of the chapter, only after demonstration of what should be noncontroversial results—a strategy in the best tradition of welfare economics.

6.1 Formalizing Endogenous Preferences

We seek a formalism expressing the fact that activities not only fulfill existing needs or preferences but change or develop those preferences as well. The first step is to stipulate that while the fulfillment individuals derive from participating in a particular set of activities obviously depends on their preferences, those preferences in turn depend on the human characteristics individuals possess at the time. In other words, individuals' "instantaneous" preference orderings are parameterized by their "instantaneous" human characteristics. In this way individuals' "needs" change whenever any of their human characteristics change—which is what we mean by "derived needs."

6.1.1 Model 1: An Individual with Endogenous Preferences

M 1.1. Let $U(t)$ represent an individual's instantaneous preference ordering at time t, and

M 1.2. Let $C(t)$ represent the whole array of personality traits, skills, knowledge, and values a person has in period t. In other words

142

$C(t) = [\, P(t), S(t), K(t), V(t)\,]$ where each vector inside the brackets has many components as well, as discussed in chapter 5. For convenience we will assume $C(t)$ is a vector with C components where each component is a postive real number, so that $C(t) \in \Re_C^+$

M 1.3. The fulfillment, satisfaction, or utility achieved in period t becomes $U(t) = U\,(P(t), S(t), K(t), V(t); (.))$ or, $U(t) = U\,(C(t); (.))$ where (.) represents all the economic activities in period t that in any way affect the individual's well-being.

In general, an individual's instantaneous preference ordering should be defined on "activity space." That is, one's satisfaction is a function of all the activities carried out by groups in which one, in some sense, participates. In terms of the notation of chapter 5, (.) would be all the activities $A_k(i,t)$ carried out by groups i in which the individual participates.[1]

But for present purposes, we can adopt the traditional view that all welfare significant activities in which people participate can be interpreted as the consumption and laboring activities each carries out individually, which in turn are assumed to be fully described by the quantities of different "consumption goods" each consumes, and the number of hours each works in different kinds of job categories. While the more general conceptualization of individuals participating in various elements of group activity space is more appropriate to treatment of issues such as public goods and the labor process, for many issues that have been the primary focus of welfare theory, the traditional formulation is sufficient, and these are the issues we address first. So for now,

M 1.4. Let $Q(t) = [\, q_1(t), q_2(t), \ldots q_Q(t)\,]$ be a vector whose elements represent quantities of each commodity consumed by the individual at time t so that $Q(t) \in \Re_Q^+$ and

M 1.5. Let $L(t) = [\, l_1(t), l_2(t), \ldots l_L(t)\,]$ be a vector whose elements represent hours of different kinds of labor the individual carries out at time t, $L(t) \in \Re_L^+.$[2]

And instead of describing the welfare significant activity space for an individual at time t as (.) $= A_k(i,t)$ where k ranges over all activities, and i ranges over all the groups the individual "participates in"—broadly defined—we describe it as the commodities consumed and labor done by the individual in period t or:

M 1.6. (.) $= \left(Q(t), L(t) \right) \in \Re_{(Q+L)}^+$

M 1.7. In sum $U(t) = U\,(C(t); Q(t), L(t))$. And for convenience we define $U(t)$ as a continuous, differentiable function mapping elements from $\Re_{(Q+L+C)}^+ \to \Re$ for each period t.

The second step, which makes preferences "endogenous," is to stipulate that these various human characteristics are potentially functions of economic activities previously carried out. In this way participating in any economic activity has both what we call a "preference fulfillment effect"— it fulfills present preferences to a greater or lesser extent—and what we call a "preference development effect"—it influences future character structures, which in turn influence future preference orderings.

M 1.8. For each element i of an individual's personality characteristic vector $P(t)$:

$$p_i(t) = p_i\Big(Q(t-1), Q(t-2), \ldots Q(0); L(t-1), L(t-2), \ldots L(0)\Big)$$

And, similarly, for the other individual human state variables:

$$s_i(t) = s_i\Big(Q(t-1), Q(t-2), \ldots Q(0); L(t-1), L(t-2), \ldots L(0)\Big)$$

$$k_i(t) = k_i\Big(Q(t-1), Q(t-2), \ldots Q(0); L(t-1), L(t-2), \ldots L(0)\Big)$$

$$v_i(t) = v_i\Big(Q(t-1), Q(t-2), \ldots Q(0); L(t-1), L(t-2), \ldots L(0)\Big)$$

And for convenience we define each characteristic formation function at each point in time, as a continuous, differentiable function mapping elements from $\Re^+_{t(Q+L)}$ to $\Re^+$.

M 1.9. Finally, the well-being an individual enjoys over his or her life would simply be some function of the well-being achieved in all time periods so that: $W = W(U(0), \ldots U(T))$.

M 1.10. But for our purposes nothing is lost by specifying an overall well-being function that is a linear function of fulfillment in each time period where τ_t represents the individual's subjective rate of time discount for fulfillment in period t. So W is a linear function mapping elements in $\Re_{(T+1)}$ to $\Re$.

$$W = \sum_{t=0}^{T} \tau_t\, U(t)$$

We complete our model of an individual with endogenous preferences with the budget constraint. We abstract from two complications irrelevant to our present purposes: income from initial stocks other than laboring capacities and borrowing and lending. For now there is no harm in specifying that expenditures in each period must be paid out of earnings in the same period.[3]

M 1.11. Let $I(t)$ be income in period t, a continuous, differentiable function mapping elements in $\Re^+_{t(C+L)}$ to $\Re^+$, where

$$I(t) = I\left(C(t); L(t)\right) = \sum_{i=1}^{Q} \pi_i(t)\, q_i(t) \quad \text{for } t = 0, 1, \ldots T$$

where $\pi_i(t)$ is the price the individual must pay for a unit of good i in period t, and the nonsatiation axiom justifies the equality. Or, using vector multiplication $I(t) = \pi(t) \cdot Q(t)$ is our budget constraint in each time period.

Although we agree with Gintis that a host of uncertainties is involved in any individual's estimation of these parameterized utility functions and human characteristic development functions, we choose to ignore these "uncertainty" issues. This is not because we think they are uninteresting, but because we have "other fish to fry." The theorems of this and subsequent chapters are our justification for the strategic decision to abstract from uncertainty by extending the assumption of "perfect knowledge" of traditional welfare theory to the new context of endogenous preferences. We will grant people "perfect knowledge" not only of the degree to which different "consumption-work bundles" fulfill their preferences of the moment and the relative prices and wages of different goods and jobs today, but "perfect knowledge" of how different consumption-work bundles chosen today will modify their future characteristics and how these new characteristics will change their preferences. Once again, the mere statement of the assumptions reinforces the reasonableness of Gintis' practical objections. But Debreu had already extended the perfect knowledge assumption to future prices and preference fulfillment effects in the spirit of the traditional welfare project—uncovering the implications of informed, individual, rational choice. In the same spirit we waive Gintis' objection.

6.2 Endogenous Preferences and Welfare Theorems

Traditional welfare theory teaches us how to estimate the welfare effects of economic choices. It interprets coincidence of relative supplies and desires as worthy of praise. And it establishes three "fundamental" theorems concerning the welfare characteristics of competitive, private enterprise market economies. Under appropriate assumptions:

1. At least one general equilibrium exists for any competitive, private enterprise market economy

2. Any general equilibrium of a competitive, private enterprise market economy is Pareto optimal

3. Any Pareto optimal outcome can be achieved as the general equilibrium of a perfectly competitive, private enterprise economy with the appropriate initial endowments

But traditional theorems assume exogenous preferences, so our first task is to reexamine traditional lessons under the assumption of endogenous rather than exogenous preferences as we model the phenomenon. In addition to being a matter of standard procedure in the development of what Kuhn termed "normal science," reexamination is necessary because Gintis claimed traditional welfare theory systematically misestimates and misinterprets welfare effects and that the second fundamental theorem of welfare economics is false under the assumption of endogenous preferences. Pollak, El Safty, and Hammond claim no fundamental conclusions are altered by treating preferences as endogenous unless welfare conclusions become impossible to draw altogether. Clarification is in order before we present our own view of how endogenous preferences are related to the fundamental issues of welfare economics.[4]

6.2.1 *Round One: Endogenous Preferences Do Matter*

Treating preferences as endogenous certainly changes estimation of the welfare effects of specific actions and undermines the traditional interpretation of the welfare significance of coincidence between supplies and demands in partial equilibrium settings.

Misestimating Welfare Effects. Gintis was perfectly correct in pointing out that traditional theory misestimates the welfare effects of economic choices if consumption-work choices not only fulfill present preferences more or less satisfactorily, but also change future preferences by changing future human characteristics, thereby affecting the possibilities of obtaining satisfaction from future consumption-work possibilities. We formulate and demonstrate this proposition as Theorem 6.1.

> THEOREM 6.1: MISESTIMATING WELFARE EFFECTS. A neoclassical welfare theory that ignores the fact that present choices of consumption and work activities not only fulfill present preferences but also generate changes in future preferences will systematically misestimate the welfare effects of economic choices.[5]

The theorem is intuitively plausible since any theory that fails to consider a significant relationship would be expected to misestimate effects of related actions. However, to prove the proposition requires some effort and the results are illustrative.

First, if we adopt the conventional assumption that all functions are continuous and differentiable, and the convenient assumptions of an interior solution point and binding budget constraints, we can model the individual's welfare maximization choice as a "classical programming problem."[6] We write the Lagrangian

$$\psi = \sum_{t=0}^{T}\left\{\tau_t U\Big(P(t),\, S(t),\, K(t),\, V(t);\, Q(t),\, L(t)\Big)\right\}$$

$$-\,\sigma_t\left\{\pi(t)\!\cdot\! Q(t) - I\Big(P(t),\, S(t),\, K(t),\, V(t);\, L(t)\Big)\right\}$$

Remembering that the choice variables are simply the quantities of each good to consume in each period and the number of hours to work at each different kind of labor activity in each period, we write the first order necessary conditions for a welfare maximum

$$\tau_t\frac{\partial U(t)}{\partial q_q(t)} + \sum_{i=t+1}^{T}\sum_{p}\left\{\tau_i\frac{\partial U(i)}{\partial p_p(i)} + \sigma_i\frac{\partial I(i)}{\partial p_p(i)}\right\}\frac{\partial p_p(i)}{\partial q_q(t)} + \tag{6.1}$$

$$\sum_{i=t+1}^{T}\sum_{s}\left\{\tau_i\frac{\partial U(i)}{\partial s_s(i)} + \sigma_i\frac{\partial I(i)}{\partial s_s(i)}\right\}\frac{\partial s_s(i)}{\partial q_q(t)} +$$

$$\sum_{i=t+1}^{T}\sum_{k}\left\{\tau_i\frac{\partial U(i)}{\partial k_k(i)} + \sigma_i\frac{\partial I(i)}{\partial k_k(i)}\right\}\frac{\partial k_k(i)}{\partial q_q(t)} +$$

$$\sum_{i=t+1}^{T}\sum_{v}\left\{\tau_i\frac{\partial U(i)}{\partial v_v(i)} + \sigma_i\frac{\partial I(i)}{\partial v_v(i)}\right\}\frac{\partial v_v(i)}{\partial q_q(t)} - \sigma_t\,\pi_{q(t)} = 0$$

For $t = 0\ldots T$ and $q = 1\ldots Q$ there would be $(T+1)$ times Q equations of the above type. And

$$\tau_t\frac{\partial U(t)}{\partial l_l(t)} + \sum_{i=t+1}^{T}\sum_{p}\left\{\tau_i\frac{\partial U(i)}{\partial p_p(i)} + \sigma_i\frac{\partial I(i)}{\partial p_p(i)}\right\}\frac{\partial p_p(i)}{\partial l_l(t)} + \tag{6.2}$$

$$\sum_{i=t+1}^{T}\sum_{s}\left\{\tau_i\frac{\partial U(i)}{\partial s_s(i)} + \sigma_i\frac{\partial I(i)}{\partial s_s(i)}\right\}\frac{\partial s_s(i)}{\partial l_l(t)} +$$

$$\sum_{i=t+1}^{T}\sum_{k}\left\{\tau_i\frac{\partial U(i)}{\partial k_k(i)} + \sigma_i\frac{\partial I(i)}{\partial k_k(i)}\right\}\frac{\partial k_k(i)}{\partial l_l(t)} +$$

$$\sum_{i=t+1}^{T}\sum_{v}\left\{\tau_i\frac{\partial U(i)}{\partial v_v(i)} + \sigma_i\frac{\partial I(i)}{\partial v_v(i)}\right\}\frac{\partial v_v(i)}{\partial l_l(t)} + \sigma_t\frac{\partial I(t)}{\partial l_l(t)} = 0$$

For $t = 0...T$ and $l = 1...L$ there would $(T+1)$ times L equations of the above type. And finally

$$\sum_q \{ \pi_q(t) \, q_q(t) \} \ - \ I\Big(P(t), S(t), K(t), V(t); L(t)\Big) = 0 \qquad (6.3)$$

where for $t = 0...T$ there would be $(T+1)$ "budget constraint" equations of the above sort. The result we are seeking follows directly from observing that if preferences are endogenous we cannot assume that the first set of terms under the double summation in both (6.1) and (6.2) are zero. Quite the contrary, in the presence of "preference development effects" there is every reason to believe their sum can be either positive or negative.

Von Weizsacker, Hammond, and especially Pollak were not primarily concerned with the welfare effects of endogenous preferences—particularly conceived as fully informed rational self-molding. But it is difficult to imagine they would disagree with this conclusion. That few, if any, traditional theorists would disagree is even more apparent once one recognizes the similarity between this result and analogous results in human capital theory that have been long acknowledged.

Prior to the advent of human capital theory all the terms under the double summation signs were ignored in expressions (6.1) and (6.2). Human capital theory recognized the need for including the effects of the second set of terms under the summation signs. In (6.1) those effects are interpreted as "consumption" choices that are, at least in part, "investments" in "human capital." In (6.2) those effects are conceived as "on-the-job training" effects of work activities.

Human capital theory pointed out that a welfare theory that ignored the human capital and on-the-job training effects of consumption and work activity choices misestimates welfare effects by ignoring the effects on individuals' future budget constraints. A theory of endogenous preferences makes a completely analogous point; a welfare theory that ignores the effects of consumption and work activity on individuals' future preferences necessarily misestimates welfare effects by ignoring the effects on individuals' capacity to extract satisfaction from future options.

Presumably the only difference between Gintis, on the one hand, and von Weizsacker, Hammond, and Pollack, on the other, would be how much importance they attach to this new revelation—and whether to consider it reason to look for a new welfare paradigm. In any case, Gintis would no doubt agree that the necessary "correction" can easily be made as it was in the case of human capital theory, and as he, himself, has done.

Misinterpreting Coincidence of Supplies with Demands. Gintis' observation is correct. If people mold their desires to better coincide with the terms of availability that exist independently of those desires, the positive welfare implications of a coincidence between relative supplies and desires vanish. We demonstrate this claim as Theorem 6.2.

In traditional theory it was possible to "separate" supply and demand. As long as we treated preferences as exogenous, there was no possibility that demands could adjust to supplies. In this case, equality between ratios of marginal costs of supplying activities and ratios of marginal utilities for those activities was of great welfare significance because it occurred only if the "economy" supplied activities according to people's relative desires.[7] But Theorem 6.2 challenges the welfare significance traditionally imputed to "consumer sovereignty" as judged by people's "instantaneous preference orderings." Once demand is a function of supply, traditional partial equilibrium welfare theory goes by the wayside.

THEOREM 6.2: MISINTERPRETING COINCIDENCE OF SUPPLIES AND DESIRES. In general, not only will rational individuals who recognize their preferences are endogenous adjust to changes in relative terms of supply by changing the relative amounts of those goods they consume, but they will also change their preferences—reducing their preference for relatively more expensive items and increasing their preference for relatively less expensive items—by changing consumption-work choices in earlier periods to change their future human characteristics and the preferences that depend on them.

For convenience, our demonstration of Theorem 6.2 concerns a change in the relative prices of two goods in the last period, T. Then we explain why the result can be generalized to a change in relative prices in any period.

Suppose there is a change in the relative prices of the mth and nth commodities in period T, $\pi_m(T)$ and $\pi_n(T)$. A superscript A signifies prices after the change and a superscript O signifies original prices. We change the relative terms of supply by increasing the price of m relative to n in period T.

$$\frac{\pi_m(T)^A}{\pi_n(T)^A} > \frac{\pi_m(T)^O}{\pi_n(T)^O}$$

Since we are in the last time period, no terms are inside the double summation sign for T and commodity m and for T and commodity n in expression (6.1) under either the new or the old price system. So if the individual maximizes his or her welfare in each situation we are led directly to the conclusion

$$\left\{ \frac{\partial U(t)}{\partial q_m(T)} \bigg/ \frac{\partial U(t)}{\partial q_n(T)} \right\}^A > \left\{ \frac{\partial U(t)}{\partial q_m(T)} \bigg/ \frac{\partial U(t)}{\partial q_n(T)} \right\}^O$$

The assumption of diminishing marginal utilities[8] yields

$$\frac{q_m(T)^A}{q_n(T)^A} < \frac{q_m(T)^O}{q_n(T)^O}$$

But a change in the relative proportions of commodities m and n consumed in period T will change the values of partial derivatives of utility in period T with respect to all the human characteristics found under the summation signs in all the necessary conditions for all the previous time periods since these partials are still functions of the quantities of commodities m and n in period T. Letting $\alpha(t)$ stand for any of our human characteristics, we can conclude that if $\alpha_i(t)$ increases enjoyment of commodity m relative to commodity n, then:

$$\frac{\partial U(\ldots q_m(T)^A \ldots q_n(T)^A)}{\partial \alpha_i(T)} < \frac{\partial U(\ldots q_m(T)^O \ldots q_n(T)^O)}{\partial \alpha_i(T)}$$

Alternatively, if $\alpha_i(t)$ increases enjoyment of n relative to m, then:

$$\frac{\partial U(\ldots q_m(T)^A \ldots q_n(T)^A)}{\partial \alpha_i(T)} > \frac{\partial U(\ldots q_m(T)^O \ldots q_n(T)^O)}{\partial \alpha_i(T)}$$

Although it is possible, there is no reason to suppose that the sum total effects of changes in the values of these partials in any one of the necessary conditions for $q = 1 \ldots Q$ and $t = 0 \ldots (T-1)$ would be such as to exactly cancel out at the old values of consumption and work activity choices for those periods. So, in general, we would expect that $q_i(t)^A$ would not equal $q_i(t)^O$ and $l_j(t)^A$ would not equal $l_j(t)^O$ for $i = 1 \ldots Q, j = 1 \ldots L$, and $t = 0 \ldots T-1$. But our model implies different sets of human characteristics will develop under economic choice patterns $\{q_i(t)^A, l_j(t)^A\}$ and $\{q_i(t)^O, l_j(t)^O\}$ and, therefore, a different set of preference patterns for various commodity-work bundles will develop as well.

This concludes the demonstration of Theorem 6.2 provided the proof does not rest on choice of the final period, T, as the starting point. But the only convenience offered by this starting point is that a particular change in relative prices can be translated into a shift in the relative amounts of the two commodities consumed whose sign is determinant under the assumption of diminishing marginal utilities. Had we begun with a change of relative prices in any earlier time period, the direction of the shift in the consumption bundle for that time period would not have been determinant due to the many terms of indeterminate signs under the double summation signs. However, it should be clear that, in general, changes would be required in the values of any $q_m(t)$ and $q_n(t)$, for $t = 0 \ldots (T-1)$ to reestablish the necessary conditions after a change in the relative prices $\pi_m(t)$ and $\pi_n(t)$. Once the ratio of prices in period t for any two commodities has changed, no matter in what direction, changes will be required for all earlier consumption and work activity choices with consequent changes in human characteristics and preference structures exactly as argued above.

The phenomenon of rational adjustment of preferences, toward wanting what is presumed will be most readily available and away from wanting what is presumed will be difficult to obtain, should not be confused with another way that "utility" might be a function of "price"—namely "snob effects," "keeping up with the Joneses," or "conspicuous consumption."[9] The clear difference between the phenomena can be appreciated by noticing that the direction of the individual's adjustment is exactly opposite in the two cases. Whereas the phenomenon we are discussing would lead rational individuals to diminish their desires for goods whose future price was expected to be high, the phenomenon of conspicuous consumption would lead individuals to value goods with high prices more. We might point out there is no reason both phenomena could not exist in the real world. But where it has been relatively easy for neoclassical welfare theory to dismiss "snob effects" as irrational, if not aberrant behavior, in which the individual at least "pays" for his snobbery, the phenomenon we refer to is characterized precisely by its rationality and, therefore, very much a "legitimate" focus of concern according to traditional welfare criteria.

6.2.2 *Round Two: Endogenous Preferences Do Not Matter*

If traditional theory, by ignoring endogenous preferences, both misestimates welfare effects and misinterprets the matching of supplies and desires, how can one possibly argue that the conclusions of traditional welfare theory stand intact?

We already demonstrated that a simple correction—completely analogous to the correction introduced by human capital theory—is sufficient to yield theoretically sound estimates of all the welfare effects of economic choices. And while it is possible that desires are molding to supplies, rather than vice versa, it is also possible that relative supplies adjust to relative desires, which themselves are adjusting in an optimal pattern as judged by the overall satisfaction they generate in light of overall possibilities. In other words, while it is possible that a match between relative supplies and desires is merely a sign of social stability, it is also possible that a match is of welfare significance. Theorem 6.2 cautions us not to jump to the conclusion that a good match deserves high welfare marks. But if the match is the result of supplies adjusting to preferences, which themselves are developing along an optimal trajectory, then presumably the traditional practice of awarding high welfare marks is warranted.

It follows that we should now consider whether this superior form of "good match" is, in fact, what private enterprise competitive market economies would yield if they contained no "other" sources of nonoptimality. This entails reexamining traditional welfare theory's three fundamental theorems under the assumption of endogenous preferences.

Below, we present a model of what we will call, for now, a private enterprise, competitive market economy in which people recognize that their preferences are endogenous. This is a general equilibrium, Debreuvian model consistent with all aspects of traditional welfare theory's treatment of such economies except that preferences are treated as endogenous. In other words, no "other problems" are presumed in the model—no "other conditions" besides endogenous preferences that would result in any change in the traditional conclusions. We adopt such a model not because we believe such economies do not have other problems, or that traditional conclusions are warranted, but because we wish to see if endogenous preferences alone reverse any of the fundamental theorems of traditional welfare theory when examined in a general equilibrium setting.[10] After all, a reasonable reaction to the implication of Theorem 6.2 that matches between supplies and desires are not necessarily deserving of praise is that partial equilibrium conclusions are frequently not sustained by general equilibrium analysis.

It is convenient to adopt the general equilibrium model developed by Debreu in his *Theory of Value*. Although Debreu's assumption of a fixed number of firms in each industry, perfect knowledge of all future conditions, and treatment of all present and future choices as being made and contracted in the momentary present, are totally unrealistic and crucially misleading to attempts to uncover many mysteries of private enterprise market systems, they are appropriate to our interests of exploring the general equilibrium consequences of endogenous preferences modeled as informed self-development. We adopt Debreu's analysis of the "production" side of the economy intact, and need only concentrate on implications of endogenous preferences for the "consumption" side. Building on Model 1 of an individual with endogenous preferences, we now define Model 2:

*Model 2: A Debreuvian Economy Inhabited
by Individuals Aware of Their Endogenous Preferences*

M 2.1. Let $\{Q, L\}^i$ be the set of all possible consumption/work activity choices over all periods for the ith consumer, where, with Debreu, we assume this set is closed and bounded and therefore compact. Let $(q, l)_{ij}$ denote a typical (jth) element of this set, and note that such an element specifies a particular amount of each good and each work type in each time period that person i experiences.

M 2.2. Let $\{C\}^i$ be our name for the set of all possible human characteristics of the ith consumer over all periods. Again, we let c_{ij} denote a typical element of $\{C\}^i$ remembering that this specifies every human characteristic i has in each time period from $t = 0...T$.

M 2.3. Let $\{U\}^i$ be the set of possible "instantaneous" utility functions with U_{ij} a typical element listing i's instantaneous utility function for every time period.

M 2.4. As in Model 1, M 1.10, let W^i be the overall welfare function for individual i that tells us how much satisfaction i enjoyed over his or her entire lifetime given the amount of satisfaction i experienced in each time period $t = 0...T$.

M 2.5. Since the choice variables for individual i are to select a $(q, l)_{ij}$ from $\{Q, L\}^i$, we can also define an overall well-being function on consumption/work activity space. We define what we explain below is the composite mapping $\varphi = WB^i[\ (q,l)_{ij}\ ]$ and note that the value of W^i must equal the value of WB^i for the same consumption/work activity "history," or the same $(q,l)_{ij}$.

Existence of Equilibria. Having specified our model, we prove:

> THEOREM 6.3: EXISTENCE OF GENERAL EQUILIBRIA. If all traditional assumptions are maintained except the assumption of exogenous preferences, and if the assumption of perfectly informed endogenous preferences is substituted for exogenous preferences, the existence of a general equilibrium in a private enterprise, competitive market economy is assured provided we can extend the usual convexity assumptions to individual consumers' overall well-being functions.[11]

In other words, endogenous preferences, in and of themselves, do not affect the existence theorem for private enterprise market economies except to the extent they undermine the plausibility of the convexity assumption. In the existence proof the crucial questions about preferences concern their insatiability, continuity, and convexity because if appropriate assumptions are postulated in these areas it is possible to demonstrate that individual consumer "demand" correspondences (functions) are upper semi-continuous (continuous). When combined with upper semi-continuous (continuous) supply correspondences (functions) from individual producers and the aggregate production side of the economy, aggregate excess demands for all commodities and work activities can be shown to be upper semi-continuous (continuous) correspondences (functions).

After the appropriate definition of an upper semi-continuous (continuous) correspondence (function) from the price simplex to the set of excess demands and formation of the cartesian product of this set of excess demands with the price simplex, it is possible to apply Kakutani's (Brouwer's) fixed point theorem thereby establishing the existence of at least one general equilibrium. Once upper semi-continuity (continuity) of the excess demand mappings is established, the remaining steps in the existence proof are well known and we can leave interested readers to consult familiar formulations.[12] We, therefore, need only concern ourselves with the upper semi-continuity (continuity) of individual consumers' demand correspondences (functions).

INSATIABILITY: The traditional view of the insatiability assumption is misleading in its focus on a tautological and obvious aspect of the human condition, namely that more of something good is better than less, and its neglect of a more intriguing aspect of the human condition, namely that each of us has only a limited amount of time to undertake our consumption and work activities so that engaging in "more" of one activity has an opportunity cost in terms of other activities that must be foregone. But this problem need not concern us here. For nothing about endogenous preferences changes the reasonableness (or unreasonableness) of the insatiability assumption. Specifically, there is no more reason to question the insatiability assumption for our well-being functions than for Debreu's traditional preference orderings, both of which are defined on the sets $\{Q, L\}^i$.

CONTINUITY: Although a number of technical details must be analyzed concerning continuity of the correspondence from the set $\{Q, L\}^i$ to the "possibility" set for an individual consumer with a given vector of initial endowments and "stock" ownership under a given price system, assuming endogenous preferences does not affect any of these details.[13] The important issue is how to conceptualize the process of character formation and derivation of satisfaction from consumption-work choices. We have already motivated an approach that envisions activities in one period as affecting human characteristics in subsequent periods and satisfaction as depending on the state of one's human characteristics as well as one's activities. Obviously, nobody can hope to specify the precise functional nature of these incredibly complex cause-effect relations. To do so would imply that psychologists had solved all the problems of their discipline! And for most purposes it is probably inappropriate to view these relations in precise, mathematical, functional forms. Yet there is a long tradition among welfare economists of treating complex psychological processes as if they could be modeled in precise mathematical ways. The lack of hubris is justified on the basis of the nonintuitive insights gained.

In this spirit we postulate that the mapping of human characteristic formation from $\{Q, L\}^i$ to $\{C\}^i$ is continuous, and that the mapping from $\{\{C\}^i; \{Q, L\}^i\}$ to $\{U\}^i$ is continuous. At least there is nothing intrinsic to endogenous preferences that precludes this. In which case, we can conclude that $\{C\}^i$ is compact since $\{Q, L\}^i$ is compact and the mapping is continuous; that $\{\{C\}^i; \{Q, L\}^i\}$ is compact since the cartesian product of two compact sets is compact; that our utility set, $\{U^i\}$, is compact since a set of elements generated by a continuous mapping from a compact set is compact; and finally, that our overall welfare function, W^i, is a linear, continuous function defined on the compact set, $\{U\}^i$. Hence the composite "well-being" function, WB^i, mapping directly from $\{Q, L\}^i$ space to the set of real numbers giving us what we interpret as the individual's well-being is continuous. In sum, our well-being function, WB^i, that is expressive of perfectly informed endogenous preferences, can be reasonably attributed the same continuity properties usually assumed for exogenous utility functions. At least there is nothing inherent in the notion of endogenous preferences to indicate otherwise.

FIG. 6.1. A CONCAVE INDIFFERENCE CURVE

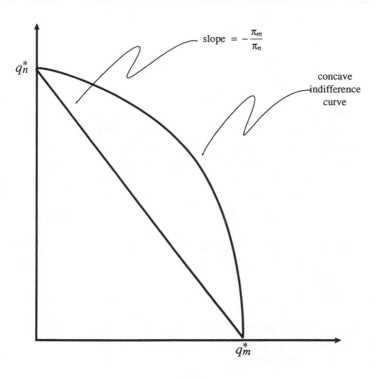

CONVEXITY: From the diagram in Fig. 6.1 we can see that some form of convexity is necessary to assure continuity of an individual's demand correspondences. If the set of consumption/work activity bundles preferred to a given bundle is concave, as pictured above, a slight shift in relative prices of two items can produce a "jump" discontinuity in demand for those goods. In this case, a shift in the relative prices from

$$\frac{\pi_m + \varepsilon}{\pi_n} \quad \text{to} \quad \frac{\pi_m - \varepsilon}{\pi_n}$$

for $\varepsilon > 0$ would produce a change in demand from $(q_n*, 0)$ to $(0, q_m*)$. The question, therefore, reduces to whether or not it is inherently less reasonable to assume the set of bundles giving equal or greater well-being according to our endogenous preference well-being function is convex, than to assume that the set of bundles giving equal or greater utility according to an exogenous preference utility function is convex. Does endogeneity of preferences increase the likelihood of concave indifference curves like that pictured in Fig. 6.1?

If we grant the assumption of convexity, then taking it together with the continuity and nonsatiation assumptions, it can be deduced that every individual consumer's demand correspondences are continuous.[14] Unfortunately, it would appear there are additional reasons to fear nonconvexities once we recognize preferences are endogenous to economic choices.

It has been argued that all convexities are the consequence of some form of indivisibility, since the full benefits of something can only be realized when a certain amount is consumed, this amount being greater than a single unit.[15] Of course, all nonconvexities could be eliminated by appropriate redefinition of the unit of account, but unfortunately, this "way out" produces equally disconcerting problems in the form of discontinuous preferences over the new units and ultimately complicates the question of whether markets can reasonably be assumed for all commodities and work activities in the units as we newly define them. One is free to redefine units of account but not free to assume that units that are convenient for eliminating nonconvexities will necessarily coincide with units convenient for purposes of continuity of preferences and existence of markets.

One of the implications of the paradigm we developed in chapter 5 is precisely that there are excellent reasons for believing that the real human world is not such that so happy a coincidence results. Moreover, our paradigm is quite consistent with mainstream modern social theory, which recognizes that the content of social structures cannot be reduced to the sum of separate individual participations. And while few economists realize the implication, the interactive view of society entails widespread opportunities for nonconvexities.[16] So, rather than being "neutral," the traditional welfare paradigm flies full in the face of mainstream social theory by projecting the kind of individualism necessary to justify the assumption of convexity.[17]

But the additional cause for concern about nonconvexities in consumers' preferences due to endogenous preferences is more mundane. One of the few reasons for nonconvexity that has received attention from traditional theorists is increasing returns to scale. As soon as consumption is recognized as having an "investment" aspect in changing human characteristics, more serious concerns of indivisibility in the form of increasing returns become apparent.

To cite one example, the immediate satisfaction derived from taking music lessons might exhibit diminishing returns, but the longer term benefits derived from further "investments" in music lessons now, in the form of appreciation of symphony concerts over one's entire life, could easily exhibit increasing returns over lengthy periods of consumption. The conception of endogenous preferences as myopic habit formation suggested by von Weizsacker and studied by Pollak and others is another obvious example. Although arguments have been advanced concerning diminution in the size of the discrepancy from equilibrium for a given nonconvexity as the size of the economy increases, it is well recognized that nonconvexities prevent demonstration of the existence of general equilibria.[18] In any case, our demonstration of Theorem 6.3 is complete under prescribed, admittedly dubious, conditions.

But we waive the right to quibble over existence theorems in order to focus on more substantive issues. We are happy to interpret Theorem 6.3 as extending the first fundamental welfare theorem: Equilibria exist under the usual assumptions, even if we treat preferences as endogenous. But will equilibria in a competitive, private enterprise market economy be Pareto optimal if preferences are endogenous?

Pareto Optimality.

THEOREM 6.4: SOCIAL EFFICIENCY. If all traditional assumptions are maintained except the assumption of exogenous preferences, and if the assumption of perfectly informed endogenous preferences is substituted for exogenous preferences, any general equilibrium of a perfectly competitive, private enterprise, market economy will be judged a Pareto optimum by our overall individual well-being functions. Moreover, in this case there is no reason to expect an endogenous view of preferences to make the necessary assumptions less plausible.

In other words, treatment of preferences as endogenous does not affect the conclusion that any general equilibrium of a perfectly competitive, private enterprise economy is a Pareto optimum provided all other traditional assumptions hold. Endogenous preferences, of themselves, do not affect the efficiency theorem for private enterprise market economies.

The proof of this theorem is well known, and the critical assumptions are the absence of externalities and "thick" indifference classes.[19] The absence of "thick" indifference curves is necessary to assure equivalence of the statement that a particular consumption/work activity bundle maximizes WB^i subject to the individual i's budget constraint and the statement that a particular consumption/work activity bundle minimizes expenditure required to achieve a given level of well-being. Absence of externalities is necessary to assure that if particular consumption/work activity bundles for each consumer and particular input/output vectors for each firm minimize a certain function on appropriately defined sets for each actor, their sum will minimize that function on the sum of those individual sets. If there were any externalities, the possibility would arise that a particular choice from one actor's set would change the production possibility set for some other firm or the "at least as preferred to" consumption set for some other consumer, and therefore, the independence of all actor's sets must be postulated. It is well known that no convexity assumptions, either for production possibility sets or "at least as preferred to" consumption sets, are required for the derivation since the existence of an equilibrium is hypothesized in this theorem, so related reservations are irrelevant in this proof. Since we postpone "other" problems with private (and public) enterprise market institutions until later chapters, here we can accept familiar assumptions regarding the nature and meaning of "competitive" labor markets and the absence of externalities. Therefore, our continuous, endogenous preference well-being functions, WB^i, which admit of no satiation activity bundles, are sufficient for the proof of Theorem 6.4 via the usual argument. While nonconvexities in the "equal to or greater than" well-being providing consumption/work activity sets may render the optimality theorem vacuous by making it impossible to prove the existence of an equilibrium, convexity considerations play no direct role in the optimality theorem.

Distributional Flexibility. We can now complete our resurrection of traditional welfare theory's holy trinity of fundamental theorems by proving:

THEOREM 6.5: DISTRIBUTIONAL FLEXIBILITY. If all traditional assumptions are maintained except the assumption of exogenous preferences, and if the assumption of perfectly informed endogenous preferences is substituted for exogenous preferences, any Pareto optimum is an equilibrium of an appropriate private enterprise, competitive market economy.

In other words, endogenous preferences, in and of themselves, do not affect the flexibility theorem for private enterprise market economies. Once again, the proof of this theorem in the case of exogenous preferences is well known.[20] In this case, "all the usual assumptions" include assumptions necessary for both Theorem 6.3 and Theorem 6.4. We must assume appropriate convexity properties to guarantee existence of equilibria and we must assume absence of "thick" indifference curves, accept the traditional characterization of labor markets, and stipulate the absence of externalities, to be sure the Pareto optimum can be reached via a general equilibrium. But beyond noting the need for these assumptions, there is nothing new to be discussed about their character in the case of Theorem 6.5. We have already stated that nothing intrinsic to endogenous preferences precludes accepting traditional assumptions concerning externalities and "thick" indifference curves. We have also already discussed how endogenous preferences generate well-being functions, WB^i, for which "at least as preferred to" consumption and work activity sets of individuals may not be convex. Waiving objections to the convexity assumption that endogenous preferences do make less plausible, Theorem 6.5 extends the traditional conclusion of distributional flexibility of private enterprise market economies under the assumption of endogenous preferences.

Interpretation of Theorems 6.1 Through 6.5. Our resurrection of all three cornerstones of traditional welfare theory under perfectly informed endogenous preferences is complete. Under the usual assumptions the existence and optimality of an equilibrium for any competitive, private enterprise market economy is assured, and any Pareto optimum can be achieved as the equilibrium of a competitive, private enterprise market economy with the appropriate initial endowments even if preferences are endogenous. Moreover, in the process of reestablishing the fundamental theorems, we have alleviated any anxiety about the implications of multiple equilibria.

Gintis believed endogenous preferences made multiple equilibria far more likely. Apparently he assumed many of these equilibria would not be Pareto optimal, since he argued that efficiency would require a Central Planning Board to choose among the equilibria and promulgate the set of prices and wages necessary to generate a socially efficient equilibrium. But Theorem 6.4 clearly states that should there be multiple equilibria they would all be Pareto optimal under the usual assumptions.[21] So there is no need to append a Central Planning Board to a Debreuvian free market economy whose inhabitants are perfectly informed regarding their own particulars to "guarantee" the "correct" equilibrium. Were a Central Planning Board necessary, this would certainly violate the spirit of a free market system. But Gintis' "technical" critique of private enterprise market economies based on the greater likelihood of multiple equilibria under endogenous preferences, which he erroneously believed implied a need to centrally plan such an economy in any case, disappears under the assumption of *individual* perfect knowledge.

Theorem 6.2 certainly points out the necessity of extending the insights of human capital theory to preference development and falsifies the usual "separability" assumption necessary to justify partial equilibrium applications of neoclassical welfare theory. But, more importantly, Theorems 6.3, 6.4, and 6.5 reestablish traditional welfare conclusions concerning relations between competitive equilibria of private enterprise market systems and Pareto optima in context of endogenous preferences. It appears we have formally confirmed what were only speculations for von Weizsacker, Pollak, and Hammond—taken alone perfectly informed endogenous preferences do not affect fundamental conclusions of traditional welfare theory. In Kuhn's language, were we to stop here, our demonstration of Theorems 6.3, 6.4, and 6.5 might well be interpreted as "normal scientific development" in which the traditional paradigm accommodates to a more general context in which old conclusions are reaffirmed.

6.2.3 Round Three: Endogenous Preferences Do Matter

Appearances can be deceiving. Let us clarify the meaning of Theorems 6.3, 6.4, and 6.5. If we assume no other aspects of private enterprise, competitive market economies produce nonoptimalities, treatment of preferences as endogenous does not affect the fundamental theorems of traditional welfare economics. Put this way, and with the benefit of hindsight, we might consider the result hardly surprising. If private enterprise market systems were totally flexible and efficient in meeting people's desires, why should they not be totally flexible and efficient satisfying people's preferences for alternative desires themselves? Why shouldn't a system that gives people what they care about, in proportion to the degree they care about it, give people the desires as well as the goods they want? Indeed, upon reflection, it would be surprising if treating preferences as endogenous, by itself, could affect the optimality properties of any economic system. This may explain von Weizsacker, Pollak, and Hammond's confidence in their speculations.

Suppose we generalize and then state our growing suspicion as a hypothesis. For any possible economic system we can ask whether the system has an equilibrium (or generates a feasible plan) and call this the existence theorem for the system. If the system does have at least one equilibrium, we can ask if any equilibrium (or feasible plan that results) will be a Pareto optimum and call this the optimality theorem. Finally, we can also ask if the system, under some arrangement, is capable of generating any Pareto optimum and call this the distributional flexibility theorem. Our analysis suggests as a hypothesis that moving from treating preferences as exogenous to treating them as endogenous will not, in and of itself, affect the truth value of these fundamental theorems for any economic system.

But even should this hypothesis prove true, it would not necessarily mean that endogenous preferences "do not matter." For example, if endogenous preferences have a profound effect on how and to what extent "other" problems generate nonoptimalities, then they certainly "do matter." In fact, it is possible that treating preferences as endogenous can completely change our view of why and how different economic institutions facilitate or obstruct well-being even though, in and of themselves, they do not affect the three fundamental theorems of welfare economics. This is the case we now argue.

Theorem 6.2 suggests the kind of results we will present in this section. We interpreted Theorem 6.2 earlier as meaning that rational people will adjust their desires to accord to expected future availabilities. Theorem 6.4 demonstrated that in a general equilibrium context this does not preclude optimality. But this leaves open the possibility that while endogenous preferences do not create nonoptimalities in and of themselves, they may magnify misallocations that appear for other reasons. Before treating this possibility, we must examine Theorem 6.4 once again, because in spite of the "careful restatement" above, our interpretation of Theorem 6.4 is still potentially misleading.

We interpreted Theorem 6.4 as if it had to do with the optimality of a private enterprise, competitive market economy. In fact, Theorem 6.4 has nothing whatever to do with a private enterprise market system. By assuming away "all other problems" in a private enterprise market system, we created—by supposition—a system with no inefficiencies, a system with no distortion of the conditions of availability of different economic activities, a system with no biases in the conditions of relative supplies of different consumption goods and laboring activities. Whether or not even the most perfectly competitive private enterprise, market economy can justifiably lay claim to such qualities remains to be discussed. In fact, the main purpose of next two chapters is to resolve just this claim.

Yet this is not to say the assumption of "no other problems" was ill formulated. In light of the claims and counterclaims made about the effect of endogenous preferences, in and of themselves, on the optimality properties of private enterprise market economies, the assumption of "no other problems" was critical to laying this debate to rest. But the economy we created for this purpose—and interpreted as a private enterprise market system in which we agreed to ignore all problems other than endogenous preferences—can be more accurately interpreted as a hypothetical economy with no distortions, biases, or inefficiencies built into its institutional structures. In other words, the economy we analyzed in Theorem 6.4 was not defined by the particular institutional structures of private enterprise and competitive markets. It was not defined by any institutional structures at all. It was instead defined by the presumed absence of any distortions or biases in the conditions of availability of different economic activities.

While we pretended for the sake of a particular argument that this could occur within the institutional structures of private enterprise and competitive markets we had no reason to believe this to be the case, other than traditional attitudes. Whether or not particular institutions merit the distinction of introducing no distortions or biases is the subject matter of part 3 of this book. What we created in Theorem 6.4 was an ideal "marshmallow economy" subject only and entirely to people's desires for goods and laboring activities and their preferences for different desires once treatment of preferences as endogenous allowed these to be expressed.[22]

What we discovered in Theorem 6.4 now appears rather trivial: A perfect "marshmallow" economy that adjusts only and entirely to people's economic "wills" will generate socially efficient outcomes under the assumption of endogenous preferences just as it did under the assumption of exogenous preferences.[23]

But what would be the effect of introducing endogenous preferences in a less ideal setting in which particular economic institutions do distort the availability of economic activities? Obviously, in any chosen economy that displays a bias we will find inefficiency. But will a treatment of preferences as endogenous give us a different view of the character and consequences of such inefficiencies? Theorems 6.6, 6.7, and 6.8, below, say yes, and reveal the real significance of endogenous preferences.

Theorem 6.6 addresses the effect of perfectly informed endogenous preferences on nonoptimal allocations arising from bias in the relative terms of supply of economic activities.

THEOREM 6.6: SNOWBALLING NONOPTIMAL ALLOCATIONS. In an economy that contains a bias in the relative terms of supply of two economic activities: (1) the degree of nonoptimality will be greater than indicated by traditional welfare theory, which treats preferences as exogenous; (2) the divergence from optimality will "snowball," or increase over time, in a manner that can be precisely defined.

Theorem 6.7 addresses the effect of perfectly informed endogenous preferences on nonoptimal human development trajectories arising from bias in the relative terms of supply of economic activities.

> THEOREM 6.7: SNOWBALLING WARPED HUMAN DEVELOPMENT. In an economy that contains a bias in the relative terms of supply of two economic activities: (1) individual human development patterns will be "warped" in a manner that can be precisely defined; (2) "warped" human characteristics will "snowball" over time.

Theorem 6.8 addresses the impact of ignoring informed endogenous preferences on analysts' ability to perceive the effects of economic biases.

> THEOREM 6.8: DISGUISED DISTORTION. The full effects of any bias in the relative terms of supply of activities in an economy will be disguised to participants in the economy and to analysts who view preferences as exogenous.

Preliminary Discussion of Theorems 6.6, 6.7, and 6.8. First, we must define the concept "degree of nonoptimality." Beyond judging situations to be Pareto optimal or non-Pareto optimal, we wish to judge whether situations are closer or farther from a particular Pareto optimum. We define "degree of nonoptimality" as the divergence of actual relative supplies from the relative supplies that characterize the optimal production program. The degree of nonoptimality is measured in commodity and not utility space. "Snowballing nonoptimality" occurs when the divergence of actual from optimal relative supplies grows larger in successive time periods.

We must also define "warped human development pattern." Any outcome or "solution" in a multiperiod Debreuvian model consists of activity choices in all time periods. But in a model in which people have endogenous preferences, any solution also implies a particular pattern of development of human characteristics for each individual, along with the instantaneous preferences that depend on them. In other words, a human development outcome accompanies each activity outcome. The human development patterns that accompany activity outcomes that correspond to Pareto optima, we term "optimal human development trajectories." Human characteristic patterns that accompany activity outcomes that are not Pareto optimal, we describe not only as "nonoptimal," but as "warped" because, as we will see, they are "self-generated" by conscious choice in light of perfect information. If actual human characteristics deviate from optimal human characteristics to an ever greater extent in successive time periods, we say the "warping" of human characteristics "snowballs."

Finally, discussion of the model and the demonstration is in order. The fact that we grant people in our economy immortality by assuming that $t = 1, 2, \ldots \infty$ might appear objectionable. Besides being of generous disposition, we did this because it is more convenient than choosing "cut-off" times when dealing with "snowballing" phenomena. As people adjust in earlier periods to conditions previsioned in later periods, cut-off times that imply a diminution of the snowballing as people near the end of their appointed times would introduce unnecessary complexities. The problem is analogous to evaluating investment stocks in the final years of national planning models so familiar to economic planners, and we do not believe eliminating this complexity invalidates our results.

We also focus on only four activities and two human characteristics because this is all that is necessary. From all activities we specify that only two have what we call "developmental effects" in the sense that engaging in these activities in an earlier time period affects one's human characteristics in later time periods. And we specify that the preferences for only two other activities are "affected developmentally" in the sense that one's preferences for these activities are influenced by human characteristics that can be influenced by prior activities engaged in. The conclusions of Theorem 6.6 result if there is a bias in the relative conditions of supply individuals face for the two activities for which preferences can be "affected developmentally." If activities with "developmental effects" and activities that can be "affected developmentally" are more widespread, the "snowballing" nonoptimality would obviously be more pervasive.

We specify the single bias in the economy as follows: we assume that no productive resources are left idle, that only technically efficient methods of production are employed, and that no exchange of inputs between production units could increase the output of one without decreasing the output of another.[24] We also assume the economy supplies all activities in such quantities that the marginal social cost of producing the last unit is equal to the market demand for the activity, and that market demand is the sum of demands of individuals with a limited income out of which they purchase economic activities according to their preferences and developmental capabilities. For all goods but one the economy "charges" individuals the net marginal social cost of supplying each person with another unit of the activity.[25] The single bias is defined as a charge in excess of net marginal social cost of supply to the individual purchaser of one of the activities that can be "affected developmentally."

Demonstration of a degree of nonoptimality greater than envisioned by traditional welfare theory that "snowballs" over time amounts to showing that the total supply of the activity subject to the charge in excess of net marginal social cost, relative to the total supply of other activities, will be less than calculated assuming exogenous preferences and grow less over time. Our formal demonstration works backward and then forward again in time, mirroring the "logic" of a "rational" individual confronted by a change in the future relative conditions of supply from the "optimal" ratio to the "biased" ratio. Unfortunately, our result is not easily proven formally. We must examine five different conceivable reactions an individual might adopt to introduction of a bias in the conditions of supply. Moreover, of the four possibilities we must exclude to demonstrate our result, the most intuitively absurd proves the most difficult to exclude formally.

Model 3: An Economy with a Single Bias in the Conditions of Supply Inhabited by Individuals Aware of Their Endogenous Preferences. Model 3 is a simplified version of Model 1 deleting all unnecessary complications. It is only necessary to consider four activities and two characteristics, and we abstract from human capital "earnings" effects altogether. But characteristic formation functions, as well as instantaneous utility functions are assumed to be continuous and differentiable, as well as having the other "traditional" properties described below.

M 3.1. There are many people: $i, j = 1, 2, ...N$ (finite), and many time periods: $t = 1, 2, ...\infty$.

M 3.2. There are four activities in each time period: three activities, x, y, and z which are made available to individuals at prices equal to their net marginal social costs; and one activity, a, for which individuals are charged in excess of net marginal social cost.

M 3.3. There are two human characteristics in every time period that can be "affected developmentally" and "parameterize" the "instantaneous" utility functions.

i) S is a characteristic that enhances the individual's enjoyment of activity a and is a characteristic generated by previous engagement in activity y.

ii) P is a characteristic that enhances the individual's enjoyment of activity z and is a characteristic generated by previous engagement in activity x.[26]

We specify these relations for $i = 1...N$; $t = 0...\infty$; $k = 1...\infty$ by

M 3.4. For good x and individual i:

$$\frac{\partial P^i(t+k)}{\partial x^i(t)} > 0 \quad \text{and} \quad \frac{\partial S^i(t+k)}{\partial x^i(t)} = 0$$

$$\frac{\partial}{\partial P^i(t)} \left[\frac{\partial U^i\left(P^i(t), S^i(t); x^i(t), y^i(t), z^i(t), a^i(t)\right)}{\partial x^i(t)} \right] = 0$$

$$\frac{\partial}{\partial S^i(t)} \left[\frac{\partial U^i\left(P^i(t), S^i(t); x^i(t), y^i(t), z^i(t), a^i(t)\right)}{\partial x^i(t)} \right] = 0$$

M 3.5. And for good y:

$$\frac{\partial P^i(t+k)}{\partial y^i(t)} = 0 \text{ and } \frac{\partial S^i(t+k)}{\partial y^i(t)} > 0$$

$$\frac{\partial}{\partial P^i(t)}\left\{\frac{\partial U^i\left(P^i(t), S^i(t); x^i(t), y^i(t), z^i(t), a^i(t)\right)}{\partial y^i(t)}\right\} = 0$$

$$\frac{\partial}{\partial S^i(t)}\left\{\frac{\partial U^i\left(P^i(t), S^i(t); x^i(t), y^i(t), z^i(t), a^i(t)\right)}{\partial y^i(t)}\right\} = 0$$

M 3.6. And for good z:

$$\frac{\partial P^i(t+k)}{\partial z^i(t)} = 0 \text{ and } \frac{\partial S^i(t+k)}{\partial z^i(t)} = 0$$

$$\frac{\partial}{\partial P^i(t)}\left\{\frac{\partial U^i\left(P^i(t), S^i(t); x^i(t), y^i(t), z^i(t), a^i(t)\right)}{\partial z^i(t)}\right\} > 0$$

$$\frac{\partial}{\partial S^i(t)}\left\{\frac{\partial U^i\left(P^i(t), S^i(t); x^i(t), y^i(t), z^i(t), a^i(t)\right)}{\partial z^i(t)}\right\} = 0$$

M 3.7. And, for good a:

$$\frac{\partial P^i(t+k)}{\partial a^i(t)} = 0 \text{ and } \frac{\partial S^i(t+k)}{\partial a^i(t)} = 0$$

$$\frac{\partial}{\partial P^i(t)}\left\{\frac{\partial U^i\left(P^i(t), S^i(t); x^i(t), y^i(t), z^i(t), a^i(t)\right)}{\partial a^i(t)}\right\} = 0$$

$$\frac{\partial}{\partial S^i(t)}\left\{\frac{\partial U^i\left(P^i(t), S^i(t); x^i(t), y^i(t), z^i(t), a^i(t)\right)}{\partial a^i(t)}\right\} > 0$$

M 3.8. People have "instantaneous" utility functions in every time period, $U^i(t)$, and an overall well-being function that is a linear sum of utilities achieved in each time period with all weights equal to 1.[27] Thus individuals are assumed to maximize:

$$W^i = \sum_{t=0}^{\infty} U^i(t)$$

where, as above, for all i and t:

$$U^i(t) = U^i\left(P^i(t), S^i(t); x^i(t), y^i(t), z^i(t), a^i(t)\right)$$

M 3.9. The single bias in the economy is specified by charging individual purchasers of x, y, and z the net marginal social cost of providing them

166

the activity, but charging those who purchase a some amount in excess of the net marginal social cost. To reflect this, we can let $0 = O(x(0), y(0), z(0), a(0); \ldots x(t), y(t), z(t), a(t); \ldots)$ define the traditional production transformation locus of all efficient productions for the economy as a whole. Then the ratios of the marginal social costs of producing one more unit of b at time t in terms of the number of units of c that must be foregone at time $(t+k)$ would be

$$\frac{\partial O}{\partial b(t)} \Big/ \frac{\partial O}{\partial c(t+k)}$$

where b and c can equal x, y, z, or a; $t = 0 \ldots \infty$; and $k = 1 \ldots \infty$

M 3.10. We further define the ratios of net marginal social costs to society of making activities available to individual i. The ratio of the net marginal social costs of supplying one more unit of b to i at time t as compared to supplying i with one more unit of c at time $(t+k)$ is:[28]

$$\frac{\partial O^i}{\partial b^i(t)} \Big/ \frac{\partial O^i}{\partial c^i(t+k)} = \frac{\dfrac{\partial O}{\partial b(t)} - \displaystyle\sum_{j \neq i} \dfrac{\partial U^j(t)}{\partial b^i(t)}}{\dfrac{\partial O}{\partial c(t+k)} - \displaystyle\sum_{j \neq i} \dfrac{\partial U^j(t+k)}{\partial c^i(t+k)}}$$

M 3.11. Since we have stipulated that supplies will be responsive to market demands in our economy, our economy must charge individuals an amount equal to the net marginal social cost of supplying each person with another unit of any activity if the economy is to be efficient.[29] Whereas our economy does so for activities x, y, and z, for activity a it charges some amount in excess of net marginal social cost. We specify all this for time period $(t+k)$ in the following equation where superscript A stands for "actual" and superscript O stands for "optimal."

$$\frac{\pi_a^i(t+k)^A}{\pi_\beta^i(t+k)^A} > \left| \frac{\partial O^i}{\partial a^i(t+k)} \Big/ \frac{\partial O^i}{\partial \beta^i(t+k)} \right| = \frac{\pi_a^i(t+k)^O}{\pi_\beta^i(t+k)^O}$$

where $\beta = x, y,$ or z

Snowballing Nonoptimality. In an economy like that represented above, the degree of divergence from optimality as measured by divergence of relative supplies from the optimal production program will be greater than indicated by neoclassical welfare theory. Moreover, divergence from optimality will snowball as measured by discrepancies between actual and optimal quantities produced in successive time periods.

Our proof draws on the familiar marginal optimality conditions that the ratios of all possible pairs of marginal social costs must be equal to the ratios of their respective marginal social benefits.[30] But we will only need to examine two of the equalities:

1. One equating the ratio of the marginal social costs of production of x and y with the ratio of the marginal social benefits of their consumption in an early time period, t.

2. The other equating the marginal social costs of production of z and a with the ratio of the marginal social benefits of their consumption in a later time period, $(t+k)$.

Theorem 6.6: Proof. Initially we charge a typical individual i the "optimal" prices in all periods and deduce i's rational behavior.[31] Next we charge i the optimal prices for all goods in all periods, except we charge i some amount in excess of the optimal price for good a in period $(t+k)$ as stipulated in M 3.11. We call these latter prices the "actual" prices charged by our economy with a single bias. The question is, how will a typical individual, i, adjust to this change in relative prices. Once we deduce the nature of a rational adjustment for a typical consumer, generalizing to changes in market demand and consequent changes in market supplies and production is straightforward.

FIG. 6.2. PREFERENCE SHIFTS UNDER ENDOGENOUS PREFERENCES: FIVE POSSIBILITIES

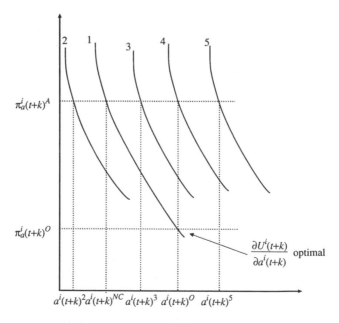

Will individual i simply reduce his or her demand for $a(t+k)$ from $a^i(t+k)^O$ to $a^i(t+k)^{NC}$ moving back up his or her given demand curve for $a(t+k)$ as neoclassical (NC) theory would predict? Or will i also change his or her preference and hence demand curve for $a(t+k)$ by shifting consumption choices for y (and hence S) and x (and hence P) in earlier time periods?

There are five possible adjustments an individual might make to respond to the change in relative prices. To prove Theorem 6.6, we must demonstrate that four of these are inconsistent with individual maximizing behavior whereas one is consistent. An individual consumer might:

1. Lower individual demand for $a(t+k)$ to curve 2 and consume at $a^i(t+k)^2$. We will demonstrate that this choice is consistent with individual maximizing behavior.

2. Keep demand curve 1 and reduce consumption along this curve to $a^i(t+k)^{NC}$. We will show this is inconsistent with individual maximizing behavior because it violates the condition that the ratio of the marginal benefit of consuming the last unit of x to the marginal benefit of consuming the last unit of y in period t to individual i must be equal to the ratio of those two goods' relative prices if i is to have maximized individual fulfillment.

3. Raise individual demand for $a(t+k)$ to curve 3 and consume at $a^i(t+k)^3$. We will demonstrate this is inconsistent with individual maximizing behavior for the same reason as choice 2.

4. Raise individual demand for $a(t+k)$ to curve 4 and consume at $a^i(t+k)^O$. We will demonstrate this is inconsistent with individual maximizing behavior for the same reason as choices 2 and 3.

5. Raise individual demand for $a(t+k)$ to curve 5 and consume at $a^i(t+k)^5$. While this choice is the most obviously absurd, to demonstrate that it cannot be an individual maximizing adjustment we must show this would imply that curve 1 and consumption $a^i(t+k)^O$ was not optimal for $\pi_a^i(t+k)^O$ so that choice 5 must be false by contradiction.

OPTION 1. Here we must show that individual i choosing to lower the personal demand curve for $a(t+k)$ and raise the individual demand curve for $z(t+k)$, and to consume relatively less of $a(t+k)$ and relatively more of $z(t+k)$ than neoclassical theory would predict is consistent with individual maximizing behavior.[32] With

$$\frac{\pi_z^i(t+k)^A}{\pi_a^i(t+k)^A} < \frac{\pi_z^i(t+k)^O}{\pi_a^i(t+k)^O}$$

to maximize individual well-being i must take steps to ensure that

$$\left\{ \frac{\partial U^i(t+k)^A}{\partial z^i(t+k)^A} \right\} / \left\{ \frac{\partial U^i(t+k)^A}{\partial a^i(t+k)^A} \right\} < \left\{ \frac{\partial U^i(t+k)^O}{\partial z^i(t+k)^O} \right\} / \left\{ \frac{\partial U^i(t+k)^O}{\partial a^i(t+k)^{O}} \right\}$$

In option 1 we have

$$\frac{z^i(t+k)^A}{a^i(t+k)^A} > \frac{z^i(t+k)^O}{a^i(t+k)^O}$$

which under the assumption of declining marginal utilities could reestablish the necessary condition

$$\left\{ \frac{\partial U^i(t+k)^A}{\partial z^i(t+k)^A} \right\} / \left\{ \frac{\partial U^i(t+k)^A}{\partial a^i(t+k)^A} \right\} = \frac{\pi_z^i(t+k)^A}{\pi_a^i(t+k)^A} \tag{6.4}$$

When we examine the second necessary condition

$$\frac{\pi_x^i(t)}{\pi_y^i(t)} = \frac{\dfrac{\partial U^i(t)}{\partial x^i(t)} + \sum_k \left\{ \dfrac{\partial U^i(t+k)}{\partial P^i(t+k)} \dfrac{\partial P^i(t+k)}{\partial x^i(t)} \right\}}{\dfrac{\partial U^i(t)}{\partial y^i(t)} + \sum_k \left\{ \dfrac{\partial U^i(t+k)}{\partial S^i(t+k)} \dfrac{\partial S^i(t+k)}{\partial y^i(t)} \right\}} \tag{6.5}$$

we observe that under option 1

$$\left\{ \frac{\partial U^i(t+k)^A}{\partial P^i(t+k)^A} \right\} / \left\{ \frac{\partial U^i(t+k)^A}{\partial S^i(t+k)^A} \right\} > \left\{ \frac{\partial U^i(t+k)^O}{\partial P^i(t+k)^O} \right\} / \left\{ \frac{\partial U^i(t+k)^O}{\partial S^i(t+k)^O} \right\} \tag{6.6}$$

since

$$\frac{z^i(t+k)^A}{a^i(t+k)^A} > \frac{z^i(t+k)^O}{a^i(t+k)^O}$$

so that the right side of condition (6.5) is greater than the left side under adjustment option 1 at the original price for $x(t)$ and $y(t)$ and the original quantities consumed. Since the prices of $x(t)$ and $y(t)$ have not been changed it follows that under option 1, to establish condition (6.5), which is necessary for maximizing W^i, individual i must change the proportions of $x(t)$ and $y(t)$ consumed. This is the only means of reestablishing condition (6.5) since changing the preferences for these two goods themselves is ruled out by our assumption that appreciation for x and y cannot be developed. Hence, under option 1 the individual acts so

$$\frac{x^i(t)^A}{y^i(t)^A} > \frac{x^i(t)^O}{y^i(t)^O} \tag{6.7}$$

thereby

170

diminishing $\dfrac{\partial U^i(t)}{\partial x^i(t)}$ and increasing $\dfrac{\partial U^i(t)}{\partial y^i(t)}$

due to diminishing marginal utility and also

diminishing $\dfrac{\partial P^i(t+k)}{\partial x^i(t+k)}$ and increasing $\dfrac{\partial S^i(t+k)}{\partial y^i(t+k)}$

due to declining marginal productivity in developmental production functions. Inspection reveals that these changes permit the reestablishing of equality (6.5). But condition (6.7) implies that

$$\left\lvert \dfrac{\partial U^i(t+k)^A}{\partial z^i(t+k)^A} \right\rvert \Big/ \left\lvert \dfrac{\partial U^i(t+k)^A}{\partial a^i(t+k)^A} \right\rvert > \left\lvert \dfrac{\partial U^i(t+k)^O}{\partial z^i(t+k)^O} \right\rvert \Big/ \left\lvert \dfrac{\partial U^i(t+k)^O}{\partial a^i(t+k)^O} \right\rvert \quad (6.8)$$

for all ratios $z^i(t+k)/a^i(t+k)$ since condition (6.7) implies that

$$\frac{P^i(t+k)^A}{S^i(t+k)^A} > \frac{P^i(t+k)^O}{S^i(t+k)^O}$$

This in turn means i has shifted his or her individual demand curve for $a(t+k)$ down—and individual demand curve for $z(t+k)$ up—which is consistent with our characterization of adjustment option 1.

OPTION 2. We must show that for individual i to retain the demand curves for $a(t+k)$ and $z(t+k)$ that were optimal under the optimal price ratios for the two goods and simply move along them to consume the amount less of $a(t+k)$ and more of $z(t+k)$ that neoclassical theory would predict is inconsistent with individual maximizing behavior if preferences are endogenous.

Under option 2 we know that

$$\left\lvert \dfrac{\partial U^i(t+k)^A}{\partial z^i(t+k)^A} \right\rvert \Big/ \left\lvert \dfrac{\partial U^i(t+k)^A}{\partial a^i(t+k)^A} \right\rvert$$

must be made equal to

$$\frac{\pi_z^i(t+k)^A}{\pi_a^i(t+k)^A}$$

by moving along the original individual demand curves. But this means it must be less than the same ratio at the optimal price

$$\frac{\pi_z^i(t+k)^O}{\pi_a^i(t+k)^O}$$

which ratio is in turn just equal to:

$$\left\{\frac{\partial U^i(t+k)^O}{\partial z^i(t+k)^O}\right\} \bigg/ \left\{\frac{\partial U^i(t+k)^O}{\partial a^i(t+k)^O}\right\}$$

But this again implies

$$\frac{z^i(t+k)^A}{a^i(t+k)^A} > \frac{z^i(t+k)^O}{a^i(t+k)^O}$$

Once again, if we go back and analyze condition (6.5) above, expression (6.6) follows for option 2 just as it did for option 1. And this again means that the necessary condition for individual maximizing behavior is not achieved by the original choice of $x^i(t)^O/y^i(t)^O$. Under our assumption that the individual's tastes for $x(t)$ and $y(t)$ are unalterable, the only conceivable way that condition (6.5) could be reestablished would be for the individual to change the proportions in which $x(t)$ and $y(t)$ are consumed. But this contradicts the characterization of option 2 that individual i's demand curves for $z(t+k)$ and $a(t+k)$ are not shifted, since any change in $x^i(t)/y^i(t)$ implies a change in $P^i(t+k)/S^i(t+k)$ and, hence, a shift in the individual's demand curves for $z^x(t+k)$ and $a^x(t+k)$. Thus, option 2 cannot be made consistent with rational individual maximizing behavior if preferences are endogenous.

OPTION 3. We next need to demonstrate that raising the individual's demand curve for $a(t+k)$ and lowering the individual's demand curve for $z(t+k)$, but not by so much that the individual does not still consume less $a(t+k)$ and more $z(t+k)$ than he or she did at the optimal price ratios is inconsistent with individual maximizing behavior.

Stipulation that under option 3 the individual reduces consumption of $a(t+k)$ and increases consumption of $z(t+k)$ gives:

$$\frac{z^i(t+k)^A}{a^i(t+k)^A} > \frac{z^i(t+k)^O}{a^i(t+k)^O} \tag{6.9a}$$

And stipulation that under option 3 the individual raises the personal demand curve for $a(t+k)$ and lowers the demand curve for $z(t+k)$ implies:

$$\frac{P^i(t+k)^A}{S^i(t+k)^A} < \frac{P^i(t+k)^O}{S^i(t+k)^O} \tag{6.9b}$$

However, the only way (6b) can occur is if:

$$\frac{x^i(t)^A}{y^i(t)^A} < \frac{x^i(t)^O}{y^i(t)^O} \tag{6.9c}$$

But conditions (6.9a), (6.9b), and (6.9c) together imply that condition (6.5)

$$\frac{\pi_x^i(t)}{\pi_y^i(t)} = \frac{\dfrac{\partial U^i(t)}{\partial x^i(t)} + \displaystyle\sum_k \left[\dfrac{\partial U^i(t+k)}{\partial P^i(t+k)} \dfrac{\partial P^i(t+k)}{\partial x^i(t)} \right]}{\dfrac{\partial U^i(t)}{\partial y^i(t)} + \displaystyle\sum_k \left[\dfrac{\partial U^i(t+k)}{\partial S^i(t+k)} \dfrac{\partial S^i(t+k)}{\partial y^i(t)} \right]}$$

necessary for maximization of individual well-being cannot be achieved since all the partial derivatives and terms in the numerator of the right side of the expression would be larger under option 3, and all the partial derivatives and terms in the denominator of the right side of the expression would be smaller, implying that the right side of condition (6.5) would be greater than the ratios of the relative prices for $x(t)$ and $y(t)$. To see this, note that under option 3

$$\frac{\partial U^i(t)}{\partial x^i(t)} \text{ is larger and } \frac{\partial U^i(t)}{\partial y^i(t)} \text{ is smaller}$$

due to declining marginal utilities. And

$$\frac{\partial P^i(t+k)}{\partial x^i(t)} \text{ is larger and } \frac{\partial S^i(t+k)}{\partial y^i(t)} \text{ is smaller}$$

due to both declining marginal productivities of utility shifting functions and the fact that the partial derivatives of utility functions with respect to human characteristics are still positive functions of the amount of goods the characteristics enhance enjoyment of. It follows that option 3 cannot be an individual maximizing adjustment.

OPTION 4. Next we must demonstrate that raising the individual's demand curve for $a(t + k)$ and lowering the individual's demand curve for $z(t + k)$ so that the consumption of $a(t + k)$ and $z(t + k)$ remain exactly what they were under the optimal consumption at the optimal price ratios is also inconsistent with individual maximizing behavior.

By stipulation of the nature of option 4, we have:

$$\frac{z^i(t+k)^A}{a^i(t+k)^A} = \frac{z^i(t+k)^O}{a^i(t+k)^O} \tag{6.9a'}$$

$$\frac{P^i(t+k)^A}{S^i(t+k)^A} < \frac{P^i(t+k)^O}{S^i(t+k)^O} \tag{6.9b}$$

$$\frac{x^i(t)^A}{y^i(t)^A} < \frac{x^i(t)^O}{y^i(t)^O} \tag{6.9c}$$

since other than the equality condition (6a'), this option is like option 3.

173

But (6.9a'), (6.9b), and (6.9c) also imply that the right side of expression (6.5) must be greater than the left side. The only difference between option 4 and 3 is the assumed constancy of the consumption bundles in period $(t+k)$ under option 4. But

$$\frac{\partial U^i(t)}{\partial x^i(t)} \text{ is still larger and } \frac{\partial U^i(t)}{\partial y^i(t)} \text{ is still smaller}$$

due to declining marginal utilities. And

$$\frac{\partial P^i(t+k)}{\partial x^i(t)} \text{ is still larger and } \frac{\partial S^i(t+k)}{\partial y^i(t)} \text{ is still smaller}$$

due to declining marginal productivities of utility shifting functions and the constancy of the consumption bundles in time period (t+k). So option 4 cannot be an individual maximizing adjustment any more than option 3 could.

FIG. 6.3. PREFERENCE SHIFT UNDER
ENDOGENOUS PREFERENCES POSSIBILITY NUMBER 5

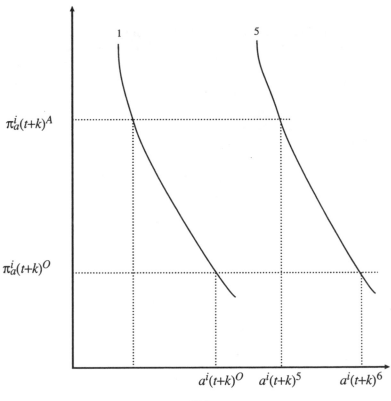

OPTION 5. Finally, we must demonstrate that raising the individual's demand curve for $a(t + k)$ and lowering the individual's demand curve for $z(t + k)$ so that consumption of $a(t + k)$ actually rises and consumption of $z(t + k)$ actually falls in response to the change in relative prices making $a(t + k)$ relatively more expensive and $z(t + k)$ relatively less expensive is inconsistent with individual maximizing behavior. This option could be dismissed out of hand as intuitively ridiculous. Yet, ironically, it proves the hardest option to formally eliminate.

Under option 5 we have

$$\frac{z^i(t + k)^A}{a^i(t + k)^A} < \frac{z^i(t + k)^O}{a^i(t + k)^O} \tag{6.9a''}$$

$$\frac{P^i(t + k)^A}{S^i(t + k)^A} < \frac{P^i(t + k)^O}{S^i(t + k)^O} \tag{6.9b}$$

$$\frac{x^i(t)^A}{y^i(t)^A} < \frac{x^i(t)^O}{y^i(t)^O} \tag{6.9c}$$

Here, we have eliminated from our earlier diagram all but the original optimal demand curve no. 1 for $a(t + k)$ under the optimal price conditions and demand curve no. 5 that represents our individual's strategy under option 5. We have also added $a^i(t + k)^6$ as the consumption of $a(t + k)$ that i would settle on if faced by the old optimal price were i saddled with demand function no. 5—a demand function that would presumably be individually nonoptimal under the optimal price.

Suppose, against our hypothesis, that demand curve no. 5 not only preserves the late period marginal equality, condition (6.4), at consumption $a^i(t + k)^5$ for price ratio

$$\frac{\pi_z^i(t + k)^A}{\pi_a^i(t + k)^A}$$

but also preserves the early period equality, condition (6.5)

$$\frac{\pi_x^i(t)}{\pi_y^i(t)} = \frac{\dfrac{\partial U^i(t)}{\partial x^i(t)} + \sum_k \left\{ \dfrac{\partial U^i(t + k)}{\partial P^i(t + k)} \dfrac{\partial P^i(t + k)}{\partial x^i(t)} \right\}}{\dfrac{\partial U^i(t)}{\partial y^i(t)} + \sum_k \left\{ \dfrac{\partial U^i(t + k)}{\partial S^i(t + k)} \dfrac{\partial S^i(t + k)}{\partial y^i(t)} \right\}}$$

In other words, we assume option 5 is an individual maximizing strategy and search for a contradiction.

Option 5 could only reestablish condition (6.5) if declines in

$$\frac{\partial U^i(t)}{\partial y^i(t)} \quad \text{and} \quad \frac{\partial S^i(t+k)}{\partial y^i(t)}$$

resulting from conditions (6.9b) and (6.9c) is exactly offset by the rise in

$$\frac{\partial U^i(t+k)}{\partial S^i(t+k)}$$

that comes as a result of condition (6.9a''), and if rises in

$$\frac{\partial U^i(t)}{\partial x^i(t)} \quad \text{and} \quad \frac{\partial P^i(t+k)}{\partial x^i(t)}$$

resulting from conditions (6.9b) and (6.9c) are exactly offset by the rise in

$$\frac{\partial U^i(t+k)}{\partial P^i(t+k)}$$

that comes as a result of condition (6a'').

But let us now examine demand curve no. 5 and consumption $a^i(t+k)^6$ under the original, optimal price conditions. Obviously, the late time period equality is satisfied with demand curve no. 5 and consumption $a^i(t+k)^6$ for $\pi^i_a(t+k)^O$. What would be the case for the early period equality, condition (6.5)?

Since we are operating with the same demand curve, no. 5, as is assumed to be optimal under the new set of actual relative prices for $a(t+k)$ and $z(t+k)$, the declines in

$$\frac{\partial U^i(t)}{\partial y^i(t)} \quad \text{and} \quad \frac{\partial S^i(t+k)}{\partial y^i(t)} \quad \text{and rises in} \quad \frac{\partial U^i(t)}{\partial x^i(t)} \quad \text{and} \quad \frac{\partial P^i(t+k)}{\partial x^i(t)}$$

must be the same as they were in the analysis above. But with

$$\frac{z^i(t+k)^6}{a^i(t+k)^6} > \frac{z^i(t+k)^5}{a^i(t+k)^5}$$

the rise in

$$\frac{\partial U^i(t+k)}{\partial S^i(t+k)}$$

must be greater with consumption bundle 6 than with consumption bundle 5, and similarly the decline in

176

$$\frac{\partial U^i(t+k)}{\partial P^i(t+k)}$$

must be greater with consumption bundle 6 than with consumption bundle 5. So if demand curve no. 5 and consumption bundle 5 left condition (6.5) an equality, as we have assumed, then instead of yielding equality, evaluating the same expression at demand curve no. 5 and consumption bundle 6 would yield:

$$\frac{\pi_x^i(t)}{\pi_y^i(t)} > \frac{\dfrac{\partial U^i(t)}{\partial x^i(t)} + \sum_k \left\{ \dfrac{\partial U^i(t+k)}{\partial P^i(t+k)} \dfrac{\partial P^i(t+k)}{\partial x^i(t)} \right\}}{\dfrac{\partial U^i(t)}{\partial y^i(t)} + \sum_k \left\{ \dfrac{\partial U^i(t+k)}{\partial S^i(t+k)} \dfrac{\partial S^i(t+k)}{\partial y^i(t)} \right\}} \qquad (6.5')$$

To move back to the equality of condition (6.5) from the inequality of condition (6.5'), individual i would have to reduce the amount of $x^i(t)$ consumed and increase the amount of $y^i(t)$ consumed. But this shift necessarily decreases the ratio

$$\frac{P^i(t+k)}{S^i(t+k)}$$

even further than was the case that produced demand curve no. 5 and would shift us to an even higher demand curve for $a(t+k)$ and an even lower demand curve for $z(t+k)$ than we had at the outset under option 5.

In other words, assuming that option 5 was optimal for the new set of relative prices and analyzing what the situation would be under demand curve no. 5 and consumption bundle 6 yields the conclusion that one would have to move even further out to the right in our diagram (Fig. 6.3) in search of the maximizing individual demand curve for $a(t+k)$ if our consumer were to again face the optimal price ratios.

But this is the opposite direction from moving from demand curve no. 5 back toward demand curve no. 1, which we assumed was optimal for the old price ratios in the first place. Hence the assumption that option 5 is optimal for the new price ratios has yielded the conclusion that the original optimal demand curves were not optimal for the old price ratios. Since the old demand curves were stipulated as optimal, this is a contradiction and establishes the fact that option 5 cannot be an individual maximizing strategy under the new price ratios for $a(t+k)$ and $z(t+k)$.

Taken together, our demonstrations that

1. Option 1—in which the individual shifts the personal demand curve for good a downward (and for good z upward) and reduces (increases)

individual consumption of good a (z) by an even greater amount than neoclassical theory predicts—is compatible with the maximization of individual well-being under the new actual relative prices, and

2. Options 2 through 5 are not maximizing adjustments to a shift in relative prices from what we have called the optimal ratio of the prices of good z and good a in period $(t + k)$ to the actual, (biased) price ratio for these goods in period $(t + k)$,

complete our proof that option 1 is, in fact, what must take place under the assumption of endogenous preferences and rational behavior on the part of individual i. What remains, in order to finalize our proof of Theorem 6.6, is to extend our conclusion from a typical individual, i, to all individuals in the economy in order to examine the aggregate trends in demand, prices, and productions for $x(t)$, $y(t)$, $z(t + k)$, and $a(t + k)$.

To summarize, we have found: If individual i is charged the optimal price for $a(t + k)$ he or she will consume an amount equal to $a^i(t + k)^O$. If i's preferences were exogenous, as neoclassical theory *presumes*, he or she would respond to an overcharge for $a(t + k)$ by moving back up the individual demand curve and consuming a lesser amount, $a^i(t + k)^{NC}$. But we have proved that if i's preferences are endogenous, the individual maximizing strategy is to shift the individual demand curve for $a(t + k)$ back to the left and move back up this lower demand curve consuming a still smaller amount, $a^i(t + k)^2$. Summing over all individuals to derive market demands yields:

$$\sum_i a^i(t + k)^O > \sum_i a^i(t + k)^{NC} > \sum_i a^i(t + k)^2 = \sum_i a^i(t + k)^A$$

and analogously

$$\sum_i z^i(t + k)^O < \sum_i z^i(t + k)^{NC} < \sum_i z^i(t + k)^2 = \sum_i z^i(t + k)^A$$

where we have now indicated that $a^i(t + k)^2 = a^i(t + k)^A$, the actual demand i will exhibit when faced with the biased price $\pi_A^i(t+k)^A$ if i maximizes and analogously for z.

Since we have assumed the economy responds to market demands, the ratios of productions for $a(t + k)$ and $z(t + k)$ will satisfy

$$\frac{z(t + k)^A}{a(t + k)^A} > \frac{z(t + k)^{NC}}{a(t + k)^{NC}} > \frac{z(t + k)^O}{a(t + k)^O}$$

since the actual market demand for $a(t + k)$ under endogenous preferences will be lower than predicted by traditional theory—and the actual market demand for $z(t + k)$ will be greater. Which finally establishes the first part of Theorem 6.6: the degree of divergence from optimality as measured by divergence of relative supplies from the optimal production program will be greater than indicated by neoclassical welfare theory.

That the degree of divergence from the optimal supply program will snowball as time goes on follows directly from the fact that the more time periods one allows people to "develop" their preferences in response to overcharges, the more people will shift their demand curves down for the items for which they are overcharged relative to the items for which they are not overcharged. More precisely, under the optimal adjustment we found

$$\left\{\frac{\partial U^i(t+k)^A}{\partial P^i(t+k)^A}\right\} \bigg/ \left\{\frac{\partial U^i(t+k)^A}{\partial S^i(t+k)^A}\right\} > \left\{\frac{\partial U^i(t+k)^O}{\partial P^i(t+k)^O}\right\} \bigg/ \left\{\frac{\partial U^i(t+k)^O}{\partial S^i(t+k)^O}\right\}$$

which is what made the right side of the expression in condition (6.5) larger than the left side until individual i increases consumption of $x(t)$ and diminishes consumption of $y(t)$. But the more time periods there are, the more terms there are under the summation sign in condition (6.5), and hence the need for ever larger adjustments in $x(t)/y(t)$.

In period 2, only $k=1$ is operative under the summation sign, but in period 3, $k=1$ and $k=2$ appear, etc. This establishes the second part of Theorem 6.6, namely that not only will divergence exist, but it will snowball, as k increases, or as time goes on, since ever greater adjustments in $x(t)/y(t)$ for larger k imply ever greater changes in $P(t+k)/S(t+k)$, which yield ever greater shifts in demand curves for $a(t+k)$ and $z(t+k)$, and hence, ever greater divergences in $z(t+k)/a(t+k)$ from optimal proportions as k increases.

Theorem 6.7, Proof. The proof of Theorem 6.7 is now trivial. First, we remember what Theorem 6.7 says: in an economy that contains a bias in the relative terms of supply of two economic activities: (1) individuals' human development patterns will be "warped" in a manner that can be precisely defined, and (2) warped human characteristics will "snowball" over time.

The first part of Theorem 6.7 follows from

$$\frac{P^i(t+k)^A}{S^i(t+k)^A} > \frac{P^i(t+k)^O}{S^i(t+k)^O}$$

which also defines "warped" human characteristics as distinct from "optimal" human characteristics.

The second part of Theorem 6.7 was established previously as well. In the last paragraph of the preceding section the argument establishing that the degree of nonoptimality in allocations must snowball over time also demonstrated that the degree of warping of individual human characteristics must snowball over time.

Theorem 6.8, Proof. The task of proving Theorem 6.8 is equally simple. Theorem 6.8 says: the full effects of the bias in the economy addressed in Theorems 6.6 and 6.7 will be disguised to participants in the economy and to analysts who view preferences as exogenous.

As we demonstrated above, neoclassical welfare theory, because it adopts an exogenous view of preferences, fails to perceive the full effects of a bias in the economy. If participants in the economy either adjust their preferences unconsciously, and/or forget that they have done so after the fact and judge satisfaction at any time only in terms of their instantaneous preferences, they will suffer under the same delusion that plagues traditional welfare theorists. If participants do not envision, or forget there were alternative development trajectories and the alternative preferences they would have generated, they will underestimate the loss of potential well-being resulting from the bias in the economy in conjunction with their individually rational responses to that bias.

Logic and Implications of Theorems 6.6, 6.7, and 6.8. The logic of the above proofs and extrapolation to broader implications is straightforward. With perfect foresight individuals will see the bias in the relative conditions of availability of activities they will face in the future. Recognizing the possibility to manipulate their preferences away from desiring activities for which they will be overcharged and toward activities for which they will not be overcharged, rational individuals will take into account "preference development" as well as "preference fulfillment" effects of present activity choices. By doing so they select present activities that tend to generate future human characteristics that in turn support instantaneous future preference structures that permit them to attain greater future satisfaction than had they not "adjusted" their human characteristic trajectories.

But the effect of all individuals making these adjustments is to shift the future market demand curve downward for activities for which individuals are overcharged. When faced with a higher price, rational individuals will lower the quantity demanded to some extent simply by moving along their initial demand curve.[33] But when afforded the opportunity to shift their future demand curve as well, rational individuals with endogenous preferences will avail themselves of a second means of adjusting to new conditions of availability.

In an economy in which production responds to market demand, this implies the production of goods for which individuals are overcharged will be even less than had individuals not adjusted their preferences. As a result the misallocation, which would have occurred in any event due to the overcharge, is aggravated by the process of rational individual adjustment.

People "mold" themselves to better cope with a bias in the economy, but the collective result is to move society farther away from the optimal production program than it would have been had people not engaged in individually rational preference adjustments.

Economists have long been intrigued by the question of whether or not "individual rationality" in particular circumstances coincides with "social rationality" formulated as Pareto optimal outcomes. Adam Smith believed he had identified an "invisible hand" in the competitive market mechanism. E. K. Hunt found an "invisible foot" in the same institution. Traditional theorists claim private production for profit guarantees technical efficiency, whereas adherents of the "conflict school" argue private profits conflict with the social goal of technical efficiency. We will continue to explore these and others claims and counterclaims regarding the coincidence of individual rationality and social rationality in part 3. But it bears noting here that theorems 6.6, 6.7, and 6.8 pose another example of a conflict between individual and social rationality, different from all others we will treat: in any circumstances in which a bias exists in the conditions of availability of different economic activities, if people's preferences are endogenous individually rational "preference development" works at counter purposes to social rationality.

It is appropriate to call the individual adjustment process "self-warping" even though we recognize it to be individually "rational." While any individual who does not make preference adjustments to economy biases is irrational in the sense of failing to maximize personal well-being under the specific circumstances faced, the adjustments are self-warping in the sense that they diverge from the optimal human development trajectory.

The conclusion that the divergence from the optimal production program and "rational self-warping" "snowball" over time follows directly. The more time people have to adjust, the greater their adjustments will be. When we increase t by one period, we add one more period during which individuals can engage in activities that have "preference development effects," thereby increasing the degree to which they will adjust their demands.

That the "snowballing" nonoptimality may become disguised to those whose actions produce it, results from the fact that people's actual, perceived preferences in later time periods do not highly value what is undersupplied and instead emphasize what is relatively plentiful. In other words, things look good from inside the system because people are getting what they want according to their instantaneous preference orderings. So to the extent that preference development is an unconscious reaction, or that people forget what they did to arrive at instantaneous preferences conforming to economic conditions, the inefficiencies in the economy can become invisible to its inhabitants. Moreover, things look just as good to any outside analyst who bases judgments on those same instantaneous preferences and, of course, this is just what traditional welfare theorists do by treating preferences as exogenous. Unfortunately, the rosy neoclassical picture is a deception that hides losses of potential satisfaction from all who fail to recognize that participants' preferences are endogenous, as Theorem 6.6 demonstrates.

Finally, we point out we did not assume that the good for which individuals were overcharged had any developmental effects itself.[34] In other words, good "a" was not assumed to be a good like "x" or "y." It would not appear implausible to conjecture that the consumption of goods in early time periods would develop preferences for those same goods in later time periods, so that "a-type" goods would also be "y-type goods," and "z-type" goods would also be "x-type" goods. In this case the snow-balling nonoptimality would obviously be even greater.

Conclusion. So what is the answer? Do endogenous preferences "matter" in a substantive rather than technical sense? The answer is: yes, they do matter in ways that are by no means only technical and of interest only to economic theorists. But they do not matter in the way previous critics suspected.

Any economy that contains no bias in the conditions upon which it makes different economic activities available to its inhabitants will generate socially efficient outcomes if people's preferences are endogenous—just as it would if people's preferences were exogenous (Theorem 6.4). Moreover, if the economy was "flexible" regarding equity under the assumption of exogenous preferences, it will remain so under the assumption of endogenous preferences (Theorem 6.5).[35] Concerns to the contrary are ill-founded.

But this does not mean endogenous preferences are of no consequence to welfare theory. To the extent preferences are endogenous, any economy that contains a bias in the conditions upon which it makes different economic activities available to its inhabitants will generate a greater degree of inefficiency than supposed under the assumption of exogenous preferences. Moreover, this greater than previously recognized inefficiency will snowball over time (Theorem 6.6). Thus, analysis of the effects of endogenous preferences reveals an entirely new way in which "individual rationality" can be counterproductive to "social rationality." In any circumstances in which a bias exists, rational individual adjustment to the bias will rebound to aggravate the bias and result in ever-increasing losses of potential well-being. In these circumstances, individually rational adjustment is actually "self-warping" because it results in losses of potential individual well-being and greater social inefficiency than would have obtained otherwise (Theorem 6.7). But the very process of individually rational adjustment, or self-warping, may be socially stabilizing if it is unconscious or forgotten, since in this case it disguises any bias in the economy from the system's inhabitants who only come to see themselves getting what they want (Theorem 6.8).

Moreover, endogenous preferences "matter" to positive economic theory as well. The logic of individually rational preference development provides a mechanism by which characteristics of an economic institutional "boundary" influence the "human center" it "surrounds." In this capacity, endogenous preferences are the conceptual key to developing a rigorous "qualitative" economic theory capable of explaining outcomes hitherto taken as given. Our treatment reveals an important mechanism whereby characteristics of the human center are brought into conformity with characteristics of the institutional boundary, the process we call "rational self-warping."

In the broader sense, endogenous preferences are a critical concept to treating what sociological theorists have called the "structure agent dichotomy." What is the relationship between social structures and individual agents within them? Should "agents" or "structures" be taken as primary? By adopting an "either/or" answer to this question sociologists have frequently divided into conflicting schools, in our view unnecessarily. Our treatment of endogenous preferences in this book is fully consistent with the views so eloquently expressed by Anthony Giddens on this subject: neither individual agents nor social structures can be taken as primary for all purposes. We have just demonstrated how economic "structures," by creating a bias in the conditions of relative supply, can lead individual agents to "self-warp" their characteristic development trajectory precisely through rational individual action. Moreover, the effect of agents doing so aggravates the institutional bias. Each has molded the other. Each exists only in the context of the other.

Regarding history in the larger sense one might pose two different research paradigms: (1) conceive of history as the result of placing people in some sort of "original position"—which presumably would be more Nozickian than Rawlsian—in which they agree to an initial set of institutional structures and analyze the "predictable" consequences that would unfold from there; (2) start from a given set of institutional structures and individual characteristics that are presumed to correspond roughly to actual historical conditions somewhere at some point, and from there analyze the "predictable" consequences that would unfold. Only the first research paradigm could be said to treat individual "agents" as primary. Since this first research paradigm seems patently ridiculous to us, we prefer Giddens conceptualization and think endogenous preferences has much to contribute.

What is most noteworthy about the above theorems from a welfare theoretic perspective is they do not assume anything in particular about what are more or less desirable human characteristics or what preference structures are more or less capable of yielding fulfillment. Of course, we have not yet proved anything with respect to particular institutional structures, but in part 3 we will show that even without judging any one set of characteristics and preferences better than another, one can derive interesting critical results regarding all major, known economic institutions. In this sense, what we have just demonstrated and much of what we will demonstrate in the remainder of this book follows the usual economic tradition of avoiding unresolved philosophical debates.

Even though a well-executed "end run" can be aesthetically pleasing, there is something disturbing about always shying away from a "plunge up the middle." As soon as it becomes apparent that economic institutions affect the pattern of human development, is it not clear we must eventually grapple with the difficult question of what kind of people we would like to become? Of course, it is possible to take the ostrich approach and ignore the issue from fear that it is intractible—as traditional theory has long done. Or we can fashion an end run around judging human development trajectories much as flexibility theorems permit an end run around controversial equity issues—as we have begun to elaborate and will complete in part 3.

Since we find this evasive strategy only partially satisfying, we favor a "two-pronged" welfare theory. Having put together the blocking patterns (Theorems 6.1 through 6.8) for an end run to be "executed" in part 3, we now turn to developing blocking patterns for a plunge up the middle. What are the thorny problems in judging human development trajectories? What different approaches are possible? What lessons are to be learned?

6.3 Evaluating Human Development

As we have begun to see, it is possible to derive powerful critical theorems without making value judgments about different human development paths. But we do not believe it is wise to make what are some of our most important evaluations without facing this issue. Yet where does one turn to find out what personality traits, skills, consciousness, and group relations are more desirable and which are less desirable? What constitutes relevant evidence in a debate over the relative merits of different characteristics? While we have argued it is no longer legitimate for economists concerned with welfare theory to avoid these questions, we by no means deny that complicated philosophical, moral, and political issues are involved. Moreover, the form in which different answers have been justified has varied greatly.

In any case, concluding that some human development trajectories are better than others is certainly problematic, so it would be of interest if a particular conclusion could be justified by more than one plausible reasoning process. Below we concentrate on what we consider the most direct approach to judging development trajectories, but also outline alternative approaches that lead to similar conclusions.

6.3.1 Development Patterns and Human Nature

An approach to evaluating human development emerges quite naturally from the paradigm we described in the previous chapter. In that chapter we presented a theory of derived human characteristics and needs that emerged from the interaction of innate natural and species needs and powers with the natural, built, and institutional environments. To argue that some set of derived human characteristics was more compatible than others with the potentials defined by our natural and species needs and powers would provide a powerful justification for that path on the grounds that those characteristics and the needs they define would provide for greater human fulfillment than any other set of characteristics and derived needs could.

In other words, different sets of economic institutions can more or less adequately express our species characteristics and thereby generate greater or lesser fulfillment. For purposes of welfare economics, the characteristics we identify as most integrally linked with human nature are self-management, solidarity, and variety. Derivative developmental criteria are straightforward: if economic institutions foster the development of self-management, solidarity, and variety in the human center, they receive "high marks," just as institutions efficiently fulfilling manifest preferences do. If economic institutions obstruct the development of self-management, solidarity, and variety in the human center, we deem those institutions flawed, just as institutions that fail to yield "static" efficiency are deemed flawed by traditional theory.

What remains, given this approach, is to define and justify each of these characteristics and relate it to our view of human nature. Self-management and solidarity are obviously related to the two aspects of human nature we identified in the previous chapter, consciousness and sociability. After discussing these attributes, we present a compatible argument for "variety" based on the complexity and breadth of human nature as well as critical human limitations.

Self-management. By self-management we mean having decision-making input in the proportion that one is affected by the outcome of a decision. Our first evaluative criteria regarding derived human characteristics is that

185

economic institutions that promote individual's desires for and capacities to engage in self-management are deemed more desirable than those that do not, ceteris paribus. To explain the uniqueness of this definition of self-management before relating it to human nature, we should distinguish it from two more common notions: individual freedom and democratic choice.

The concept of individual freedom that Locke made a cornerstone of "classical liberalism" champions the right of individuals to do as they please. Of course this "vision" of liberty was refined by the stipulation that individuals should be free to do as they please as long as this does not infringe on the freedom of others to do likewise.[36] It is crucial to note that the concept as defined may or may not be operational. Whether or not one can apply the concept as an evaluative criterion for ranking situations depends upon the social environment. For instance, if there are no instances in which person A may do as he or she pleases without preventing person B from doing likewise—and vice versa—the concept of individual freedom, at least as refined by Rawls, cannot be used to rank alternative situations. In this environment the concept is well defined but nonoperational. If, on the other hand, in all instances the "choice set" of person A is independent of the "choice set" of person B—and vice versa—the concept taken as an evaluative criterion is not only well defined, it is also operational. Granting either person A or B decision-making discretion over more elements in his or her individual choice set is preferred by the principle of individual liberty.

So what renders classical liberalism's concept of individual liberty more or less useful are the conditions of the social environment. Since we are not in the habit of commissioning factual scientific studies when dealing with lofty matters of principle like "liberty," this is where paradigms come in.[37] The paradigm behind classical liberalism is what permits one to presume that, in general, or to a great extent, or to a sufficient degree to render the concept frequently usable, individual choice sets are nonintersecting. For to the extent that they are intersecting one must either make judgments based on other criteria, or define rules of priority. Specifically the classical liberal paradigm armed all individuals with sufficient material "wherewithal" to do what they pleased and presumed that doing as one pleased entailed no particular implications for the "activity and possibility sets" of others except in cases such as murder or rape where rules of priorities of individual liberties were easy to justify. We emphasize that it was the classical liberal paradigm, an intellectual construct, that so armed people. Whether individuals were and are so armed with "sufficient material wherewithal" in actual societies is quite debatable.

In any case, it is useful to distinguish two factors when thinking of choices of economic activities. It has often been remarked that the Lockean paradigm envisions a society of independent farmers and artisans—or petty commodity producers—each possessed of necessary means of production. In this case, farmers are each presumed to possess sufficient land, and artisans each presumed to possess necessary tools, to make accessible to them all activities in their individual economic choice sets. In other words, in the Lockean paradigm, no one's choice of economic activity is limited by absence of sufficient material wherewithal. In terms of the qualitative model of economic activity described in chapter 5, values of all state variables, both material and human, are nonlimiting for everyone.[38]

In contrast, the Marxist paradigm presumes exactly the opposite: the great majority of people have their individual liberty severely constrained by lack of material wherewithal, and must submit entirely to the will of a small minority, who by exercising individual economic liberty over their "person and property" effectively abridge the individual liberty of everyone else. In other words, in contrast to the Lockean paradigm, the Marxist paradigm renders the concept of individual liberty inoperable unless clear rules of priority are defined. While Milton Friedman was not the first to clarify related priorities, he is the best-known modern exponent of the "conflict resolving rule" that individual freedom to dispose of one's legally possessed "wherewithal" as one sees fit is to take precedence over others' individual freedom to utilize their laboring capacities as they would choose. Of course, there is a more euphemistic way of stating the rule: everyone is to be granted complete individual liberty over both person and property. If this consigns most to exercising their freedom to "vote with their feet" between work sites defined by other people's property "rights"—so be it.

But there is a more subtle form of potential limitation. Even if the values of individuals' "state variables" are nonlimiting, my activity choice set can still depend on others' activities to provide necessary "input flows." Suppose person A prefers activities that are relatively self-sufficient—activities that require fewer inputs from others' activities—and person B prefers activities that are relatively less self-sufficient.[39] It will matter little to A what B does because A does not rely on B in order to do what A prefers to do. But the same does not hold for B. Apparently when A exercises individual liberty A infringes on B's individual liberty by effectively preventing B from doing what B would most like to do, whereas B is in no position to do likewise to A.[40]

The point is, to the extent technological possibilities include "divisions of labor," exercise of individual liberty by some can entail infringements of liberty for others—and this is totally distinct from the question of limitations due to lack of "material wherewithal." Moreover, if people have different preferences regarding activities ranked on a scale of "relative self-sufficiency," the exercise of individual liberty by all will result in some people infringing more on the individual liberty of others and other people being more infringed upon—in much the same way that differential owner-ship of material wherewithal grants some an edge in the struggle over whose individual liberties will be more or less infringed upon.

Whereas the Lockean and Marxist paradigms concentrate on the dis-tribution of "material wherewithal" among individuals—albeit with op-posite assumptions—the paradigm we developed in chapter 5 emphasized the view that the human world is social and that most economic activities have effects reaching beyond one or two individuals. For that reason in relatively few consequential economic decisions would self-management, as we define it, be achieved by someone exercising "individual freedom of choice," since this would allow that individual more decision-making power than effects warranted and deprive others who are also affected of any say in the matter whatsoever.

But just as there are relatively few matters where only one person is affected, there are also very few matters where all people are equally affected. Therefore, there are few economic decisions for which self-management can be achieved by simple democratic majority vote.

Most local work place decisions, such as what kind of new technology to install in a particular factory, affect workers in that factory more than far distant consumers, but affect the consumers to some extent, as well as workers in other factories that might be supplying inputs. In such a case, self-management would not exist if all had an equal say, but only if workers in the given factory had greater say but consumers and workers in other factories had some say. In conclusion, according to our proposed paradigm, self-management is seldom equivalent to either individual freedom or democratic majority vote. In rare cases it may coincide with one or the other but in most cases it will not, because in most cases the pattern of effects is more complex than the pattern of effects that would justify the common conceptions.

Now that the full implications of our definition of self-management and the paradigm that justifies its greater usefulness as an evaluative criterion than traditional alternatives are explicit, how can one justify it as an evaluative criterion based on a conception of human nature?

Though it is obvious that many humans have existed under conditions with few opportunities for self-management, it is our contention that just as denial of material means is inevitably in conflict with human "natural" needs for food, shelter, and clothing, denial of self-management oppor-tunities is inevitably in conflict with our "species" nature. The capacity to analyze and evaluate the consequences of our actions and choose among alternative actions based on analysis and evaluation in conjunction with the need to employ that capacity is what we have called "consciousness" and defined as a key component of human nature. Maximum development of the capacity and desire for self-management is nothing more than maximum development of the capacity to garner satisfaction from this innate human potential. Therefore, the greater the development of the capacity and desire for self-management in the human center, the better ceteris paribus. And if an economic institution enhances this human characteristic more than another does, it is deemed superior, ceteris paribus.

Solidarity. By solidarity we mean concern for the well-being of others and granting them equality of consideration in their endeavors. Regarding others with concern and respect has been formulated as a "golden rule" and "categorical imperative," so that outside the economics profession solidarity is widely held to be a powerful creator of well-being. Solidarity among family members, between members of the same tribe, or within an ethnic group frequently generate well-being far in excess of what we would imagine possible based on material resources alone. But in the traditional economic welfare paradigm, concern for others is defined as an "interpersonal externality"—a nasty sounding habit—and regarded as troublesome since it undermines fundamental welfare theorems for private enterprise market economies. How are we to interpret this strange schizophrenia between traditional morality and traditional economics?

Traditional morality holds we will all be better off if we treat each other decently—a remarkably simple and sensible proposition. Traditional economics holds that since we do not, we had better find economic institutions that do not rely on people doing so. Is it farfetched to imagine Adam Smith chuckling to himself somewhere between *The Theory of Moral Sentiments* and the *Wealth of Nations* over the cleverness of economic institutions he believed generated maximum human well-being when people continue to refuse to treat each other decently? Do economists tend to see their employment as contingent on the fact that the clergy have not completed their appointed task?

In our view, a great deal depends on whether one takes a static or dynamic view of human characteristics. If human characteristics are presumed exogenous to economic institutions, then the task is simply to find economic institutions that generate maximum well-being based on given human characteristics. Since we by no means deny that actual human characteristics are considerably lacking in solidarity, we cannot deny that choice of economic institutions must take this into account. Of course, the opposite holds as well. Unless one denies that actual human characteristics are totally lacking in solidarity, one cannot deny that choice of economic institutions should take this into account as well.

To put it in terms of a debate commonly heard in postcapitalist economies, to overestimate the degree of solidarity among the citizenry and reduce "material incentives" too severely, can lead to unacceptable losses in production and present well-being, not to speak of counterproductive political repercussions.[41] But another kind of "inefficiency" receives far less attention. To the extent any solidarity is present among the citizenry, to fail to "cash in" on the maximum well-being that could derive from this favorable circumstance by using economic institutions that are overly "egocentric" is no less "inefficient."[42]

This much would be true even if actual human characteristics were exogenous to the choice of economic institutions. But if more solidaritous human characteristics would make possible greater well-being than present characteristics allow, and if different sets of economic institutions have differential effects on the development of solidarity, this should be taken into account. In short, an endogenous view of human characteristics makes clear that it is also "inefficient" to fail to select economic mechanisms that develop solidarity among the citizenry, if, as we argue below, greater solidarity gives rise to greater possibilities of future well-being.

How specific economic institutions differ regarding their effect on the development of solidarity we leave to part 3. In this chapter we merely offer our own reasons for believing that the more solidarity present among the citizenry, the greater the possibilities are for well-being. Put differently, we now make our case for the wisdom of traditional morality.

In addition to consciousness, we identified sociability as a critical aspect of human nature. Our desires develop in communication with others and our needs are fulfilled in interaction with others. One of the strongest human drives is the neverending search for respect and esteem from others. All this is a consequence of our innate sociability. Because our lives are to a great extent joint endeavors, it makes sense we would seek the approval of others for our part in group efforts. Since many of our needs are best filled by what others do for/with us, it makes sense to want to be well regarded by others.

To put things in terms economists should readily understand, compare two different ways in which an individual can gain the esteem and respect of others. One way grants an individual status by elevating him or her above others, by positioning the person in a status hierarchy that is nothing more than a pyramidal system of relative rankings according to established criteria. For purposes of the present discussion, it doesn't matter what the particular criteria are. For one individual to gain esteem in this way it is necessary that at least one other—and usually many others—lose esteem. We have at best a zero-sum game, and most often a negative sum-game since losers in pyramidal hierarchies far outnumber winners.

The second way grants individuals respect and guarantees that others are concerned for their well-being out of group solidarity. Solidarity establishes a predisposition to consider others' needs as if they were one's own, and to recognize the value of others' diverse contributions to the group's social endeavors. Solidarity is a positive-sum game—or in the language of a different branch of economics, the development of greater levels of solidarity multiplies the possibilities of positive externalities.[43]

The difference is straightforward. Group characteristics that enhance the overall well-being that can result from a given set of scarce material resources are obviously advantageous. Other things equal, it would be inefficient not to maximize the development of such characteristics. Solidarity is one such group characteristic.

We have argued elsewhere that the belief that solidarity among people can be generated by eliminating the differences between the multitude of distinct "communities" that have developed through actual history and creating a single human "community" with a single shared culture is a tragic mistake.[44] The "dream" of a single "proletarian culture" that has influenced much of traditional "left" thinking is, in fact, a "nightmare" of an infantile "cultural playpen." But this is not an argument against the advantages of solidarity, it is an argument against a sadly mistaken strategy for creating solidarity. What we have championed in place of forced homogenization is the advantage of extending actual solidarity to a wider and wider range of communities. And in our view, this advantage stems from the fact that this is the only way to take fullest advantage of the potentials for well-being inherent in human sociability.

It is worth noting the very interesting relationship between solidarity and equality. Not only does solidarity mean equality of consideration for others, but in our view, a substantial equality of outcome is a precondition for generating solidarity. If material goods are generally scarce, then little solidarity can exist between people who have material abundance and people who lack the basics of life. If some people have considerable say over the decisions that affect their lives whereas others have little, it will be difficult to generate much solidarity between them. In general, to the extent that any of our human needs are unfulfillable for all, any great discrepancy of outcome that is persistent and uncompensated will diminish the possibilities of solidarity. Another way of putting it is that equality of consideration implies a commitment to rectify any social circumstances that lead to persistently unequal outcomes.

Those familiar with the nineteenth-century history of welfare economics will be quick to recognize the lineage of an "efficiency-based" justification for greater equality. Jeremy Bentham spawned a whole school of "radical utilitarians" who brandished the sword of "diminishing marginal utility of income" in the redistributive debates of their day. More recently John Rawls "deduced" his "difference, or maximin principle" as rational choice in "an original position" in which one could not know who one would turn out to be. Apparently the desire to justify greater equality of outcome on other than "simple, moralistic grounds" is powerful enough to span the centuries!

In any case, the power of Bentham's argument was supposedly undercut by strengthening the notion of the sanctity of the individual and foreswearing interpersonal utility comparisons.[45] Rawls' conclusion that "rationality" in the "original position" coincides with the maximin principle has been challenged by many as less compelling than the criterion of "maximizing expected utility." Most significantly, the latter criterion does not yield egalitarian conclusions. Not surprisingly, most economists side with Rawls' opponents in rejecting his "arbitrary assumption" of risk aversion, which is the crucial ingredient Rawls uses in cooking a more egalitarian stew.

We by no means accept the much touted virtues of foreswearing interpersonal utility comparisons as a compelling answer to Bentham's quite plausible contention. Nor do we reject Rawls' attitude toward rationality and risk aversion. But certainly, indirect justifications for greater equality are not overly popular these days. So, in the spirit of attempting to marshal abstract intellectual weaponry on the side of the forces of good, we offer yet another "efficiency based" justification for greater equality. The argument implicit above is that greater solidarity is efficient, and greater equality is a precondition for greater solidarity. Whether this argument will prove as provocative but less ill-fated than those of Bentham and Rawls is dubious since in the end, opinions are most often formed—as they should be—in "simple moralistic terms."[46]

Variety. Our last "developmental criterion" is variety. Development of a greater variety of human characteristics is better than a greater uniformity of traits, ceteris paribus. The argument is based on the breadth of human potentials, the multiplicity of human natural and species needs and powers, the "fact" that people are neither omniscient nor immortal, and the laws of "sound" ecology.

First of all, people are very different. Constraints on the degree of our genetic differences make us all members of the human species, but this does not mean there are not differences between people's genetic endowments, nor does it preclude the view that the best trajectory of human development for different people is different. Robert Nozick makes the point graphically:

> Wittgenstein, Elizabeth Taylor, Bertrand Russell, Thomas Merton, Yogi
> Berra, Allen Ginsburg, Harry Wolfson, Thoreau, Casey Stengel, the

Lubavitcher Rebbe, Picasso, Moses, Einstein, Hugh Heffner, Socrates, Henry Ford, Lenny Bruce, Baba Ram Dass, Ghandi, Sir Edmund Hillary, Raymond Lubitz, Buddha, Frank Sinatra, Columbus, Freud, Norman Mailer, Ayn Rand, Baron Rothschild, Ted Williams, Thomas Edison, H. L. Mencken, Thomas Jefferson, Ralph Ellison, Bobby Fisher, Emma Goldman, Peter Kropotkin, you, and your parents. Is there really any one kind of life which is best for each of these people?[47]

Second, we are each individually too complex to achieve our greatest fulfillment through relatively few activities. Even if every individual were a genetic carbon copy of every other, the complexity of this single human entity, the multiplicity of potential needs and capacities would require a great variety of different human activities to achieve maximum fulfillment. To generate this variety of activities would in turn require a rich variety of social roles even in a society of genetic clones. And with a variety of social roles we would discover that even genetic clones develop quite different derived human characteristics.[48]

At this point it bears pointing out that variety of human development is not intrinsically at odds with solidarity and equality of outcomes. To those who think it is let us point out:

1. Even in a society where everyone had the same human characteristics nothing precludes granting differential material reward and status on completely trivial bases. Remember, we live in a society where skin color still explains differences in income better than most "meaningful" traits.

2. Even if people have very different human characteristics—personality traits, skills, knowledge, and values—it is possible to give them all equivalent material reward, decision-making authority in proportion as they are affected, and respect and esteem for the part they play in society's joint endeavor. Thus, "meaningful" differences between people do not have to become the basis for differential material reward, unequal decision-making authority, and hierarchies of status. That presumed "meaningful differences" can serve as the basis for differential treatment is obvious. But the critical point is whether or not one believes the allocation of material reward, decision-making authority, and status is socially determined. The paradigm we champion clearly views them as such.

All of the above is a "positive" argument for variety of human development. Recognizing our lack of omniscience provides a "negative" argument in the way we hedge our bets. No individual can know for sure which development path will be most suitable for him or her, nor can any group or society be certain which development path is best. Of course, the whole logic of our evaluative theory presumes that we can come up with some sufficiently educated guesses so that acting on them is more likely to produce fulfilling results than pretending that all development paths are equally likely to prove fulfilling. But, ultimately, we must agree with John Stuart Mill that it is particularly important for human societies to exercise caution in this regard and admit the strong likelihood of majority fallibility.

This does not mean minority views concerning preferable development paths should be enforced on an unwilling majority. But it does imply that whenever possible, minority views concerning development should be enacted in parallel with majority choices by the minority believers themselves. In other words, since none of us can be perfectly sure about the best life for ourselves, it is in all our interests to encourage others who have different opinions about "the good life" to pursue their ideas. With a variety of development strategies the risk of continuing a nonoptimal trajectory is minimized to the extent that we seriously consider the lives of others.[49]

When we said mortality was an argument for variety we were not being facetious. Although each of us lives only one life, we are each able to enjoy the lives of many others vicariously. Without diverse human development, opportunities for vicarious enjoyment would be minimal. The greater the variety, the greater the possibilities of using our capacity to understand and appreciate the lives of others. Solidarity pays greater "dividends" in context of variety, and vice versa.

We close our argument regarding variety by noting that according to many analysts, "bad" ecological practice can usually be equated with an overabundance of uniformity in our environment. This is not the place to pursue the "laws" of ecology, but for now we can simply observe that if a variety of results is a requirement of ecological stability, this can best be achieved by a variety of human activities, which in turn implies a variety of human characteristics and derived needs.

6.3.2 *Alternative Approaches to Evaluating Human Development*

Prioritizing development of particular human characteristics on grounds they are capable of generating more satisfaction because they are most compatible with essential aspects of innate human potential is only one possible approach to evaluating human development. Though we find it most appealing, we outline three other approaches that have merits of their own and grow in interest to the extent one is troubled by potential stumbling blocks in the optimizing fulfillment of human nature scenario.

First, in the approach taken above we treated human nature as noncontradictory and identified specific aspects of human nature that we argued social institutions should develop. But what if different aspects of human nature are contradictory? Are there reasons to believe human nature is contradictory, and if so, how would that affect the evaluative methodology we have proposed?

One interpretation of the "laws of evolution" suggests that it is highly unlikely fundamental aspects of human nature are contradictory. The argument is straightforward: natural selection should not favor the development of contradictory attributes in a species. Evidence can be presented to the effect that "contradictory natures" are not to be found in other species, establishing a "presumption" of harmony within human nature until proven otherwise. This presumption then grants priority to alternative plausible explanations for apparent contradictions in human characteristics and/or behavior.

In other words, if we observe contradictory characteristics/behavior in people, we can propose two very different kinds of explanations. We can see contradictory characteristics/behavior as based in development of contradictory aspects of human nature itself. Or we can explain such outcomes as the result of contradictory social institutions that generate contradictory derived human characteristics and behavior, even though no contradictory elements underlie human nature itself. The above reading of the "laws of evolution" gives the benefit of the doubt to plausible explanations of the latter form.

But suppose one is dubious about this interpretation of evolution and/or the plausibility of explanations emphasizing "contradictory social institutions" in at least some cases of contradictory behavior? Certainly other social theories have found our view overly optimistic and have proceeded from the assumption of contradictory elements in human nature.[50] And, if other aspects of human nature were contradictory to any of the aspects we discussed, or if the elements we discussed proved contradictory among themselves, the evaluative approach we presented would no longer suffice. In and of itself, the above approach provides no basis for preferring a development trajectory that maximizes one aspect of human nature rather than (or at the expense of) another contradictory aspect of human nature.

Another possibility would give rise to similar problems with the approach we favor. Even if there are no contradictory aspects in human nature, suppose our genetic inheritance permits a relatively broad as opposed to narrow range of human potentials. We based our valuation of development effects of economic institutions on the criterion of their compatibility or noncompatibility with aspects of human nature. This presumes human nature is sufficiently specific that the range of human potentials permitted by our human genetic inheritance is sufficiently narrow to render such comparisons possible. In other words, in the approach presented above we not only based our evaluative criteria on an interpretation of human nature, we argued that institutions promoting the development of self-management, solidarity, and variety were uniquely compatible with human nature. What would be the effect on our theory if human nature were not so specific and if the range of human potentials was so broad that many quite different arrangements of institutional features were equally compatible with it?

We can summarize the implications of both possibilities together: if human nature should prove contradictory, then a trajectory that maximized development of one aspect of innate human potentials would necessarily fail to promote, and could quite possibly undermine, development of some other aspect of human nature. If human nature is sufficiently broad, a number of development trajectories could be equally compatible with human nature, or at least, could not be easily distinguished by the criterion of compatibility alone. In both cases the approach presented above would provide insufficient means to rank different derived human characteristics and the institutions that promote them.

We reiterate that in our opinion both logic and evidence point to a human nature that is essentially noncontradictory and sufficiently specific to permit important comparisons of social institutions based on developmental effects. Although we recognize that humans are unique among all species, we see no reason to believe the pressure of natural selection operated any differently with respect to us regarding the conformity of different aspects of our natures to one another. We are also aware of ample plausible explanations for contradictory and antisocial behavior based on incentives inherent in particular institutions that compel people to pursue fulfillment of intrinsically compatible needs in ways that nonetheless sacrifice satisfaction of some to the satisfaction of others and fulfill the needs of some members of society at the expense of leaving unmet the needs of other members.[51] And while we recognize that human nature is sufficiently broad to permit development of the diverse characters Nozick compiled to make his point above, we believe human nature is also sufficiently restrictive to permit us to draw important distinctions on developmental grounds.[52]

In sum, while the possibilities of contradictory human nature, or a human nature too broad to generate meaningful evaluative criteria, exist, we do not believe these possibilities are borne out. Therefore, we believe the evaluative approach presented above will hold up. But should we prove wrong in these judgments, what other approaches to evaluating human development are available, and what kinds of conclusions would they generate?

A Contractarian Approach. Should the criteria we have suggested prove insufficient, should more than one development path be compatible with human nature, or development paths be compatible with only part of human nature, we find the contractarian notion of choice in an "original position" with appropriately structured information a useful analytical concept. In fact, this philosophical concept seems far more appropriate and useful in this context than in the contexts in which it is usually applied.

When we criticized neoclassical theory for its failure to treat preferences as endogenous, we indicated that contractarians were not immune to such criticism, but deferred our explanation. The reason was the failure of contractarians to face the problem of endogenous preferences was less obvious because even modern contractarians have not formalized what they call the individual's "conception of the good" in mathematical terms. Since neoclassical theory has long been accustomed to treating preferences mathematically—whether as cardinal or ordinal utility functions, or preference orderings—it was much easier to formulate a criticism of the neoclassical treatment of preferences than a criticism of contractarians' treatment of the individual's "conception of the good." But now we can extend our critique to the modern contractarian form of traditional welfare theory and proceed to show how their concept of the original position can nevertheless be of use in the present context.

When modern contractarians use the concept of original position they begin by stipulating that every individual has his or her own "conception of the good." But accepting the idea that every individual has a personal conception of the good is not the same as refusing to ask where that conception came from and what might have influenced it. We have explained how not only political, cultural, and kinship institutions will have an effect on the individual's conception of the good, but economic institutions may have a strong effect as well. The crucial question we pose to modern contractarians is whether we are to presume that individuals behind the "veil of ignorance" realize that their very conceptions of the good will be so influenced, and, if so, how individuals behind the veil of ignorance take into account the effect of choice of economic and other institutions on the development of human characteristics and "conceptions of the good." In fact, modern contractarians fail to address this question, which leaves us no choice but to interpret their silence as indicative that they believe these effects are as unimportant as neoclassical theorists believe them to be.[53] Indeed, it was precisely for this reason we lumped modern contractarianism with neoclassical and classical utilitarianism as part of traditional welfare theory.[54]

In some readings, the aura of "value free objectivity" surrounding modern contractarianism is even greater than assumed by neoclassical theorists. We wish to point out that this is no more justified for contractarians than neoclassicals. Often, the original position is treated as a kind of vacuum. Contractarians admit that knowledge of general social laws is permitted behind the veil of ignorance, but this knowledge is portrayed as "objective," noncontroversial information. They imply no assumptions are made about what individual conceptions of the good are like. This is deception, though perhaps self-deception as well. In fact, what is permitted to pass through the veil of ignorance and enter the hallowed sanctum of the original position is the paradigm that underlies the theory. Once this is recognized, the question of "values" versus "objectivity" reduces to whether one accepts the paradigm as obvious and noncontroversial.

Our objection to modern contractarianism as it has been practiced is that it uncritically permits elements of the traditional welfare paradigm to enter the original position as "objective social law." There is no way market institutions can be "deduced" to satisfy the liberty and difference principles unless one has accepted as "objective social fact" the traditional paradigm's assumption of "external effect exceptionalism." And if market institutions affect people's conceptions of the good, then "deducing" market institutions from an original position implies a preference for some conceptions of the good over others. Or, put differently, if "individual's conceptions of the good" are recognized as endogenous to the choice of economic institutions, one cannot pretend to make no presumption about individual's conception of the good while deducing particular economic institutions as those that would be chosen freely by people in an original position. In other words, far from being a vacuum tainted only by "known truths," the veil of ignorance has been used to make the original position an anonymous repository for precisely the presumptions of the traditional welfare paradigm—certainly the most ideologically loaded and controversial part of the theory.

In sum, our criticism of modern contractarians is that they pretend to be "value free" when they are not; that they are seemingly unaware that many conclusions they reach can only be justified on the basis of crucial elements of the traditional welfare paradigm that are, in fact, quite controversial; and consequently that they fail to even treat the most important issues regarding choice of economic institutions. In particular, modern contractarians have permitted traditional presumptions of "external effect exceptionalism" and exogenous preferences inside the original position even while pretending that only noncontroversial social "truths" are permitted to penetrate what in this case is truly a veil of ignorance. The assumption of exogenous preferences is camouflaged but nonetheless present in the form of treating individual's conceptions of the good as if they were not affected by economic institutions.

Notice this is not a criticism of the new contractarian methodology, but a criticism of the application of that methodology to this point. Once we recognize that the veil of ignorance and original position are concepts that allow us to isolate our underlying paradigm to discover whatever conclusions may be deduced from assumptions inherent in that paradigm, we can apply those tools to investigate the hidden implications of other paradigms. And this is the role we now propose for the contractarian tools should contradictory or nonspecific human nature prove to be the case.

In short, what if we permit our paradigm to pass through the veil of ignorance and fill the original position? In that case, what those who must choose will "know" includes understanding that their choice of social (including economic) institutions will profoundly affect their "conceptions of the good," since it will affect the development of human characteristics upon which those conceptions are based. This implies the necessity of "choosing" among different development trajectories. If aspects of human nature prove contradictory, and different development paths enhance some aspects at the expense of others, those in the original position must choose which aspects they wish to favor. If many different development paths are equally compatible with human nature because human nature is insufficiently specific to provide evaluative criteria, again, those in the original position would have to decide which path they favor and base their choice of social institutions, at least in part, on whether or not those institutions propel human development in that direction or some other.

In our view the need for the additional theoretical "tools" the new contractarians afford us is minimal—choice within an original position surrounded by a veil of ignorance—assuming human nature is noncontradictory and sufficiently specific. But the contractarian methodology becomes more appealing in proportion to whatever weaknesses may develop in the human nature-based approach. How might it be applied?

What if people's acquisitive tendencies were the result of an "acquisitive instinct" that in some sense was part of our genetic endowment, as Veblen hypothesized? What if sociobiologists are right that we are aggressive, or seek to dominate others, "by nature" rather than by social conditioning? If the aspects of human nature we identified previously and the development characteristics of self-management, solidarity, and variety based upon them were no less part of our "species being," those in the original position would face an obvious dilemma. We would certainly want the veil of ignorance to function so as to allow them to be aware of their dilemma. If it should prove the case, the fact that our natures are to some extent contradictory should be permitted to pass through the veil of ignorance. And information concerning which aspects of human nature would be enhanced or retarded by particular social institutions would also be "legitimate" information we would wish to penetrate the veil of ignorance. Without this information, choice in the original position would not be "informed choice."

In this instance, the additional theoretical concepts provide a way to identify with great care what people need to know to make an informed choice about where they wish to go, and what we could not permit people to know if we want "unbiased" opinions. The new contractarian methodology does not permit me to know whether or not I would end up with a large or small "pile of possessions," if I voted for a path that developed our "acquisitive instincts." It forces me, if you will, to choose prior to knowing if I would be an aggressor or victim of aggression, a master or subordinate, if I vote for institutions that develop these potentials. If some aspects of human nature are contradictory, but development of some of those aspects implies "losers" as well as "winners," while development of other aspects implies aggregate benefits in which all receive positive allotments, a compelling criterion would appear to emerge from the structure of the new contractarian methodology.

Of course, some will object that the conclusion that self-management and solidarity would be favored over acquisitiveness, aggression, and mastery over others by vote in an original position is not a logical deduction but ultimately a statement of preference. And we do not really disagree. After all, it is at least possible to prefer a one-in-ten chance of riches or mastery accompanied by a nine-in-ten chance of poverty or subjugation to a guarantee of solidarity and self-management, assuming—against our interpretation of the evidence—that maximizing fulfillment of human nature is compatible with both paths.[55] The point here is similar to the objection raised to Rawls' "deduction" of the maximin principle by those who argue that maximizing expected utility would be preferred by those in an original position.

What about the possibility of different development trajectories equally compatible with human nature? Here as well, one reading of the "anonymity" restriction in the original position "deduces" a preference for trajectories where positive aggregate benefits are accompanied by positive individual benefits for all as opposed to trajectories where positive aggregate benefits may entail losses for some as well as benefits for others.[56] Such a reading would, in our opinion, endorse the characteristics we identify as self-management, solidarity, and diversity. Whether it would also endorse other characteristics that might be enhanced by alternative development trajectories equally compatible with human nature would, of course, depend on analysis of what those characteristics turned out to be. But as we pointed out previously, Nozick and others objected to this reading of the implications of anonymity in any case.

Even if one takes a non-risk averse or even risk-prone view, we believe the contractarian approach can improve the quality of debate. If, contrary to our judgment, a human nature-based approach is insufficient, at minimum a self-conscious contractarian approach that recognizes itself as a vehicle for isolating a particular paradigm that may contain controversial elements can elucidate matters. It can help clarify what is at stake when we surround ourselves with different institutional boundaries, and it can clarify the dilemma of people "choosing" among institutions when living under the influence of institutions that affect our preferences for what those institutions provide.

Conceiving of choice in an original position where no institutions influence our conceptions of the good is a way of reminding us that to evaluate whether institutions are giving us what we want or molding us to want what they give us, we must, in some sense, step outside our institutional environment and examine matters from a distance. Provided we remember not to unconsciously import the influence of our actual institutional environment through the veil of ignorance, the original position can provide the detachment necessary for meaningful evaluations of this kind. But should a contractarian methodology still prove insufficient to yield conclusive judgments, two other approaches can be brought to bear.

Species Survival and the Humanist Tradition. One could judge different developmental trajectories from the perspective of species survival in a nuclear age. In context of multiparty potentials to unleash mutual self-destruction, we could judge different development trajectories from the point of view of whether they are more or less likely to avoid this outcome. Obviously, institutions that enhance the spread of solidarity between groups that have historically viewed each other with suspicion and hostility would be regarded highly.[57]

Finally, if faced with more than one development trajectory believed to be equally compatible with human nature, equally likely to ensure species survival, and equally attractive to a faceless voter shrouded in an original position, we could grant such a voter a philosophical, moral, political, historical tradition. We could say one set of institutions may be chosen over another because it would be more likely to enhance human development trajectories more favored by such a tradition. In this vein we could say self-management, solidarity, and variety would be chosen in an original position by those who accept the values of a "humanist" tradition.

Indeed, in this section on judging human development patterns, we have tried to point out a variety of arguments that justify conclusions of the humanist tradition. After all, it need not be the case that evidence is equally compelling for all competing traditions. But, no doubt, as much as we have tried to argue that favoring a particular pattern of human development need not reduce to a simple leap of faith, there will be those who insist it does. For them, this section will be judged intellectual adornment for opinions already held. But even for those who view our arguments in this light, we hope they provide clarity about the kinds of approaches that can be taken to justify preferring one trajectory to another, and about what can render the different approaches compelling. In any case, for those who remain skeptical, we offer the theorems of this in subsequent chapters. The theorems presume no preferred trajectory.

6.3.3 Summary

While it is tempting to avoid arguing directly for the superiority of a particular human development trajectory, we have developed a "second track" to our welfare theory that does not duck this issue posed by an endogenous view of preferences. In fact, we have outlined more than one approach that can be used to establish the superiority of one set of characteristics over another. We presented our own approach based on human nature, and also considered approaches based on the new contractarian methodology, species survival in a nuclear age, and explicit adherence to the humanist tradition. Moreover, we have shown how each approach could be used to justify the characteristics of self-management, solidarity, and variety that form the basis for the "second track" to our evaluative methodology.

In part 3 we use both the theorems and the values of self-management, solidarity, and variety developed in this chapter to investigate the welfare attributes of the major economic institutions of our time—competitive markets, private and public enterprise, and central planning.

PART THREE

NEW RESULTS

7

MARKETS

NEVER BEFORE have so many voices shouted Adam Smith's rallying cry of laissez-faire. Never before have those aware of the liabilities of markets been so silent.

Keynesian macroeconomists who sought to improve upon free market outcomes have been sent packing in one Western economy after another, often confessing the sins of their meddling ways. Occupational health and safety economists have been stampeded by the free market juggernaut of compensating wage differentials. The notion of "comparable worth" has become almost unspeakable among economists now that we have been duly reminded that what labor markets do is precisely establish the comparable worth of different labor inputs in the only feasible way.

But most surprisingly—and to the great delight of Western economists, politicians, and journalists—even "socialist" economists are rallying to the free market bandwagon. No longer are Yugoslavs and Hungarians the only Marxists in postcapitalist economies singing in praise of markets. In China, Vietnam, and even the Soviet Union, it must appear to old-timers that the "spectre of markets" is haunting Communism! While among Western socialist scholars, proponents of planning such as Ernest Mandel are on the defensive against those such as Alec Nove who champion markets in their vision of a "feasible socialism."[1]

In sum, the view of markets as cybernetic miracles, essential to providing strong economic incentives, socially efficient allocations, and necessary bulwarks for the preservation of freedom, has been restored with a vengeance. It is in this context of a worldwide, free market jubilee that we deploy our new welfare theory to reevaluate the most hallowed of economic institutions.

Our results prove considerably more critical than the findings of traditional theory, which, in turn, are modest compared to present-day euphoria. What distinguishes our critique—beyond the fact that we dare object at all in today's highly charged atmosphere—is that it rests on problems seldom emphasized by those who previously counseled that markets should be approached with caution.

Most previous critics concerned themselves with problems of adjustment dynamics and noncompetitive structures. Until recently this lead to a kind of implicit truce between market defenders and critics; critics conceded the wonders of markets' cybernetic, incentive, and efficiency properties but only under competitive equilibrium assumptions. Defenders conceded there would be efficiency problems should structures prove noncompetitive and equilibration prove slow.[2]

Recently, defenders of unbridled markets broke the traditional truce by suggesting that government remedies for noncompetitive structures and slow equilibration were worse than the maladies themselves. The intuitions and historical assessments of free marketeers were converted into a kind of "impossibility theorem": no conceivable form of government interference can improve upon free market allocation whatever its faults may be. The rout was on when the "impossibility theorem" was replaced by a "perfection theorem": not only is it "impossible" for governments to improve on market allocation, so-called "market imperfections" and "nonequilibrium adjustments" are, in fact, mechanisms for achieving dynamic efficiency by continually selecting decision makers who prove themselves best at estimating consequences and assessing uncertainty.[3]

In other words, the new wave of free marketeers came to the conclusion that concessions previously granted traditional critics of markets were unwarranted. It was only the "comparative statics" model that gave the appearance that nonatomistic markets and nonequilibrium adjustments were inefficient. According to the "perfection theorem," a dynamic model with uncertainty would reveal that what had been conceded as market liabilities are actually market assets.

While we will concern ourselves with the information, incentive, and efficiency properties of markets, we do not wish to redebate the issues of noncompetitive structures and adjustment dynamics. We leave aside whether "Keynesian" stabilization policies can improve upon free market business cycles; indicative planning can ameliorate "bottle-neck" and "surplus" sectors; and development planning can improve prospects of less developed economies, or more developed economies for that matter. Similarly, we sidestep uncertainty by granting the perfect knowledge assumption.

But we do all this not because we believe there are no problems with markets in these areas central to the traditional debate, but because we wish to focus on what have been presumed to be markets' greatest strengths—their cybernetic, incentive, and efficiency properties under competitive structures and equilibrium conditions. In other words, we wish to re-examine the properties of markets in the most favorable settings imaginable.

7.1 Laying Old Debates to Rest

Before treating markets per se, we seek to alleviate confusion concerning certain claims that, in our view, stem from ideological bias. Some opponents of public ownership argue that while competitive markets coupled with private ownership generate social efficiency, when coupled with public ownership they fail to do so. On the other hand, some opponents of private enterprise argue that while competitive markets coupled with private ownership necessarily generate unacceptably inegalitarian income distributions, socially wasteful business cycles, increasing industrial concentration with consequent inefficiencies, and a malady dubbed "commodity fetishism," when coupled with public ownership they become innocuous.

Of course, the properties and quality of economic systems depend on the interaction of all their important institutions. But we find no reason to deny that according to traditional welfare criteria public enterprise market economies have as much claim to social efficiency as private enterprise market economies. Nor do we see any reason to believe that substituting public for private enterprise will miraculously cleanse market economies of all the problems critics of capitalism have long dwelled on. Claims to the contrary have been used by ideologues for private and public enterprise in turn to avoid conclusions they find inconvenient. In either case, we are diverted from a "matter of fact" treatment of market institutions, and with that purpose in mind we seek to lay these "old debates" to rest before proceeding.

7.2 Misconceiving Public Enterprise Market Economies

It is helpful to differentiate between two different types of public enterprise market economies (PuEMEs).

1. Combining markets and public ownership with employee management yields an economic model used by many who have analyzed the Yugoslav economy since the early 1950s and championed by some who favor "workers' self-management," public enterprise, employee-managed, market economies (PuEEMMEs).

2. Combining markets with public ownership and state-appointed management yields a model similar to that used by Lenin and the Bolsheviks in

the Soviet Union as part of their New Economic Policy in the 1920s, analyzed by Oscar Lange, Frederick Taylor, and Abba Lerner theoretically in the 1930s,[4] and championed by economic "reformers" today in many postcapitalist economies, public enterprise, state-managed, market economies (PuESMMEs).

Proponents of private enterprise have based their argument against public ownership in part on grounds that neither version of public enterprise market economy permits markets to perform their efficiency function completely. According to this view, while replacing central planning with markets in public enterprise economies improves efficiency dramatically, retaining public ownership ensures that at least some inefficiency will remain. Put differently, many champions of private enterprise argue that while the second and third fundamental theorems of traditional welfare economics hold for private enterprise market economies, they do not hold for public enterprise market economies of either the employee-managed or the state-managed variety. First we present their argument. Then we explain why traditional welfare theory does not sustain their conclusion.

7.2.1 Employee-Managed Market Economies

A public enterprise, employee-managed, market economy (PuEEMME) is an economy in which publicly owned, employee-managed production units engage in free market exchange of goods and services with one another as well as with final consumers. Ownership is public in the sense that production units are legally owned by the whole nation and cannot be sold or shut down without permission of the state. Management is by employees in the sense that all decisions concerning enterprise functioning are ultimately controlled by a council of current employees in which each employee has one vote and majority decision rules. Of course, councils may form subcommittees or hire managers and supervisors to whom they delegate authority, but ultimately all committees and managers are answerable to the employees' council that may hire and fire them at will.

Goods exchanged on markets include consumer goods, intermediate goods, investment goods, and nonlabor primary factors. Terms of employment can be conceived in diverse ways, but it is convenient to assume that individual applicants and enterprise personnel departments negotiate wage rates and job descriptions, while implementation of agreements falls to whatever supervisory system is established by the workers' council. In a very real sense there is a labor market in PuEEMME since people are free to seek and leave employment whenever they choose, while enterprises are free to hire or fire whomever they like. But once hired, every employee is a member of the workers' council and, therefore, plays a "managerial" role as well. So while employees may receive differential wages (as negotiated with their personnel departments) they are all on equal footing as voters in the workers' council.[5]

Enterprises obtain revenues by selling outputs and incur costs by purchasing inputs. If they fail to attract sufficient revenues to cover contractual obligations, they must sell bonds to the public or obtain loans from publicly owned, employee-managed banks that accept deposits (paying interest) and make loans (charging interest). Money can never be raised by sale of stock because stockholding is not permitted in a public enterprise, employee-managed market economy. If enterprises' revenues exceed their contractual obligations, the workers' council is free to use the excess for investment in the enterprise, purchase of "collective" consumption goods for employees, payment of bonuses to employees, or saving, as it decides.

Birth and demise of enterprises is admittedly complicated in real world economies that pursue the model. But for theoretical purposes, it is easy enough to simply say that new enterprises are born when a group of workers declare themselves a new employee-managed enterprise and start selling something. The initial employees might come from other enterprises from which they resign, from among the unemployed, or from new entrants into the labor force. In the likely event that inputs needed in advance of initial sales cannot be entirely obtained on credit from their suppliers, "start up" loans would be required. While members of the initial group might provide part of the "start up" loan, this merely establishes a contractual obligation of the enterprise to them as creditors. It is as if an original employee purchased a bond from the new enterprise. Risk "capital" establishes neither ownership nor managerial prerogatives different from those of employees who arrive later.

Enterprises die by declaring bankruptcy, or by merging with some other employee-managed enterprise. When an enterprise goes bankrupt, its employees become unemployed and must seek employment with some other employee-managed enterprise, while its creditors recoup what they can just as they would from a private enterprise that went bankrupt. If two enterprises merge, all employees from both become full members on equal standing in the new enterprise's workers' council, and the assets and liabilities of both become the sum total assets and liabilities of the new enterprise.

Traditional Criticism of Employee-Managed Market Economies. Critics using traditional welfare theory have argued that employee-managed market economies are inherently less efficient than private enterprise market economies. But this charge is ill-founded. The claim is that PuEEMMEs do not achieve Pareto optimality in their general equilibria. Or, more specifically, that the second and third fundamental theorems of welfare economics do not hold for PuEEMMEs whereas they do for PrEMEs.[6]

Originally, Benjamin Ward and Evsey Domar based these conclusions on short-run, partial equilibrium models of PuEEMME in which labor is the sole input in production and workers' councils are assumed to attempt to maximize average income per employee.[7] Before criticizing their conclusions, we will extend them to a more general model.

We can create a "multiperiod" general equilibrium model of PuEEMME equivalent to the model of perfectly competitive capitalism developed by Gerard Debreu in chapter 6 of his *Theory of Value*, by substituting the assumption that enterprises maximize profits per employee for Debreu's assumption that enterprises maximize profits. Since conclusions that hold in short-run, partial equilibrium models do not always hold in multiperiod, general equilibrium settings, this strengthens the arguments of Domar, Ward, and others critical of PuEEMMEs.

Though the elasticities and even the signs of both individual firm and aggregate supply functions might change under the new assumptions, there is no reason to expect any change in the continuity (semi-continuity) properties of the supply functions (correspondences). Therefore, Debreu's conclusions about existence of general equilibria in perfectly competitive capitalism can be directly extended to a similar version of PuEEMME. But the traditional criticism of PuEEMME does not concern the existence of equilibria, but their lack of optimality.[8] That the second and third fundamental welfare theorems will not hold in a Debreuvian model of PuEEMME is readily apparent: since the number of firms in Debreuvian models is taken as given, there is no reason they should not have different levels of profits per employee.[9] But this implies the opportunity cost of labor will vary from firm to firm in a Debreuvian model of PuEEMME, because in such a model firms must pay each employee his or her share of the enterprise profits in addition to a market-determined wage. In loose terms, this implies that firms with higher than average profits per employee will underhire labor relative to nonlabor inputs compared to firms with lower than average profits per employee, which will overhire labor relative to nonlabor inputs. If firm i has higher profits per employee than firm j, and if L stands for a labor input, NL a nonlabor input, MP for marginal product of the nonlabor inputs, W for the wage, P for price, and $\$$ for the difference between total revenues and total costs, or profits, the first order conditions for the optimization problems of firms i and j, assuming both firms use total inputs,

$$\frac{MP_L^i}{MP_{NL}^i} = \frac{W + \left(\frac{\$}{L}\right)^i}{P_{NL}} \neq \frac{W + \left(\frac{\$}{L}\right)^j}{P_{NL}} = \frac{MP_L^j}{MP_{NL}^j}$$

Nonoptimality is immediate since the ratios of marginal products for two inputs are not equal for two PuEEMME enterprises using some of each with different levels of profits per employee. The outputs of both firms i and j could be increased by an appropriate transfer of labor from j to i and of the nonlabor input from i to j.[10]

A Poor Defense. In the late 1960s and early 1970s, Branko Horvat and Jan Vanek both defended PuEEMMEs from this criticism by challenging the assumption that workers' councils in PuEEMME would seek to maximize profits per worker.[11]

Horvat proposed instead that PuEEM firms would try to maximize $pq-[(d+\delta)x+cz+k]$, where p is the price of the firm's output, q is the amount of that output, "d is last year's or some standard personal income, delta a change, normally an addition to that income per worker to be achieved in the given year," x is the number of employees, c the price of nonlabor inputs, z the quantity of those inputs, and k any fixed costs.[12] Alternatively, Jan Vanek proposes a list of nineteen possible indices a PuEEM firm might be interested in furthering.[13]

If Horvat's criterion were accepted, then PuEEMMEs would achieve optimality, as he claims, since Horvat's necessary conditions for a PuEEM firm's maximization problem are precisely the same as those for privately owned firms. If, instead, PuEEM workers' councils attempt to balance a long list of goals, as Jan Vanek argues, then they do not attempt to maximize profits per employee, and the traditional "proof" of nonoptimality vanishes as well.

Both Horvat and Jan Vanek defended their hypotheses for PuEEMME firm decision-making criteria as better explanations for Yugoslav firms' actual behavior than the hypothesis of maximizing profits per employee, and evidence tends to suggest they might well be correct about the greater realism of their criteria as measured against Yugoslav practice, particularly since many of the perverse adjustment dynamics predicted by critics' modeling had not been observed. However, even if a different criterion than maximizing profits per employee proves a better approximation to actual Yugoslav behavior, this is irrelevant to the question of what rational behavior would require of the members of a workers' council in an idealized PuEEMME economy according to traditional welfare theory.

More recently, Horvat has attempted to defend the efficiency of PuEEMMEs by turning the tables on its critics. He points out that if PrEMEs were modeled under the assumption that capitalist enterprises attempted to maximize the *rate* of profit on invested capital rather than the magnitude of profits, we would obtain the same "equally absurd results" critics have proclaimed for PuEEMMEs.[14] While Horvat is correct in sensing a bias in neoclassicists' choice of models begging an explanation from the theory of the sociology of knowledge, his counterattack is wide of the mark again. The problem is simple. Under traditional assumptions of no external effects, fully compensating wage differentials, and perfect "capital" markets in which firms can borrow infinitely at a market rate of interest, maximization of stockholder well-being in PrEMEs translates into maximizing profits, whereas maximizing employee well-being in PuEEMMEs translates into maximizing profits per employee. Hence the criticisms originally formulated by Ward and Domar, which we confirmed in the more general "Debreuvian" model of PuEEMMEs, withstand the original and more recent rebuttals of Horvat and Jan Vanek.

A Better Defense. Jaroslav Vanek voiced a much better response to traditional criticisms of the efficiency properties of PuEEMME, but never proved his intuition. Jaroslav Vanek accepted that as seen from the traditional paradigm maximizing profits per employee is the rational criterion for employee-managed enterprises. But he hypothesized that "a multi-sectoral perfectly competitive general equilibrium of a pure labor-managed economy is Pareto optimal in the long-run provided that free entry is guaranteed."[15] In other words, the "problem" theoretically elaborated above is not in PuEEMME, but in the use of inappropriate models for analyzing the optimality properties of PuEEMMEs.

Both Ward and Domar's partial equilibrium models are short-run models where entry and exit do not equalize profits per employee. They are the PuEEMME analogues of short-run, partial equilibrium models of private enterprise market economies in which entry and exit have not had time to equalize the rate of profit between different firms and industries. In the Debreuvian model of PuEEMME we used above, the number of firms in the economy is a fixed datum. A firm is nothing more than its production possibility set. There are only so many of them, and even should the workers in one firm receive very high profits per employee, it is not possible for new enterprises to replicate their activities. It is the analogue of Debreuvian models of private enterprise market economies in which what are called different profit rates, but in fact are different quasi rents achieved due to unique technological possibilities, are not competed away.

In the case of private enterprise market economies, no damage was done to an analysis of social efficiency under the assumption of a fixed number of firms because the opportunity costs for all arguments in the production functions of all firms were the same regardless of the firms' "profit" positions. But in PuEEMMEs, the opportunity cost of labor inputs depends on the firm's rate of profit per employee, and in a model where the number of firms is fixed and, therefore, different rates of profit per employee will not be "competed away," the implications for misallocation of resources are evident.

The problem is not that the assumption of a fixed number of firms is any less realistic for PuEEMME than for private enterprise market economies, but that the simplifying assumption of a fixed number of firms is inappropriate for an analysis of the efficiency properties of PuEEMME, whereas, for very special reasons it was not inappropriate for a similar analysis of private enterprise market economies.

Thus Jaroslav Vanek was correct when he insisted that though PuEEMME must appear to be non-Pareto optimal in the simplified context of a fixed number of firms where there is no reason for profits per employee to equalize among firms, the same might not be true in models permitting free entry and exit of enterprises.

Unfortunately, at the time Jaroslav Vanek wrote, no one had developed a multisector, general equilibrium, multiperiod model of either PrEMEs or PuEEMMEs in which the number of firms in an industry is determined endogenously under the assumptions of free entry and exit. That is no longer the case since Dilip Madan, followed by William Novshek and Hugo Sonnenschein, have developed such a model for private enterprise market economies where the equilibrium number of firms in each industry as well as the uniform rate of profit in the economy are determined endogenously.[16] With such a model, it is finally possible to demonstrate Vanek's intuition rigorously. But since the adaptation of the Madan/Novshek/Sonnenschein model to PuEEMME is simple and straightforward, and since Vanek's conclusion is immediate once there is an equal rate of profit per employee for all firms—as there would be in the Madan/Novshek/Sonnenschein model of PuEEMME, just as there is an equal rate of profit for all firms in the Madan/Novshek/Sonnenschein model of PrEMEs—we leave it to the interested reader to reproduce Madan, Novshek, and Sonnenschein's work with the single modification that firms attempt to maximize profits per employee instead of profits.

7.2.2 *State-Managed Market Economies*

In the 1930s Oscar Lange, Frederick Taylor, and Abba Lerner all contributed to theorizing a model of public enterprise, state-managed, market economies (PuESMMEs), for the express purpose of refuting the traditional criticism that public enterprise economies could not be socially efficient. Since their economy was designed precisely for this purpose and literally incorporated necessary conditions for social efficiency from microeconomic texts as decision-making criteria, it is surprising they failed.

In some respects Lange, Taylor, and Lerner improved upon private enterprise market economies as "efficiency machines." By directing state-appointed enterprise managers to obey the rule, minimize the cost of producing any level of output always calculating the cost of inputs according to going market prices, the ability of PuESMME to achieve efficient allocations is unaffected by monopsonistic input markets.[17] By directing state-appointed managers to obey the rule, produce the level of output at which marginal cost is equal to market price, the ability of PuESMME to achieve efficient allocations is unaffected by monopolistic product markets.[18] In other words, PuESMME is socially efficient whether or not markets are competitive provided managers obey the above rules.

To those who reasoned managers would maximize profits rather than obey the rules whenever there was a discrepancy between the two courses of action, champions of PuESMME replied there was no reason for them to do so. First, enterprises in PuESMME do not retain any "profits" they generate. And second, since they were state appointed, presumably the state would fashion incentives for enterprise managers to reward rule-obeying behavior and punish profit-maximizing behavior in the event of discrepancies.

The creators of PuESMME also sought to improve upon the ability of real market economies to reach equilibria and, thereby, avoid the inefficiencies that nonequilibrium outcomes imply. In Lange, Taylor, and Lerner's economy a planning board manipulates prices to eliminate excess demands and supplies for intermediate goods rather than leaving price adjustments to the "free market mechanism"—which the Western economies of the 1930s did little to recommend! But whether or not there is any reason to believe the Lange-Lerner-Taylor system would equilibrate any more quickly than free markets generated remarkably little discussion.[19]

Traditional Criticism of State-Managed Market Socialism. Criticism of PuESMME on efficiency grounds centered on its presumed misallocation of society's resources over time. What proportion of society's resources would be used for present consumption and what proportion used for investment? As designed by Lange, Taylor, and Lerner, all enterprise profits were to be turned over to the state. Out of this pool of profits the state first pays bills of enterprises for which costs exceed revenues.[20] The remainder is then divided into two parts. One part is sent to a state investment bank, and the other part is distributed as bonuses to workers.

Lange believed the bonuses should be paid as a percentage of workers' wages to avoid distorting incentives to offer services in different labor categories. Ironically, while this bonus system accomplishes Lange's aim, it distorts the incentive to work rather than use one's time in leisure.[21] The key to distributing bonuses without disturbing efficiency is to hand out bonuses totally unrelated to work time or wage rate. Equal bonuses to all members of society (working and nonworking) is the simplest system of "efficient" bonuses. But this does not solve all problems.

The part of the state's profit pool that was turned over to the state investment bank was to be loaned to state enterprises for investment. The interest rate was to be set just like prices of all intermediate goods in PuESMME—raised in case of excess demand for loans, and lowered in case of excess supply. Although there was no explicit discussion, presumably Lange, Taylor, and Lerner would not have objected to permitting individual citizens to deposit some of their income in this same bank and receive the same rate of interest. But the question is how the division of the profit pool between a part earmarked for bonuses and a part earmarked for investment was determined in the first place. In Lange, Taylor, and Lerner's description, the division was arbitrary. But an arbitrary division may bias society's present versus future consumption.

Critics argued as follows: suppose society's citizens have a strong preference for present as opposed to future consumption, but the arbitrary division of the state profit pool is heavily weighted toward the investment bank and away from citizen bonuses. In this case, a large proportion of society's resources would go to investment—since the large supply of funds would generate low interest rates and greater loans to enterprises—despite society's preference for greater present consumption. The point was well taken. To our knowledge few advocates of public enterprise market economies of this type have bothered to reply beyond noting that the alternative notion that the rate of time preferences of the wealthy in private enterprise economies should govern the rate of investment and, therefore, growth and development prospects for all of society is obscene. While this argument is compelling on its own grounds, it is hardly an adequate response to critics of PuESMME.

A Simple Defense. There is a simple way to salvage the efficiency properties of PuESMME as judged by traditional welfare theory.[22] If all of the state profit pool is distributed as bonuses, and citizens are free to deposit whatever part of their total incomes they wish in the state investment bank in return for interest payments, society's "rate of time discount" will be left to determine the division between present and future consumption. Alternatively, the state profit pool can be arbitrarily divided between bonus payments and deposits in the state bank as long as citizens are free to take out consumer loans at the same rate of interest enterprises take out investment loans. In other words, the profit pool can be arbitrarily divided between the state bank and bonuses, but then the state bank cannot be an investment bank in the sense that its only loan customers are enterprises. In any case, citizens must be free to make deposits and receive interest and take out loans paying interest, and the rates of interest paid cannot be different for loans out of state funds and loans from consumer deposits, and the rates of interest charged cannot be different for enterprise and

215

consumer loan customers if PuESMME is to achieve social efficiency according to traditional welfare theory.

This concludes our analysis of public enterprise market economies from the point of view of traditional welfare theory. When corrected and analyzed using appropriate models, both PuEEMME and PuESMME prove just as capable of generating efficient outcomes as private enterprise market economies. While we have not taken the time to generate every analagous theorem, the demonstrations are all perfectly straightforward; the first, second, and third fundamental theorems of welfare theory all hold for both PuEEMME and PuESMME, just as for private enterprise market economies, according to the norms of traditional welfare theory. If we wished we could even extend the theorems under the assumption of endogenous preferences provided there were no reasons to suspect PuEEMME and PuESMME of biasing conditions of supply of different goods and/or work roles. And according to the traditional paradigm, there are no more reasons to suspect PuEEMME and PuESMME of any such biases than their private enterprise counterparts.[23] In the eyes of traditional welfare theorists, therefore, PuEEMME and PuESMME should appear equally meritorious as private enterprise market economies—provided those eyes are not blinded by ideological prejudice against public ownership. In fact, from the point of view of welfare theoretic results, according to traditional theory the three systems are indistinguishable!

7.2.3 An Overzealous Defense of Public Enterprise Market Economies

While both versions of public enterprise market economies can be defended from charges that they are inherently less efficient than private enterprise market economies, the claim that they are not subject to a familiar catalog of other complaints voiced by leftists about private enterprise market systems cannot be defended. In our opinion, there is every reason to believe public enterprise market systems suffer from many of the maladies leftist critics have long cited in arguments against capitalism. In this case, what is bad for the goose is bad for the gander as well.

To focus on what we believe to be the most theoretically significant and least recognized deficiencies of markets, we will say little about a number of problems others have dwelled on. Yet to claim these problems would plague private enterprise market systems but not public enterprise market systems is not our intent. Before proceeding to our main argument, we wish to disassociate ourselves from such overzealous defenses of the use of markets in public enterprise economies.

We leave the question of whether or not there is reason to believe public enterprise market economies would or would not be plagued by unacceptably inegalitarian distributions of income to chapter 8 where we examine ownership and income distribution in detail. And we defer the question of whether or not public enterprise market economies would generate the kind of "false consciousness" Marxists call "commodity fetishism" to follow our treatment of the cybernetic characteristics of markets later in this chapter. Here we disassociate ourselves from the notion that public enterprise market economies would be immune to business cycles and increasing industrial concentration.

Economists have long been concerned with the obvious inefficiency associated with the kind of gross disequilibria typical of alternating cycles of boom and bust. Economists have also long been aware of the obstacles industrial concentration pose for efficiency. Since the "anarchy of capitalist production" and the "law of ever-increasing concentration of capital" are fundamental precepts of Marxist economics it is hardly surprising that Marxists associate these maladies with private enterprise market economies. But there was never any compelling theoretical reason to believe public enterprise market economies would be immune to these maladies. And empirical evidence is now accumulating to the contrary. While influenced to some extent by ownership, business cycles and increasing industrial concentration are fundamentally market phenomena.

This is not the place to review competing theories of the business cycle. While there are "political economy" theories in which the struggle over capital and labor's share play a critical role,[24] the self-feeding nature of aggregate market expansions and contractions has received increasing theoretical attention as well.[25] But more convincing is the clear empirical evidence of a business cycle in the Yugoslav economy over the past thirty years.[26] And for those who think PuESMMEs might be less susceptible to cycles than PuEEMMEs, the Hungarian experience is proving sobering. In any case, real world public enterprise market economies have not proven immune to the cycles that plague their private enterprise counterparts, making a strong prima facie case that cycles are associated with markets per se.

One might argue that industrial concentration is irrelevant to at least some versions of PuESMMEs since it does not interfere with their efficiency.[27] But such is not the case for PuEEMMEs. Nor are increasingly popular PuESMME "reform" models in which enterprises are encouraged to maximize profits, at least part of which they are permitted to retain, rather than obey the Lange/Lerner/Taylor "rules" immune to inefficiencies should monopolistic market structures develop. In these cases in which enterprises do compete against one another for profits, or profits per employee, it strikes us as naive to presume they would not avail themselves of tactics that have always proven highly successful in such endeavors. Arrangements in which a small number of sellers face a large number of buyers have seldom proven damaging to sellers' profits. We see no reason for public enterprises competing with one another to find differently.

The empirical evidence here is also overwhelming. There has been a lively debate in Yugoslavia since the early 1950s over how to combat the effects of monopolistic behavior where some recommend price controls, others favor increased foreign competition, and still others call for breaking up large enterprises.[28] And it is common knowledge among Soviet economic historians that monopolistic factors played an important role in the famous "scissors crises" that followed implementation of the NEP in the 1920s.[29]

In sum, while we will overlook problems with market dynamics and market imperfections to focus on other matters, there is no reason to believe substituting public for private enterprise solves these very real problems.

7.3 New Criticisms of Markets: Snowballing Individualism

We are now ready to examine the cybernetic, incentive, and efficiency properties of markets with our new valuative theory. As we will see, a very different picture develops than the one celebrated by the free market jubilee. Instead of cybernetic miracles, optimal incentive devices, and efficiency machines, we will find that markets bias and obstruct the flow of essential information, promote antisocial incentives over equally powerful motivations that need not be socially destructive, and generate increasingly inefficient allocations of resources. In sum, we will find that markets promote snowballing individualism that is demonstrably nonoptimal regardless of whether they are combined with private or public enterprise.

7.4 Markets as Cybernetic Disasters

In both production and consumption, a group of people aided by physical implements act on inputs to generate outputs. In the process they transform not only the tools they use, but the individual and group characteristics of the people who undertake the activity as well. The qualitative model of the economic sphere we developed in chapter 5 was designed to highlight all this. But the inputs and outputs of economic activities we usually conceptualize separately actually connect each activity to others. No activity is possible without inputs that must be generated as outputs by other activities. And the meaning of an activity hinges on the uses to which others put the outputs it generates.

Another way of saying this is that the economic activities of different groups of people at different times are parts of an extensive network of activities that extends through space and time. Each activity is connected to countless others implying extensive relationships between both things, the inputs and outputs passed, and people—those who generate outputs for others and use inputs others produce. This has been referred to casually as "the division of labor," which Adam Smith celebrated as the engine of ever-greater productivity. And it has been analyzed with great care under the title of "commodity fetishism" by Karl Marx, who was concerned that the very people related to one another might be blinded to the nature and importance of those human, social relationships under particular arrangements for carrying them out.

In any case, those who carry out economic activities and who are integrally related to one another may be more or less aware of those relations and their complexities. And depending on the allocative mechanism used, people may receive more or less appropriate and useful information for developing such an awareness. One important question to ask concerning any allocative mechanism is whether or not it facilitates awareness of the interconnection of economic possibilities between groups of people who carry out activities in different times and places.

It might be objected that this is not an appropriate question for all economies. While different allocative mechanisms have different cybernetic qualities, they also have different cybernetic needs. The ability of groups of separated producers and consumers to sensibly select and coordinate their efforts obviously hinges on their knowledge of the interrelations between those efforts. But if instead of producers and consumers deciding how to organize their activities, a central planning agency is going to make those decisions for them, then it is not the producers and consumers but the central planners who need to understand the interconnections.[30] And if the coordination is going to be achieved by market interactions without conscious planning and coordination on anyone's part, then there is no need for anyone to have the information.[31]

While it is obvious that different allocative mechanisms have different cybernetic needs as well as qualities, this does not preclude asking evaluative questions about the cybernetic qualities of allocative mechanisms regardless of their internal information needs. The evaluative theory developed in chapter 6 awards high marks to decision-making processes characterized by self-management and solidarity, ceteris paribus. So regardless of who needs to know what for any particular decision-making framework to function, it bears asking what people would have to know to engage in self-managed decision making, what information would facilitate solidarity among economic actors, and to what extent any particular allocative mechanism provides that information to the economic actors themselves. In sum, what economic actors need to know to do what is required of them is a valid analytical question about any decision-making system. Whether economic actors will receive the information necessary for self-managed, solidaritous decision making is a no less valid valuative question and we can reasonably pose it for any allocative mechanism.

The market mechanism coordinates economic activities taking place in different places and times by providing all individual units with the opportunity to offer the material outputs of their activities in exchange for the material outputs of other units' activities, with a general assumption of noncoercion.[32] This exchange of material inputs and outputs between units is an expression of the fact that people in those separate groups are actually engaged in social activity with one another. Although the two units involved in exchange are separated by distance and/or time and likely lack information about the nature of each other's roles in their shared activity, neither of their activities is possible or makes sense without the other. We have no difficulty understanding that workers at the beginning and end of an automobile assembly line are engaged in the social activity of making a car. And even though the workers in a blast furnace are not connected by a physical assembly line to the workers in the rolling mill, we see their activities as integrated and part of the joint endeavor of making steel. But in a market system it is more difficult to recognize that workers in a steel mill and workers in an automobile assembly plant are similarly involved in a shared activity.

The reason for our blindness is that within individual units the activities of different individuals are consciously planned and coordinated to achieve a conceived goal. But as we have seen, the great miracle of market economies is precisely that the activities of different units are not consciously coordinated and planned by anyone. Those working in auto plants do not appear to be engaged in a social activity with steel workers, or bound by a specific set of production possibilities with steel workers. Instead it appears they are engaged in isolated productive activity and have relations only with other things, i.e., the sheet metal they use as inputs and the automobiles they create as outputs. The relations between people and things—people consuming inputs and people producing outputs—are readily visible, as are work relations between people in the same unit. But in market systems, the relations between groups of people working in different places and times can easily escape notice because people do not consciously plan and coordinate these relations. Instead they take the form of an exchange of things.[33]

But the "problem" of "commodity fetishism" as it has been treated by Marxists is overly abstract and philosophical. If one were concerned to eradicate this particular misconception among producers in "commodity producing societies," the simple solution would appear to be including introductory price theory in the high school social science curriculum. Then people could be taught that commodity exchange is the form in which important economic social relationships are expressed in market economies, just as people are taught now that the earth revolves around the sun although it appears otherwise.[34]

The more important question is whether market cybernetics would help separated producers and consumers discover much about the complexities of their actual interrelations in market systems should they realize there was something to be discovered! Having argued that self-management and solidarity are desirable welfare goals, it is only logical to inquire whether or not the cybernetic qualities of markets are conducive to these ends. For our auto workers to evaluate their work in human terms they would have to know the human-social implications for others of providing them with the steel they need to work with, the human-social consequences for them of their own work process, and the human-social consequences for others of consuming the cars they produce. Let's assume our auto workers know (perhaps more than they care to) about the human-social effects of their own work process. How can they discover the human-social implications of supplying them with steel, rubber, and the human-social consequences of driving the cars they produce?

The only information the market provides is the prices of steel and cars. Even if these prices accurately represent the total human and social costs and benefits associated with supplying rubber, steel, and cars—and we will argue shortly that this is not the case—this information is totally insufficient if auto workers are to develop the kind of understanding that can serve as the basis for a realistic and empathetic evaluation of the full consequences of their activity. Market institutions "efficiently" delete all this information about the concrete relations between separated activities that is necessary for developing a humanized awareness of interconnected possibilities. And while a humanized awareness may not be necessary for some kinds of decision making, it certainly is necessary if separated groups of economic actors are to develop a sense of solidarity for one anothers' aims and predicaments.

"Information economy" means deleting information that is not needed by decision makers. Deleting information about the drudgery and unpleasantness of work in steel mills and auto factories and deleting information about the injuries from accidents in unsafe cars is not "economy" of information if the goal is a self-managed decision-making process characterized by solidarity, because such information is needed for informed collective self-management.[35] As cybernetic devices markets are systematically destructive of the development of solidarity based on understanding and concern for the situation of others.

We can summarize using the qualitative economic model of chapter 5. Assume actors understand their own activity possibility set, $\{A\,(i,t)\}$. How can they come to understand $\{A\,(j,t)\}\,j{\neq}i,t{=}0,1,\ldots T$, that is, the activity possibility sets for all the other actors and times their activity is, in fact, related to? Do they receive sufficient information? Is it organized in ways that are usable? For fully informed self-managed decision making based on solidarity with others' problems and desires, we would ideally wish every producer-consumer to know as much about others' situations as they do about their own. But not everybody can work-consume everywhere and everything. And while people can read novels by Upton Sinclair, this is not the point. The question is how well the market itself serves the information needs of a self-managed, solidaritous decision-making process by economic actors. Perhaps we need not have belabored the answer so; at best markets systematically delete qualitative human information necessary for solidaritous decison making. At worst, as we will explore further, they provide inaccurate summaries of overall consequences. The cybernetic "miracles" of markets looks more like a disaster from the perspective of our welfare criteria.

Moreover, we see no reason to believe the information deficiences of markets should be any less serious in public enterprise than private enterprise settings and wish to disassociate ourselves from contrary claims.

For example, in one of the more sophisticated defenses of employee-managed, public enterprise market economies Arthur DiQuattro specifically argued they would not suffer the malady of commodity fetishism that plagues their private enterprise cousins. According to DiQuattro:

> Not the market, but class structure and class-determined technological mis-development, are responsible for alienated labor. It's true enough that in market socialism workers produce for exchange and not directly for use, but why must production under such an arrangement result in alienated labor, false consciousness, and the estrangement of individuals from one another?...If workers succeed in supplanting capitalist control with socialist productive relations, they would at the same time abolish the class basis of "commodity fetishism."

And,

> With the transformation of work and other spheres of social life (e.g., education, community and political organization), is there any reason to believe that market operation need generate "false consciousness," casting a fog over the social character of production, and subjecting producers to its sway? In market socialism, the working community freely chooses, with a thorough and reasoned comprehension of the automatic workings of market arrangements, to rely on those arrangements for the purpose of allocating economic resources. The idea that production for exchange must engender false consciousness is a metaphysical "must," based on a confusion between productive relations

and modes of allocation, ruling out a priori the distinct analytical fact and historical possibility of diminished alienation in market socialism.[36]

In our view, DiQuattro's defense of "market socialism" from the charge that it too would be plagued by commodity fetishism is another example of an overzealous defense that cannot be justified.[37]

First DiQuattro conflates two distinct Marxist concepts, "commodity fetishism" and "alienation," arguing that if alienation is not present then commodity fetishism will not be either. While this line of reasoning may appeal to many Marxists who do not believe alienation exists in public enterprise economies, it is a non sequitur. Even if employee-managed market economies were immune to alienation, this would not imply they were necessarily immune to commodity fetishism. For the question remains whether markets hinder or aid the process of expanding one's understanding of the full effects of one's economic activities from $\{A(i,t)\}$, to $\{A(j,t)\}$ for $j \neq i$ and $t = 1,...,T$. DiQuattro offers no direct rebuttal to our argument that markets hinder actors' abilities to achieve a full understanding of their economic activities. And his indirect rebuttal hinges on a proposition he does not demonstrate, namely that alienation is a necessary condition for fetishism. In this, he assumes his conclusion.

Second, DiQuattro seems to believe that as long as institutions are "freely" chosen "with a thorough and reasoned comprehension of their automatic workings," any deficiences in those workings disappear! DiQuattro presumes that if workers are aware of the cybernetic deficiencies of markets when they choose to use them for allocative purposes, they will not suffer from those cybernetic deficiencies. Hardly a compelling argument, when recognized for what it is. And while we might agree with DiQuattro that the more thorough and reasoned our understanding of the automatic workings of market arrangements the better off we will be, the same could be said about slaves' comprehension of slavery! This would not be because slaves' greater awareness would dull the negative effects of slavery, but because the more thorough their understanding of slavery the more capable slaves become of overthrowing the institutions that oppress them! In the same vein, a thorough comprehension of the workings of markets does not lessen the negative effects of market institutions, but makes more likely their replacement by a superior cybernetic mechanism.

Finally, it is DiQuattro who suffers from a "metaphysical" confusion not uncommon to Marxists that only "productive relations" can generate effects as profound as "false consciousness." But there is no a priori reason "allocative relations" cannot have consequences as profound as those of "productive relations," no matter what a majority of Marxists may believe. In any case, a successful argument downgrading the importance of allocative relations would merely diminish the importance of the criticisms voiced in this chapter rather than alter any of its conclusions.

7.5 Market Roles and Incentives

According to the traditional paradigm, markets economize on unneeded information. Our new paradigm sees them as deleting information critical for self-managed, solidaritous decision making. The traditional paradigm celebrates the motivational miracle of competition that supposedly harnesses egotism and greed for socially beneficial tasks. Our new paradigm helps elucidate how market roles undermine cooperative behavior and relationships built on mutual respect and solidarity.

Markets simultaneously require competitive behavior and prohibit cooperation (not to be confused with collusion) as irrational by creating a direct opposition of interests between seller and buyer. The interest of the seller is to sell a good or service that is least troublesome to provide at the highest possible price. The interest of the buyer is to buy the most beneficial good or service at the lowest possible price. Since "least troublesome" seldom coincides with "most beneficial" the opposition of interests is complete over both the good or service exchanged and what is paid for it. In market exchange, neither party can afford to be concerned with the needs and desires of the other, except in a mercenary sense. To be concerned with the well-being of one's "partner" in exchange undermines the functioning of the market mechanism. To put it starkly, market allocation establishes a war of each against all.

It is interesting that markets' greatest critics and admirers have agreed on this point. While the critic writes:

Every product is a bait with which to seduce away the other's very being, his money; every real and possible need is a weakness which will lead the fly to the gluepot...every need is an opportunity to approach one's neighbor under the guise of the utmost amiability and say to him: "Dear friend, I give you what you need, but you know the conditio sine qua non; you know the ink in which you have to sign yourself over to me; in providing for your pleasure, I fleece you."[38]

The admirer concurs:

It is not from the benevolence of the butcher, the brewer, or the baker, that we expect our dinner, but from their regard for their own interest. We address ourselves, not to their humanity but to their self-love, and never talk to them of our own necessities but of their advantage.[39]

Market competition motivates economic effort based on self-interest, not concern for others who are similarly concerned for you. Market competition forces people to think of ways to take advantage of others they buy from and sell to and with whom they compete for suppliers and buyers. In sum, market roles require participants to practice antisolidaritous behavior on a daily basis, which cognitive dissonance then translates into consciousness. And while solidarity is expressed by the maxim "do unto others as you would have them do unto you," market competition expresses the maxim "do in others before they do you in."

Karl Marx summarized the problem succinctly over 130 years ago when he wrote that those who wanted markets in socialism want competition without the pernicious effects of competition.[40] More recently Gar Alperowitz pointed out that "as long as the social and economic security of any economic unit is not guaranteed, it is likely to function to protect (and out of insecurity, to extend) its own special stuatus-quo interests—even when they run counter to the broader interests of society."[41] But this is precisely the situation a market system creates. Under market competition managers of plants that pollute—whether they be managing in the interests of stockholders or workers—dissimulate with good reason since pollution taxes and more ecological technology would lower profits. Managers of plants that create shoddy and dangerous products have an incentive to engage in deceptive advertising to preserve demand for their products. And those whose livelihoods depend on the automobile industry will continue to oppose changes they know to be desirable in transportation systems as long as market competition means they would bear the burden of the social costs of transition in the loss of income and dignity that comes from unemployment.

To generalize, markets systematically establish divergences between individual and societal well-being. They establish an incentive to pursue individual interest at the expense of social interest because they guarantee that the rest of society cannot be relied on to safeguard one's individual welfare. Markets create a kind of lowest common denominator consciousness. "Under market conditions a minority of the workers in an industry—perhaps even one enterprise—can impose its preferences on all the rest." If one firm chooses to use deceptive advertising or lower the quality of the product in imperceptible ways, "all the other firms must follow suit—or find themsleves driven out of business."[42]

In sum, the information markets delete, the roles they define, and the incentives they establish all combine to reward pursuit of narrow self-interest at others' expense. It is not that self-interest and competition against others are the only forms of behavior of which people are capable. It is that these are the only forms of behavior rewarded by markets! Just as markets systematically delete information necessary for self-managed, solidaritous decision making, markets establish roles and incentives that penalize solidaritous behavior and reward its opposite.

At a minimum, it is important to recognize these properties of markets irrespective of whether or not better allocative mechanisms exist. That is, even should all other feasible allocative mechanisms have worse failings, that is no reason to deny weaknesses inherent in market institutions. The cybernetic and incentive properties of markets not only do not promote solidarity, they are systematically destructive of any solidarity that may arise from other spheres of social intercourse. This is true regardless of whether or not they are the least of the allocative evils. And this is true irrespective of whether or not the prices generated by competitive markets are accurate reflections of the relative social costs and benefits associated with the production and use of different commodities. But, as we will see, markets are far less deserving of this reputation for accuracy than commonly supposed.

7.6 Market Inefficiency

Traditional theory holds that equilibrium prices in competitive markets represent accurate evaluations of the relative usefulness of society's scarce human and nonhuman resources, the relative benefits of different goods produced, and the relative burdensomeness of different work situations. If this were so markets would, indeed, possess one important positive quality. For while our valuative theory makes clear that more is required to facilitate self-managed, solidaritous decision making, our theory, like others, recognizes the importance of accurate summaries of social costs and benefits associated with economic decisions.

As we discussed in chapter 3 there has long been a caveat to the thesis that competitive market prices are efficiency prices: namely, that no externalities or public goods are involved. At the risk of belaboring the commonplace, the problem with market prices in the case of externalities and public goods is that the balancing of costs and benefits in market transactions is done only by the buyer and seller. If others beside the buyer and seller are affected, there is every reason to believe that market competition excludes their interests from consideration. In this case, effects on others beside the buyer and seller are not captured by market prices.

Buyers evaluate the worth of a commodity in terms of how its consumption affects them alone, paying the price if the benefit is deemed more than the loss of other commodities the purchase out of a limited income implies. Sellers sell a commodity if their loss in well-being is deemed less than their gain from other commodities the sale enables them to purchase. For either to do otherwise—for either side to take account of benefits or costs to others—would be to engage in acts of charity with no reason to expect reciprocation and, indeed, with every reason to expect a "fleecing."

"With no reason to expect reciprocation" is crucial here. We are not saying people are unable to make decisions that take others' interests into account—though as discussed above they have little relevant information that would enable them to do so in market economies. But we agree with

226

conventional wisdom that people are unlikely to be mutually supportive when they have every reason to expect that others are not reciprocating. To extend oneself, at cost to one's self-interest, in full knowledge that reciprocation will not be forthcoming and that, indeed, one will simply be taken advantage of, is to engage in the "saintly" behavior of continuously turning the other cheek. But this is not to say that people are incapable of taking others' interest to heart when they are free from fears of being taken advantage of, or better, when they have every reason to expect others to take their interest into account. More to the point, it is not to say that if people find themselves in a situation in which it is unlikely they can succeed in advancing their own interests except by taking the interest of others as seriously as their own, that they will be unable to do so.

In any case, if markets misestimate the social worth of commodities whose production or consumption by one agent generates effects for other agents because they do not provide means for joint, or social expression of desires, why can't a number of affected agents band together and become joint buyers of goods whose consumption has external effects? The answer is that they can and will whenever the result of failure to do so is so grossly inadequate as to drive them to forge a "makeshift social structure"[43] outside the institutional structures provided by the market. Which brings us to the questions posed in chapter 3:

1. How rare, or how prevalent are externalities and public goods?

2. Do market mechanisms create incentives for people to generate negative externalities?

3. To what extent can previously known makeshift social structures be expected to resolve these problems?

4. To what extent could these problems be ameliorated by any of the "incentive-compatible mechanisms" that have been recently proposed?

We now discuss what our new welfare paradigm has to contribute in these regards.

7.7 The Prevalence of Externalities and Public Goods

Put simply, our new welfare paradigm undermines the traditional conclusion of external effect exceptionality and supports E. K. Hunt's claim that external effects are pervasive. This is not to suggest that "paradigms" settle such issues. Ultimately this is an empirical matter. But in situations where conclusive empirical testing is difficult to even envision, paradigms play important roles in establishing presumptions. The traditional paradigm suggests the presumption of external effect exceptionality, until proven otherwise. It allows a vision something like that depicted in Fig.

227

7.1 where most goods are private goods, and public goods and externalities are exceptional. Our paradigm suggests a presumption of pervasive external effects, until proven otherwise. It envisions a spectrum between the extreme of pure private and pure public "goods," where pure cases of either kind are relatively few, and most "goods" fall somewhere in-between, as depicted in the frequency distribution in Fig. 7.2. And while it sees fewer and fewer activities as the external effect becomes stronger, as in Fig. 7.3, activities with the exact average external effect are insignificant compared to the sum of all those above or below the average.

FIG. 7.1. TRADITIONAL VIEW

FIG. 7.2. ALTERNATIVE VIEW 1

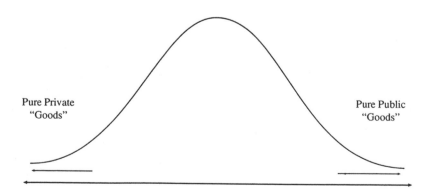

FIG. 7.3. ALTERNATIVE VIEW 2

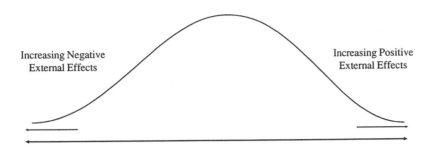

Hunt claims:

The fact is…most of the millions of acts of production and consumption in which we daily engage involve externalities.…Externalities are total-ly pervasive.[44]

In chapter 5 we elaborated a theory of human sociality emphasizing that most of our needs and potentials were developed and satisfied only through social interaction, and that human consciousness contributes special fea-tures to our sociality beyond what is enjoyed by other social animals. We explained how even Robinson Crusoe—of great fame in the traditional welfare paradigm—was unintelligible apart from the society from which he had become separated.

Moreover, our paradigm makes clear that it is not the nature of goods that is at issue. It is not that some goods are public and others are private, that some goods have externalities and others do not. To think in terms of the supposed properties of goods is to misconceive the issue. The question is to what extent various kinds of human activities have more or less pervasive effects on others that go unconsidered in the decision-making system established by markets in conjunction with a particular definition of property rights. To what extent do the choices and actions of economic actors cast a wider or narrower net of effects on others than we can reasonably expect to be evaluated by a market-organized, decision-making process?

The issue is best conceived not as one of the characteristics of goods, but as one of the characteristics of markets. It is markets in the context of a system of property rights that establish who gets to make what decisions in market economies. If the markets and property rights confer on an economic actor the right to make a decision that affects the well-being of other economic actors, we have an external effect. And this will be the case whenever the market-property-rights system grants economic actors the right to make a decision that changes the state of the world in some way that matters to someone other than themselves.[45]

Moreover, in assessing "breadth of effects," our paradigm reminds us that economic actions have human as well as material inputs and outputs and transform the states of both individual and group human characteristics as well as physical implements. This conception of human activity broadens the possibilities for external effects considerably. One actor's choice may affect flow or state variables of relevance to other actors, and those flow or state variables may be physical or human in form. Any time actors affect the state of the world we all live in they affect the possibilities we all face. It is not so much whether external effects do or do not exist, but how strong the external effects of any particular action may be.

Our paradigm makes this point symbolically by defining individual well-being functions, $U(t)$, on the activity space of all human action, $A_k(i,t)$ for $i = 1..., H$, rather than only on the activity space of actions in which the individual participates directly, that is where i ranges only over those groups in which i directly participates.[46] But the emphasis on human sociality and the implication that much of what determines our individual well-being hinges on the situations of others with whom we will/can interact implies a subtle problem that few traditional theorists have confronted. As is frequently the case, Arrow is an exception:

> There is one deep problem in the interpretation of externalities which can only be signalled here. What aspects of others' behavior do we consider as affecting a utility function? If we take a hard-boiled revealed preference attitude, then if an individual expends resources in supporting legislation regulating another's behavior, it must be assumed that that behavior affects his utility. Yet in the cases that students of criminal law call "crimes without victims," such as homosexuality or drug-taking, there is no direct relation between the parties. Do we have to extend the concept of externality to all matters that an individual cares about? Or, in the spirit of John Stuart Mill, is there a second-order value judgement which excludes some of these preferences from the formation of social policy as being illegitimate infringements of indiviudal freedom.[47]

While this dilemma is more often than not ignored by traditional theorists, it is a real dilemma. And as Arrow implies, the traditional paradigm offers very little help in resolving the dilemma other than posing an arbitrary choice of whether or not to impose a "second-order value judgement." Certainly there is nothing in the traditional paradigm that helps us decide when and where to impose such a value judgment, even should we decide it were justifiable to do so.

While paradigms neither create nor resolve real dilemmas, they can be more or less helpful in clarifying their origins and what is at stake in their resolution. Our paradigm implies that the dilemma occurs far more frequently than the traditional paradigm would lead one to suspect. Whereas the traditional paradigm disguises conflicts between different economic actors' "individual freedom," ours highlights the prevalence of the problem. Our paradigm also suggests that the degree of conflict varies widely. We do not expect that an individual's potential well-being will be affected to an equal extent by all other human activity irrespective of who is directly involved in performing the activity and how distant the activity is in time and space. We would expect, ceteris paribus, individuals would be more affected by activities that they and their closer acquaintances are involved in and by activities taking place closer to them in space and time. Our paradigm casts doubt on the plausibility of the impermeable membranes the traditional paradigm envisions surrounding individual members of our species and suggests that the problem is twofold.

First, a universal interdependence is denied by the traditional paradigm, which is inadequately accounted for by market/property rights, decision-making systems, thereby leading to demonstrable inefficiencies. Second, the universal interdependence is highly unequal. Any particular decision and economic activity has greater effects on some than others. For this reason, we defined the valuative concept, self-management, to serve as a more useful guide[48] to this ever-present dilemma than the traditional notion of individual freedom. Whereas the traditional paradigm establishes no clear-cut goal in the context of external effects,[49] the valuative imperative of our welfare paradigm is clear: try and approximate, as best possible, a self-managed, decision-making system, that is, a system in which all actors have decision-making input to the extent they are affected by the outcome. Whether or not this is easily done is another matter.

Although we have deliberately chosen to conduct our welfare analysis, for the most part, under the assumption of perfect knowledge, we emphasize an important implication should that assumption be relaxed. If everyone knew exactly how development would translate into later fulfillment and what kind of derived characteristics and activities best suited them, there would be nothing beyond self-management to aim for. But while we would expect people possessed of perfect knowledge to frequently "exchange proxies" created by the reality of external effects so as to allow variety in others' development for all the reasons discussed in chapter 5; in the world of doubt, there is even more reason to weight decision-making authority in the direction of those most directly involved. In general, there is good reason to believe the more directly one is involved in an activity, the less imperfect one's knowledge about the consequences is likely to be. So the only dilemma implied by our welfare theory is how to apply the principle of self-management in a context of unequal knowledge about consequences—which amounts to determining the extent to which those most immediately involved should be granted extra authority due to their greater knowledge as well as the greater effects.[50]

Finally, we will discover that it is the unevenness of external effects, more than their existence, that makes it difficult to construct desirable economic decision-making mechanisms. Our paradigm emphasizes not only the high likelihood of the prevalence of external effects, but the unevenness of those effects as well. The breadth of the net of effects cast by any particular decision and action can fall any place on a continuum ranging from zero effects on others to equally powerful effects on all. As we will see, it is unfortunate for simple economic decision-making mechanisms (like markets and central planning) that there is every reason to believe that the degree of external effects of most economic decisions falls somewhere between the two extremes.

7.7.1 *Market Incentives to Create Negative External Effects*

Hunt dubbed this phenomenon the "invisible foot," which he argued must logically accompany the "invisible hand" in market systems.

> Each man will soon discover that through contrivance he can impose external diseconomies on other men, knowing that the bargaining within the new market that will be established will surely make him better off. The more significant the social cost imposed upon his neighbor, the greater will be his reward in the bargaining process.[51]

What is of interest here is that taking an endogenous rather than exogenous view of preferences turns what was already a bad dream for Hunt into a full-blown nightmare. Not only will different preferences over the state of the world create opportunities for self-advancement by choosing so as to maximize others misery, ceteris paribus, the market "solution" to external effects creates incentives for individuals to magnify preference differences over social outcomes to enhance their ability to extract greater "reward in the bargaining process" in the future.

If my preferences over the state of the world are the same as my neighbors', there is little opportunity to "contrive" to impose external diseconomies on them (that they will have to bargain with me to cease) without cutting off my own nose to spite my face. In the tradition of using trivial examples, if we both strongly prefer azaleas to forsythia, planting forsythia in the hopes that my neighbor will bribe me to replace them with azaleas is a dubious strategy. Of course, not everyone has the same preferences over the state of the world. What interested Hunt was how inevitable differences between individuals' preferences over the state of the world give rise to the logic of maximizing one's own well-being by maximizing others' misery. If I am truly indifferent between forsythia and azaleas, I can "contrive" to receive a bribe from my forsythia-hating neighbor by threatening to plant forsythias rather than azaleas even though I would be just as happy with azaleas. Any divergence of preferences over flora between me and my neighbor creates an opportunity that an individual "maximizer" is "honor bound" to pursue.

Our new paradigm makes very clear that people's preferences are not exogenous, but amenable to conscious manipulation. As soon as we recognize that preferences are endogenous, and that all choices have preference development as well as preference fulfillment effects, the (socially negative) possibilities multiply. As an individual maximizer I must not only take into account to what extent a choice will satisfy my present desires (traditional theory) and thwart the desires of my neighbor (Hunt's insight), I must also weigh the extent to which it will mold my future preferences to be as contrary to those of my neighbor as possible in order to enhance my opportunity for "conniving" greater bribes out of my neighbor in the future. In other words, even if my neighbor and I were fortunate enough to begin with similar preferences over flora, so that Hunt's invisible foot did not initially conspire to maximize our joint misery, we would each have an incentive to undo our good fate and develop preferences in the most contradictory directions possible!

By viewing preferences as endogenous, our new paradigm deepens another of Hunt's insights. Hunt complained that traditional welfare theory "simply takes the externalities, for which property rights and markets are to be established, as somehow metaphysically given and fixed. In ignoring the relational aspects of social life their theory ignores the fact that individuals can create externalities almost at will."[52] Hunt meant that individuals with different preferences over the state of the world they must share can create negative externalities for one another (or withold positive externalities) for bargaining purposes "almost at will." In this sense those externalities are not "given and fixed." But in a world of exogenous preferences the opportunity costs (to me) of the negative externalities I can choose to cause others is fixed. However, in a world of endogenous preferences they are not. People can expand on their effective ability to do each other harm by "rationally" developing their preferences in contradictory directions. Of course, in this case the "invisible foot" comes down with an even heavier thud as people who "seek only their private gain, and neither intend to promote the public misery nor know how much they promote it" nonetheless make it increasingly impossible for everyone to be satisfied in the one world in which they must all live.

7.7.2 *The Inadequacy of Traditional Solutions*

In chapter 3, we briefly summarized the traditional view of the source of the "problem" posed by public goods and externalities, as well as the consensus that prevailed prior to the advent of incentive-compatible mechanisms regarding the inadequacy of all "solutions." We quoted Richard Musgrave to the effect that just as markets and voluntary associations were demonstrably inefficient, so too were all "solutions" that had been proposed whether they were of the "benefit" approach, the "ability to pay" approach, or any of a variety of voting systems. Moreover, Musgrave categorized Tiebout's "solution" as irrelevant to issues of central finance irrespective of its merits regarding local finance. We refer to all these approaches as "traditional solutions" to distinguish them from the more recent solutions proposed as part of the literature on incentive-compatible mechanisms. Here we reexamine the "problem" posed by external effects, and reevaluate the "traditional solutions" in light of our new welfare theory before considering incentive-compatible mechanisms.

For theorists such as Richard Musgrave, the key to the public good "problem" was nonexclusion.

> In the satisfaction of private wants, the market functions as an auction place, forcing individual consumers to reveal their true preferences: Unless I bid, I shall not be able to get what I want. In the satisfaction of social wants, this reasoning does not hold. The services supplied are not subject to the exclusion principle. Consumers will be able to obtain the benefits whether they contribute or not. Since the exclusion principle cannot be applied, there is no reason why consumers should reveal true preferences.[53]

Kenneth Arrow pointed out that "market-thinness" was possibly as important as "nonexclusion" in preventing market systems from achieving efficient allocations in the presence of public goods and externalities. It was Arrow who originally suggested the delightfully simple device of including the amount of all commodities consumed by every individual as an argument in the utility function of each individual.[54] Of course, this is tantamount to reversing the presumption of the traditional welfare paradigm that all goods are to be treated as private goods until proven otherwise and adopting the presumption suggested by our new paradigm that all economic activities potentially have (differing) external effects. Arrow proceeded to point out that by this "suitable and indeed not unnatural reinterpretation of commodity space, externalities can be regarded as ordinary commodities, and all the formal theory of competitive equilibrium is valid, including its optimality."[55] But Arrow also pointed out the "catch 22": "[In this case] each commodity...has precisely one buyer and one seller. Even if a competitive equilibrium could be defined, there would be no force driving the system to it; we are in the realm of imperfectly competitive equilibrium."[56]

Let us try to summarize the traditional assessment of the source of the external effects problem in a way that unifies the treatment of "public goods" and "externalities" in market economies whether they occur in "consumption" or "production" and whether their effect is "direct" or "indirect." Whenever a decision is taken in any economy without regard to some of the effects of that decision, we have external effects and the high probability of social inefficiency. In market economies, economic decisions are taken by individual actors who have limited information about the effects their decisions may have on others and certainly no incentive to advance others' interests at their own expense. When this occurs, an obvious incentive exists for those whose interests are being disregarded in the decision-making process to seek to negotiate with the actor whose activity affects them. Not only does this imply an incentive for the actor to contrive to thwart the desires of others in order to maximize the side payment he or she receives; even if we ignore Hunt's "invisible foot," there is little reason to believe the results of negotiations would generate Pareto optimal outcomes. There are at least two different reasons for this pessimism.

1. If many actors are affected, while they may attempt to band together to express their views jointly, the coalition of affected partners will be plagued by the problem of nonexcludability. The coalition cannot effectively challenge individual members' deliberate misrepresentations of the degree to which they are affected in efforts to minimize their individual assessments.[57] For the only way to challenge the veracity of coalition members' suspicious estimate of the degree to which they are affected is to exclude them individually from the benefits of the negotiations. And the only way to do this is to break off negotiations with the actor whose decision generates external effects for the coalition. But this implies that all other members of the coalition will be excluded from any benefits that could have been obtained as well. In more colloquial terms, the coalition cannot effectively challenge members' dissimulation without cutting off its own nose to spite its face.[58]

2. Even if the external effect is confined to one other actor in the economy (thereby eliminating any problems of dissimulation within the coalition of affected parties), it is not obvious that Pareto optimal outcomes should be expected from negotiations between two parties. Without the "discipline" of competitive markets to structure their negotiations (more exactly, to do away with negotiations entirely), tactics and strategies of

"gamesmanship" are perfectly rational. While some have argued that unrestricted bargaining may result in efficient outcomes, the consensus seems to be that this need not be the case.[59]

It is worth noting that the problem of market thinness applies to negotiations between coalitions of affected parties and a single actor as well—beyond whatever internal problems the coalition may face in truthfully assessing the extent to which members are differentially affected. It is also worth noting that if such unrestricted bargaining could be relied upon to generate socially efficient outcomes, one of the principal virtues of competitive markets would disappear. For while competitive markets might still be convenient—as a way of saving the trees that would be consumed by greatly lengthened classified sections in daily newspapers—they would no longer be necessary for generating socially efficient outcomes. After all, the chief virtue of competitive markets that led Adam Smith to ascribe to them the properties of an omniscient, beneficent invisible hand was that by eliminating the indeterminacy of unrestricted, individual negotiations they drove negotiations to socially efficient outcomes that might not otherwise have arrived there.

For flood control projects, sanitary campaigns, national defense, or pollution, the greater problem is clearly that the group cannot effectively challenge individuals' underestimation of benefits without being willing to do without the benefit themselves. In other words, the fact that all will end up "consuming" the same amount of a public good (bad) creates an incentive for individuals to underestimate (overestimate) the benefit (cost) they enjoy (suffer) from a public good (bad) in hopes of minimizing (maximizing) the payment (subsidy) they will be assessed as a member of the coalition of affected partners.

For parks, bridges, or lighthouses[60] "exclusion is perfectly possible...but there would be only one buyer [each individual user] and one seller [the supplier of the public good]" and no reason to believe the two would arrive at a Pareto optimum since there are "no competitive forces to drive the two into a competitive equilibrium."[61]

In Meade's classic example of an apple farmer and a beekeeper both problems pertain. The apple farmer could not exclude the beekeeper from benefiting from any expansion of his orchard without giving up the benefits of that expansion himself. But the fact that there were only two individuals negotiating over the sharing of payments also contribute to the unlikelihood that the two would agree to an optimal expansion of the orchard.

In conclusion:

1. There is every reason to expect that markets, even should they be accompanied by voluntary associations, will misallocate resources in the case of public goods and externalities.

2. There is no qualitative difference between public goods and externalities and no reason to treat them differently at a theoretical level. Public goods or bads are simply externalities whose effects are more pervasive than what convention has chosen to call an externality. Externalities are simply public goods or bads whose effects are too circumscribed to merit the label public.

3. The primary intentions of the economic actor whose decision generates external effects for others and the private or public status of that actor, are of no theoretical consequence as far as social efficiency is concerned.

4. The issue is not the characteristics of goods but the characteristics of markets, since it is the market/property right system that establishes who gets to make what decisions.

How is it that "traditional solutions" that involve a government with coercive powers might improve matters? And why have economists concluded that while "traditional solutions" might improve upon market allocation and voluntary association, they are all, to some extent, inevitably flawed? Here we will uncover a very peculiar lack of rigor in the analysis by traditional welfare theorists.

Suppose we substitute a government for the market-property-right system of allocating resources in all cases where external effects exist and instruct the government to do so in a socially efficient manner. The goverment must decide two things: how much of each activity that generates effects external to the market decision-making process should occur, and how much to assess each citizen to defray whatever costs may arise from implementing its first decision. In language more familiar to students of public finance, the goverment must make (1) a decision about expenditures—how much to spend on the provision of different public goods, and (2) a decision about taxation—how to collect the revenues necessary to cover the expenditures.

The common approach of actual governments is to determine how much of different public goods to provide (and how much to subsidize or tax externalities) through some political process, paying the cost out of general tax revenues. Here we can permit our theoretical government to contemplate what might be more time-consuming and less practical options. On the expenditure side, the government could ask individuals to report the benefits they feel they would receive from different amounts of each public good and provide the amount of each that equalizes the reported marginal social benefit of another unit with the marginal social cost of providing it.[62] On the revenue side, the critical question is whether the government should correlate the size of individuals' tax assessments with the size of the benefits they report they would receive.

What Musgrave and others describe as the "benefit approach" holds that individuals' assessments should correlate with benefits. The motivation for this approach is obvious. Why should an individual benefited little by a package of public goods pay as much as an individual benefited greatly? But Musgrave points out the equally obvious difficulty of implementing a "benefit approach": the government is in no better position to elicit truthful information about the degree to which individuals are benefited than a voluntary coalition of affected agents once citizens become aware that tax assessments are positive functions of individuals' reported benefits. For if tax assessments are positive functions of reported benefits, while citizens could not decline membership in the coalition of affected partners, we cannot avoid the conclusion they would have every incentive to lie about their true preferences. And if people underrepresented their true "marginal willingness to pay," the government would end up doing just what markets in conjunction with voluntary associations do; it would undersupply goods with positive external effects compared with a socially efficient allocation. So we agree with Musgrave and the traditional consensus regarding the apparent dilemma of the "benefit approach."

However, when Musgrave and others analyze what they term "the ability to pay approach" and "voting systems together with a compulsory application of the budget plan thus decided upon," they display what we believe is a remarkable lack of rigor. Remarkable because they apparently confuse "Pareto efficient" with "Pareto improvement"—two fundamental concepts of traditional welfare theory—in a way that implies they allowed their instincts about equity to blind them about issues of efficiency!

According to Musgrave, the "very necessity for compulsory application of a general tax formula means that the resulting solution will not be optimal."[63] We take this to mean that if tax assessments are based on any formula that ignores differences between individuals' benefits the package of public goods and assessments cannot be Pareto optimal. But this is wrong. If tax assessments are independent of reported benefits, there is every reason to believe that the outcome will be Pareto optimal, for there is no incentive for individuals to misrepresent their true preferences when their tax assessments are independent of their reported marginal willingness to pay. And there is (at least a slight) incentive for them to report truthfully since that is the best way for them to influence the package of public goods they (along with everyone else) will have to live with, no matter how slight that influence may be.

The fact that separating assessments from benefits preserves the efficiency properties of a government allocative procedure is so obvious that it begs an explanation for why so many traditional theorists would have thought otherwise. Such speculation is problematical, but we can only imagine that what Musgrave and others mean is that compulsory application of a general tax formula cannot be a Pareto improvement over the market (mis)allocation. For this is certainly true as well. Undoubtedly, citizens who care little for public goods are made worse off if we move from a market allocation with no public goods and no assessments to a situation with public goods and assessments that are as great for them as for others who are greatly benefited by the public good package.[64]

But this is most certainly not the point. It is well known that a move from a particular non-Pareto optimal situation to a particular Pareto optimal situation may not be a Pareto improvement,[65] just as it is well known that the number of Pareto optimal situations is infinite. But this is the case whether or not external effects exist. So, Musgrave appears to be off the mark as well when he concludes:

> The basic problem in the theory of public economy, therefore, is not that social wants are generated in some different and mysterious fashion; rather it is that the same amounts of services are consumed by all, so that (1) true individual preferences for such wants are not revealed at the market, and (2) there is no single solution that is optimal in the Pareto sense.[66]

It is true there is no unique Pareto optimum when the same amount of services must be consumed by all. But if this is all Musgrave means it hardly bears saying because there is no unique Pareto optimum even if all goods are private. If, instead, he means no Pareto optimum exists, he is simply wrong. The fact that we all must live in the same public good world does not imply there are not packages of public goods and individual assessments in which any change would make at least some individual worse off. In other words, public goods have no bearing on the existence of Pareto optima, which was the sum of what Samuelson demonstrated in his famous article.[67]

It seems Musgrave simply confused Pareto improvement and Pareto optimum, a confusion that plagued the literature on "compensation effects" as well. Moreover, this confusion is related to the traditional welfare paradigm. If one's paradigm fosters a vision of individual actors immersed in free-market exchange who notice instances of social inefficiency associated with external effects and then try to negotiate a government that would intervene on their behalf; and if one's paradigm poses the question of whether or not there is any government that imposes a "compulsory general tax formula" they would unanimously agree to; then the answer is "no." The answer is "no" because if every citizen must believe that he or she could only become better off, and never worse off, under the rules a government would apply, then presumably some citizen who expected to be little benefited by the public goods that would be provided would veto any government that applied a "compulsory general tax formula."

To state it differently, a path from free-market anarchy to any government that taxes according to a forumla not based on individual benefit that consists only of Pareto improvement is highly improbable. Yet any government that makes a reasonable attempt to determine and abide by citizens' preferences regarding public goods and taxes on other than a benefit basis can reasonably expect to achieve Pareto optimality.

On the other hand, if citizens immersed in free-market anarchy became aware of the "free-rider problem" and tried to negotiate a government that taxed on a benefit basis, they might well be able to establish a government by unanimous agreement. For at worst the government would replicate their present predicament. And any difference in outcome the government made could be arranged so as to benefit each individual at least as much by the public goods provided as it inconvenienced him or her through tax assessment. But this is not to say such a government would achieve Pareto optimality. Prior to the revolution in incentive-compatible mechanisms it was believed governments that taxed on a benefit basis would inevitably lead people to misrepresent their preferences and therefore be unable to generate Pareto optimal allocations even if some such government were unanimously agreed to by people who sought to improve upon their situation in free-market anarchy.

The last variety of "traditional" solution was outlined by C. M. Tiebout in his famous 1956 article in which he proposed that citizens could express their preferences regarding different packages of public goods by "voting with their feet."[68] In other words, there would be a competitive market in local finance. Besides the fact that this solution begs the question concerning problems of central as opposed to local finance, which Musgrave among others duly noted, the conditions under which "voting with ones' feet" would generate Pareto optimal outcomes in local finance are highly bizarre. There would have to be an infinity of different local communities within costless walking distance exhibiting an infinite variety of choices on every single issue of public good provision and payment. That is, there would have to be a different community for every possible choice on any single issue and for every other possible set of choices on every other issue of local finance. While we economists have been undaunted by no less far-fetched assumptions in our theorizing, the real problem in this case is the need for a law to prevent members of communities from voting by ballot to change the mix for their own community to keep Tiebout's "local finance market" from collapsing. More than anything else, the necessity of outlawing democratic collective action within communities made Tiebout's "solution" unattractive for many, even for problems of local finance. In retrospect it is apparent that rather than solve the problem of social choice, Tiebout merely suggested using our feet to run around it.

7.7.3 Incentive-Compatible Mechanisms

In chapter 3 we reviewed the seminal contributions to the literature on "incentive-compatible mechanisms" that literally burst upon the theoretical economic world at the beginning of the 1970s. We explained how, in the eyes of the pioneers, the key was severing the link between reporting high preferences and receiving high tax assessments in order to eliminate the incentive to report untruthfully. But as we have just seen, this is actually not all that difficult to do. The most simple and commonplace systems of taxation such as head, property, wealth, and income taxes sever the link between benefits reported and taxes assessed.[69] Dozens of complicated new schemes were hardly necessary if all that was needed was to make taxes independent of benefits.

And the truth is this was all that was needed in order for governments to be capable, in theory, of supplying Pareto optimal allocations in the presence of external effects. But it is obvious traditional theorists desired more. Although many traditional theorists may have been confused about why they found taxation unrelated to benefits less than satisfying, it is clear they did find it so. And even though we have demonstrated that the conviction that such governments cannot generate Pareto optimal situations is misfounded, there may be other reasons to object.

Clearly, what traditional theorists wanted was a system of taxation that would permit the government to discover people's true preferences in order to provide public goods in socially efficient ways while at the same time collecting the necessary revenues from people according to the degree to which they were benefited. In other words, they wanted not just an efficient solution to the public goods problem, but an efficient benefits approach. While traditional theorists may have erroneously believed the problem with nonbenefit approaches was lack of efficiency, their real objection was that they did just what they were designed to do: they divorced assessments from benefits. While this is an objection on equity rather than efficiency grounds, it has an obvious appeal nonetheless. Why should someone little benefited pay as much as someone greatly benefited? What many theorists wanted was an efficient benefits approach, and this was what the profession had come to believe was impossible. When Richard Musgrave concluded that neither markets and voluntary associations, nor any alternative procedures were fully adequate to resolving the problem of public goods, this is what he meant. He could not foresee an efficient benefits approach. And he was by no means alone. This was the overwhelming consensus among experts in the theory of public finance prior to the advent of "incentive-compatible mechanisms."

What those who unleashed the revolution in incentive-compatible mechanisms did was conceive efficient "benefits" approaches. They accomplished what their peers had come to believe was impossible. However, the opinions of a majority of traditional theorists notwithstanding, "incentive-compatible mechanisms" were not the first procedures for providing and funding public goods with reasonable claims to efficiency but they were the first that taxed according to benefit and still could lay reasonable claims to efficiency. There is no need to treat the various innovations in greater detail here than in chapter 3 because we do not propose to offer new procedures, nor engage in technical critiques of others' mechanisms. In our opinion the innovations are far more than clever. They recognize that efficient provision of public goods requires truthful reporting of preferences. And they accept the conclusion that if people are placed in a position in which they will be penalized by reporting truthfully, they may lie. But where others concluded this implied an irreconcilable conflict between efficiency and taxation according to benefits, contributors to the incentive-compatible mechanisms literature saw a flaw in what had become an implicit impossibility theorem.

Individuals must be rendered unable to influence their tax assessments by the preferences they report to elicit truthful reporting of preferences. But the same truthful preferences that permit the government to calculate efficient supplies of public goods can be used to adjust individuals' assessments so that those benefited more will pay more and those benefited less will pay less provided the preferences used for adjustment purposes are the preferences of others. "Pivot mechanisms" use the reported preferences of others to calculate how much others are inconvenienced by the degree to which I influence the provision of public goods, and then charge me for the inconvenience I cause others. "Demand-revealing mechanisms" use the reported preferences of others to calculate the net benefit others will receive from the public goods provided, if they pay their proportional share, and deduct their net benefits from my assessment.

In either case, incentive for me to manipulate the reporting of my preferences is negligible since what I report does not enter into the calculation of my tax assessment. But in both cases, individuals who benefit more (or cause others greater inconvenience) will be assessed higher taxes, and individuals who benefit less (or cause others lesser inconvenience) will pay less. If pivot mechanisms are used, those who cause others greater inconvenience will be charged more. If demand-revealing mechanisms are used, those whose net benefit is less will receive larger tax abatements, so to speak, because their abatements are based on the net benefits of others who benefited more. With the benefit of hindsight the idea appears perfectly simple. But this could be said about many brilliant ideas. The obstacle to correlating taxes with benefits without inducing an incentive to lie had been removed; compensations must be based on the effects others' report.

The clarification of what is accomplished by incentive-compatible mechanisms and how they achieve it has little to do with our new welfare paradigm and theory. But the new welfare paradigm contributes to the interpretation of incentive-compatible mechanisms a better understanding of the importance of the issue. What is at stake is whether or not individuals with "minority" preferences for public goods should be compensated or penalized in some way. The issue is important because:

1. If such compensations should be deemed warranted, the calculations necessary for carrying them out efficiently must be applied to the entire allocative system

2. Beyond its distributive effect, compensation, penalization, or tax "neutrality" affects the degree of variety or uniformity that will evolve in people's preferences with respect to external effects

Since the reader may find these interpretations novel, we elaborate.

Everybody "consumes" the same public goods, but not everyone is equally benefited by doing so. People's preferences can vary with regard to how much public goods they would like provided and what they would like those public goods to be. An individual who enjoys the good fortune of having preferences that coincide closely to the package finally provided will enjoy greater benefits than individuals who would have preferred more (or less) and different kinds of public goods. Since what will be provided corresponds to average preferences, those whose preferences are closer to the average will benefit more than those whose preferences regarding public goods are farther from the norm.[70]

In one view, the question is whether individuals who are less benefited by the package of public goods all receive should be compensated for their "misfortune." In other words, should "odd balls" receive positive compensations? Should those whose preferences deviate farther from the social norm be compensated for the fact that they got less of what they wanted than those whose preferences were closer to average? Should the "preference minority" be compensated for the fact that their "candidates" lost in the public goods elections?[71]

At one level this is an equity issue—having verified that efficiency could be preserved in either case. If we implement proportional taxation our implicit answer is "no." If our answer is "yes" we should tax on a benefit basis, which could be accomplished without loss of efficiency by using a "demand-revealing mechanism," such as Groves and Ledyard developed.

Similarly, everybody influences the package of public goods provided,[72] but the extent to which everyone's influence inconveniences others, by skewing the package from what it would have been without their influence, is not the same. Those whose preferences are farther from the average will exercise a greater influence on the outcome than those whose preferences more closely approximate the norm. Moreover, if preferences are distributed normally, outliers' influence will inconvenience more others, causing a greater inconvenience. Seen in this light the question is whether individuals who inconvenience others to a greater extent should be penalized for doing so. Should "odd balls" be penalized? Should those whose preferences deviate farther from the social norm pay for the fact that they imposed their will on others to a greater extent than others imposed their will on them with regard to public goods? Should the "preference minority" be penalized for the fact that their "vote" counted for more in the public goods elections despite the fact that their "candidates" lost by larger margins? Again, at one level this is simply an equity issue. The implicit answer of proportional taxation is "no," while the implicit answer of a "pivot mechanism" is "yes."

But regardless of which view one takes and how one decides to answer the question in either case—that is, regardless of one's conception of what constitutes an "equitable" procedure for financing the provision of public goods—our paradigm implies the issue is of much greater importance than the traditional paradigm would lead one to suspect. For our paradigm emphasizes the reasons for believing that external effects are prevalent rather than exceptional. If one believes that compensations or penalties are warranted on equity grounds with regard to public goods, then our paradigm suggests that an appropriate "demand-revealing" or "pivot" mechanism must be implemented as the general mechanism for resource allocation. Since not even their most fervent supporters claim demand-revealing mechanisms are highly practical and easy to implement, this is a highly significant conclusion.

Our paradigm also suggests important consequences beyond equity are involved in the choice of a principle of taxation. If people's preferences are to some extent endogenous, and any advantage can be obtained by molding them in one direction rather than another, our welfare theory highlights why it is rational for people to do so. What preferences over "public good commodity space" would it benefit me to have? From the perspective of maximizing fulfillment from the package of public goods provided, it is advantageous to have preferences as close as possible to the social average. Here the incentive is always toward a greater conformity of preferences regarding public goods. From the point of view of minimizing tax assessments, it is advantageous to have whatever kind of preferences are compensated and not penalized, but that will depend on what principle of taxation is adopted. A pivot mechanism penalizes minority preferences, pushing preference development toward greater conformity. Any mechanism unrelated to benefit or inconvenience to others provides no incentive to develop either conformist or deviant preferences for public goods. A demand-revealing mechanism rewards minority preferences and establishes an incentive for individuals to develop diverse preferences.

But presumably it is the overall package of the public good "consumption" effect and the "payment" effect that is relevant. In this light, taxation unrelated to benefit or inconvenience to others exhibits a single conforming influence on preference development. A pivot mechanism contains a double conforming influence. And a demand-revealing mechanism "compensates" the conforming influence of the "consumption" effect with the diversifying influence of the "payment" effect. If compensation were complete, there would be no net influence toward greater diversity or conformity. Presumably overcompensation could be arranged to provide a net diversifying impact.

In any case, the preference development effects of taxing principles and the implication for greater conformity or variety of human preferences with regard to public goods appear to be as interesting as the implications for equity. And just as one might conclude there is no clear-cut case for one version of equity over another regarding payment for public goods, the case for greater variety or conformity of preferences for public goods appears ambiguous as well. For all the reasons we examined in chapter 6—uncertainty, vicarious enjoyment, etc.—greater variety is better, ceteris paribus. But in the case of public goods greater conformity of preferences has an advantage in efficiency. Since we all have to consume the same public goods, the advantage in having similar preferences is that more people get closer to what they want. The greater the variety of preferences for public goods, the more disappointed more people must be. We hasten to point out that this "trade-off" pertains only in the case of public goods. To the extent that goods are private, or can be suitably handled via local finance, there is no disadvantage to greater diversity of preferences. But for truly public goods greater variety of preferences implies a loss of well-being. All our new welfare paradigm can do is make us better aware of this trade-off. It does not imply any particular solution.

So, where does all this leave us regarding the efficiency properties of competitive markets?—the question we began with. At one level we only wish to borrow a conclusion that, until recently, no serious economic theorist would have denied: market allocations are demonstrably inefficient for public goods and externalities. While this opinion is no longer unanimous, we attribute recent dissenting opinions to the overexuberant atmosphere of the free-market jubilee. We are fully confident that a return to normalcy will restore the time-honored consensus among reputable economists that voluntary associations appended to markets must still fail to yield efficient allocations when external effects are present.

At a second level, we wish to point out that this very traditional conclusion is of far greater consequence than usually supposed. While the traditional paradigm confines the problem to a small number of exceptional "goods," our new paradigm projects the problem to be the general case. In general, human activities have external effects on others' possibilities—to a greater or lesser degree. The vision of economies as millions of isolated Robinson Crusoes connected only through the material goods they interchange is precisely the view we have criticized as grossly misrepresenting the human condition. While in market economies maybe only material "outputs" are exchanged, in fact what is shared is the physical and human environment in which we all must live, which is the joint outcome of all economic activities engaged in. Instead of seeing only the physical objects of market exchange we should see them as proxies for all the human activities that stand behind them. And while the effects of any particular activity may be much greater for some than others, the effects seldom are entirely confined to a single economic actor.

Moreover, since resource allocation in the context of external effects is the general resource allocation problem rather than a special case, the subject matter of the recent literature in incentive-compatible mechanisms becomes far more important. Some alternative to the market mechanism is required, in general, if there is to be any hope of allocative efficiency. The most important point is that this already takes us beyond the subject matter of this chapter. Market allocations will be, in general, inefficient. The efficiency, equity, and preference developmental properties of various alternative allocative procedures are another set of questions made interesting precisely because of markets' failures.

Finally, we have sought to throw some light on what is at stake in considering different proposals. Efficiency in the traditional sense becomes a rather trivial concern that can be satisfied by perfectly common approaches to financing public goods. And while one's notion of "equity" is of great importance in defining desirable allocative mechanisms, the effects of different procedures on preference development and the relative advantages and disadvantages of variety and conformity may be of equal or greater interest. We will comment briefly on criteria for an alternative desirable allocative mechanism in our conclusion, but return now to the allocative mechanism under consideration in this chapter, markets.

7.8 An Imperfection Theorem

Here, we formalize the only conclusion we require from the previous section and reformulate it as a theorem in a slightly unusual form that will be useful in the analysis that follows.

Market institutions have an inherent tendency to provide a relative overabundance of private goods compared to public goods. More exactly, markets can be expected to allocate too much of society's scarce productive resources to the production of private goods, goods with negative external effects, and public "bads," and too little of society's resources to the production of public goods and goods with positive external effects, resulting in a relative oversupply of the former kinds of goods and relative undersupply of the latter.

The usual way of seeing this is to note that social efficiency requires that output of every good be such that the marginal social cost of production be equal to its marginal social benefit. In private goods the marginal social benefit is simply the additional benefit enjoyed by a single purchaser. But for public goods the marginal social benefit incorporates the benefits enjoyed by everyone when the supply is expanded by one unit. Because free markets, even in conjunction with voluntary associations, are unable to overcome the free-rider problem, the effective demand expressed for public goods underestimates the true marginal social benefits.

The inefficiency can be seen from the perspective of the aggregate market as follows. The actual demand expressed in the marketplace for a public good, a, lies everywhere below the marginal-social benefit curve, yielding the well-known result that the actual amount of the public good, a^A that would be supplied under a market allocative mechanism would be less than the socially optimal amount, a^O. From the suppliers' perspective, the actual market price, π^A, they will receive is less than the price that would elicit an optimal supply, π^O, so they supply less than the socially optimal amount of the public good as depicted in figure 7.4.

FIG. 7.4. MARKET FOR PUBLIC GOOD "a"

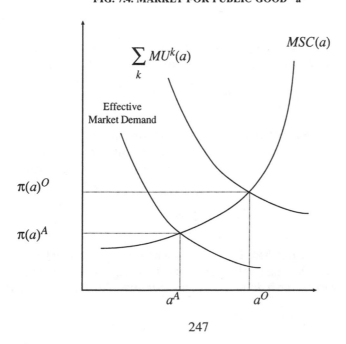

However, in the following section we will analyze the adjustments of rational individuals to the terms upon which markets make "goods" available when some have external effects. For this reason it is convenient to translate the traditional analysis of the resource allocation problem of public goods at the level of the aggregate market into terms of the supply price individual demanders will face. Strange as it may seem at first, whereas the problem with public goods from the point of view of suppliers is that they are priced too low (in comparison with private goods), the problem with public goods from the point of view of individual demanders is that they are priced too high.

An individual, i, should only be charged an amount equal to the net marginal social cost of supplying him or her with another unit of the public good, a. That is, individual consumers should be charged all additional costs to society of supplying another unit minus the marginal social benefits to all others. To charge individuals otherwise necessarily generates social inefficiency. To see this consider that

$$MSC(a) = \sum_k MU^k(a)$$

is the usual condition for social efficiency for public goods.[73]

As long as the right side is at least as large as the left side in this expression, it is socially inefficient not to supply the marginal unit. This can be rewritten as

$$MSC(a) = \sum_{k \neq i} MU^k(a) + MU^i(a)$$

where we separate the marginal benefits of all others from the marginal benefit to individual i. Suppose i is charged an amount in excess of

$$MSC(a) - \sum_{k \neq i} MU^k(a)$$

Then she or he may not purchase an additional unit of the good, even though the marginal social benefits of another unit are as great as the marginal social costs of providing it. On the other hand, if i is charged less than

$$MSC(a) - \sum_{k \neq i} MU^k(a)$$

then she or he may purchase units even when the marginal social benefits are smaller than the marginal social costs. This implies that the socially optimal price to charge individual i for another unit of a, $\pi^i(a)^O$, is exactly

An Imperfection Theorem

$$\pi^i(a)^O = MSC(a) - \sum_{k \neq i} MU^k(a)$$

Charging i either more or less than $\pi^i(a)^O$ can lead to socially inefficient outcomes.

But since suppliers of goods with positive external effects (or public good a in our example) cannot collect all of

$$\sum_{k \neq i} MU^k(a)$$

from others—for the reasons explained above—they make each individual, i, pay some actual supply price, $\pi^i(a)^A$, in excess of the optimal individual supply price, $\pi^i(a)^O$, in their efforts to cover costs. In other words, the inability to force others to pay for the benefits they actually obtain means private market suppliers must charge purchasers prices that are higher than would be socially optimal as pictured in figure 7.5.

FIG. 7.5. INDIVIDUAL DEMAND FOR PUBLIC GOOD "a" IN PERIOD $(t+k)$

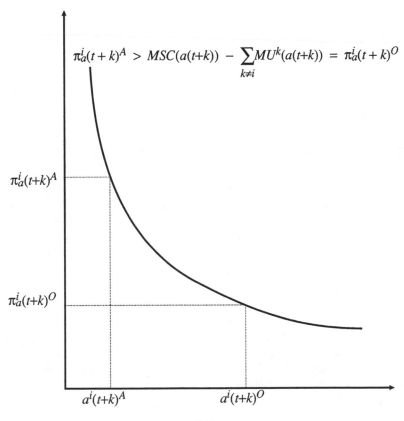

$$\pi^i_a(t+k)^A > MSC(a(t+k)) - \sum_{k \neq i} MU^k(a(t+k)) = \pi^i_a(t+k)^O$$

In figure 7.5 we formulate the situation for period $(t+k)$ to apply our theorems from chapter 6 directly. As can be seen, the actual supply price to individuals—the price that will be charged buyers under market allocations of goods with positive external effects—yields individual demands for the good, $a^i(t+k)^A$, that are less than the optimal individual demands would be, $a^i(t+k)^O$. If we compare this situation with the situation with a good displaying no (or less) positive external effects we can formulate the following useful theorem:

THEOREM 7.1: MARKET OVERCHARGES. Markets overcharge purchasers of goods with greater than average positive external effects. In other words, if good a has greater positive external effects than good b then: $\left[\pi^i(b)^A/\pi^i(a)^A\right] < \left[\pi^i(b)^O/\pi^i(a)^O\right]$ where $\pi^i(a)^A$ or $\pi^i(b)^A$ stands for the supply price individual i would actually face under market allocations and $\pi^i(a)^O$ or $\pi^i(b)^O$ stands for the supply price that would be socially efficient to assess individual i.

7.9 "Snowballing" Nonoptimality

We are finally ready to combine results here with results from chapter 6. The insight that markets overcharge purchasers of goods with positive external effects and consequently misallocate resources should not surprise traditional theorists. The claim that this is general, rather than occasional, is more novel. But there is reason to believe the situation is worse.

In chapter 5 we argued preferences are endogenous to economic systems, and in chapter 6 we explained that people can be expected to orient their future needs toward goods and activities that will be relatively easy to obtain and away from goods and activities that will be hard to obtain. We proved Theorem 6.6, establishing that if there is a bias in the conditions of supply of a good or activity, the resulting degree of nonoptimality in the economy will be greater than indicated by a traditional welfare theory that treats preferences as exogenous, and that the divergence will "snowball," or grow, over time. In Theorem 6.7 we demonstrated that "rational" people can be expected to influence their own development in a direction that mirrors any bias in the conditions of supply, or that individual rationality dictates a kind of "self-warping" in response to biases in the functioning of economic systems. And in Theorem 6.8 we demonstrated that any such biases will tend to be disguised to the economy's inhabitants to the extent that their "rational self-warping" is unconscious or forgotten after the fact. We have just reformulated a well-known theorem regarding public goods and externalities as our Theorem 7.1 that markets generate a bias in conditions of supply for goods with external effects.

But the sum of these theorems implies that if people have reason to believe that markets will be used as allocative institutions in the future, they also have reason to expect a bias in the conditions of future supply of goods with external effects. Combining yields the following result:

THEOREM 7.2: SNOWBALLING NONOPTIMALITY OF MARKET ALLOCATIONS. Not only will markets misallocate resources in some initial time period—undersupplying goods with greater than average positive external effects as compared to goods with less than average positive external effects—but there will be a cumulative divergence away from optimal allocations in future time periods as individuals "rationally" adjust their personal characteristics to diminish their needs for goods with positive external effects and expand their needs for goods with few external effects and negative external effects.

The proof of Theorem 7.2 is immediate, applying Theorem 6.6 to Theorem 7.1 written for period $(t+k)$. What the theory and theorems of this and chapter 6 permit us to see that was not apparent to traditional theorists is not only the prevalence of the problem of effects external to market decision making, but the full consequences of market failure. Not only are misallocations due to external effects pervasive in market economies, the severity of the misallocations worsens over time as people pursue the "individually rational" strategy of molding their characteristics and preferences to better conform to institutional biases, thereby producing the "socially irrational" outcome of allocations that diverge even farther from efficient allocations than would have occurred had people not adjusted.[74]

Beyond theorems concerning social efficiency, we have tried to pinpoint the mechanism whereby people's perceived needs and desires come to correspond with the individualizing characteristics of market institutions. In our terms, we clarified the mechanism of "rational" self-manipulation or warping of personality structures, skill development, and consciousness that reproduce the core characteristics of market institutions in the human center of people's personalities as they evolve in market economies. While the effects of institutions on the characteristics of those whose activities they organize has been apparent to many, there has been a lack of clarity about the mechanisms through which those effects are exerted. Moreover, it has not been apparent how one could draw conclusions about the welfare consequences of such effects since the institutional influence affected people's preference structures as well as their characteristics. We hope our new welfare theory clarifies both how the characteristics of institutions affect the characteristics of inhabitants and why this need not subvert prospects for drawing welfare conclusions.

251

We hope our first application of these new tools contributes to a fuller evaluation of markets—an evaluation that highlights liabilities of markets under the most generous assumptions of how they may function. And we hope our analysis also clarifies what has frequently been only a vague "intuition" of those critical of markets. More than a few social critics have voiced the sentiment that markets have an undesirable effect on the people who use them—that markets tend to make us into people we would rather not become. Critics have sometimes implied that besides whatever else markets do or do not do, they have a destructive effect on the quality of social life. Traditional welfare theory ridicules such sentiments as unscientific—the sentiments of fuzzy-minded romantics—that does not withstand the rigors of clear-thinking analysis. Our theory suggests that such intuitions about markets are perfectly well founded, and that the criticisms of "romantic visionaries" of certain effects of modern economic institutions can be expressed and supported by rigorous "scientific" analysis.

This chapter has attempted to identify the cybernetic, incentive, and allocative characteristics of market institutions. We claim to have uncovered a pervasive bias in market institutions against discovering, expressing, and developing needs that require social rather than individual activity for their fulfillment. Markets do not provide concrete information about how my decisions affect the life prospects of others. They do not even provide accurate summaries of the social benefits and costs associated with what I decide to do. Markets establish an incentive structure that rewards competitive behavior and penalizes cooperative behavior. And actual market allocations undersupply social goods and activities and oversupply individual goods and activities. They thereby establish the kind of individually rational incentives described in Theorem 7.2 to wean myself of needs that require socially coordinated intercourse for their fulfillment and accentuate needs that can be met through individualized activities.

In any case, we have demonstrated the logic that would lead "rational" people to mold their own characteristics to better conform to market biases. And we have demonstrated that this "individually rational process" is "socially irrational." By doing the best they can within the limiting environment of market institutions, individuals will adjust in ways that imply even greater losses of potential fulfillment than if they did not adjust to markets' limitations. As time goes on, the preferences that are "individually rational" for people to develop combine with the biases inherent in market allocations to yield allocational outcomes increasingly farther from those that would have maximized fulfillment. In the end, the worst fears of "romantic" critics of the "socially alienating" affects of markets prove more to the point than the endless volumes of "scientific equations" produced by academic economists claiming to "prove" that markets are ideal allocative institutions.

252

8

PRIVATE
ENTERPRISE

OUR PRINCIPAL AIM in this chapter is to use our new welfare theory to
examine the effects of private enterprise on the production process. We
analyze weaknesses in previous criticisms of the traditional analysis and
focus our attention on how the "conflict theory" of privately owned firms
can be better formulated using our new paradigm. But before tackling that
agenda, we have some unfinished business from chapter 7 on markets. In
our discussion of overzealous defenses of PuEMEs we mentioned that
some claim PuEMEs would be immune to income distribution "problems"
that plague PrEMEs. While set in a market environment, the question is
what, if any, are the implications for income distribution of public as
opposed to private ownership. We treat income distribution in conjunction
with ownership in this chapter.

8.1 Ownership and Income Distribution

Opponents of private enterprise economies frequently object that
PrEMEs generate unacceptable distributions of income. Of course, the
third fundamental theorem of welfare economics is the ultimate defense
against this charge. As we saw in part 1, this theorem is traditionally
interpreted as guaranteeing that private enterprise market economies are
completely flexible with regard to income distribution. However, critics
have refused to accept these assurances on grounds that while this may be
the case in theory, there is little reason to believe it will be so in practice.

Besides the difference between income flexibility in theory and practice, we believe there has been some confusion regarding exactly what the

253

third fundamental theorem of welfare economics means and what conditions guarantee income flexibility even in theory. Since our new paradigm highlights complications infrequently considered, we will treat them here as well.

Broadly speaking, critics argue it is hard to imagine a private enterprise market economy with a highly inegalitarian income distribution undergoing a radically egalitarian redistribution of income. Critics reason this would first require a successful "revolution" in which the "have nots" succeed in expropriating the property of the "haves." Then, if private enterprise market institutions were maintained after such an upheaval, the vagaries of luck and talent in combination with ample opportunities to accumulate assets would require that lump-sum redistributions be repeated over and over again to maintain an egalitarian outcome. As conservative opponents of such practices hasten to point out, even should sufficient political "will" be forthcoming repeatedly,[1] predictable redistributions necessarily affect incentives when "rational expectations" catch up to redistributive manipulations.[2]

In our view, egalitarians' intuitions are sound. To expect real, private enterprise market economies to generate acceptably equitable income distributions that are stable over time is naive.[3] But some who criticize private enterprise market economies on these grounds claim their public enterprise counterparts are not plagued by similar problems. We will end by disagreeing, but let us reexamine income distribution in private and public market economies step by step.

8.1.1 The Flexibility Theorem Reconsidered

Returning to the level of pure theory, it is important to distinguish between "initial endowments" that prove to be income generating assets that are transferable and those that are not. The difference between alienable and nonalienable productive assets is hardly highlighted by the traditional paradigm.[4] In fact, our ready acceptance of the meaningfulness of the third fundamental theorem of welfare economics for PrEMEs results in no small part from the fact that the traditional paradigm blurs this distinction. The third theorem states only that any Pareto outcome can be achieved as the equilibrium of an appropriate PrEME. The translation of this theorem into the language of "under an appropriate redistribution of initial endowments" presumes that all initial endowments can be transferred. Shares of ownership in firms and stocks of physical goods can obviously be transferred, in theory. But productive initial endowments in the form of human talents and skills presumably cannot be so easily transferred, even in theory.[5]

It appears the existence of productive assets that are inalienable even in theory casts a new light on the most common interpretation of the flexibility theorem for PrEMEs. But at first sight the implications for public enterprise market economies are more striking. If PrEMEs are only flexible to the extent that alienable productive assets can be transferred, how are PuEMEs to have any flexibility since individuals gain no income through ownership of nonhuman productive assets in public enterprise economies?

While the dilemma is only temporary in both cases, it does highlight common misperceptions. Even if we imagine private enterprise market economies achieving income flexibility by arranging transfers of alienable assets to compensate for differences in nonalienable assets, strictly speaking this does not guarantee complete income flexibility. Complete income flexibility requires that we be able to reduce an individual with a productive nonalienable asset to zero income. In other words, in PrEMEs complete income flexibility requires more than reshuffling alienable assets in the presence of nonalienable assets. It must be possible to reduce peoples' income through negative lump-sum assessments.

But once the existence of inalienable productive assets forces us to recognize that full income flexibility of PrEMEs ultimately rests on the possibility of lump-sum assessments, some of which may be negative, the appearance of income inflexibility in PuEMEs vanishes as well. For while there are no alienable productive assets that can be transferred to compensate for differences in nonalienable assets in PuEMEs, complete income flexibility can be achieved via an infinitely flexible system of positive and negative lump-sum assessments. In fact, complete income flexibility in both private and public enterprise market economies hinges on an infinitely flexible system of positive and negative lump-sum assessments.[6] The "redistribution of initial endowments" is neither a sufficient nor necessary mechanism for complete income flexibility in either system.

So rather than think in terms of redistributing initial endowments, it is more appropriate to think of income flexibility via a system of handicapping. The pre-race potential of all the horses is determined by preferences, technology, and economic as well as noneconomic institutions, which combine to determine the "productivities" of the different inalienable human assets each possesses. With no handicapping, free labor markets will translate this into a particular pattern of income distribution. If we wish to be able to achieve all conceivable income distributions, we must be able to supplement or subtract from individuals' incomes to whatever extent necessary to alter how our "horses" finish. That is, we must have a free hand in handicapping that does not affect how fast our horses try to run. If we handicap once, for races in all periods, prior to any races taking place, all horses must run to their full potential in every race to maximize their income. The only remaining subtlety is that as soon as we change the income distribution by our handicaps we change the weights attached to different individuals' preferences, which affects the "productivities" of assets (the "natural speeds" of our steeds). But this merely complicates the job of handicapping, and perfect knowledge on the part of our handicapper was already required in order to handicap all races before any were run.

Of course, in PrEMEs individuals can be permitted to receive income from alienable, nonhuman assets—whose "productivities" are determined by the same interaction of preferences, technologies, and institutions that determine the "productivities" of human assets. But this is just a particular kind of handicapping. Positive and negative assessments are like starting horses ahead and behind the starting line. Doling out inalienable assets is like pulling weights out of saddlebags or giving injections of drugs. In general, in either a PrEME or PuEME would be a prehandicapped outcome. In PuEMEs the prehandicapped outcome is determined only by the natural speeds of steeds. In PrEMEs, weighted saddlebags and drug injections modify "natural potentials." In either case, to get any other outcome we must have flexible handicapping that does not induce horses to perform below their capabilities in hope of influencing their handicap. In either case, to have complete income flexibility we must be able to start some horses ahead and others behind the starting line. In theory, a one-time-only system of lump-sum positive and negative assessments calculated with perfect knowledge will do the trick for both public and private enterprise market economies.

To recapitulate, what the third fundamental theorem of welfare economics says for PrEMEs is that a particular initial endowment will generate any possible Pareto optimum. What the third fundamental theorem says for PuEMEs is that a particular initial endowment will generate any possible Pareto optimum. But once we recognize that income-generating assets in PuEMEs are almost entirely inalienable, it is obvious that it may be impossible, even in theory, to achieve a particular Pareto optimum as the equilibrium of a PuEME via a reshuffling of existing endowments. But the presence of inalienable productive assets in PrEMEs implies that reshuffling is incapable of generating the endowments necessary to generate some Pareto optima as the equilibria of PrEMEs as well. Fortunately (or not) a substitute flexibility Theorem 6.5 saves the day for both kinds of economy—at least in theory.

ALTERNATIVE FLEXIBILITY THEOREM 6.5. An appropriate one-time-only system of lump-sum (positive and negative) assessments will give us any Pareto optimum we desire as the equilibrium of any PrEME or PuEME under all traditional assumptions with either exogenous or perfectly informed endogenous preferences. In other words, under any set of initial endowments in either PrEME or PuEME we can still get any Pareto optimum by appropriate handicapping.

256

This leaves us with the following conclusion: at the purely theoretical level, in a world of perfect knowledge and "Debreuvian" rather than "real" time, PuEMEs and PrEMEs are both completely flexible—although not via the mechanism usually presumed. On what basis, then, might one argue that PuEMEs would be less likely to generate "unacceptable" income distributions in practice than PrEMEs?

8.1.2 *Income Distributions in Practice*

There are two issues here:

1. While both PrEMEs and PuEMEs are completely flexible regarding income distribution in theory, as we have just verified, are there reasons to believe that in practice each system has tendencies to "gravitate" toward a particular pattern of income distribution?

2. What income distributions are deemed "acceptable," "approved," or "appropriate," and what distributions are deemed "objectionable," or "inappropriate"?

If one adopted the view that income differentials based on differences of human productive assets were appropriate, whereas income differences resulting from unequal ownership of nonhuman productive assets were objectionable, one would have every reason to conclude that PuEMEs have "practical" immunities to income distribution "problems" that plague PrEMEs. In other words, under this definition of appropriate and inappropriate, while theoretically PuEMEs could deviate from the "approved" distribution by "inappropriate" handicapping, there would be little reason to expect them to do so.

In PuEMEs "inappropriate" handicaps in the form of privately held alienable assets are ruled out by the substitution of public for private enterprise. And the translation of economic wealth into political power should work against the possibility of establishing "inappropriately" egalitarian handicaps in the form of redistributive lump-sum assessments that modify the "natural" outcome of the "free" labor market as those with greater wealth exert greater political influence to block such initiatives. Moreover, the complications of real time and uncertainty impose the practical necessity of continual reassessments if more egalitarian distributions were to be preserved. This would necessarily affect incentives and efficiency, which opponents of redistribution would presumably explain in very convincing ways. In any case, in the real world "inappropriately" egalitarian redistributions would require unlikely repeated political victories of "have-nots" over "haves." So those who approve of income differentials based only on differences in productive human assets have every reason to expect the practical conditions of PuEMEs to militate against handicaps they deem "inappropriate."[7]

But on what basis are unequal incomes that result from unequal distributions of human productive assets deemed appropriate? Just because the operation of a "free" labor market generates differential wages and salaries due to differences in talent, training, and/or education, why are these considered acceptable?

At this point, especially those who have "invested" in more than the average number of years of education would likely remark on the importance of differentiating between inherited talent and training/education, insisting that time and effort (of trainee and trainers alike) spent in training and education should be compensated. It is certainly a common view that this is fair, as well as an important incentive for people to "better" themselves. Feelings run so strong on this subject we prefer to defuse the situation through a device. Let us stipulate that all training and education is paid for at public expense, that the time spent in such endeavors is time that otherwise would be spent working,[8] and that time spent in training/education is at least as pleasurable as time spent on the job.[9]

Under these circumstances we see no reason to accept the proposition that unequal incomes deriving from unequal endowments of human productive assets are justified. In our view, genetic advantages and education or training that were in no sense obtained through individual sacrifice are no more justifiable excuses for differential economic well-being than inheritance of property. In neither case is there anything particularly fair about the birth lottery.

The view that differential income based on differential genetic endowments is justified is the PuEME analogue of Nozick's thesis that historical initial endowments of alienable productive assets give rise to just distributional outcomes in PrEMEs. That is, Nozick and supporters of PrEMEs implicitly defend the maxim:

DISTRIBUTIVE MAXIM 1. From each according to genetic inheritance, to each according to genetic and property inheritance.[10]

Supporters of PuEMEs implicitly defend the maxim:

DISTRIBUTIVE MAXIM 2. From each according to genetic inheritance, to each according to genetic inheritance.

In our view, both maxims are arbitrary and unjustifiable. In theory they merely rationalize the outcome of different random lotteries. In actual historical settings they rationalize the status quo which serves the interest of those who benefit from obstructing redistributions that would benefit the disadvantaged. For us, equal effort is a sufficient and necessary condition alike to merit receiving an equal share of whatever the economy has to offer, while in the long-run it is desirable if people become sufficiently trusting and empathetic to adopt distribution according to need. To put it in terms of alternative maxims that have received some attention and, in our opinion, have much to recommend them:[11]

DISTRIBUTIVE MAXIM 3. From each according to genetic inheritance, to each according to effort.

DISTRIBUTIVE MAXIM 4. From each according to genetic inheritance, to each according to need.

8.1.3 *Economic Systems and Implicit Maxims*

The point here is not to debate the relative philosophical merits of different distribution maxims. We merely seek to identify the maxims implicit in different distribution outcomes, and determine whether there are practical reasons to expect different maxims to be achieved by different economies. The "practical" considerations to which most allude reduce to: (1) a positive correlation between economic and political power, (2) uncertainty requiring continual readjustments to preserve any of the "infinitely possible" income distributions other than the one that would prevail without "assessments," and (3) the undeniable incentive implications of predictable readjustments. We have discovered that these same practical considerations imply: PrEMEs' "natural tendency"—although we hesitate to use the terminology—is to "gravitate" toward an income distribution expressive of the maxim for which Nozick sought to provide a philosophical justification (distributive maxim 1). While PuEMEs' "natural tendency" is to "gravitate" toward an income distribution expressive of distributive maxim 2.

Moreover, the link between economic institutions and ideology is strong. While this is not a matter of concern in the traditional paradigm, it is something our new paradigm takes more seriously. Private enterprise market economies induce people to maximize return on all their assets. That is what competition in PrEMEs enforces. But people have a strong propensity to rationalize what they do. In people's minds, the outcome of what they strive for must be justified, and they tend to ensure that it is by molding our thoughts and values accordingly. Hence private enterprise market economies are likely to generate an ideology for which the likes of Nozick have merely provided refined philosophical elaboration, i.e., historic endowments of productive assets are nothing more than fruits of prior efforts and are thereby justified. Further, to be constantly "expropriating" those fruits is unjustifiable—except, perhaps, in cases of extreme humanitarian concern.

Similarly, public enterprise market economies induce people to maximize return on their human productive assets. That is what competition in PuEMEs enforces. And once again, people have a strong tendency to

259

justify the distributional outcome of what they strive for. In this case, the fruits of maximizing return on one's stock of "human capital" in the labor market come to be seen as justified, and arguments for egalitarian "compensating differentials" come to be seen as "expropriation." All of which simply adds to the list of reasons to doubt that sufficient political will could be mobilized in stable PuEMEs in practice to generate outcomes we would consider sufficiently egalitarian.

In conclusion, if opponents of private enterprise who claim public enterprise market economies would not be subject to income distribution "problems" that plague private enterprise market systems mean that PuEMEs can be expected to gravitate toward distributions expressive of maxim two rather than maxim one, we are in agreement. Moreover, it is obvious the number of income-generating assets that can lead to inegalitarian outcomes is greater in private than public enterprise market economies. And since inalienable assets must be "embodied" in mere mortals, the possibilities of vastly inegalitarian distributions of "initial endowments" through accumulation is far greater in the case of private enterprise economies as well. So PuEMEs may well prove less likely to yield distributions as inegalitarian as their PrEME cousins, thereby lending credence to claims of greater egalitarianism on their part.[12]

But if supporters mean that PuEMEs will not be plagued by distributional "problems"—specifically inegalitarian tendencies that in practical terms would be most difficult to overcome—we do not agree. For we personally do not accept the definitions of "appropriate," and "objectionable" implicit in distributive maxim 2, and see no reason to expect real PuEMEs to generate distributions that are sufficiently egalitarian to be expressive of distributive maxim 3, much less sufficiently humanitarian to be expressive of maxim 4.[13]

8.2 Weaknesses in Conflict Theory

In chapter 2 we reviewed criticisms by a number of authors of the traditional treatment of production under private enterprise. According to the traditional theory of production, profit maximization under the restraining influence of competitive labor and product markets should lead to: (1) choice of efficient production techniques, (2) job design in accord with the principle of "producer sovereignty," and (3) wage differentials reflective only of differences in marginal productivities and desirabilities of jobs. What has come to be known as the "conflict school" has challenged these conclusions as we elaborated in chapter 2. We begin our efforts to strengthen the theoretical argument of the "conflict school" by discussing weaknesses in previous formulations.

8.2.1 *Rebuttal to "Labor Power" versus "Labor"*

A traditional theorist might respond to criticisms based on the distinction between "labor power" and "labor done" along the following lines.

Granted the labor market in PrEMEs is formally a market for "labor power" rather than actual labor services, but this is of no practical consequence. Just as employees whose expectations about working conditions are unfulfilled will find out soon enough, and move on to another job where their expectations are realized, employers have a clear enough idea of the work services they expect to receive, and should those expectations go unfulfilled the employer will change employees soon enough. In other words, while the market is formally a market for labor power, it is implicitly a market for labor services. Of course, all this assumes competitive, anonymous, labor markets. But in any other context traditional theory has always admitted "all bets are off."

Similarly, if critics want to insist on labeling the decision-making process under private enterprise "dictatorial," and point out that the labor exchange leaves important aspects of the situation unsettled by binding contract, so be it. But to imply that "dictatorial" employers can settle such matters entirely to their own satisfaction after employees show up for work, without taking employee preferences into account, is to ignore the fact that competitive labor markets permit unsatisfied employees to vote with their feet if their expectations are unmet. Competition for labor means that employers must offer a wage/work effect package that continues to attract employees in the context of uncountable other employers' demand for workers. Likewise, competition for jobs means that employees must abide sufficiently by the implicit integrity of the labor contract not to be replaced by uncountable others looking for the best wage/work effect package they can find.

In general, a plausible traditional rebuttal is to appeal for a reasonable assessment of "expectations." Especially in a "steady state" model there is no reason the full consequences of decisions and actions that are repeated over and over again would not become fully known to all involved. Hence we have the traditional conclusion that the formal distinction between labor and labor power disappears in a full information world.

8.2.2 *Rebuttal to Asymmetrical Information*

This same line of defense can be used to good effect against theorists who base their "conflict theory" of the firm entirely on asymmetrical information sets of employees and employers. In a steady state model there is no answer to the question why the "principal" would not find out anything he or she did not know at first. To put it in Coase/Simon terms: the worker who disappointed the boss' expectations by shirking or disobeying orders would be sent packing after two or three periods. And if the problem is that the employer does not know what expectations to have regarding capabilities of employees, competitive labor markets will take care of that problem over the long run. With enough competition among workers for jobs, employers will be able to discover what employees are capable of doing, if not through repeated observation of performance in their own firm, from studying the results other employers are able to elicit.

In this context it is worth noting that those who have treated the employment situation in a multiperiod, principal-agent model have been very careful not to assume that the principal comes to full knowledge as time goes on.[14] If this were the case one of the conditions requiring principal-agent modeling in the first place would disappear. But in any case, the final rebuttal to this line of criticism is that traditional welfare theory never claimed that organization of the production process via private enterprise institutions would be efficient if one of the contracting parties was systematically and continuously deprived of information available to the other.

So while any conclusions of inefficiency deriving from asymmetrical information are perfectly interesting to the extent that employers and employees do have asymmetrical information in a real world characterized by continual changes in productive possibilities, they do not contradict the conclusions of traditional welfare theory under a perfect knowledge assumption.

In our introduction we warned the reader we would not be reviewing a considerable new literature in welfare theory on uncertainty, because we did not believe progress in this area required a major shift in paradigm. This is an appropriate place to clarify this issue. Many have remarked on the extent to which the "real" world of uncertainties diverges from the "steady state" world, which implies full and symmetrical knowledge within which traditional welfare theory has long operated. In the last decade many have responded by reworking traditional welfare theory under assumptions of uncertainty. But this work has yielded few "surprises." Reworking welfare theory under assumptions of uncertainty has proved to be "normal science" in Kuhnian terms—reaffirming the original vision and conclusions in slightly more complex settings, requiring no substantial change in paradigm.

At the risk of oversimplifying, if uncertainty is symmetrical, agents who maximize the expected value of utility or profits replicate the welfare theoretic results of traditional theory. If uncertainty is asymmetrical, certain traditional welfare theoretic conclusions no longer hold, but the social inefficiencies are intuitive rather than surprising, and principal agent theory is well suited to elaborating these complexities. Moreover, these results contain few critical implications for major economic institutions because they apply generally to all economic systems. Rather than clarify fundamental characteristics and/or weaknesses of economic institutions, such work demonstrates that welfare losses can be diminished in any economic system by diminishing uncertainty in general and by eliminating any asymmetrical uncertainties that grant some agents "uncompetitive" advantage over others. But work on this frontier of welfare theory neither requires nor compels a major change in welfare paradigm, whereas work on other frontiers does. It was for this reason we ignored the numerous recent advances in this area and not because we do not appreciate the advances that have been made.

8.2.3 Rebuttal to Alienated Labor

The criticism that private enterprise production dooms most to the status of "alienated labor" has not moved traditional theorists to respond. While putting words into people's mouths is always of questionable value, we might hypothesize that traditional theorists find this charge naive. They might argue the criticism stems from a romantic comparison of modern economies to the presumed "golden age" of craft production in which self-sufficient, independent producers could conceive and direct their own work activities. And they might argue that what seems to be "formal" alienation from control over work process, product, and whatever else, upon more sophisticated analysis, turns out not to be a "practical" alienation at all.

In the traditional view, workers have control over the work process through their supply of labor function that will be different for activities whose "process" or "products" the workers evaluate differently. If the work is debilitating or boring, presumably workers will insist on a sufficient wage premium to exactly "compensate" the differential displeasure. If the work "product" is deemed less worthy than average, presumably here as well employers will demand compensating differentials.[15] In the traditional view, as long as labor markets are competitive, the worker has "practical" control in the same sense that the consumer has "practical" control over what products private employers "choose" to produce.

As a matter of fact, traditional theory suggests the influence permitted workers over the work process and product through their supply of labor functions backed by their freedom to "vote with their feet" is all they should be permitted. Even within the framework of working for an employer, different kinds of jobs and occupational categories permit varying degrees of self-direction over one's laboring efforts. Carpenters engage in more self-directed work than assembly-line workers, and if "self-determination" is important to people this should be reflected in compensating differentials between jobs that differ in this respect.

Moreover, contrary to what traditional Marxist analysis implies, the dividing line between employer and employee in private enterprise economies is not completely impermeable.[16] Presumably, if self-directed labor were sufficiently important to individuals they would work, as many do in all private enterprise economies, as self-employed, accepting compensating differentials in income. And if the desire to conceive and coordinate activities involving more than one's own efforts is strong enough, perfectly competitive capital markets permit people to take out loans and start their own businesses. In any case, in the traditional view to allow any greater control over the product by individual workers would rob consumers of their say over what they will consume. One might even say that if we "de-alienate" workers from their products we necessarily "alienate" consumers from the objects of their consumption!

In fact, as soon as one concludes that private entrepreneurs' freedom to manuever is nil within the "black box" because they are completely hemmed in by competitive labor and product markets, the "problem" of "alienation" vanishes. In this traditional view, producer and consumer sovereignty are the appropriate concepts concerning influence over decision making, and the Marxist concept of alienation, which focuses exclusively on an individual worker without reference to other workers or consumers, is seen as an inappropriate concept for evaluating effective influence over decision making in modern, integrated economies.

8.2.4 Malfeasance Is Universal

As we saw in chapter 2, Bowles argued that private enterprise aggravates the problem of malfeasance. But this amounts to the claim that there are alternative ways to organize production that either alleviate the problem of malfeasance or reduce the costs of combating it. A skeptic might counter that people will shirk unpleasant work under all organizations of production. More specifically, a skeptic might ask why a worker would shirk less in a publicly owned, employee-managed enterprise than in a privately owned and managed enterprise.

The skeptic's point is not that malfeasance is independent of surveillance, punishment, and reward, but precisely that these are the factors, and the only factors, that affect the amount of shirking a rational, self-interested actor will engage in. Consequently, the rebuttal to Bowles' critique would be that under the same system of surveillance, punishment, and rewards, malfeasance would be the same under either private or public ownership. In which case, the social costs of combating malfeasance would be equal in both systems of ownership—provided individuals behave as rational, self-interested actors.

Of course, this is precisely the position Bowles, to his credit, identified as the "Neo-Hobbesian" view. And in fairness to Bowles, he did not so much intend to rebut the Neo-Hobbesian view in his *American Economic Review* article as to clarify and contrast that view with what he called the "Marxian" class conflict view. But if what we prefer to call the "radical" class conflict school is to have anything to contribute beyond a "Neo-Hobbesian" analysis of malfeasance, it must explain why workers would not be just as likely to "cheat" on one another as on a private employer. While Bowles hints at the answers, we show below how our new paradigm helps clarify the reasons. Of particular interest is whether or not the reasons given by the radical conflict school assume that workers behave other than as rational, individual maximizers in public enterprise, employee-managed environments. For if this is the nature of the explanation, no matter how reasonable the argument, traditional theorists would be justified in concluding that it lies outside welfare theory proper, that a Neo-Hobbesian view of malfeasance is sufficient in welfare theoretic terms, and that Bowles' critique of private enterprise rests on the assumption that workers' behavior in some environments is influenced by factors other than rational, individual maximization.

8.2.5 *Limitations of Single Period Models*

As we saw, Michael Reich's model responds directly to the traditional objection to "divide and conquer" theories of racially motivated employer behavior that they are, ultimately, "conspiracy theories." As Kenneth Arrow explained, while employment discrimination may well be in the interests of employers as a class, one must provide compelling reasons for why it would not be profitable for individual private employers to cheat on the discriminating employer cartel in order to avoid concluding that competitive private enterprise economies tend to alleviate, rather than aggravate, racial and sexual discrimination.[17] Put differently, if class-dividing effects of individual employer actions are merely positive externalities for an employer's classmates, then traditional theory teaches us not to expect such effects to be taken into consideration. And if there is one point on which our new theory agrees with traditional theory it is that effects external to a decision-making process will not be taken into account! But Reich provides a reason why the effects are not external to the individual employer.

If an employer could get the same work done by paying whites no more skilled than blacks the same wage rate, it would be unprofitable to pay whites more. And if an employer could get the same work from an equally capable all black work force as employing more than a proportionate share of whites, it would be unprofitable to hire whites at a higher wage rate. But Reich voices a reason to doubt the assumption that an employer can get the same work done in both situations and, therefore, gives a reason employers might do just what traditional theory suggests they will not, except at the expense of their own individual profits. What Reich's argument boils down to is that since wage discrimination and employment discrimination increase the amount of work an employer can extract from labor hired, doing so up to the point where the increased costs equal the benefits is part and parcel of profit-maximizing strategy for individual employers, rather than contrary to profit maximization, as traditional theory would have us believe.[18]

In our view, Reich's argument succeeds in overcoming the "conspiracy theory" rebuttal of traditional theory. Moreover, Reich points the way toward a more general view of how the conflict of interests between employers and employees works itself out in ways that are not necessarily socially efficient. But we believe his model fails to suggest the extent to which employers have an individual profit incentive to engage in discriminatory actions. Nor does his model enable us to assess all the factors that play important roles in the battle between employers and employees as each pursues individual interests.

By treating the issue in a single time period model, Reich limits the extent of benefits that accrue to discriminating employers regarding extracting labor from labor power and fails altogether to show how such actions can benefit employers in wage negotiations as well. A traditional theorist might well respond to Reich's argument by admitting the logic of his demonstration, but challenging the significance of the effect. If the only benefit to the employer of what Reich admits is cost-increasing behavior is to make employees more manageable in the present, one might wonder just how much extra cost would be warranted.[19] What Reich's model, which should be seen as a pathbreaking first step, fails to indicate is that by far the most important beneficial effects to employers of discriminatory actions today are greater divisions among their employees throughout the future.

By choice of technology and reward structure employers can affect the human and group characteristics their employees will have in the future, thereby affecting what they must pay their employees in many future time periods in addition to the effort they can extract from the labor they hire during many time periods. Choice of technology and manipulation of reward structures that affect the individual and group characteristics of employees in ways that weaken their ability to resist future efforts to extract greater work effort are also likely to permit employers to pay less for that labor power in many future time periods. In sum, Reich's model correctly identifies the "wage increasing effect" of employer discrimination since this is the effect on the wage bill in the period in which the discriminatory actions are taken. But his model is blind to the "wage diminishing effect" of employer discrimination since this effect occurs in periods after the discriminatory actions.

Moreover, expanding our view of what is at stake for employers and employees alike in discriminatory behavior clarifies the importance of factors not highlighted in Reich's model. Most obviously, the importance of the rate of labor turnover becomes immediately apparent. A multiperiod view of what is at stake in discriminatory behavior is no different from a single period view if there is 100 percent labor turnover in each time period! For with 100 percent turnover all future "beneficial" effects of discriminatory behavior that employers might carry out would vanish for those employers and accrue only to their classmates as "positive" externalities. But the traditional claim that discriminatory actions only generate positive externalities for other employers is most certainly not valid if labor turnover is less than 100 percent each time period and if employers compete for profits over the long haul rather than simply in the present. In the far more realistic case of competition for profits over the long run and less than 100 percent labor turnover, the benefits of discriminatory behavior to individual employers are far greater than suggested by Reich's limited model, as we will see when we embed Reich's logic in the formal model we developed in chapter 6. In our model it is much easier to see why the total future profit-enhancing effects can provide a powerful incentive capable of outweighing substantial present costs. Moreover, the critical nature of labor turnover on employer incentives is readily apparent in our formulation, while it was invisible in Reich's model without a future.

8.2.6 *The Importance of Human Characteristics*

More fundamental is the importance of the individual and group characteristics of employees. What is really at stake is nothing less than the fact that employers and employees have directly opposed interests not only with respect to the real wage, but also with regard to the human characteristic transforming effects of the production process.[20]

Without a paradigm and welfare theory that explicitly identifies individual and group characteristics as "state variables" for which private employers have important interests in determining values quite different than those employees would choose, the generality of the problem, the critique of "producer sovereignty," and the profit-enhancing logic of economic discrimination are not apparent. The conflict between employer and employee in private enterprise economies is a complicated battle waged over time. In any period what is at stake is not only the present outcome in terms of wage rates and effort extracted, or "real wage," but changes in employee characteristics that powerfully affect the terrain of future battle. While implicit in Reich's reasoning, he never defines the key variables—the human characteristics of the employees.

In other words, while it is an important response to the "conspiracy theory" rebuttal to "divide and conquer" theories of discrimination, Reich's model is not sufficient for our purposes. But by embedding his idea in a more general framework we strengthen the conclusions he drew.

In sum, as previously formulated, many challenges to the traditional analysis of production under private enterprise are subject to rebuttal. Criticisms based on the distinction between "labor power" and "labor performed," on the formally dictatorial nature of entrepreneurial prerogatives, and on asymmetric information sets for employers and employees are less than compelling in steady state models with their full information implications. And the ethical imperative to eliminate "alienated labor" appears less than categorical upon closer inspection, leaving in doubt whether or not private enterprise misapportions decision-making influence regarding production. Reich's critique can be greatly strengthened and expanded in a multiperiod model in which the critical role of changing human characteristics can become apparent. The same might be said for the pioneering work of Gintis. While Gintis' critique loses bite in a steady state world in which employers and employees learn what to expect from one another, it gains significance in a multiperiod model where the battle over the human characteristic transforming effects of production is waged for higher stakes.

8.3 Reformulating Conflict Theory

What, after all, is really at stake in the conflict between private employer and employee? From the employer's perspective, division of the net product, or the wage rate, is of great importance, as is the degree of effort and diligence employees exert in concert with their capabilities. From the employees' perspective, their wage rate is important, as is the extent to which they receive positive or negative satisfaction from their work. All of which can be summarized as a direct conflict of interest over the "real wage." What we might call the human fulfillment effect of their work is a function not only of the meaning and interest the activity holds for them, but of the extent to which they are compelled to exert greater or lesser effort. This implies a "double" conflict of interest between employer and employee over division and extraction, which can be usefully summarized as a "struggle" over the "real wage."[21]

8.3.1 Human Characteristics and Conflict of Interest

But the struggle over division and extraction is waged over time. And both the individual and group characteristics of the employees in each time period play a critical role in the outcome of that struggle. Moreover, the characteristics employees will have in future periods[22] are influenced by the nature of their productive activity in this time period. So, while the conflict of interest is ultimately over division and extraction, there is also an all-important conflict of interest over the human characteristic transforming effects of laboring activity, since these will largely determine the advantages and disadvantages of employees and employers in their future struggles over division and extraction.[23] So the double conflict of interest over division and extraction implies a third conflict over the human characteristic transforming effects of the labor process.

We might pause to consider how traditional theory missed such an obvious conflict of interest. While the traditional paradigm ignores the human development effects of economic activities, under some circumstances this is justified. And the labor process under private enterprise has some of the markings of just such a situation. In traditional theory employers had no interest in opposing organizations of work that fulfilled employees' preferences provided they did not diminish productivity. As a matter of fact, the conclusion of "producer sovereignty" hinged on the assumption that employers would seek such improvements in working conditions in their efforts to pay lower wages, which competitive labor markets would provide in the form of compensating wage differentials. Had the traditional paradigm permitted traditional theorists to see the preference development effect of work activity, they no doubt would have come to the same conclusion: employers have no reason to oppose, and a wage-reducing reason to seek, changes in work that generate future preferences that employees prefer.

Moreover, traditional theorists are quite aware of the difference between PrEMEs and slavery. While slave owners have every reason to concern themselves with the effects of the work process on their slaves since they may sell their slaves as well as the products they produce, private employers do not own and cannot sell the workers who bear the imprint of the work activity they carry out under their employers' direction. Herein lies temptation to conclude that employers have no axe of their own to grind regarding the human characteristic transforming effects of labor activity, but only an incentive to search for arrangements employees most prefer.

But as we have just explained, employers have a very big axe to grind in this matter because their employees' characteristics will have an important impact on their ability to lower wage bills and extract greater effort from these employees in the future. Private employers cannot "cash in" on the extent to which they organize production in ways that enhance the attractiveness of those who have worked for them to other employers by selling their employees to other private employers; in PrEMEs workers must sell themselves and only for a limited time. But individual employers can benefit from producing transformations of human characteristics advantageous to employers simply by rehiring those they employ today, tomorrow!

The qualitative economic model we developed in chapter 5 facilitates a careful analysis: any economic activity, including production, can be characterized by its material and human inputs, by the transformations in the "state" of the physical productive machinery and the individual and group human characteristics of those who carry out the activity, and by the material and human outputs of the activity.

Beyond caring about the wage they receive, employees are also logically concerned with (1) the number of hours of different kinds of work as well as the degree of effort exerted, or what we have called the human inputs of the production process, E^i; (2) the transformation of their human characteristics, or what we have called the difference between the beginning and final values of the "state" variables representing their individual and group human characteristics, (P^f-P^b), (S^f-S^b), (K^f-K^b), (V^f-V^b), and (G^f-G^b); and (3) the degree to which their needs are met or unmet, or they are satisfied or unsatisfied by their work activity, which we have called the human outputs of the production process, U^o.

The E^i matter to employees because the kind of work affects their well-being and because the time spent and degree of effort expended affects their well-being. Changes in human characteristics matter to employees both because (1) changes in individual characteristics parameterize their preferences and earnings functions and, therefore, future abilities to enjoy different activities and earn labor income, and (2) because changes in individual and group characteristics affect their future bargaining strength regarding division and extraction vis-a-vis their employer. U^o represents the obvious direct preference fulfillment (traditionally termed the "disutility of work") effects of their work activities.

Beyond caring about how much they pay for inputs, including labor time, and how much they are paid for material outputs, employers are also logically concerned with (1) the quantities of inputs used, R^i and X^i ; (2) the number of hours and the degree of effort employees put forth, E^i ; (3) the transformation of their employees' human characteristics, (P^f-P^b), (S^f-S^b), (K^f-K^b), (V^f-V^b), and (G^f-G^b), that occurs at work; and (4) the quantities of material outputs produced, X^o. Since employers pay positive prices for inputs they wish to minimize quantities used. Because the labor contract does not guarantee the effort that employees will exert, employers must seek to induce employees to exert maximum effort. Since changes in the individual and group characteristics of their employees will affect their future bargaining strength regarding division and extraction, employers wish to maximize the erosion in future bargaining strength among their employees. And because employers gain revenues only from the sale of material outputs, they wish to maximize the quantities of material outputs produced.

We can assume that the prices of nonhuman inputs and outputs are fixed exogenously if they are bought or sold on competitive markets. But to some extent the price of human inputs, or wages, is endogenous to the production process in the sense that future wage rates may be affected by present decisions provided labor turnover is not 100 percent. This is not to deny that competitive labor markets place limits on wage rates. Competitive labor markets presumably guarantee, among other things, compensating wage differentials for work that generates different degrees of satisfaction, which in turn implies that employers will have an interest in the kinds of work employees do and the degree to which they garner satisfaction from that work to the extent such factors are translated into market wage differentials. But traditional theorists are correct to see this kind of interest as being in harmony rather than conflict with the social interest. However, to some extent the wages an employer must pay are not totally determined by labor market conditions, no matter how competitive they may be. To some extent, wage determination is endogenous to the organization of the production process.

Interestingly enough, the relation between extraction and competitive labor markets is totally analogous. Competitive labor markets place both lower and upper limits on the degree to which employers can extract effort from their employees, just as they place limits on wage rates. As a matter of fact, competitive labor markets place limits on the wage/effort package, or real wage, since just as even the most competitive labor markets permit a degree of indeterminacy in payments that can be affected by the organization of production in previous periods, they permit a degree of indeterminacy in the degree of effort that can be extracted as well. Which means in a multiperiod model in which the possibility of influencing payments emerges along with the possibility of affecting extraction, Reich's assumption of exogenous payments (to which employers can add a discriminatory bonus for whites if they choose) but endogenous degrees of extraction was arbitrary. The two are equally exogenous, to the extent that competitive labor markets hem employers in, and equally endogenous, to the extent that present choices of technology and reward structure can transform the human "state" variables in ways that affect the relative bargaining strengths of employees and employers in the future.[24]

Our model allows us to pinpoint the difference between a fully elaborated "conflict theory" and the traditional analysis of the production process. In the traditional view, employers do not care about transformation of the human "state" variables. (Private employers are not, after all, slave owners.) And it is precisely this omission in traditional theory that renders the real wage just as exogenous as the prices employers must pay (and receive) for nonhuman inputs and outputs under the assumption of competitive markets. In complete information worlds, competitive markets do limit decision making within the black box so severely as to eliminate all room for maneuver. In other words, perfect information, competitive models generate determinate solutions. But recognition of the human characteristic transforming effects of production changes our view of what decisions are eliminated by competitive labor markets and what decisions are "predestined" for employers who are to succeed in competition with others.

The decision that is compelled by competitive labor markets takes into account the degree to which future profits can be enhanced by diminishing the bargaining power of one's employees through appropriate choice of technology and reward structure today. And, of course, the definition of appropriate choice is precisely the technology and reward structure whose marginal loss of present profits from lost output or higher costs is exactly as great as the discounted marginal gain in future profits from enhanced leverage over division and extraction. The decision that is eliminated by competitive labor markets is precisely the one traditional theory believes is compelled: a decision in which the employer abides entirely by employee preferences regarding human characteristic transforming effects of the production process eschewing the possibility of expanding profits by contributing toward human characteristics that weaken employees' bargaining power.

8.3.2 *Competition and Power*

Ultimately the issue reduces to the question of the relative power of employers and employees—something traditional theory implies is irrelevant under competitive circumstances. So it is important to clarify the relation between competition and power and exactly what we are arguing here. A traditional theorist might formulate the following rebuttal to our argument, similar to the rebuttals to previous contributors to the conflict theory we reviewed previously.

> If an employer offers lower payment than other employers, don't competitive labor markets imply workers will seek, and find, better employment elsewhere? If an employer tries to extract more effort than other employers without paying a wage premium, don't competitive labor markets imply workers will seek, and find, better employment elsewhere? If an employer structures work roles in ways that have less desirable preference fulfillment and/or development effects for employees than jobs offered by other employers, don't competitive labor markets imply workers will seek, and find, better employment elsewhere?[25] And finally, if an employer manipulates choice of technology

and reward structure to affect employee characteristics in ways that diminish their ability to secure favorable employment circumstances in future negotiations, don't competitive labor markets imply workers will seek, and find, better employment elsewhere?

We wish to respond to this line of reasoning explicitly and precisely, because in our view this is the "bottom line" to the debate over the welfare theoretic properties of private enterprise.[26] Suppose the competition among employers for employees was so strong that the answer to all of the above questions was "yes." In our view, this amounts to stipulating that circumstances are such that the balance of power between employers and employees over all the conflicts of interest between them is entirely in the employees' favor. It amounts to assuming labor markets are so "tight" that employees' threats to vote with their feet are sufficient to extract any and all concessions from employers short of ones that would literally bankrupt them. Of course, if this were the case we would expect employees to leave employers no part of the net product[27] and insist that the work-roles/payment/effort trade-off be entirely in accord with employee preferences. As a matter of fact, if this were the case, there would be no difference between a private enterprise market economy in which employers hired employees and one in which employees hired employers.[28]

But this could not be the case unless, among other conditions favoring employee power, the human characteristics of the work force were such as to maintain a monopoly of power in employees' hands. So we logically expect such a situation to coincide with a condition in which employees have whatever individual and group characteristics guarantee them advantage in their negotiations with employers. And if this situation is to persist as a steady state, we naturally assume employees are taking care to reproduce these characteristics as reproductive transformations of human characteristics that are "empowering" for employees.

So our answer to the question, "Isn't this what competitive labor markets imply?" is, "Yes, this could be what competitive labor markets imply,[29] but they might imply something very different." Let us pose the following questions:

If an employee tries to insist on higher payment than other employees, don't competitive labor markets imply employers will seek, and find, lower cost workers? If an employee tries to get away with less effort than other employees without accepting a wage reduction, don't competitive labor markets imply employers will seek, and find, more willing employees? If employees insist on work roles that have more desirable human consequences than those offered by other employers, don't competitive labor markets imply employers will seek, and find, more reasonable employees? And finally, if employees only tolerate technologies and reward structures that affect employee characteristics in ways that maximize their ability to secure favorable employment circumstances in future negotiations, don't competitive labor markets imply employers will seek, and find, less combative employees?

If the competition among employees for employers were sufficiently strong, wouldn't the answer to all these questions have to be "yes"? And doesn't this amount to saying that circumstances are such that the balance of power between employers and employees over the conflicts of interest between them lies entirely in employers' favor? Haven't we simply stipulated that the competition for jobs is so fierce that the threat of unemployment is sufficient to extract any and all concessions from employees short of ones that would not permit them to sustain themselves and their families? And if this were the case, couldn't we expect employers to leave employees no part of the net product beyond subsistence needs and insist that the work-roles/payment/effort trade-off be entirely in accord with employer preferences?

But, once again, this could not be the case unless the human characteristics of the work force were such as to maintain a monopoly of power in employer hands. And we would logically expect such a situation to coincide with a condition in which employees have whatever individual and group characteristics are required to grant their employers full negotiating advantage. If this situation were to persist as a steady state, we would have to assume employers are taking care to reproduce these human effects of the production process. In other words, all this is also consistent with "competitive" labor markets.[30]

The issue here is the same as the issue of the normal rate of profit to which traditional theory has not exactly provided a clear-cut answer. In most traditional treatments, the long-run normal rate of profit is zero on the assumption that any activity that generates positive profits will be expanded until those profits are "competed away." But traditional theorists seldom consider competitive circumstances under which long-run profits may not be "competed away." If financial capital is sufficiently scarce,[31] and inputs must be financed in advance, activities may not be expanded to the point that normal profits are competed away. If employers have been accustomed to earning a positive normal rate of profit and labor's bargaining strength does not increase, productive potentials may go unleashed unless they continue to generate positive profits.

While "Sraffians" expend little more effort than neoclassical theorists analyzing the particular circumstances that generate higher or lower rates of profit, they do not presume the long-run rate of profit will be zero. Instead, the normal rate of profit in Sraffian models is seen as determined jointly with the wage rate by the relative bargaining strengths of employers and employees. What we are arguing here is implicit in Sraffian theory, namely that many wage rates and normal rates of profit are consistent with "competitive" labor (credit) markets. Moreover, we claim the individual and group characteristics of the work force go far toward establishing the relative bargaining power of employers and employees and that they are, therefore, important determinants of what the "competitive" wage rate and "normal" rate of profit will be. More to the point, unless labor holds a complete upper hand, the kind of employer tactics envisioned by the conflict school which we have attempted to clarify are part and parcel of the employer behavior that is compelled by competition among them.[32]

The point is that stipulating "competitive labor markets" does not answer the question of relative power between employers and employees.[33] Instead the "assumption" of "competitive labor markets" neatly sidesteps this question—which in some situations is highly ingenious! If we are examining a situation where the relative bargaining strengths of an employer and his or her employees does not matter, then sidestepping an admittedly ticklish but irrelevant issue is totally justified.[34] But the problem here is we are dealing with a situation in which the issue at stake depends precisely on the balance of power between employer and employees. And since stipulating "competitive labor markets" merely sidesteps the question rather than answering it, the "assumption" of competitive labor markets has nothing to contribute whatsoever. To proceed we employ a different, but productive simplifying assumption.

For the unproductive assumption of "competitive labor markets" we substitute the explicit assumption that employees have something less than a complete upper hand in their bargaining with employers.[35] For in a private enterprise economy, under any of the infinite possible relative bargaining strengths between employers and employees consistent with competitive labor markets, other than the extreme case in which employees have employers entirely at their mercy, the conclusions drawn by traditional welfare theory do not hold. Instead, as we demonstrate next, the conclusions of the "conflict theory" obtain.[36]

In sum, if employers rehire at least some of their employees, and if employers are not completely at the mercy of their employees, employers will be able to achieve a positive normal rate of profit.[37] And in doing so they will choose technologies and reward structures that equalize the (long-term) profit gains from influencing employee characteristics in ways that reduce their bargaining power with the (short-term) profit losses of less productive technology and higher cost wage bills. All of which sustains the conclusions of the conflict theory that we cannot rely on private employers to choose the most productive technologies available, nor can we trust them not to engage in discriminatory systems of rewards. Competition among profit-maximizing employers will drive them to search out ways to transform the human characteristics of their employees in ways beneficial to employers. And there is every reason to believe this will be, to some extent, at the cost of social efficiency.

But before examining what human characteristics we can expect employers to foster to promote their interests in the conflict over division and extraction, we reconsider the conclusions of Gintis and Katzner concerning sufficient conditions for profit maximization to coincide with social efficiency. At first glance they seem to contradict the conclusions we have just drawn.

8.3.3 Gintis and Katzner's Invisible Hand Revisited

Gintis and Katzner found that profit-maximizing employers would make socially efficient decisions if:

1. Employees permit their employers to choose whatever activity they wish from the set of all activities employees formally agree to provide in return for their contractual wages.

2. Employees, of their own volition, choose to behave in ways that conform perfectly to the wishes of their employers.

3. Employees are influenced exclusively by their immediate supervisor's goals and premises.

4. Employees have no preferences regarding what activity they perform but are motivated exclusively by monetary incentives.

In chapter 2 we merely remarked upon the implausibility of these sufficient conditions for a correspondence between profit-maximizing decisions and socially efficient decisions. But now we are in a better position to offer a more meaningful interpretation, and explain why we do not believe these conclusions contradict our conclusion that unless employees are all powerful vis-a-vis employers, profit maximization will not generate social efficiency—first appearances to the contrary.

None of the above conditions are likely to be met in full—which was Gintis and Katzner's point. Conditions two and four both stipulate that employees have no reason to oppose employers' desires regarding what they actually do for their wages. They essentially stipulate no conflict of interest over extraction and, therefore, no squabble to potentially disrupt social efficiency. Conditions one and three stipulate, in effect, that employers are all powerful in their ability to extract whatever performance they desire from their employees. They essentially certify that the labor exchange is, in fact, a quid pro quo exchange in which the buyer receives a known quantity of labor services for a payment. In this case, there is no more reason to expect inefficiencies to result from the exchange between employees and employers than there would be from quid pro quo exchanges of physical commodities between firms and consumers, or among firms facing one another under "competitive" conditions.

So, do the Gintis/Katzner theorems contradict our conclusion that only total employee power is consistent with Pareto optimal outcomes? While their conclusions appear to contradict ours, we think the inconsistency is only apparent. In the first place, we took for granted that the preferences of employees and employers over work activity space generate nonidentical orderings.[38] In other words, we implicitly assumed a conflict of interest over what employees actually do in exchange for their wages—a conflict of interest over extraction—thereby ruling out the feasibility of conditions two and four. All we can say to someone who believes there are no conflicts of this sort is to suggest they get a job![39]

How can the Gintis/Katzner theorems be reconciled with our assertion? The key is to note that the Gintis/Katzner theorems are derived in a single period model in which there is no question of how the conditions of employer power were established. These conditions either do or do not exist, and there are no costs to employer or society for establishing them. Our conclusion, in contrast, is set in a multiperiod model in which employers establish their power in later periods by actions taken earlier.

In our model, the actions employers take to enhance their power later entail present costs in the form of lost profits due to choice of less than the most efficient technique. These are not only costs to the employer in lost revenues, but costs to society as well in lost output. And while the employers "balance" their losses against greater profits later due to enhanced bargaining power, there are no "balancing" gains for society. Enhanced employer power carries no social benefits, which is why efforts undertaken to establish high levels of employer bargaining power necessarily imply nonPareto optimal outcomes in our model. Infinite employer power over extraction does not imply social inefficiency in the Gintis/Katzner model, however, because no social (or private) costs are entailed to establish this condition. Moreover, once the condition exists, infinite employer power over extraction turns the labor exchange into a quid pro quo exchange guaranteeing it will produce social efficiency if there are no other considerations.

Besides reconciling our conclusions, the important point is to focus on what will determine employer bargaining power. What will determine the degree to which actual conditions fall short of the Gintis/Katzner conditions? The answer, of course, is that what will largely determine the extent to which conditions diverge from full compliance with any of the four Gintis/Katzner conditions are the individual and group characteristics of employees. The characteristics our model identifies as "human state variables," such as personality traits, knowledge, and values, are precisely the traits that will determine to what extent employees do or do not distinguish their interests from those of their employers (conditions two and four), or find themselves in a position able or unable to oppose their employer's will (conditions one and three). Moreover, the employee traits that determine the extent to which these conditions are fulfilled are not "given," but are instead endogenous variables subject to influence by the choice of technology and reward structure the employer makes in earlier time periods.

8.3.4 *Malfeasance Reconsidered*

In our view, public enterprise and employee management[40] might be expected to improve upon private enterprise and management to reduce malfeasance and the social costs of combating it for two different reasons. One reason is easily formulated without the aid of our paradigm and models, but the second is not.

Even if individuals are equally tempted to shirk in both circumstances, the cost of surveillance to combat this tendency is less to the extent that other productive employees can be relied on to monitor their fellow workers' performance. To the extent that shirking adversely affects the "rational self-interests" of fellow employees—rather than the interests of a private (or state) employer—the greater will be the incentive for other productive employees to monitor each other's performance. In this case the need for supervisory workers who produce nothing themselves is diminished.[41] This is an argument easily formulated with traditional welfare theoretic concepts. It focuses only on how rational, individual self-interest can be expected to affect the costs of surveillance.

But Bowles and other adherents of the conflict school have also implied that private enterprise aggravates the temptation to shirk. We agree that, irrespective of the system of surveillance, punishment, and reward, private enterprise contributes to the tendency toward malfeasance, but feel the case can be strengthened. Specifically, we think our paradigm helps explain why the Neo-Hobbesian view of the impluse to malfeasance is insufficient, even in strictly welfare theoretic terms.[42]

By identifying the importance and origins of human characteristics and treating preferences as endogenous, the concept of "rational individual self-interest" becomes more complex. In the first place, one's preferences toward work effort are seen to depend on the human characteristics one has developed. If a history of participating in production decision making creates characteristics that generate preferences more favorable toward effort, there is reason to believe that more participatory environments should lessen the impulse to shirk. Similiarly, if a history of cooperative relations with fellow workers creates characteristics that generate empathetic preference structures among workers,[43] while a history of combative relations with an employer creates characteristics that generate hostile preferences toward the interests of one regarded as a disinterested tormentor; there is reason to believe that more cooperative and less hostile work environments lessen the impulse to shirk.

After all, "rational, individual self-interest" is only meaningfully interpreted as rational pursuit of one's preferences. Once we recognize those preferences are influenced by characteristics, which are influenced by previous activities, which are influenced by the structure of interests and conflicts of interest that exist among and between different participants in the social organization of production, there is every reason to expect different individual preferences for shirking in different social environments. Put differently, nothing is necessarily irrational about individuals having different motivations to engage in malfeasance under different circumstances, even if we assume that they are motivated entirely by personal utility maximization. The Neo-Hobbesian view reduces to the assertion that preferences for shirking are exogenous, so that the amount of shirking that will occur depends only on the extent of the opportunity. Our paradigm helps clarify why this presumption is an unwarranted oversimplification.[44]

8.3.5 Reducing Solidarity

We now turn to an abbreviated discussion of the kind of characteristics that might be expected to enhance employer bargaining power. The stronger the employees' group characteristic we call "solidarity," the worse employers chances of achieving wage reductions and extracting greater effort are. This is in large part the attraction of unions to employees in private enterprise systems and the reason employers go to considerable cost to prevent unionization.

Aggravating Racial Antagonisms. One way employers can prevent or dilute employee solidarity is by aggravating racial antagonisms. In our model the divide and conquer strategy many have alluded to, and Reich modeled, is seen as an attempt on an employer's part to prevent development of or erode the group characteristic of solidarity by pitting one race of employees against another. The strategy is to systematically favor one race over another to establish a situation in which employees of neither race will support efforts of the other to resist employer pressure over division and extraction. Sometimes the reasons racial discrimination would be destructive of employee solidarity are assumed to be obvious. Sometimes it is implied that it is simply a matter of stirring up bad feelings from historical antagonisms. We prefer to spell out the dynamic in the following terms: the race that knows itself to be discriminated against will rightfully blame the race that either overtly or tacitly colludes with the employer by accepting unfair advantage. The favored race will be precluded from

279

establishing open and supportive relations with members of the race that is discriminated against because of the compromised position their privileges from collusion place them in. Understood this way, while the result is that neither race will support the other, the reasons are fundamentally asymmetrical.

We are not suggesting that PrEMEs "invented" racism. We recognize that what usually occurs is better seen as employers playing upon an oppressive historical relation whose roots can most often be traced to a noneconomic sphere of social life we call the community sphere.[45] We are discussing here whether or not predictable dynamics of the economic institution of private enterprise are co-reproductive, rather than destructive (as traditional theorists claim), of racist dynamics and characteristics in other spheres of social life. Nor do we insist that favored races must necessarily "gain" or "lose" compared to a situation without discrimination. It is possible that the discriminatory "premium" enjoyed by the favored race is less than the loss they incur as employees in a weakened bargaining relation with their employer. But it is perfectly possible that the opposite may hold.[46] In any case, it is possible racially dominant groups of employees might enjoy a net "gain" from the racial practices of employers and, therefore, engage in "rational" collusion, just as it is possible racially dominant employees delude themselves to think this is the case.

Of course, employer discrimination can take many forms. To enumerate a few: members of subordinated races can be discouraged from applying for employment. Members of subordinated races can be hired less than in proportion to their representation among qualified applicants. Employees of subordinated races can be paid lower wages for the same work, fail to receive promotions as rapidly as equally qualified members of favored races, or be assigned to job categories that pay less, are less healthy, less enjoyable, or less skill developing. Or, employees of subordinated races can simply be harassed to a greater extent than employees of favored races. Nor is manipulation of reward structures the only way employers can aggravate racial antagonisms. By choosing technologies that imply a wide variation in the pleasantness of different job roles over technologies with relatively uniform human effects, or by choosing technologies that isolate employees from one another rather than require frequent cooperation, employers can establish conditions that favor aggravation of racial divisions. But in all cases, the social dynamic generated between favored and subordinated races is roughly what we described above, and the effect is to diminish employee solidarity.

Aggravating Sexual Antagonisms. Theoretically, the logic of employer discrimination on the basis of gender or sexual preference is completely

280

parallel to racial discrimination. This is not to imply the two dynamics are equally productive to employer ends in all circumstances. (It would be most surprising if they were.) Nor is it to imply that the forms used most often to aggravate sexual divisions are the same as the forms most frequently employed to aggravate racial divisions. (The form of job "ghettos," which gives rise to the response of pay according to "comparable worth," for example, appears more prominent in the case of sexual discrimination.)[47] But in both cases we have the possibility of manipulating divisions that predate private enterprise economies, and originate in noneconomic spheres of social life, to expand future profits by diminishing employee solidarity. In both cases, competitive labor markets compel employers to adopt such tactics, rather than provide incentives against their use. And in both cases, the usefulness of such tactics to profit-maximizing employers hinges on the assumption that at least some of those they will hire tomorrow are in their employ today.[48]

Artificial Hierarchies in a Homogeneous Labor Force. Even if a society were devoid of racial, religious, and sexual divisions, and the labor force were completely homogeneous with respect to productive capabilities, it might well be in the interest of profit-maximizing employers to create artificial hierarchies among their employees. By artificial hierarchies we mean establishing distinctions in remuneration and treatment that are completely without basis in skill and totally unnecessary to the organization and supervision of production. While such distinctions could not play upon historical antagonisms among the work force, they could still sew the seeds of justified resentment and rationalization of unmerited privilege among employees that would enhance employer power. Below we demonstrate that totally artificial wage differentiation that has this effect is a necessary condition for profit maximization.

8.3.6 *Reducing Self-management Capabilities*

In addition to "divide and conquer" strategies, employers might profitably seek to produce other kinds of effects on employees' characteristics when they decide how to organize production. While "divide and conquer" tactics seek to diminish the group characteristic of solidarity, there are individual characteristics employers would do well to erode, and others they should try and promote.

De-skilling. As we noted in chapter 2, Harry Braverman reanalyzed a dynamic originally treated a century ago by Henry Babbage. Braverman charged that private employers would attempt to "de-skill" the content of work to reduce their wage bill, and that while this was undoubtedly a profitable policy for employers it was socially inefficient because it prevented society from fully utilizing available productive human skills. In other words, according to Braverman "private profit rationality" does not correspond to "social rationality" with regard to the use of human productive skills.

But traditional theorists have long argued just the opposite. In their view, the incentive for employers to substitute cheaper, less skilled labor for more expensive skilled labor serves the social interest of "economizing" on scarce productive resources. Traditional theorists, once again, see the invisible hand of competition neatly arranging for employers' private greed to serve the interest of social efficiency. We hope to use our model to clarify the assumptions behind both lines of reasoning and to assess more accurately whether an invisible hand or foot is at work here.

Everyone agrees profit-maximizing employers' have an interest in reducing the use of any expensive input. If expensive labor can be replaced by cheaper labor, profit-maximizing employers will presumably do so. If costly productive knowledge and skills can be concentrated in the hands of relatively few employees rather than spread among many, employers will presumably prefer to pay fewer a "knowledge" premium. The question is to what extent such behavior serves the social interest and to what extent, if any, it is contrary to the social interest.

Obviously, much depends on what happens to those whose skills are "economized." If they are reemployed elsewhere and their skills are utilized as productively as before, society has benefited. If they are left unemployed, society does not benefit even though their employer will have succeeded in raising profits.[49] In our view, traditional theorists would be justified in accusing Braverman of implicitly assuming an unemployed scenario in deriving his "antisocial" conclusions, although it is important to realize the unemployment can take a variety of forms. In addition to literal unemployment for victims of de-skilling (or skill-consolidating) automation, their skills could be underemployed if they are retained in the new organization of production but in capacities in which their skills are underutilized. But the inefficiency would be the result of a kind of unemployment in any case.

Clearly, this immediately suggests a highly reasonable rebuttal to Braverman's criticism. Traditional theory never claimed PrEMEs would be socially efficient out of general equilibria. And a general equilibrium rules out the unemployed scenario in all its guises. Does this mean Braverman's concern that private employers would "go beyond the call of social duty" in their attempts to economize on scarce productive skills is unwarranted in full employment scenarios?

Now that we have clarified that employers inevitably struggle with their employees over relative bargaining power—irrespective of how competitive labor markets may be—and that the human characteristics of employees are a highly contested terrain, we are better able to use our model to define and compare the employer's interest, employees' interest, and society's interest in the skill-enhancing and dispersing effects of the labor process. First, a multiperiod model makes clear that skills are not mere givens; they can be expanded, eroded, or transformed. Second, skills are not merely accidents of birth magnified by education or training outside production, they are also generated as "joint outputs" of production.

With this in mind, society's interest is to allocate scarce productive skills to their most useful task at every point in time. And in this sense traditional theory is perfectly correct; "economizing" on scarce productive skills (in a full employment context) is socially beneficial. But it is also in society's interest to maximize the creation of productive knowledge and skills that emerge from the production process, ceteris paribus. That is, as long as there is no loss in useful outputs or diminution in job satisfaction, the more skills developed in the greater number of employees the better from society's point of view. Otherwise, there is a trade-off between more skills and other beneficial effects. But the crucial point is that more skills are socially beneficial.

The employer's interest is to "economize" on expensive scarce skills at every point in time,[50] but it is not to maximize generation of skills among employees. Recalling the distinction between private enterprise and slavery is once again in order. In this case, employers of wage labor have no interest in maximizing the skill-enhancing effects of the work process because, unlike slave owners, they are in no position to reap the benefits of the employees' increased productivity. The employer cannot sell the employee who has become more valuable. And if the employer attempts to reap the benefits by rehiring the employee without paying him a wage differential fully commensurate with his increased skill, the same competitive labor markets necessary to negate Braverman-type inefficiencies will permit the employee to reap the benefit of the difference between wage labor and slavery by "selling himself" to another employer—temporarily.[51] But more importantly, to the extent employees with greater productive skills and knowledge of the production process are more formidable opponents in negotiations over division and extraction, the employer has an incentive to minimize skill-enhancing "joint products." This was the logic Braverman rediscovered, and it is now clear that it needn't hinge on an "unemployment" scenario.

Suppose an employer must decide whether or not to implement a technology that requires no more inputs, yields the same outputs, but increases the skills and knowledge of productive possibilities of his or her employees in the future. Suppose, as well, labor markets are not particularly tight, so the employer will be able to retain most employees without being compelled to pay fully compensating wage differentials for their enhanced productivity, which we assume will be fully utilized and result in greater future output.

It is obviously in society's interest to implement the new technique. But even though there is a future profit gain effect since we stipulated that employees are not (initially) in a position to capture 100 percent of the increased revenues through compensating "knowledge" premiums, a profit-maximizing employer might still reject the change. In addition to the "productivity" enhancing effect, there may well be a "bargaining strength" enhancing effect. Employees may become more productive as a result of their greater skills, but also better able to expand their share of the net product due to their greater knowledge of productive possibilities. So, even if the employer would be in a position to capture part of the "productivity" effect at the original level of relative bargaining strength, the "bargaining strength" effect may outweigh the "productivity" effect in the long run.

We can generalize the problem as follows: any change in the organization of production that expands the "net product" is socially beneficial. If the change does not affect how the "net product" will be divided between employers and employees, we can rely on employers trying to maximize their part of the net product to implement the change. But since employers are concerned only with their part—not with the whole net product—they will not approve changes that augment the whole net product but diminish their part. What our model makes apparent is that changes in the organization of production, in general, affect both the size of the net product and how that product will be divided among employers and employees. Therefore, potential output-expanding changes may not be implemented by private employers if the effect on the human characteristics of their employees is sufficiently deleterious to employer bargaining power.

So, in a dynamic context, "de-skilling" may be quite different from "economizing on scarce skills." And while both may be in the interests of profit-maximizing employers, only "economizing" is in society's interest. "De-skilling" definitely is not.

Employees obviously share society's interest in maximizing skill development, but to claim they share society's interest in economizing on scarce skills at any point in time would be deceptive. If loss of job entails costs for employees—because they cannot immediately walk into another job of equal or greater "value"—then they do not share society's interest in shifting skilled employees out of positions where they are no longer most valuable. It would be tempting to adopt the view of traditional theory that "competitive labor markets" imply no employee-cost of job loss, but we do not believe this to be the case. It would probably not even be true if employees completely dominated employers, but it is certainly not so under other conditions. So we also cannot have our cake and eat it too!

Which leaves us with the following provocative conclusion: an invisible foot accompanies the invisible hand in both unemployment and full employment scenarios of private enterprise management of productive skills. Moreover, neither employers nor employees' interests coincide completely with society's interest regarding generation and use of scarce productive skills under private enterprise conditions. If employers are all-powerful, skills that could have been developed will not be. If employees are all-powerful, existing skills that could be better utilized probably will not be. At intermediate positions on the power spectrum, we will get a mixture of the two inefficiencies that upon reflection jibes nicely with many empirical assessments of reality!

Nonartificial Hierarchies. We already explained how totally artificial hierarchies might enhance profits by "dividing and conquering" employees. But in a different sense hierarchies that are not totally artificial can enhance employer power. Employers have a special interest in "compartmentalizing" knowledge of the production process. If employees only know what is necessary to implement a particular task, and if the knowledge of how to combine these particular tasks is reserved to a small number of employees known as management, employee bargaining strength will in all likelihood be less than if large numbers of employees are aware of how to run the show. The more complete the fragmentation of productive knowledge the better from the employer's perspective.[52]

But this means that no matter how necessary hierarchies might be and no matter how much hierarchy might improve efficiency, hierarchies also contribute to the fragmentation of productive knowledge in a way that is beneficial to employers but not to society. Which is not to say we concur with the dominant view that hierarchical forms of production are unavoidable without great losses in productivity—as is abundantly clear from our other writings. We simply mean that regardless of what view one holds on these matters, one must recognize that private employers have an incentive to become excessive consumers of hierarchy. Therefore, private employers have reason to exaggerate the division of labor beyond the extent to which it is socially useful, whatever that may be. Once we recognize the importance of power relations between employers and employees and that employee characteristics affect their power and that these characteristics are affected in turn by the organization of production in previous periods, exaggeration of hierarchical divisions that define differential distribution of information and different degrees of control over decision making become a logical means of diminishing the self-managing capabilities of employees and, thereby, their power in negotiations over division and extraction. These hierarchies are not totally artificial in the sense that they do define different jobs and responsibilities. But there is every reason to suppose they are to some degree socially unproductive in situations where employers expect to retain at least some of their employees from period to period. Moreover, our analysis makes clear there is no reason to suppose the wage differentials attached to different positions in hierarchies are reflective of marginal productivities alone.

8.3.7 *Internal and External Labor Markets*

According to traditional theory the wage structure inside a firm should not differ from the wage structure in labor markets outside the firm. For employers to pay more when they could recruit identical replacements on the outside would be irrational. And for employees to work for less than they could get for the same work elsewhere would be irrational. That is, "internal labor markets" should be identical to "external labor markets." Moreover, both should reflect only differential productivities and desirabilities of different jobs.

But our argument above goes far toward explaining why there will be differences between external and internal wages beyond relocation costs, and why wages reflect more than differential productivities and desirabilities of jobs—even under the most competitive conditions. If both artificial and nonartificial, but "exaggerated," hierarchies are part of profit-maximizing strategies, there is every reason to believe wage rates attached to different categories of work will form a wage structure inside the firm that differs from wages in "external" markets. Wage discrimination entails paying whites and/or men higher wages than the external labor market establishes for equivalent minority and/or female workers. Totally artificial hierarchies mean employers will pay some "internal" employees higher wages than equivalent "external" workers. But our focus on the importance of employees' characteristics makes apparent a more general criterion for wage determination invisible to traditional theory.

Greater productivity is grounds for higher wages, ceteris paribus, as are less pleasant work conditions. But employee characteristics that improve their employers' bargaining power are logical grounds for higher wages as well, ceteris paribus. Just as any employee characteristic that enlarges the net product is worth paying more for (as long as the employer receives part of the net gain), any characteristic that enlarges the employers' share of the net product of the production process is worth paying more for. In other words, we should expect employee traits that tend to enhance employers' share of the net product to be rewarded by higher wages just as characteristics that make employees more productive are.

For example, employee consciousness that readily accepts employers' "right" to adequate compensation in the form of generous profits is obviously likely to increase profits. But while this trait may be "profit expanding" it is not in any way "socially productive." There is no reason

286

to believe an increase in this trait would increase the size of the social net product. Which leads us to the following conclusion: in general, traits that diminish employee bargaining power may be as valuable to employers as traits that expand the social net product. But whereas traits that expand the social net product are socially valuable, traits that merely diminish employee bargaining power are not. Yet there is just as much reason to expect wage "premiums" for traits that diminish employee power in private enterprise economies as there is to expect "skill premiums," and "disutility premiums." Instead of the traditional vision of competitive wages reflecting only productivity and disutility—both legitimate criteria for social efficiency—we arrive at a vision of competitive wages under private enterprise reflecting productivity, disutility, and characteristics that favor employer bargaining power. And to the extent the third factor enters wage determination, wage rates will not coincide with "efficiency" wages.

In any case, the logic of the demand-side explanation for internal labor markets that differ from external labor markets, which is invisible to the traditional paradigm, is as follows: employers have an incentive to develop internal job ladders with pay rates influenced by factors other than productivity and desirability, and that vary from the pay rates for equivalent labor categories in external markets. The incentive derives from the internal ladder's usefulness in diminishing employee solidarity and de-skilling the work force as important employer tactics to "preserve the integrity of the labor exchange" and reduce future wage bills. This entails two consequences: (1) If much worker mobility occurs within job ladders of large firms rather than between firms,[53] employers can create a degree of monopsony power for themselves with internal job ladders, even if external labor markets are competitive; and, (2) if the participation in the economy of large firms with such internal job ladders is significant, over time the internal structures will necessarily shape the demand structures of the external labor markets, which are ultimately nothing more than the aggregate of the internal structures. Hence emerges a demand-side explanation of segmented external labor markets.

We can only hope our discussion of the logic of internal job ladders based on factors other than productivity and desirability and their relation to external labor markets helps answer important questions critics have raised. For while what has been mostly empirical work by modern institutionalists has done much to advance the importance of "internal labor markets" and "segmented labor markets," the field has been marred by theoretical ambiguities and contradictions.

A successful challenge to the traditional treatment on its own terms—which is to say in a steady state or perfect knowledge model—requires emphasizing either (1) that the choice of job organization/pay structure (i.e., organization of the production process) affects worker solidarity in the same period with implications for extracting labor effort after the wage has been settled (Reich); or, (2) that organization of the production process affects human characteristics with consequent implications for negotiations and extraction and wage rates in the future in a world with less than 100 percent turnover. We find the latter track more suggestive of important real world dynamics.

8.4 An Imperfection Theorem

In this section we express the arguments of the preceding sections as an imperfection theorem, thereby formalizing our reformulation of the conflict theory in terms of the new welfare paradigm.

We examine the implications of profit maximization for a competitive employer who hires people to work in two different kinds of jobs. In addition to the traditionally recognized effects of greater output and revenue and higher labor costs in the employment period, our treatment recognizes the effects of time spent in work activities on the future human characteristics of employees, the effects of employee characteristics on employer bargaining power, and the effects of employer bargaining power on effort and wage determination. Since the argument is for a typical competitive employer, we can easily extrapolate to the implications for market demands for labor, which yields our imperfection theorem. Moreover, the form of the imperfection theorem is familiar and permits immediate application of Theorems 6.6, 6.7, and 6.8 on snowballing nonoptimality from chapter 6.

Our competitive employer produces only one output in each time period, which we denote by $x(t)$. For convenience we set the price of this output equal to 1 in each time period. And since nothing is lost by stipulating that x is produced by means of labor inputs only, we write that x is a positive function of work efforts of type-1 and/or type-2:

$$x(t) = x\left(E_1(\%)(t), E_2(\%)(t)\right); \quad \frac{\partial x(t)}{\partial E_k(\%)(t)} > 0; \quad k = 1, 2$$

Work effort, or what Reich calls "labor done," is expressed as a positive function of both the number of hours worked, h, and the degree of effort expended, e.

$$E_k(\%)(t) = E_k(\%)(h_k(t), e(t)); \quad \frac{\partial E_k(\%)(t)}{\partial h_k(t)} > 0, \frac{\partial E_k(\%)(t)}{\partial e(t)} > 0; k = 1, 2$$

The degree of effort, e, is expressed as a positive function of the bargaining power of the employer vis-a-vis the employee, BP. And we also note the negative effect of employer bargaining power on the wage rate, $W_k(t)$.[54]

288

An Imperfection Theorem

$$e(t) = e\,(BP(t));\quad \frac{de(t)}{dBP(t)} > 0$$

$$W_k(t) = W_k\,(BP(t));\quad \frac{dW_k(t)}{dBP(t)} < 0;\ k = 1, 2$$

And employer bargaining power, BP, is expressed as a negative function of an employee human characteristic, C. In other words, C is a trait that makes employees more powerful in their negotiations with employers. It is an employee empowering characteristic that weakens employer bargaining power.

$$BP(t) = BP(C(t));\quad \frac{dBP(t)}{dC(t)} < 0$$

The characteristic C is stipulated as a function of hours previously engaged in work activities of type-1 and type-2. Specifically, time previously spent in work activity 1 enhances trait C, and time spent in work activity 2 reduces C.

$$C(t) = C(h_1(t-1), h_1(t-2), \ldots h_1(0); h_2(t-1), h_2(t-2), \ldots h_2(0))$$

$$\frac{\partial C(t)}{\partial h_1(t-j)} > 0\quad \frac{\partial C(t)}{\partial h_2(t-j)} < 0\ \ j = 1, 2, \ldots t$$

We complete our notation by using $\tau(t)$ to represent the employer's rate of time discount for profits in period t, and $\theta(t+j)$ to represent the probability that an employee hired in period t will still be employed by the same employer in period $(t+j)$. We express the employer's profits:

$$Profits = \sum_{t=0}^{T} \left\{ \tau(t)\,[x(t) - (W_1(t)h_1(t) + W_2(t)h_2(t))] \right\}$$

We need only examine two first order profit-maximizing conditions. We take the derivative of profits with respect to hiring another hour of labor type-1 and labor type-2 in some representative period t

$$\frac{\partial(Profits)}{\partial h_1(t)} = \tau(t)\left\{ \frac{\partial x(t)}{\partial E_1(\%)(t)}\,\frac{\partial E_1(\%)(t)}{\partial h_1(t)} - W_1(t) \right\} + \tag{8.1}$$

$$\sum_{j=1}^{T-t} \sum_{k=1}^{2} \theta(t+j)\tau(t+j)\left\{ \frac{\partial x(t+j)}{\partial E_k(\%)(t+j)}\,\frac{\partial E_k(\%)(t+j)}{\partial e(t+j)}\,\frac{\partial e(t+j)}{\partial BP(t+j)} - \frac{\partial W_k(t+j)}{\partial BP(t+j)} \right\}\frac{\partial BP(t+j)}{\partial C(t+j)}\,\frac{\partial C(t+j)}{\partial h_1(t)}$$

$$\frac{\partial(Profits)}{\partial h_2(t)} = \tau(t)\left\{ \frac{\partial x(t)}{\partial E_2(\%)(t)}\,\frac{\partial E_2(\%)(t)}{\partial h_2(t)} - W_2(t) \right\} + \tag{8.2}$$

$$\sum_{j=1}^{T-t} \sum_{k=1}^{2} \theta(t+j)\tau(t+j) \left\{ \frac{\partial x(t+j)}{\partial E_k(\%)(t+j)} \frac{\partial E_k(\%)(t+j)}{\partial e(t+j)} \frac{\partial e(t+j)}{\partial BP(t+j)} - \frac{\partial W_k(t+j)}{\partial BP(t+j)} \right\} \frac{\partial BP(t+j)}{\partial C(t+j)} \frac{\partial C(t+j)}{\partial h_2(t)}$$

The first line in expressions 8.1 and 8.2 represents the traditionally recognized effects of hiring another unit of labor of each type: the discounted increase in revenues in period t that results from greater output coming from another hour worked, and the discounted increase in wage that must be paid in period t. The second line expresses the effects that are not recognized by traditional analysis: in every future time period there is some probability of changes in both revenues received and wages paid because working an hour in one kind of job or the other in period t will affect the employee's characteristic in all future periods and, thereby, the employer's bargaining power and ability to influence the wage/effort outcome in all future periods for which the employee is retained.

For $0 < \theta(t+j) < 1$ for all j, in expression 8.1, the nontraditional affects are unambiguously negative. That is, hiring another hour of work type-1 contributes less to profits than would be recognized by traditional theory. In expression 8.2, the nontraditional effects are unambiguously positive implying that hiring type-2 labor contributes more to profits than recognized by traditional theory.

But our concern is less with correcting the estimations of traditional theory than the implications of our analysis for social efficiency. If the employer's rate of time discount can be presumed to be the same as the social rate of time discount, the first term in the first line of expressions 8.1 and 8.2 represents the marginal social benefit of another hour of labor of each type, MSB $(h_k(t))$. But, we have just seen, the marginal private benefit to the employer of hiring another unit of labor, MPB $(h_k(t))$, is equal to the sum of the first term in the first line plus the entire second line, that is, the sum of the traditionally recognized benefit and the nontraditionally recognized effect. The critical point is that the nontraditional benefit is not a benefit for society, but only a benefit to the employer. The nontraditional effect simply affects the relative bargaining power of an employer vis-a-vis his or her employees. It affects only how the net product will be divided and the extent to which employees will have to exert effort to collect their wages. And while this is no doubt critical to employer and employee individual interests, it is irrelevant from the perspective of social efficiency.[55]

Profit-maximizing employers will hire labor up to the point where the marginal private benefit equals the wage rate, not up to the point where the marginal social benefit equals the wage rate, and herein lies the imperfection of private enterprise production. The marginal private benefit of an hour of type-1 labor is less than the marginal social benefit, and the marginal private benefit of an hour of type-2 labor is more than the marginal social benefit. Since the discrepancy is precisely the sum of terms in the second lines of 8.1 and 8.2, and the number of these terms will be greater the lower the rate of labor turnover, that is, the higher $\theta(t+j)$ all j, we see that the discrepancy will exist in any private enterprise economy in which the rate of labor turnover is less than 100 percent per period, but is all the more powerful the lower the rate of labor turnover.[56]

For type-1 labor the market demand, which is the sum of the marginal private benefits to employers, will be less than the sum of the marginal social benefits. And for type-2 labor the market demand, which is also the sum of the marginal private benefits, will be greater than the sum of the marginal social benefits. These market relations are expressed in Figs. 8.1 and 8.2.

FIG. 8.1. LABOR MARKET FOR $h_1(t)$

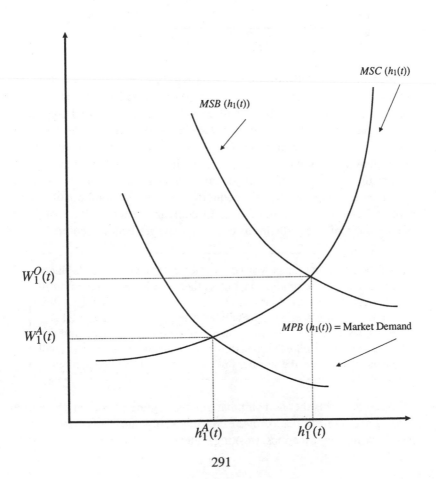

FIG 8.2. LABOR MARKET FOR $h_2(t)$

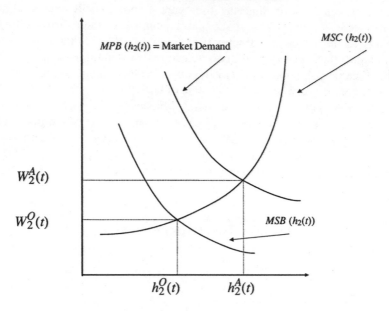

Since outcomes will presumably be the equilibrium outcomes determined by actual conditions of market demands and supplies, the actual wage paid for an hour of type-1 labor will be lower than the optimal wage that equates marginal social benefits and marginal social costs of another hour of work 1; and the actual wage paid for an hour of type-2 labor will be higher than the optimal wage. If we make the traditional assumption that the marginal disutility of labor of any kind is rising, then we can also conclude that private enterprise production will employ too little of type-1 labor and too much of type-2 labor in comparison with what would be socially optimal. We state this as our second imperfection theorem.

THEOREM 8.1: BIASES IN WAGES UNDER PRIVATE ENTERPRISE. Under private enterprise production, unless there is 100 percent labor turnover each time period, any kind of laboring activity that generates employee-empowering traits will have an actual market wage that is less than the socially optimal wage and be undersupplied. And any kind of labor activity that weakens employee-empowering traits will be paid more than the socially optimal wage and be oversupplied.

To see how this theorem summarizes the arguments of the preceding sections in our reformulation of the conflict theory one needs only to make the following identifications: working under conditions of (1) participatory decision making, (2) cooperation among employees, and (3) fairly perceived distribution of duties and rewards among employees,[57] are all type-1 laboring activities, which are underpaid and undersupplied; whereas working under conditions of (4) wage discrimination, (5) employment discrimination,[58] and (6) artificially created hierarchies are all type-2 laboring activities, which are overpaid and oversupplied.

In our interpretation, the common thread in different representations of the conflict school is that socially counterproductive practices such as wage and employment discrimination, the creation of artificial hierarchies and overexaggeration of nonartificial hierarchies, and the erosion of self-management capabilities and de-skilling of employees are part of rational profit-maximizing strategies of employers who compete with one another for profits over the long run in economies where employee turnover rates do not approach 100 percent. Theorem 8.1 clarifies the basis for such behavior and its implications for social efficiency.

These practices are all cases of working conditions that tend to erode employee bargaining strength and enhance employer bargaining strength. The mechanism through which this occurs is that working under such conditions affects both the individual and group characteristics of employees in future time periods, which redefines the relative bargaining strength (power) of employees and employers in future negotiations (daily struggle) over the wage/effort package (real wage). To the extent that employers can influence the choice of technology and reward structure (organization of the work process) it would be "individually irrational" for them not to take these effects into account in doing so.[59]

By taking these effects into account, because they are part of the calculation of the employer's private benefits,[60] they will establish wage rates that diverge from "efficiency prices" for labor services and misallocate human productive resources. The social inefficiency is transparent once we recognize the divergence between private and social benefits.

8.5 Snowballing Nonoptimality

Once again we can combine the above results with the results of chapter 6 to provide a fuller picture of the consequences of "individual, rational self-interest" under particular institutional conditions. Theorems 6.6, 6.7, and 6.8 connect allocative biases with snowballing nonoptimal allocations that will go unnoticed if preferences are assumed to be exogenous. Theorem 8.1 establishes that the institution of private enterprise generates a bias in the conditions of supply of different kinds of laboring activities, as we have just seen. Private enterprise economies will overpay and oversupply work activities that have the effect of disempowering employees vis-a-vis employers, and underpay and undersupply work activities that have the effect of empowering employees vis a vis employers. In the view of adherents to the conflict school, and we certainly include ourselves in this category, working under conditions of wage and employment discrimination, artificial and exaggerated hierarchies, and discouragement of participatory and cooperative impulses are precisely activities that tend to disempower employees. Whereas working under conditions that encourage employee participation and cooperation, which employees perceive to be a fair distribution of duties and rewards among them, are activities that tend to empower employees. Combining Theorem 8.1 with Theorem 6.6 we have Theorem 8.2:[61]

THEOREM 8.2: SNOWBALLING NONOPTIMALITY OF PRIVATE ENTERPRISE PRODUCTION. Not only will production under private enterprise fail to deliver optimal job mixes in some initial time period, oversupplying work conditions that empower employers vis-a-vis employees, but there will be a cumulative divergence away from optimal allocations in future time periods as individuals "rationally" adjust their personal characteristics to diminish their need for work opportunities that are underpaid and enhance their preference for work opportunities that are overpaid.

Again, combining our "snowballing" theorems from chapter 6 with our "imperfection" theorem expressing the logic of the conflict school in this chapter permits us to see not only the generality of private enterprise inefficiency, but the full consequences of this failure. Not only are laboring capacities systematically misapplied, the severity of the misallocation of productive potentials worsens over time. In this case, workers will mold their characteristics and preferences to more readily accept discriminatory conditions, unwarranted hierarchy, and what we might call "other directed" work. But again, such "individually rational behavior" is "socially irrational" since the inefficiencies that result will diverge even farther from efficient organizations of work efforts than had people not adjusted.

Moreover, our results highlight a mechanism by which the dynamics of competition for profits between private employers contributes to the development of particular characteristics in what we call the human center of society. Our analysis explains why workers' "participatory impulse" should diminish over time under conditions of private enterprise. And while our analysis begins with an assumption of racial antagonisms, it explains not only why employers might act to inflame those antagonisms, but why individual consciousness might become more racist or sexist as people "rationalize" situations for which there are positive incentives to accept.

8.6 **A Double Indictment**

We conclude this chapter with a summary of our "full case" against private enterprise market economies.

In formal terms our case is summarized by Theorems 7.1, 7.2, 8.1, and 8.2. PrEMEs are characterized precisely by two economic institutions that will guide and govern economic activity: markets and private enterprise. Theorem 7.1 reformulates a result well known to the traditional theory of public finance, namely that even competitive markets misallocate resources in the presence of external effects. Theorem 7.2 establishes that under the assumption of endogenous preferences misallocations from this source will become worse over time. Theorem 8.1 establishes what we consider to be the essential result of the conflict school, namely that private enterprise production misallocates human productive potentials. Theorem 8.2 establishes that under the assumption of endogenous preferences inefficiencies from this source will grow over time.

In other words, each of the principle economic institutions that characterize what is more commonly known as perfectly competitive capitalism is inherently flawed. Each exhibits a particular bias regarding the terms of availability of different kinds of economic activities from which people can choose. Each is characterized by a particular kind of "imperfection" that will become magnified over time in response to individually rational behavior.

Moreover, there is absolutely no reason to believe that the two biases and socially inefficient trajectories "compensate" or "correct" each other. Therefore, we are left with the conclusion that, contrary to traditional beliefs, the equilibrium trajectories of private enterprise, competitive market economies will diverge from socially efficient trajectories in a kind of "double" snowballing nonoptimality.

Of course, unless we have made errors of logic in the deduction of our theorems, the difference between our results and those of traditional analysis must reduce to differences in assumptions that we might usefully summarize here. Regarding private enterprise we assume only that turnover rates are less than 100 percent, that employer discretion over choice of technology and reward structure is greater than zero, that employee characteristics are not totally unaffected by work conditions, that employers' bargaining power is not totally independent of their employees' individual and group characteristics, and that workers' preferences are not totally exogenous. Regarding markets we assume only that some external effect is not completely corrected and that consumer preferences are not totally exogenous. These assumptions are sufficent to generate our conclusions. Of course, to the extent that any of these assumptions is strengthened, the greater will be the cumulative divergence from socially efficient uses of resources.

We hasten to point out that we do not assume noncompetitive market structures or imperfect or asymmetric information, and that we confine ourselves to an equilibrium analysis. In other words, we confine ourselves to what has long been the welfare theoretic project of investigating the consequences of perfectly informed rational individual behavior under the most favorable conditions imaginable for a particular institutional context.[62]

In less formal terms, our "double indictment" is far more sweeping. We find that the cybernetic and role properties of markets can be expected to contribute toward "snowballing individualism." We expect external effects to be pervasive rather than exceptions to the rule. We judge the income flexibility of private enterprise economies to be largely illusory for multiple reasons, not all of which had been previously clarified. And we expect the degree of employer power consistent with the preservation of real private enterprise economies to generate powerful impulses toward racial and sexual antagonisms, apathy, and enmity—a far cry from the vision of flexible efficiency machines!

9

CENTRAL
PLANNING

$\mathbf{W}$E BEGIN by reviewing the "old" debate about whether or not central planning can be efficient. In the context of modern mathematical programming techniques and computer capabilities, the "old" debate, brought into focus by Barone's essay "Ministry of Production" published in 1908, has been resolved in the affirmative.[1] We will extend this conclusion to the case where individuals' preferences are endogenous. But the "old" debate assumed that the Central Planning Board would have perfect knowledge of all resource availabilities, all technical capabilities of all production units, and society's social welfare function, and that all the Central Planning Board's instructions would be carried out.

Next we review the "modern" debate about information gathering difficulties and incentive problems in central planning. We analyze a number of iterative techniques designed to help the Central Planning Board gather technical data from the separate units in the economy. We review a number of approaches to formulating society's social welfare function. And we discuss incentives that might be used to induce managers and workers to carry out the plan once it is calculated. We conclude that many information and incentive problems emphasized by critics of central planning are resolvable, and that the most intractable problem—obtaining accurate information from management about productive capabilities—is not unique to centrally planned systems.

Having reviewed the "old" and "modern" debates—both conducted in terms of traditional welfare theory—we reevaluate the different iterative techniques for gathering technical information using our new welfare criteria and discover that all these techniques are cybernetic disasters from a social point of view, regardless of how successful they might be for informing central planners. This leads to our first new criticism of central planning: as necessary as consolidating data from individual production units in the hands of central planners might be for central planning to achieve efficiency, the primary cybernetic task of economic institutions appropriate for achieving self-management is to disseminate information about other production units so the members of each unit can expand their understanding of how their choices impact on others and vice versa. The techniques for processing information in central planning not only fail to do this, but accomplish just the opposite.

Next we discuss the roles inherent in central planning using our new evaluative criteria. We find the interunit roles to be irresolvably authoritarian and discuss the likelihood that their authoritarianism would spread to intraunit roles as well. We point out that apathy is the other side of the authoritarian coin and that the roles defined by central planning relegate individual production units, and most often workers within those units, to just such a condition. In this respect our work provides a theoretical basis for criticisms often voiced by analysts of central planning in practice.

But our most important new criticism of central planning derives from reanalyzing the problems associated with estimating society's social welfare function. We discover that central planning is incapable of providing self-managed work activities in accord with their true social opportunity costs. Even giving central planning every benefit of the doubt—eliminating the Central Planning Board from any decision-making role, formulating the social welfare function through strictly democratic procedures, and including different kinds of work activities as well as different final goods in the social objective function to be voted on—we find that central planning is inherently biased against supplying self-managed work roles.

Worse still, treating preferences as endogenous we prove that central planning's inherent bias against supplying self-managed work activities leads to a "snowballing divergence" from optimality in which the economic plan proceeds farther and farther from an optimal use of society's laboring capacities as time goes on. When viewed in terms of human development, this snowballing divergence displays itself as an ever-increasing apathy of the executors of economic activities as they accommodate to the absence of opportunities for self-managed work activities.

We conclude with some observations on how the institutions of central planning might be expected to affect the disposition of classes in public ownership economies. We suggest that the institutions of central planning contribute to the development and strengthening of a coordinator class separate from, and with interests opposed to, ordinary workers in such economies.

9.1 A Centrally Planned Public Enterprise Economy

We begin with a moderately complex model that could be used to calculate a central plan for an economy.

9.1.1 Model 4: The Central Planning Problem

M 4.1. The time horizon for the plan in Model 4 is $t = 1, 2, \ldots T$.

M 4.2. The gross outputs of produced goods i and j in period t are $x_i(t)$ and $x_j(t)$ respectively, where $i, j = 1, 2, \ldots c$.

M 4.3. The number of different processes for making good i are $p = 1, 2, \ldots P(i)$. The number of different ways to add to capital stock s are $r = 1, 2, \ldots R(s)$.

M 4.4. There are L different kinds of labor and primary (nonproducible) factors of production, $l = 1, 2, \ldots L$, and for each time period there exists a certain amount of each of these factors including man/woman hours for labor categories and physical quantities for land, minerals, etc. The available supplies are taken as "given." $\dot{Z}_l(t)$ stands for the amount of factor l available in period t. $Z_l(t)$ stands for the amount of factor l actually used in the production program in period t.

M 4.5. $x_{jp}(t)$ stands for the amount of good j produced in period t via process p. The total amount of good j produced in period t is:

$$x_j(t) = \sum_p x_{jp}(t)$$

M 4.6. $a_{ijp}(t)$ stands for the amount of i needed to make one unit of j via process p in period t.

M 4.7. $S_s(t)$ stands for the stock of capital good s in existence at the outset of period t, where $s = 1, 2, \ldots m \leq c$.

M 4.8. $\delta S_s(t)$ stands for the addition to stock of capital good s in period t. And $\%S_s(t)$ stands for the fraction of capital good s that physically depreciates in period t, which we assume to be independent of usage.

M 4.9. $a_{ljp}(t)$ stands for the amount of primary factor l needed to make one unit of good j via process p in period t.

M 4.10. $S_{sjp}(t)$ stands for the amount of stock of capital good s we must have on hand to produce one unit of good j via process p in period t.

M 4.11. I_{isr} stands for the total amount of good i that must be set aside (invested) in all prior periods to obtain one unit increase in the stock of capital good s via process r.

M 4.12. $i_{isr}(t|t')$ stands for the fraction of I_{isr} that must be invested in period t to help produce one more unit of capital good s in later period t' via process r. Thus, $[i_{isr}(t|t')]$ $[I_{isr}]$ stands for the amount of i that must be set aside in period t to help get one more unit of stock of s in period t' via process r, where:

$$\sum_t i_{isr}(t|t') = 1$$

M 4.13. $Q_i(t)$ stands for the final consumption of good i in period t.

The Central Planning Board is provided society's "social welfare function" containing society's relative valuation of all final consumption goods and labor activities.[2]

The simplest case would be a linear social welfare function where $v_i(t)$ stood for the relative social value of one unit of consumption good i at period t, and where $w_l(t)$ stood for the relative social value of one unit of primary factor l at period t. For all l that correspond to a specific kind of labor activity, the $w_l(t)$ would represent the relative disutility of performing an hour's worth of that activity. For all l that stand for nonlabor primary factors there is no reason they would not have $w_l(t)$'s equal to zero, for even with T a finite time period, we do not accumulate stocks of these nonproductive inputs in our model; they simply appear in certain quantities each time period, and would presumably do so in the future.

In the case of a finite time period, however, we would have to set some positive social values on the different stocks of produced goods in the last time period if we are not to totally ignore the well-being of generations to live after time period T. For now, assume the planners know the valuations for capital goods s, $y_s(T)$, as well.

An easy way to handle the more general case of a nonlinear social welfare function, where the relative social value of a unit of any final good or labor activity depends on both the absolute and relative amount of the good or activity that was being consumed, would be to simply interpret the $v_i(t)$'s and $w_l(t)$'s as functions of all the $Q_i(t)$'s and $Z_l(t)$'s.

M 4.14. That is

$$v_i(t) = v_i(Q_1(t), Q_2(t), \ldots Q_c(t); Z_1(t), Z_2(t), \ldots Z_L(t))$$

$$w_l(t) = w_l(Q_1(t), Q_2(t), \ldots Q_c(t); Z_1(t), Z_2(t), \ldots Z_L(t))$$

where this formulation allows for the usual substitutes and complements.

Finally, we are ready to state the Central Planning Board's programming problem: Maximize social welfare

$$\sum_t \sum_i v_i(t)Q_i(t) + \sum_t \sum_l w_l(t)Z_l(t) + \sum_s y_s(T)S_s(T)$$

subject to the following constraints

1. Producing enough of each good in each year to meet its intermediate, investment, and final consumption uses as expressed by the $c{\times}T$ inequalities (for $i = 1, 2,\dots c$ and $t = 1, 2,\dots T$):

$$\sum_p x_{ip}(t) - \sum_j \sum_p a_{ijp}(t)x_{jp}(t) - \sum_r \sum_{t'} \sum_s i_{isr}(t|t')I_{isr}\delta S_s(t') - Q_i(t) \geq 0$$

2. Having at least the minimum amount of all the necessary capital stocks available at each time period for the production of each good as expressed by the $m{\times}T$ inequalities (for $s = 1,\dots m$ and $t = 1,\dots, T$):

$$\sum_j \sum_p S_{sjp}(t)\, x_{jp}(t) \leq S_s(0) + \sum_{\tau=0}^{t-1}\delta S_s(\tau) - \sum_{\tau=0}^{t-1} \%S_s(\tau)\, S_s(\tau)$$

3. Having at least the minimum amount of all the necessary primary, nonproducible factors like labor, land, etc., available at each time period for the production of all goods as expressed by the $L \times T$ inequalities (for $l = 1, 2,\dots L$ and $t = 1, 2,\dots T$):

$$Z_l(t) = \sum_j \sum_p a_{ljp}(t)\, x_{jp}(t) \leq \dot{Z}_l(t)$$

For this problem, the givens are the $a_{ijp}(t)$'s, $a_{ljp}(t)$'s, $S_{sjp}(t)$'s, $i_{isr}(t|t')$'s, I_{isr}'s, and $\%S_s(t)$'s, which are production, investment, and depreciation coefficients; and the $\dot{Z}_l(t)$'s and $S_s(0)$'s, which are stocks of primary factors and initial capital goods; and the $v_i(t)$'s, $w_l(t)$'s and $y_s(T)$'s, which are the relative values of different goods, work activities, and final stocks. The "decision" variables for the Central Planning Board are the $x_{jp}(t)$'s and the $Q_i(t)$'s, which imply the $Z_l(t)$'s and $S_s(t)$'s.

9.2 Round One: Efficiency of Central Planning

9.2.1 Calculating the Plan

Although the only feature essential to our purposes is that the planning model be multiperiod, we have included a limited number of complications that hint at the complexity any realistic situation entails. Model 4 allows:

1. Planning over many time periods

2. A number of different nonproducible, or primary inputs, including different kinds of labor services

3. The necessity of having stocks of different "capital" goods in place as well as intermediate and primary inputs for production to take place

4. A variety of different production techniques for producing a variety of different intermediate and final goods

5. A variety of different processes by which the stocks of "capital" goods can be increased allowing variation in inputs and in the timing of their application

Although we included in Model 4 the possibility that different kinds of labor activities might have different effects on social welfare, and will discuss this case in a later section, the "traditional" debate about the efficiency of central planning considered only final consumption goods to be of welfare significance. It treated different categories of labor only as limiting primary factors. Model 4 can be easily adapted to the "traditional" debate by excluding the second set of terms in the planning board's objective function in the definition of the planner's problem.

The central planner's problem can be formulated as a linear programming problem where the different social evaluations of final goods are presumed constant and production technology is presumed to exhibit constant returns to scale. In the more realistic case of relative valuations of final goods being functions of relative amounts of final goods provided, and nonlinear production technologies, two approaches are available.

We could reformulate the planning problem as a nonlinear programming problem in either the objective function, the constraints, or both. Or, more practically, we could incorporate the more realistic elements within the framework of linear programming by using a variety of well-known artifices. To account for economies of scale within a linear framework one can define new activity vectors and new units of output for larger and smaller scale operations. To account for nonlinear social preferences one can define new variables in the objective function for different ranges of output and introduce new constraints limiting the range of possible values these new output variables can take. In this case Model 4 can be interpreted as allowing for these additional elements of realism within a linear framework.

But whether we use artifices to retain linear forms, or explicitly formulate a nonlinear programming problem, solutions maximizing social welfare, and a number of algorithms for finding them, are known to exist,[3] and there is no need to belabor these technical matters here.

The point is that in light of modern mathematical programming theory and computer capacity, the "old" debate about whether a centrally planned

302

economy can be efficient is settled in the affirmative provided one can assume the planning board

1. Has perfect knowledge of initial capital stocks and primary resource and labor availabilities

2. Has complete information about the technical coefficients of all the different production processes

3. Possesses an accurate social welfare function to be used as the objective function in the programming problem

4. Has a sufficiently large computing facility

5. Will have its plan carried out

The "modern" debate about the efficiency of central planning has revolved precisely around whether or not these assumptions can be justified. But before considering various schemes for solving information and incentive problems in centrally planned economies, we first need to address the distribution of final goods among the different consumers and the assignment of particular individuals to specific jobs. For while a Central Planning Board might achieve a socially optimal production plan, this does not guarantee Pareto optimality unless the assignment of work and distribution of final goods is also carried out efficiently.

When the Central Planning Board calculates an optimal plan, it arrives at a complete list of all the inputs each unit is to receive and the outputs each unit should produce. Included among the list of inputs are the number of hours of different categories of labor services that each unit is to use, but this is not the same as a list of who will be assigned to which units. Similarly, when the amount of each product needed in production and for investment is subtracted from the gross output of that good we arrive at the net output of each good available for consumption. But this is not the same as a list of the amounts of each final good to be distributed to each consumer. In other words, even if we assume that an optimal plan has been calculated and carried out, some system of distribution of final goods and job assignments is needed. Obviously inefficiencies could arise in these aspects of a centrally planned economy as well. Next we describe a few ways by which distribution and job assignment could be carried out, along with the necessary conditions for them to achieve Pareto optimality, to illustrate just how markets are, and are not, related to efficiency in central planning.

9.2.2 Distribution of Final Goods

1. The Central Planning Board could distribute arbitrary portions of each final good, in each time period, to each member of society.

Of course giving equal portions of each good in each time period to each citizen would be one such distribution. But less egalitarian possibilities abound. To preserve optimality under any chosen scheme, all citizens would have to be free to trade whatever goods they initially received (both within and across time periods), and we would have to assume that the absence of any prohibition on such trading resulted in the successful conclusion of all mutually beneficial transactions. In other words, the government would have to sanction a "white market" in final goods rather than confining such operations to a "black market."

2. Alternatively, the Central Planning Board could create a number of distribution centers to which people were assigned and distribute some particular quantity of each final good to each distribution center in each time period.

Assigning an equal number of people to each center and supplying each center with an equal portion of each good in each time period, again, is one possibility among many. In any case, the members of each distribution center could be left to decide how to distribute whatever goods the center received. But even if we assume that the distribution among members leaves no possible mutually beneficial transactions between members, we would have to assume that centers were permitted to trade their goods (both within and across time periods), and that this trading opportunity resulted in the conclusion of all mutually beneficial transactions between centers in order to guarantee Pareto optimality.

Under both these methods of distribution any degree of egalitarianism is theoretically possible. There are no formal markets in either system. (There is not even any currency.) But as anyone trained in economics will have recognized, the absence of markets is something of a sleight of hand. There are no markets only because all Pareto improvements achievable through exchange are left to individuals to work out for themselves. It is not difficult to visualize how individual barter exchange would quickly lead to more and more extensive "classified" sections in newspapers and eventually monetized markets for final goods. After all, for all the faults we found with money and markets in chapter 7, we never claimed they did not serve a practical cybernetic function in particular situations. In a cybernetic vacuum it is predictable markets would appear. And if the alternative is no information, or information only at great expense of time and effort, it is reasonable to consider the emergence of markets a social improvement. In light of which

3. The Central Planning Board could introduce currency, retail outlets, and savings and loan banks.

Each individual could be given some amount of currency in each time period, and all final goods could be sent to retail outlets. The managers of retail outlets could be directed to adjust prices to ensure that each good disappeared from the shelf on the last day of each month, just prior to next month's deliveries. People would freely loan or borrow from the banks, whose managers would. have to finance loans out of savings deposits, adjusting interest rates to eliminate excess deposits or loan applications. Provided the retail (and bank) managers perfected the art of having "empty shelves" just prior to new deliveries, this method would also result in Pareto optimality. And this holds, of course, without regard to how much currency each individual is allotted.[4]

Obviously, a number of different criteria could be used in deciding how much currency to give each individual, but the Pareto optimality of central planning would be preserved under any currency distribution provided we assume the production plan is carried out. If one were concerned with economic equality

3a. Each individual could be given the same amount of currency.

On the other hand, if one were concerned that the plan may not be carried out unless individuals are provided strong material incentives to exert effort in their work assignments and develop productive skills, other differential currency disbursements come to mind. For instance:

3b. The Central Planning Board could give out different amounts of currency to employees in different production units according to how closely the unit came to fulfilling its part of the production plan

3c. The Central Planning Board could distribute different amounts of currency to different categories of labor depending on how many years of education were required on average to achieve a certificate of competence in that field

3d. The Central Planning Board could do studies to rate different jobs according to relative difficulty and burdensomeness and design pay scales accordingly

3e. The Central Planning Board could give currency to the personnel departments of production units with which to hire workers. Workers would freely seek employment wherever they chose, and personnel departments would freely hire any they wished from among those who applied. Since this last "criterion" for differential currency disbursement is also one way of assigning people to jobs, we will discuss different systems for allocating labor via "free" labor markets next.

305

9.2.3 *Job Assignment*

In examining different possible systems of job assignment we should remember that the Central Planning Board was assumed to have perfect knowledge of the amount of all different "primary" inputs available—including the number of people capable of performing each different kind of labor service. Moreover, as part of calculating an optimal production plan the Central Planning Board calculated the number of people in each labor category to be assigned to work at each production unit. What is less obvious is that in calculating an optimal production plan the Central Planning Board also necessarily calculates the social value (or opportunity cost) of each scarce input used in producing the optimal production plan, including each category of labor. In mathematical programming language, those opportunity costs are called "shadow prices" and are the well-known solutions to the "dual" programming problem. They are easily (and often automatically) generated along with the optimal production plan that is the solution to the "primal" programming problem. This means that the Central Planning Board also knows the opportunity costs of different categories of labor when they are employed to produce an optimal production plan.

1. The simplest method of job assignment would be for the Central Planning Board to send a letter to each individual in each labor category telling him or her where to report to work. The Central Planning Board could make the assignments on any basis they wished—randomly, alphabetically, etc.

2. The Central Planning Board could leave the specific assignments up to associations of individuals in each labor category. The Central Planning Board would send the associations a list of how many of their members should report to each production unit in the economy and let the associations decide who goes where. This might be done within any given association by lottery, seniority, or voting, or with an eye to work and educational incentives. It might be done according to members' work ratings in their previous employment(s) or their academic standing in the educational process that qualifies them as members of the association.

Although the "old" debate did not countenance differential welfare effects of different work assignments, in fact the situation is theoretically symmetrical to that of differential welfare effects of different consumption bundles. In this context, for either of the above systems of job assignments to be Pareto optimal, one must assume that all mutually beneficial trades of work assignments between similarly qualified individuals were both permitted and exhausted before people showed up to work. But under this assumption of ex post "white markets" within

306

labor categories, both assignment system 1 and 2 would satisfy the criterion of efficiency without resort to formal labor markets.

3. The Central Planning Board could establish a "free" labor market in the sense that individual workers would be "free" to search and apply wherever they chose, and the personnel departments of different units would be "free" to hire whomever they preferred.

It is important to realize, however, that such a "free" labor market could operate in three very different ways.

3a. Under one system the number of workers hired in each category by each production unit, as well as the pay rates for each category of worker, would be determined by the Central Planning Board as part of the overall production plan. The only decisions left up to individual personnel departments would be which individuals to hire into positions and pay rates already determined by the central plan.

Personnel departments would not be authorized to hire fewer workers of one category and more of another. Nor would they be authorized to pay wages different from those set by the Central Planning Board. In other words, production units would not be permitted to make "input" substitutions or payments differing from nationwide pay scales which the Central Planning Board could set equal to the labor "shadow prices" calculated from the optimal production plan. This would be analogous to the management of a privately owned firm telling its personnel department how many positions of each kind it was to fill, what wages those individuals would be paid, and leaving only the hiring of particular employees to the personnel department.

3b. Alternatively, the Central Planning Board could allocate to each production unit a wage fund and leave to the units all decisions about how many workers to hire in each category and what to pay them.

To determine the size of the wage fund to be given each unit the Central Planning Board would calculate the number of employees in each category who should work in that production unit according to the Central Planning Board's optimal production plan, multiply the number in each category by what the CPB calculated to be the "shadow price" of that particular scarce labor resource, and deliver the sum total as the wage fund of the production unit. Then the personnel department of each production unit could hire whichever individuals in whatever labor categories it wished, paying them whatever it wished, subject only to the constraint of not exceeding its total wage fund. This would be analogous to the management of a private firm giving its personnel department a budget and allowing it to hire and pay from that budget as it deemed fit.

3c. A third system is a combination of the first two. The Central Planning Board would fix the number of employees to be hired in each category in each production unit, as in the first case. But the personnel departments would have discretionary powers over wages they contracted to pay particular employees out of a wage fund that was calculated by the Central Planning Board as in the second case.

This system would be analogous to the management of a private firm determining how many of each kind of worker to be hired, but allowing the personnel department to decide who to hire and how much to pay them within an operating budget.

Although the "free" labor market obviously differs in the three different cases, each has a claim to efficiency under a particular set of assumptions. Under the assumptions of Model 4, planners are assumed to have perfect knowledge about the desirabilities of all goods and work activities, the availabilities of all primary inputs including labor, and the technologies available to all units. Moreover, the quantities of different categories of labor supplied as well as the effort exerted are assumed independent of wage rates. Under these assumptions the Central Planning Board is in a position to calculate optimal allocations of labor as well as "efficiency" wage rates. But once labor supply is assumed exogenous, not only is system 3a perfectly efficient with "efficiency" wages, the Central Planning Board would be free to set wage rates according to any equity criterion without affecting economic efficiency,[5] permitting maximum flexibility regarding the degree of equality (or inequality) in the distribution of labor income.

On the other hand, if the central planners lacked accurate information about the possibilities of substitution between different labor categories in individual units, as well as information about differential preferences for different kinds of work, system 3b would have greater claim to efficiency. But while system 3b is highly flexible in the sense that it allows maximum room for individual negotiation for both prospective employees and employers, it would be inflexible regarding the degree of equality or inequality of labor incomes that could be arranged since the distribution of labor income would be determined by the forces of supply and demand.[6]

Finally, if the central planners had accurate information concerning labor availabilities and the production possibility sets of the units, but lacked accurate information on differential work preferences, system 3c would have greater claims to efficiency.

Before proceeding, we consider a final issue regarding labor assignments totally ignored in the "old" debate about central planning and efficiency. Whether the central planners fix hiring quotas and pay rates, allocate wage funds to production units, or fix hiring quotas but leave pay rates to production unit discretion within a budget, if the differential desirabilities of work in different units (units in Siberia versus units in Moscow) are ignored, less attractive units will have difficulty competing with more attractive units for the better workers within categories. The "old" debate did not consider differential preferences regarding work location any more than it did differential preferences for job types. But once we recognize this issue, it is clear all the above "labor market solutions" to the job allocation problem of central planning would be subject to inefficiencies if any such differences were not accounted for. To correct this failing, central planners would have to enable units that proved only able to hire from the bottom of the various labor category barrels to pay higher than average wage rates. In system 3a this would entail authorizing higher pay scales in all categories of employment in relatively less attractive enterprises. In systems 3b and 3c planners would have to allocate larger wage funds to less attractive units.

9.2.4 *Summary of the "Old Debate"*

We hope our treatment of final good distribution and job assignment served to illustrate the following points:

1. From the perspective of traditional welfare theory and under the terms of the "old debate," not only can efficient plans be calculated via central planning, but the distribution of final goods and job assignments can be carried out in efficient ways that do not necessarily employ currency, formal markets for final goods, or formal labor markets.

2. Although centrally planned systems deemed efficient by traditional welfare theory can, in theory, operate without markets of any kind, the vision is artificial. If one accepts traditional welfare theory's view of the possibility of Pareto improvements through exchange of anything that individuals might value (goods or jobs), any system of central planning that does not employ markets to distribute goods or assign people to jobs would quickly generate them or suffer from distributional inefficiencies.

3. Final goods markets and labor markets can be part of a centrally planned system without affecting the mixture of final goods and job roles. The optimal mixtures can be determined by the central planning procedure with markets used only for distribution and assignment.[7]

4. On the other hand, final goods and labor markets can be used in a way that allows them not only to distribute goods and assign jobs that have already been planned, but to influence the quantities of different final goods and jobs the system settles on. We defer explaining exactly how this can be done to our discussion of different ways for deter-

mining the relative social values of different final goods and work activities in the social welfare function. But it is important to distinguish here between these two very different uses of final good and labor markets in centrally planned systems.

5. An improved version of the "old" debate, still from the perspective of traditional welfare theory, would be to recognize the symmetry between differential preferences for final goods and differential preferences for different kinds of work by including different job types and locations, along with final goods, in the social welfare function.

6. Still, our major conclusion is that if the central planners are presumed to have all relevant information, an optimal plan can be calculated, and distribution and job assignment could be handled in a number of different ways that would preserve the efficiency of central planning as judged by traditional welfare theory.

But before leaving the "old" form of the traditional debate to focus on the "modern" debate concerning information and incentive problems, we consider the efficiency of central planning under the assumption of endogenous preferences.

9.2.5 The "Old Debate" and Endogenous Preferences

If the Central Planning Board is assumed to know both the developmental as well as fulfillment effects of economic activity—that is, if the Central Planning Board knows the true social welfare function—the demonstration that the central planning can be efficient even under the assumption of endogenous preferences is straightforward. In this case, the different social evaluations of final goods and labor activities in the objective function are interpreted to be not only functions of the relative amounts of different final goods and labor activities consumed in the given time period, but functions of the relative amounts of different final goods and labor activities to be consumed in later time periods as well. In this way the future developmental effects of different production plans would be included in the social welfare function as well. In other words, in our Model 4 we would want 4.14 to become:

$$v_i(t) = v_i(\, Q_1^t \ldots Q_c^t; \ldots Q_1^T \ldots Q_c^T; \, z_1^t \ldots z_L^t; \ldots z_1^T \ldots z_L^T \,)$$

$$w_l(t) = w_l(\, Q_1^t \ldots Q_c^t; \ldots Q_1^T \ldots Q_c^T; \, z_1^t \ldots z_L^t; \ldots z_1^T \ldots z_L^T \,)$$

If we extend this further knowledge to the Central Planning Board, the plan they calculate would obviously be optimal under endogenous preferences, just as when preferences were assumed exogenous. This completes our review of the "old" debate about the efficiency of centrally planned economies where informational and incentive problems are "assumed away."[8]

9.3 Round Two: The "Modern Debate"

The planning bureau cannot be aware of all the information needed for a perfect description of techniques. These are too numerous, complex, and diverse. Only the individual firms or highly specialized industry offices can have precise knowledge of the conditions governing production in their particular field. Some way must, therefore, be found for these firms and offices to participate in the preparation of the plan.[9]

What Malinvaud means here by "participate" is to provide information to the Central Planning Board that will allow the Central Planning Board to calculate an optimal production plan. We now investigate procedures for accomplishing this aim.[10]

9.3.1 Discovering the Technical Coefficients of Production

The method of "material balances" has been the most common way of gathering information in the actual practice of central planning, though it is least interesting from our point of view, because irrespective of some of its practical advantages, it is demonstrably inefficient. Various iterative procedures involving trial prices, trial quantities, and a gradient search are more theoretically interesting because they can provide sufficient information for the Central Planning Board to calculate an efficient plan under specified conditions, assuming the Central Planning Board knows the social welfare function. We now consider these methods in turn.

Material Balances. As Benjamin Ward explains:

The planning bureau starts with a known bill of final demands for each sector. Its task is to find a bill of gross outputs for each sector which is consistent with this bill of final demands and with the production technology. The procedure is as follows:

1. The bureau reports to each sector its corresponding final demand.

2. Each sector calculates its input requirements if it is to produce this final demand. To do this it simply multiplies each coefficient in its column of A [the input-output matrix for the economy] by the final demand. [He assumes that each sector knows its own technology, that is, its own column in A, but no other columns; and that the Central Planning Board does not know any of the columns at all.] The results are reported to the bureau.

311

3. The bureau adds the input requirements for each good in each sector together and reports these to the sectors as additions to the previously assigned output level [the final demands in the first round].

4. The process continues until further additions to requirements become insignificant. The bureau then takes its total requirements for each sector as the desired plan and assigns these as production targets to the individual sectors.[11]

Ward observes that "this process is equivalent to the power series expansion solution to a system of linear equations" and that "the process converges for reasonable technologies."[12] But whereas "the calculations are extremely simple," and "a minimal amount of communication is involved," "the scheme is inflexible (in that) there are assumed to be no technological options for the sectors," "no account is taken of limitations on the attainable level of production," and most importantly, "there is no optimizing (since) the final demands are given a priori, and opportunities that may exist for achieving higher performance levels are ignored."[13]

In conclusion, the method of material balances allows the Central Planning Board to come up with a plan without knowing in advance the production technologies of any of the individual sectors. And in this process the Central Planning Board certainly comes to know the matrix of input-output coefficients for the economy. But regardless of some of the practical advantages discussed above and others pointed out by J. M. Montias in his original analysis,[14] the process is not efficient. It is unable to allow for alternative technological processes within the sectors and for substitution between different goods in the bill of final demands in light of production possibilities. It remains, however, the most common way of planning in centrally planned economies.[15]

Trial Prices. Danzig and Wolfe[16] were the first to propose an iterative procedure where "the center proposes tentative resource prices, the producing units develop corresponding profit-maximizing production programs (with prices treated parametrically),"[17] and the center then proceeds to revise its proposed prices in light of the production programs received. An optimal solution to the economic programming problem can be reached using this procedure although it is necessary to assume that there are no technological externalities, that all constraints are linear, both at the level of single production units and at the overall level of the economy, and that "the objective function and the overall constraints are 'additively separable.'"[18] It is because of the assumed linearity of individual unit constraints that the units can use linear programming techniques to solve the "primal" problems posed to them at each iteration by the Central Planning Board. And it is because of the assumed linearity of economy wide resource constraints that the Central Planning Board can use linear programming techniques to solve the "dual" problems posed at each successive iteration. The presumed absence of externalities and assumption of "additive separability" guarantees that the equilibrium reached in a finite number of steps will be an economy wide optimum.

Baumol and Fabian[19] extended Danzig and Wolfe's procedure "to situations where constraints pertaining to single producing units are non-linear, while the overall constraints pertaining to resources needed by all units remain linear."[20] Obviously, the individual units can no longer use any of the well-known algorithms for solving linear programming problems, but must instead use some effective algorithm for solving nonlinear programming problems to calculate their individual production plans at each iteration.

However, the best-known procedure for arriving at an optimal production plan through the use of trial prices is that of Malinvaud.[21] In Malinvaud's procedure:

the center proposes prices to the producing units which, in turn, determine production plans maximizing the value of the firm's output in terms of those prices. The center then builds up its picture of each unit's production set by taking all convex mixtures of its previous proposed input-output vectors, together with the initial feasible vector, assumed known to the center....Treating its pictures of the production sets as if they were the actual sets, the center then maximizes its utility function subject to the resource availability constraint and proposes a new set of prices corresponding to the relevant marginal rates of substitution.[22]

In this manner the Central Planning Board can formulate an optimal plan under the following conditions:

the bureau knows the set X of acceptable final consumption, the vector representing available resources, and the utility function $u(x)$ [which is what we have called the social welfare function]; but...it does not know a priori the specifications of the sets Y_k (the production possibility sets for the individual production units). On the other hand, firm k has perfect knowledge of its own set of technical possibilities Y_k, but does not know the sets which apply to other firms; nor the set X, the [resource] vector, or the function $u(x)$.[23]

The assumptions necessary are that the individual production sets are closed, bounded, and convex; the set X is closed, convex, and bounded from below; the function $u(x)$ is continuous and concave; and the planning bureau knows a feasible program to begin with. Under these conditions, Malinvaud's procedure of trial prices yields a feasible plan at every iteration, is "well defined," "monotonic," and "convergent." "Well defined," meaning that "there always exist solutions to the operations according to which the firms' proposals, the prospective indices, and the plan can be determined"[24] yielding a feasible program. "Monotonic," meaning that the value of the social welfare function is never lowered in any successive iteration. And "convergent," meaning that as the iterations increase indefinitely the value of the social welfare function "tends to the value $u*$, the least upper bound of $u(x)$ over the set of feasible programmes."[25]

Trial Quantities. Kornai and Liptak make very similar assumptions concerning the economy as in the Danzig and Wolfe model, namely that there is "block angularity," or subsets of constraints each pertaining to a given sector, as well as resource constraints affecting the whole economy.[26] In the Kornai and Liptak procedure, however, the kind of proposals made by the center and the units are reversed.

> In the dialogue, the center proposes allotments of scarce resources to the various sectors: then each sector responds with shadow prices (marginal rates of substitution) minimizing the value of the allotment subject to sectoral dual constraints (nonprofit condition for every sectoral activity). The center's aim, on the other hand, is to maximize the contributions of the sectors to the objective function, i.e., to maximize the value of the allocated resources at the shadow prices received from the sectors, subject to the limitation of available resource totals.[27]

Although Kornai and Liptak are able to establish convergence to an equilibrium with any desired degree of accuracy by structuring the dialogue as a fictitious game, they are not able to guarantee that the equilibrium will be achieved in a finite number of steps; nor is their procedure completely informationally decentralized "since each sector's resource sectoral allotments must be large enough ('evaluable') to assure the existence of a feasible solution for that sector."[28]

A number of other "quantity-guided" procedures are designed specifically for nonlinear economies. One of S. A. Marglin's[29] mechanisms requires "the center to allocate the scarce resources on the basis of information obtained from the producing units concerning their marginal productivities and their excess demands, adjustment ceasing when aggregate excess demand is zero and the marginal productivities of producers are equalized."[30] G. M. Heal developed a similar process in which

> the Central Planning Board proposes an allocation of inputs amongst firms, and these latter respond by informing it of the outputs that these would make possible, and of the marginal productivities of the inputs at

this allocation. In the light of this data the Central Planning Board proposes a new allocation of inputs in which, by comparison with the previous one, resources have been shifted towards the uses where they are most marginally productive, and away from those where their marginal contribution is least.[31]

Heal's first procedure (1969) is capable of handling both intermediate goods and joint products. Dreze and de la Vallee Poussin[32] and Malinvaud[33] also developed "quantity-guided" procedures that are interesting in their ability to handle mixtures of public and private goods. Weitzman developed a quantity-guided procedure that is a sort of dual to that of Malinvaud.

While Malinvaud's center is rather timid and only considers plans known to be feasible for the units, Weitzman's central planning agency constructs imaginary production sets it knows to be too ambitious, formulates targets that are, in general, infeasible and then lets the units scale down the proposals to feasible levels....Convergence is assured (even in a finite number of steps when the production sets are polyhedral).[34]

Whereas the procedures of Marglin, Heal (1969), and Dreze and de la Vallee Poussin all maintain feasibility, are convergent, and monotonic, Malinvaud's "quantity-guided" mechanism (1970) does not maintain feasibility or monotonicity, and Weitzman's procedure fails to maintain feasibility. Finally, none of the procedures that are of a pure "price-guided" or pure "quantity-guided" variety are applicable in cases where individual production units' possibility sets are nonconvex and are specifically not applicable in the presence of increasing returns to scale. This is not the case with some of the procedures that mix price-guidance with quantity-guidance discussed next.

Mixtures of Price-Guidance and Quantity-Guidance. In 1971 Heal described a procedure using mixed price and quantity guidance that "locates a local maximum of the objective function even in the presence of increasing returns to scale, that satisfies Malinvaud's feasibility and monotonicity criteria, and has some of the informational economy of price-guided procedures."[35] The "essential informational feature" of Heal's second procedure "is that certain functions of each producing unit's marginal productivities (roughly, its shadow prices for particular resources) must be conveyed to the center." But whereas in Heal's first mechanism the center's only response was to "calculate improved resource allotments" and issue them as new trial quantities, in his second method the center may also "calculate and send to the units a resource price (the same for all units) and so enable them to determine their respective resource requirements."[36] This added flexibility at the center, combined with a procedure requiring agents in the economy "only to raise rather than maximize the magnitudes in which they are interested (is what) gives ...the procedure added stability and allows it to converge to an optimum even in the presence of increasing returns."[37]

The interesting feature of Aoki's[38] procedure is that it can handle mixtures of private and public goods by using "price-guidance for private goods and quantity-guidance for public goods." In Aoki's procedure, producers

> develop production plans that maximize net revenue given the central "guide-lines" (prices for the private goods and quantities for the public goods), and convey to the center their demands for private goods and marginal evaluations, including marginal cost, for public goods. The center, in turn, adjusts the price of each private good according to the difference between its marginal utility and price....The targets for public goods are increased in proportion to the net aggregate of marginal valuations (users' minus producers').[39]

Gradient Procedures. We conclude with a brief description of a particular kind of price-guidance, gradient procedures. For a linear economy, Koopmans[40] described an

> allocation game to be played...by a helmsman (setting the prices of final goods)...commodity custodians (adjusting the prices of resources according to excess demand), and activity managers who determine the production programs. Koopman's adjustment rule...is that managers expand profitable activities and curtail those bringing losses.[41]

Unfortunately, Samuelson[42] demonstrated that this procedure yields nonconvergent results in constant returns economies. But

> in an economy where all functions (including the utility indicator) are strictly concave (i.e., we have diminishing returns) similar rules produce a process with the desired stability properties. Utilizing the notion of gradient approach to the saddle point of the Lagrangian expression, Arrow and Hurwicz (1960)[43] used the following rules: the helmsman, taking the prices of desired commodities as given, changes each final demand at a rate equal to the difference between its marginal utility and price; each manager, again taking prices as given, changes the scale of his process in proportion to its marginal profitability; each commodity custodian varies the price of his commodity in proportion to excess demand.[44]

316

Although this gradient process converges to an optimum, the strict concavity assumptions are critical, and none of the intermediate plans are feasible. The original gradient process of Arrow and Hurwicz was formulated in continuous time, but Uzawa[45] constructed a discrete time parameter counterpart that overcame this undesirable feature of the Arrow-Hurwicz process.

Summary of Information Gathering Procedures. We have gone to great lengths to describe different ways in which a Central Planning Board might arrive at an optimal plan without being aware, initially, "of all the information needed for a perfect description of techniques, [since] only the individual firms...can have precise knowledge of the conditions governing production in their particular field" for three reasons. Our immediate purpose was to demonstrate that this particular kind of information problem, often referred to in the "modern debate" over the efficiency of central planning, can be overcome, at least in theory. Although the particular assumptions necessary for the application of the different procedures are far from totally realistic, the widening of the set of procedures to meet situations ever farther from "classical" conditions is sufficiently impressive, in our opinion, to conclude that technical information problems should no longer be considered theoretical obstacles to the efficiency of central planning. The criticism was well taken when material balances was the only known method for generating the central plan, but this is no longer the case.

However, these technical procedures for solving the "information problem" of transferring knowledge of local productive potentials to the Central Planning Board suggest an associated "incentive problem." Are there incentives for managers to report truthfully or not? The above procedures simply assume truthful reporting. A primary concern of the "modern" form of the traditional debate is examination of this assumption. We offer only limited observations on this subject since our primary concern with central planning lies elsewhere.

1. There certainly appear to be incentives for managers to lie about unit capabilities in order to influence the production targets and input allocations they receive and, thereby, their possibilities of winning reward and avoiding punishment. In our view, recent attempts to treat this issue as the most important "principal-agent" problem in centrally planned economies are right on the mark.[46] And ample evidence in the historical literature supports claims of incentives to misinform.[47]

2. But the incentive for management to dissimulate to "higher authorities" is not unique to centrally planned economies. As Pak-Wai Liu observed, "The nature of the problem of the socialist planner in

motivating and rewarding socialist managers...bears much similarity to the problem of motivating branch or divisional managers of a capitalist corporation."[48] Moreover, it is not obvious that the problem is structurally any different from the problem stockholders in PrEMEs have knowing whether the managers they hire are really maximizing profits. Is there an incentive for managers of privately owned enterprises to "downplay" potentials and expectations to stockholders in order to enhance their rewards and avoid punishment?

3. It would appear the outcome of the central planning principal-agent model—and in particular the accuracy of information transferred—should depend on the ability of the central planners: (a) to punish or reward managers for the veracity of information provided, and (b) to judge the veracity through either independent investigation or "competitive" comparison with similar units. Regarding rewards and punishments, there need be no problem in theory. Regarding comparative evaluation, central planners are not altogether without means.

4. Whether or not central planners are in a less advantageous position than superiors to local management in other kinds of economies to elicit accurate information, and exactly why and to what extent this may be the case, is under active investigation. We remain "agnostic" to date.

In any case, we went to such lengths to discuss information eliciting procedures for two reasons beyond demonstrating that, at least theoretically, matters have progressed considerably beyond material balances. First, in a later section of this chapter we will return to an analysis of the cybernetic properties of central planning from the point of view of the new welfare theory developed in chapter 6. In that context it will prove very useful to have at least a moderately detailed understanding of the informational procedures that have been formalized to date. Second, in our concluding chapter we assert the need to devise a new, decentralized planning procedure, different from both market and centrally planned allocation. And while none of the above procedures for consolidating information in the hands of central planners can be adopted "as is" for decentralized planning, we believe they contain useful ideas for developing procedures appropriate for participatory planning.

9.3.2 *In Search of the Social Welfare Function*

In the previous section we discussed a number of ways a Central Planning Board could calculate a central plan without knowing the productive capabilities of production units in advance, but we assumed throughout that central planners at least knew the social welfare function (or what was often referred to in the literature as the "utility function"). As Malinvaud stated explicitly:

> I shall not consider the problems which may be posed in defining the collective choices to be made; these choices will be represented here by a utility function which is known by the central agency.[49]

We now turn to how a central agency might come to know the social welfare function. We discuss three different approaches, but we might note in advance that at least one method leaves centrally planned economies with as much claim to Pareto optimality as either private or public enterprise market systems—provided we use traditional welfare theory as our basis for judgment and confine our attention to traditional concerns.

Authoritarian Political Determination. Joseph Stalin or Mao Tsetung might know what is best for the people of their societies. They might know which economic activities are most fulfilling to the citizens, which economic activities develop people's capacities best for greater fulfillment in the future, which economic activities generate "socialist citizens," or "communist men," etc. And they might have sufficiently detailed knowledge in all these regards to be able to set down a quantitative function relating all these different fulfillment, development, and political effects. We are not suggesting that Mao ever considered himself capable of such a heroic feat, but it is one possible way that the Central Planning Board could obtain the social welfare function; it could be handed to the central planners by a maximum leader. Or, the social welfare function could be elaborated in a more subtle process by a "collective" political leadership such as a politburo, or central committee, or an entire vanguard political party. In any case, one approach is to obtain such a function from some such group of Revolutionary Philosopher Kings.

Market Determination. In our description of how the optimal bill of final goods might be distributed to particular individuals, we described how retail outlets might be established, individuals given currency with which to buy goods, and prices set by retail managers to eliminate excess demands or supplies.

In essence, a centrally planned economy can resort to the "revealed preferences" of individuals in the marketplace to determine the social welfare function. Central planners need simply use the most recent relative prices from the retail outlets (and banks) as the relative social valuations of different final goods (and time) in society's social welfare function. With this method of determining relative weights to be given different final goods (and times) in the social welfare function, a centrally planned economy would exhibit the property known in traditional welfare theory as "consumer sovereignty." Of course, if different individuals entered the retail outlets and banks with different amounts of currency, the result would be different than if everyone had the same number of "dollar votes." But the resulting social welfare function, when successfully maximized by the Central Planning Board, would yield a Pareto optimum no matter what the distribution of currency.

If different kinds of labor activities were considered to be welfare significant, one would have to establish a market in labor services to use differential market wage rates as weights for different work activities in the social welfare function. But again, we have already described how such a market could be arranged.

The first system of labor markets we discussed, 3a, is obviously not such a solution since in 3a wage rates can be arbitrary. System 3a assumes the central planners already have the weights, which they combine with the constraints when they solve the planning problem yielding shadow prices for different labor activities as part of the solution to the dual, which the Central Planning Board may or may not choose to use.

But either of the other two labor market systems, 3b or 3c, in which personnel departments hire out of a wage fund allocated by the Central Planning Board, could be used to generate weights incorporating differential disutilities of different kinds of labor in the social welfare function. Moreover, this method of determining the relative weights assigned to different kinds of labor exhibits the property known in traditional welfare theory as "producer sovereignty."

In any case, determination of the social welfare function through revealed preferences in the markets for final goods and labor services places central planning on the same exalted pedestal that private enterprise competitive market economies have long occupied, at least according to traditional welfare theory. That is, a centrally determined plan can be a Pareto optimum.[50]

Political Determination by Voting. A final way to arrive at society's social welfare function would be for every citizen to vote for the weights to be assigned to final goods and labor activities. Each citizen could be given, say, 1000 points to distribute among arguments in the social welfare function. Or, as in the case of market determination, different citizens could be given different numbers of points to vote (according to their highest degree earned, IQ, hair color, etc.). In any case, points voted would be tallied by the Central Planning Board, and the sum of points voted for each good or work activity would be used as its weight in the social welfare function.[51] We leave discussion of the advantages and disadvantages of democratic voting procedures for estimating the social welfare function to a later section.

320

9.3.3 *Material Incentives for Carrying Out the Plan*

It has been argued that in well-run, public ownership, centrally planned economies since no capitalists exploit workers, since the central plan maximizes social well-being if all carry out their assignments, and since the distribution of work assignments and consumption benefits is just, no incentives beyond enlightened self-interest are needed. Again, we defer discussion of the extent to which all this might or might not be plausible to a later section. But suppose—for purposes of concluding the "old debate" from the point of view of traditional welfare theory, and in line with practical experience—that enlightened self-interest and solidarity were not sufficient incentives to bring a centrally calculated plan to fruition. Are other means available to centrally planned economies to motivate compliance with targets and work assignments?

There is no reason centrally planned economies cannot use the same kind of material incentives that are presumed sufficiently motivating to bring PrEMEs to Pareto optimality. In a centrally planned system with markets for labor and final goods, workers would have the same material interests to carry out production tasks as workers do in PrEMEs. If personnel departments included some form of bonus system in the labor contract, workers in centrally planned systems might even come to have material interests closely approximating those of workers with stock ownership plans, or workers in PuEEMMEs!

As far as managers of production units are concerned, the problem as we discussed previously of establishing incentives for them to perform in accord with Central Planning Board criteria is theoretically no different from the problem of motivating branch managers within privately owned corporations, or the problem stockholders have getting CEOs of privately owned firms to behave in accord with stockholders' criteria, or, for that matter, the problem a workers' council has getting managers they hire to behave in accord with the council's criteria. In all cases the possibilities of material rewards, bonuses, fringe benefits, and advancement in the managerial hierarchy, are all available, as are the same set of material punishments, pay cuts, elimination of perquisites, demotion, and firing. All three economies—PrEMEs, PuEMEs, and PuECPEs—embody similar problems of determining the extent to which managers are doing the best possible job of maximizing their superiors' criteria. Contrary to popular opinion, we see nothing inherent in central planning making "accountability problems" more serious than in other economies we have analyzed, and the most recent literature applying principal-agent theory to central planning environments cited earlier appears to be confirming this opinion.

To summarize: one kind of incentive problem is how "superiors" are to get "subordinates" to carry out superiors' wishes. Whether superiors are stockholders and subordinates managers (PrEMEs), or superiors are CEOs and subordinates division managers (PrEMEs), or superiors are central planners and subordinates unit managers (PuECPEs), or superiors are employees in a council and subordinates managers (PuEEMMEs), or superiors are in a central bureaucracy and subordinates are state-appointed plant managers (PuESMMEs), or superiors are managers and subordinates are workers (any of the economies we have considered); the problem is to induce subordinates to "execute" superiors' "goals." What we have discussed in this section are conceivable incentives superiors in centrally planned economies might use to hold their subordinates "accountable," and we have concluded that the same range of "material incentives" presumed to guarantee accountability in the other economies we have discussed is available to central planners as well. A different kind of incentive problem is how "superiors" can elicit information from "subordinates" about subordinates' true capabilities when subordinates know something about this their superiors may not. This is also not a problem unique to central planning, although it may have more far-reaching implications in centrally planned economies than in others. In any case, in the context of central planning the "information" incentive problem is logically prior to the "accountability" incentive problem because the first involves calculating an optimal plan and the second involves getting people to execute the plan. But while logically prior, information incentives are not logically separable from accountability incentives, which poses difficulties others have pointed out and we are by no means oblivious to. Just as work by Western economists in the early 1970s on iterative planning pointed the way for how central planners might gather information on unit capabilities, work by Western economists on the principal-agent relationship in the 1980s is shedding light on incentive schemes to induce unit managers to "play" interactive planning games truthfully.

Finally, to argue that central planning lacks the "disciplining force" of unemployment is to forget the full employment context in which we have been discussing market systems and to underestimate the flexibility of central planning. In real world market economies a certain probability of unemployment exists. But we have been discussing the optimality properties of market economies in general equilibria. Neither private enterprise nor public enterprise market economies have any claim to efficiency whenever any of their markets fail to clear—the labor market hardly being an exception. In equilibria market economies do not have the disciplining force of unemployment any more than full employment versions of central planning do. Moreover, there is no reason a Central Planning Board could not "plan" to create a "reserve army of the unemployed" for motivational purposes should it be deemed necessary.[52]

9.3.4 *Summary of the "Modern Debate"*

The neoclassical economist who has "broken out of his traditional limits" and "enlarged his field of vision...to avoid a narrow focus on the status quo, whether East or West,"[53] may think of himself or herself "as taking part in a contest to design a 'superior' mechanism."[54] For an economist such as Leonid Hurwicz the name of the game is still to evaluate what he terms different possible "economic mechanisms" from the perspective of traditional welfare theory. But he is willing to go beyond the "cease search" sign in front of PrEMEs to give equal consideration to variants of public enterprise market economies and different planning schemes as well.

In this more refreshing but still traditional context, we have argued that, in theory, when all complications are assumed away, publicly owned, centrally planned economies can lay equal claim to efficiency as can privately or publicly owned competitive market economies. Moreover, the much discussed problems of gathering technological data, estimating a social welfare function, and providing sufficient incentives to carry out the central plan are far less intractable, at least in theory, than usually assumed. In fact, if one weighs the practical limitations on the different procedures discussed above, including the possibilities of self-interested concealment of information in those procedures, against the difficulties of hopping from general equilibrium to general equilibrium infinitely quickly in market economies and the analogous information and incentive problems that are present in private and public enterprise market economies as well, one might conclude—if one were an economist such as Leonid Hurwicz—that the efficiency-oriented economist's dream just may lie closer to a PuECPE than either a PuEME or PrEME!

At any rate, that is the case we have attempted to present in order to demonstrate that even if this were all true—even if central planning won the traditional welfare theory sweepstakes, or came in a "dead heat"—it is still an economy inherently incapable of collecting and dispersing economic information, organizing productive roles, and estimating relative social values in ways that maximize human fulfillment and development.

9.4 Round Three: The "New Debate"

It is finally time to reexamine the different procedures for generating a central plan from the perspective of the information goals indicated by the welfare theory developed in chapter 6. To give central planning every possible benefit, let us assume that price-guided, quantity-guided, mixed price and quantity-guided, and/or gradient procedures are completely successful in allowing the central planning agency to acquire all information concerning technical possibilities of production. What is the nature of the information consolidation and dispersion patterns they generate in the process of plan formulation?

9.4.1 *Central Planning as a Cybernetic Disaster*

The cybernetic essence of Malinvaud's price-guided mechanism (1967) is that "the information concerning the production functions (of the individual units) is being transferred to the center, although on an installment plan."[55] The Central Planning Board is gathering ever more information about production possibility sets of individual units by issuing prices and receiving feasible production plans that maximize the value of the firm's net output in terms of those prices. The Central Planning Board retains unit responses and formulates an ever more accurate picture of individual units' production possibility sets by forming the convex hull of all previous proposals. The only difference between Malinvaud's procedure and other price-guided mechanisms[56] is that Malinvaud's Central Planning Board must retain and utilize all previous information about units to calculate its next set of trial prices. In the case of other price-guided mechanisms, the Central Planning Board receives similar responses from units with which it could generate an ever more accurate image of the units' possibility sets, but the center does not need to retain and use past information to calculate its next proposal.

So the information consolidation and dispersion effects for all price-guided mechanisms, including gradient procedures, is essentially the same; information about individual units' technical production possibilities is transfered piece-meal to the center, while the extent to which units receive information about the rest of the economy is limited to a series of price vectors, giving them no more information than units receive in market economies, whose cybernetic inadequacies we discussed in chapter 7. In Malinvaud's scheme, the Central Planning Board must retain all information and construct ever more accurate images of units' technical possibilities. In other procedures, this information could be thrown away. But in any case, information centralization (or potential centralization) is the essence from a cybernetic point of view.

As we explained earlier, assuming that a group of workers, i, "sees" $\{A(i,t)\}$ with all its material and human inputs, outputs, and characteristic transformations, to understand how their activity fits with the activity of others they need a vivid picture of all $\{A(j,t)\}$ for all $j \neq i$ and $t = 0,1,...T$, where the human inputs and outputs of the other processes are particularly crucial to understand. We already explained how information conveyed by a price vector is insufficient to permit members of different groups to achieve this understanding. Price vectors do not explain how the activities of others define what is possible for one to do, nor how one's choices affect the possibilities of others thereby weakening each group's ability to exercise self-management and develop solidarity with others. Since this is the total information provided units under price-guided central planning, the same criticism made of market systems applies here as well.

It is important to notice that price-guided central planning does not even fully inform the Central Planning Board concerning all critical aspects of economic potentials and activities. Information accumulated in Malinvaud's scheme (or that could be accumulated in the other price-guided mechanisms) is entirely technical. There is no communication regarding many of the human inputs and outputs of units' proposals, and none whatsoever regarding the transformation of human state variables. In other words, the so-called "production possibility sets," $\{Y(i,t)\}$, the Central Planning Board estimates with greater and greater precision, are woefully inadequate subsets of the full human productive activity sets, $\{A(i,t)\}$, which are necessary if the Central Planning Board is to understand the full implications of its decisions.

But the cybernetic qualities of quantity-guided mechanisms are even worse when viewed from the perspective of the new welfare theory. As a kind of dual of Malinvaud's 1967 mechanism, Weitzman's quantity-guided procedure is the most instructive to analyze in detail. In his own words:

> the approach taken…views the planning procedure as a learning process whereby the center iteratively comes to understand more and more exactly the relevant parts of the production possibility sets without ever requiring any firm to transmit the entire set.[57]

It follows that the information consolidation process is the exact equivalent of the one discussed previously. The Central Planning Board develops an ever more accurate image of the technical possibilities of the units, although in this case the learning process entails scaling down infeasible productions to feasible ones, rather than expanding an initial feasible production possibility into the set of all feasible productions. But the understanding the center develops is still entirely technical and highly limiting as discussed above.

On the other hand, the information dispersed from the center gives individual units even less idea how they are connected to the rest of the economy. The units do not receive a series of price vectors transmitting some notion of the comparative social costs and benefits of different material inputs and outputs. Instead they receive a series of production orders, with no further information about the reasons these orders are being sent. And in the case of Weitzman's procedure, the orders are all infeasible until the very last one.

The other quantity-guided procedures differ from Weitzman's in that

1. The units respond with feasible quantity proposals rather than a price vector of resource evaluations to the quantity proposals from the center.

2. The information received from the units must be retained and built into an ever more accurate image of individual unit's technical possibility sets in order for Weitzman's center to calculate its next quantity proposal; whereas the information received in dual form in the other quantity-guided procedures could be thrown away after each iteration.

But once it is recognized that retaining information sufficient to build an image of each unit's dual is the equivalent of being able to build an image of the technical possibility sets themselves, our analysis of the cybernetic deficiencies of Weitzman's procedure extends to all other quantity-guided mechanisms.

Mixed-price and quantity-guided mechanisms do not improve the situation, leaving us with the conclusion that central planning fails to provide the executors of economic activity sufficient information to exercise self-management, even if they were permitted to do so, and none of the information required for developing empathy and solidarity between members of different units in the economy. Furthermore, central planning does not even provide the Central Planning Board with the information necessary to evaluate the full, human consequences of their choices. Instead, central planning bestows an information monopoly limited to technical aspects of the economy only on the Central Planning Board.

So paradoxically, while central planning teaches us to treat the economy as "one big factory," all of whose parts are interconnected in an effort to maximize social well-being, it does not provide those who carry out economic activities knowledge concerning how their efforts contribute to the final outcome. It succeeds only in creating a monopoly of technical information, which can contribute to new social divisions and differential power and wealth, as we explain below.

9.4.2 *Central Planning and Authoritarian Roles*

We have just seen that during the iterative procedures of central planning the individual units are not participating in the social generation of an economic plan, but are instead supplying data to the Central Planning Board so that the CPB can calculate a plan for the units to carry out. The only "management" central planning leaves to the individual economic units is to "manage" to fulfill the centrally planned targets with the inputs they are allocated. So the essential characteristic of the interunit roles of central planning is a command relationship between the Central Planning Board and each individual unit. The Central Planning Board issues marching orders; units obey.

Benjamin Ward describes this kind of role structure as a hierarchic organization in which "there is a partial ordering of participants...such that each is either a superior to or a subordinate of some other participant, or both, and such that no participant, directly or indirectly, is both superior to and a subordinate of another."[58] In the specific case of the interunit roles of central planning, every unit is a subordinate of the Central Planning Board and is superior to no other participant, and the Central Planning Board is superior to all individual units and a subordinate of none. In other words, if we abstract from ministries representing aggregate sectors, no intervening layers in the chain of command characterize the hierarchic interunit institution of central planning.[59] Ward uses the term "command economy" to "refer to this type of economic organization where the allocation of resources is carried out by the extensive use of orders to produce and deliver goods," and points out that centrally planned economies "are distinctive in that they use the command economy extensively in inter-enterprise allocation processes."[60]

Moreover, the authoritarian character of the interunit roles in central planning is likely to spread to intraunit roles for two reasons. First, an authoritarian relationship requires that the superior agent have effective means for holding the subordinate agent accountable for carrying out directives. This entails establishing methods of surveillance and verification as well as incentives for subordinates to obey orders. In our opinion, it will quickly become evident to the Central Planning Board that it is easier to hold a manager accountable for carrying out directives than to try and establish complicated methods of surveillance, verification, and incentives sufficient to hold an entire democratic council of workers accountable. Of course, if the Central Planning Board chooses to deal with a manager whom they appoint, rather than a workers' council in each production unit, they must logically grant the manager authority over the workers in the production unit. In this way the hierarchy spreads downward in the economy, with many intervening layers of participants who are superiors to some but subordinates to others, as the managers of each enterprise establish an authoritarian hierarchy beneath them in each unit.

But, in addition to the need for compatibility within the institutional boundary of central planning—in this case between the interunit and intraunit roles—if central planning is to be socially stable, strong forces also push for compatibility between the human center and the institutional boundary. Authoritarian interunit roles tend to act on people's consciousness and personalities to create a human center more compatible with authoritarian intraunit roles. Once we recognize that apathy among the ranks of subordinates is the flip side of the authoritarian coin, it is easier to see why the authoritarian interunit institution of central planning makes all the more likely the emergence of authoritarian intraunit forms and tends to obstruct democratic and participatory impulses wherever they might arise in society.

9.4.3 *Central Planning's Inherent Bias against Self-management*

We described three different approaches to finding the social welfare function: political determination, market determination, and voting. The first two can be rather easily rejected from the point of view of our new welfare theory. The authoritarian implications of any of the nondemocratic political determinations are obvious. And in combination with the inherently authoritarian role structures of central planning, the results are predictably disastrous. The tension we expect to exist between fulfillment and development might suggest the desirability of combining political determination with market or voting procedures. Revolutionary "philosopher kings" would presumably represent a "developmental" counterweight to the "fulfillment" pole expressed through market or voting procedures. But we can think of no reason to grant a nondemocratic political force any authority beyond its ability to influence the outcome of either market or voting determinations through persuasive argument and any respect it might deserve due to past insights.

The problem with using market prices in the planners' objective function is simple. Markets are no more able to handle problems of public goods and external effects under central planning than in private or public enterprise market economies. There would be no retail prices to use for obvious public goods like national defense, environmental protection, parks, education, etc., for which some alternative decision-making mechanism would have to be employed. But more importantly, using market prices to estimate relative social values for those goods that can be sold in retail outlets incorporates the same bias against goods with some external effects and the consequent snowballing nonoptimality we explained in chapter 7. In other words, retail prices can no more accurately convey the relative social benefits of the great majority of goods and services in central planning than they can in pure market systems. Markets are simply ill-suited to the task of preference expression given the fuzzy border between personal and social effects—irrespective of what economic system employs them.

This leaves determination of relative social values in central planning to some form of voting scheme. We will give voting every benefit of the doubt, and attempt to show that even at their best, voting procedures will be biased against the provision of self-managed work activities.

First, we assume complete democracy; every member of society will have the same number of points to vote. Second, we assume "informed" voting, based on the fullest possible discussion of the merits of different arguments in the social welfare function and complete knowledge of both the fulfillment and development effects of all goods. Third, we assume no elements of "gamesmanship" or "coalition formation" corrupt the voting process. Fourth, we rule out all manner of complications much discussed in the literature on majority voting such as the problem of "cyclical majorities" or the "paradox of voting."[61] Fifth, we assume the voting process exhibits no bias against goods with external effects.[62] We now argue even in this "best case" scenario that central planning is inherently flawed because perfectly informed "democracy" is not the same as "self-management."

The paradigm in chapter 5 highlighted the likelihood that the effects of different economic activities are not usually confined to single individuals or units in the economy, but neither are they evenly spread over all members of society. With this in mind, we defined self-management to be having decision-making input, or authority, with respect to a certain choice in the proportion that one is affected by the outcome of that decision. And we pointed out that self-management would not be the same as individual freedom of choice except in those relatively exceptional cases where the effects of a particular activity were confined entirely to a single individual—the case of "pure private goods." But self-management is also not synonomous with majority rule except in those rare cases where the effects of a particular choice are spread equally over everyone in society— the case of "pure public goods."

In other words, in most situations self-management lies somewhere on the continuum between "individual freedom" and "democratic majority rule." And just as market institutions exhibit a bias against self-managed decision making for activities with some degree of "public" external effects, a democratic voting procedure for determining the social welfare function, which will be mechanically translated into production orders for every unit, exhibits a bias against self-managed decision making for activities with some degree of "private" effects.

The problem can be put in terms of choice of production technology: to achieve self-management the economy must provide greater decision-making authority than the social average to those working in a particular production unit over the choice of technology in their unit. I would want such "extra" authority in the voting process when we come to questions about my work place. And in return, I would happily grant more authority to others concerning their work place. This is not simply because of differences in information about what the outcome is likely to be—I understand better the consequences in my factory; others understand better the consequences in their factories—though that too might be a factor. More fundamentally, it is because in one case I am more affected, so my preferences should count for more, and in the other case, other people are more affected so their preferences should count for more.

But "democratic" central planning gives everyone equal say in determining the social welfare function and then mechanically translates that social welfare function into specific production plans for each unit in the economy. This implies that workers in other plants have as much say in determining the choice of technology in my work place as I have, and I have as much say about technology in their work places as they have. Since the effects are unequal, equal decision-making input is not self-management.

The difficulty is that the choice of technology in any one plant has some private aspects because it affects the workers in that plant more than people elsewhere. But even the most perfectly democratic, centrally planned system exhibits a bias against self-managed work by treating this choice as if it were a pure public good.

Although some of the bias against "self-managed" work roles can be alleviated in central planning by including different categories of work activities along with different consumption goods in the social welfare function, this in no way solves the problem discussed above. To the extent that a skilled carpenter has more power to define the nature, organization, and pace of his or her work activities than an assembly-line worker, people could record their preference for self-managed work situations by voting fewer negative points to carpentry than assembly-line work when distributing their points among different arguments in the social welfare function. But as a carpenter or assembly-line worker in a particular enterprise, he or she has no more say over choice of technology in that unit than a carpenter or assembly-line worker in a unit thousands of miles away. That problem cannot be overcome by simply including the list of different labor activities in the social welfare function and permitting people to indicate their preferences for occupational categories characterized by more self-management. The problem is that all work carried out in centrally planned economies, in all occupational categories, will have less self-management than would be desirable.[63]

In sum, even if the Central Planning Board has overcome incentives for local management to dissimulate and discovered the production possibility sets of all individual units, even if the CPB knows all the primary resource availabilities and initial stocks of capital goods, even if every member of society votes an equal number of points in determining the social welfare function and makes no mistakes in their evaluations of both the fulfillment and development effects of all arguments in that function, even if there are no problems with gamesmanship, voting paradoxes, and external effects, even if sufficient incentives guarantee that the plan is carried out to the letter, and even if we include different kinds of labor activities, or occupations, in the social welfare function, central planning still has a bias against provision of self-managed work activities. Work activities in centrally planned economies will be characterized by less self-management than under some conceivable, alternative organizations of production.

9.5 An Imperfection Theorem

We formally express this inherent bias against self-managed work by stipulating that a centrally planned economy's supply curve for work activity characterized by any degree of self-management is everywhere above the true marginal social cost curve for supplying that activity. In a model where we conceive of individuals "purchasing" jobs with desirable characteristics, this translates into a higher than optimal supply price individuals must pay for jobs with self-managed characteristics.

9.5.1 Model 5: An Economy with a Bias against the Supply of Self-managed Work

M 5.1. There are many time periods: $t = 0, 1, \ldots T$

M 5.2. There are four goods in each time period: three consumption goods, x, y, z; and a labor activity that has some degree of self-management, a.

M 5.3. We stipulate supply prices equal to true marginal social costs for the three consumption goods. But in the case of good a the supply price is something in excess of the true marginal social cost, expressing the bias inherent in even "best case" central planning as discussed previously.

M 5.4. More precisely, we let $O(x_0, y_0, z_0, a_0; \ldots x_T, y_T, z_T, a_T)$ define the production transformation locus of all efficient productions for the economy as a whole. Then the ratios of the marginal social costs of supplying one more unit of b at time t in terms of the number of units of d that must be foregone at time $(t+k)$ would be

$$\frac{\partial O}{\partial b(t)} \bigg/ \frac{\partial O}{\partial d(t+k)}$$

where b and d can equal x, y, z, or a

M 5.5. But whereas for all $(t+k)$

$$\frac{\partial O}{\partial x(t+k)} \bigg/ \frac{\partial O}{\partial y(t+k)} = \frac{\pi_x(t+k)^A}{\pi_y(t+k)^A}$$

M 5.6. The structural bias is expressed by

331

$$\frac{\partial O}{\partial z(t+k)} \Big/ \frac{\partial O}{\partial a(t+k) + \mu} = \frac{\pi_z(t+k)^A}{\pi_a(t+k)^A}$$

with $\mu > 0$.

The market for $a(t+k)$ as it would equilibrate both with and without the structural bias against self-managed labor activities is represented in the above graph

FIG 9.1. SUPPLY AND DEMAND FOR
SELF-MANAGED WORK UNDER CENTRAL PLANNING

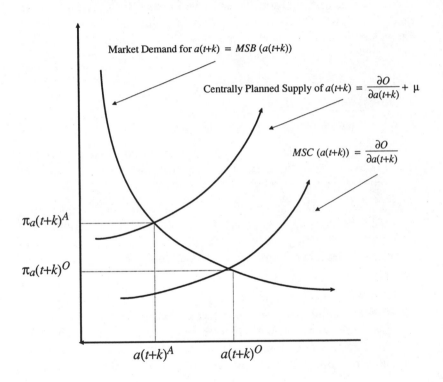

For our purposes, the important result is that with the bias

$$\pi_a(t+k)^o < \pi_a(t+k)^A$$

and assuming no bias in the supply curve for $z(t+k)$

$$\frac{\pi_z(t+k)^A}{\pi_a(t+k)^A} < \frac{\pi_z(t+k)^o}{\pi_a(t+k)^0}$$

And, therefore,

$$\frac{a(t+k)^A}{z(t+k)^A} < \frac{a(t+k)^o}{z(t+k)^0}$$

Which establishes our third, and last, imperfection theorem:

THEOREM 9.1: CENTRAL PLANNING BIAS AGAINST SELF-MANAGE-MENT. Centrally planned economies will "charge" individual job seekers more for self-managed work activities compared to other activities than is socially optimal, resulting in less self-managed work being performed than is socially optimal.

9.6 Snowballing Nonoptimality

When we combine the inherent bias of central planning against the provision of self-managed work activities with a view of people as having endogenous preferences, we find that not only will central planning be inefficient in its organization of work at any point in time, but that the degree of inefficiency will increase, or "snowball" as time goes on.

THEOREM 9.2: SNOWBALLING AUTHORITARIANISM IN CENTRAL PLAN-NING. In a centrally planned economy not only will self-managed laboring activities be overpriced and undersupplied at some initial point in time, but the degree of divergence from optimality will be greater than indicated by traditional welfare theory and grow, or "snowball," over time. Accompanying the snowballing nonoptimal allocations will be a "snowballing" apathy consisting of "warped" human characteristics which undervalue self-managed work activity.

By conceiving of individuals as "buying" jobs with different charac-teristics, we have proved Theorem 9.1 in a form that permits immediate application of Theorems 6.6 and 6.7. Once the self-managed labor activity is recognized as activity a of Model 3 in chapter 6, these theorems can all be applied to the bias inherent in a centrally planned economy specified in Theorem 9.1, yielding Theorem 9.2.

It is worth pointing out that Theorem 9.2 is valid assuming only

1. The supply-side bias against self-managed labor is operative to the tiniest degree

2. There is a single individual who has the slightest preference for self-managed work activity

3. That such an individual has the slightest degree of endogeneity in his or her preferences

In other words, snowballing nonoptimality results even under these extremely lenient assumptions and without specifically stipulating the degree to which any individual is capable of being fulfilled by self-managed work or the proportion of people who have this capability. Of course, the greater the capacity of fulfillment through self-management, the greater the bias against the supply of self-management, and the more room people have to maneuver their preferences, the worse the situation becomes.

Moreover, as we pointed out in chapter 6 in discussion of Theorems 6.6, 6.7, and 6.8, Theorems 9.1 and 9.2 are proved without assuming that the activity of engaging in self-managed work itself in earlier time periods enhances the appreciation of self-management in later time periods. In other words, we assume only that the desire for self-managed labor could be affected developmentally, not that the self-managed activities have "auto" developmental effects themselves. In the not unlikely event that engaging in self-management generates ever greater appreciation for self-management, and/or that performance of other-directed work increases tolerance for other-directed work, the snowballing nonoptimality would have a "double" aspect and be aggravated.

9.6.1 An Important Caveat

The theorems of chapter 6 demonstrate that to the extent people's preferences are endogenous, rationality dictates orienting future desires toward activities that one has reason to believe will be available on relatively better terms and away from activities that one has reason to expect will be available only on relatively worse terms. That is, if the expected conditions of future supply of particular kinds of activities is biased, people can be expected to influence their own development in a similarly biased direction. The imperfection theorem of this chapter translates the argument that central planning has an inherent bias against provision of self-managed labor activities into the proposition that citizens of such economies will be charged too high a price, so to speak, for work roles characterized by some degree of self-management.[64] In combination the two arguments imply a cumulative divergence from "producer sovereignty."

Moreover, the argument implies that the process of people molding their characteristics to conform with the core characteristics of a centrally planned economy is not only a process entailing loss of potential fulfillment and warping of the optimal human development pattern—a process in which private rationality yields social irrationality—it is a process that reinforces the core characteristics of central planning. Our analysis, therefore, predicts not only a "snowballing" divergence from the optimal organization of human laboring capacities, but an increasingly dominant and entrenched central planning mechanism.

But the results of formal arguments are easily misconstrued. What we have been able to capture in our formal models and theorems is the logic of the system stabilizing effect whereby various institutional boundaries "mold" the human center toward greater conformity. The degree to which this is not possible—or the extent to which resistance will build—is not so easily modeled. In any case, it should not be inferred from what we have just proved that the citizens of real centrally planned economies are forever doomed to ever-increasing domination and apathy. Fortunately, the real world is more complicated than simple models and not nearly so determinant. There is always some resistance to inefficient social mechanisms and always a possibility that such mechanisms will be corrected. In this regard the question of momentum is critical. In the struggle between the criterion of developing ever-greater passivity among the executors in the economy (implicit in the core characteristic of authoritarianism inherent in the interunit mechanism of central planning) and the criterion of maximizing human fulfillment through the free development and expression of self-management among the participants in the economy, the perception of the likelihood of institutional change has a powerful impact on "individually rational" adjustment strategy.

If the core characteristic of central planning increasingly dominates the actual conditions of work, it will be increasingly rational for people to accelerate their adjustment to authoritarian conditions. But if the momentum should begin to reverse, if groups of workers should begin to place constraints on the choices of technology available to the central planners, the disjuncture between centrally planned work roles and people's perceived needs and expectations will widen, until central planning might be replaced by some alternative form of interunit economic institution. Central planning is not unique among major social institutions in being reinforced by the individually rational choices of those whom it oppresses. And to recognize this discouraging potential is not to deny the possibility of more encouraging potentials and prospects for change.

9.6.2 Summary: Snowballing Authoritarianism

The problem with central planning, as seen from every vantage point of our new welfare theory, is that it generates authoritarian dynamics. Central planning minimizes the amount of knowledge that direct producers have about how they fit into the rest of the economy and generates a monopoly of technical information in the Central Planning Board. The interunit roles of central planning are command relationships that promote similar hierarchical relationships within production units. No matter how democratic the process of choosing the social welfare function, central planning still has an inherent bias against provision of self-managed work activity since the best it can offer is equal say over the choice of technology in every production unit to every worker in the economy. In context of endogenous preferences this initial bias leads to a snowballing away from optimal organizations of the work process as people continually lower their desires for self-managed work activity. In this way the authoritarian characteristics of the interunit institution of central planning come to pervade the human center of society, generating ever greater apathy and passivity among the work force.

We have concerned ourselves with evaluating the mechanism of central planning to focus on what we believe to be its "tragic flaw"—its bias against self-management with all this entails. While highly critical of central planning, this has never been the focus of traditional analysis. The early debate focused on the "calculation problem." When mathematical programming theory and modern computer capacity rendered this criticism obsolete, traditional theorists turned their critical gaze toward information and incentive problems. While we do not mean to belittle the practical importance of dissimulation by local managers or the theoretical problems of majority voting, we do believe they are irrelevant to the most fundamental deficiency of central planning. To put it differently, under equally generous assumptions as those afforded PrEMEs, it seems to us traditional welfare theory should find central planning equally as "efficient" and "flexible" as public and private enterprise market systems, at least in theory.[65] In contrast, our evaluation distinguishes central planning from other economic mechanisms on welfare theoretic grounds and provides a critique of "best case" central planning on theoretical as well as practical grounds. This completes our "evaluative" task regarding central planning: it is an inherently flawed economic mechanism. But in light of the importance of central planning in real economies, we close on an "analytic" note with a brief treatment of the predictable impact of central planning in the real world contexts in which it has been deployed.

9.7 Central Planning and the Coordinator Class

As we have seen, the informational and role biases of central planning generate a group within the economy with a monopoly of technical information and a habit of playing the superior role in command relations. Moreover, the absence of information available to workers, their role experiences, and "individually rational" adjustments to the scarcity of self-managed work situations, generate a condition of increasing apathy among those who must "execute" economic decisions.

In comparable circumstances some have seen fit to argue that these are "objective" conditions ripe for formation of an exploiting "class":

1. A position of strength for a minority stemming from a common relationship to the means of production, which provides the minority the possibility of directing economic activity to reinforce their power and satisfy their own desires

2. A situation in which the great majority of actors find themselves with little motivation and or means to resist the dominance and exploitation to which they become subjected

In short, central planning tends to empower a class of central planners and high-level plant managers and foment apathy among those who are disempowered. Central planning eases the road of central planners and the plant managers who serve them to power.

But this is not the place to address the details of class theory. Nor do we wish to present here the full case for identifying a potential ruling class besides the capitalist and working classes, a third class whose power is based on a monopoly of economic information and control over economic decision making.[66] Without delving into the debate over classes in public enterprise, or postcapitalist economies,[67] we simply observe:

1. In the context of powerful authoritarian dynamics in noneconomic spheres of social life that have accompanied most anticapitalist revolutions, the authoritarian dynamics of central planning should be viewed as particularly dangerous to prospects for self-management and democracy.

2. Many leftists have singled out the political institution of a single "vanguard" political party with bans on internal factions—or the "flawed practice" of democratic centralism by a particular ruling party—as the internal flaw that combined with "objective circumstances" and "external pressures" to yield authoritarian outcomes in any number of postcapitalist experiences.[68] And even leftists who admit the existence of a "ruling class"—in addition to whatever political and military ruling "elites" they may also recognize in postcapitalist societies—frequently avoid any criticism of the institution (as opposed to practice) of central planning.[69] In our view, while criticisms of political authoritarianism are on the mark, there is every reason to include the economic institution of central planning in the list of culprits when trying to explain authoritarian outcomes in postcapitalist societies.

Howard Sherman, a Marxist expert on the Soviet Union, described the interactive, overlapping segments of the ruling elite in the Soviet Union:

There are four main hierarchies in the Soviet Union: the Communist party, the government apparatus, the economic pyramid, the military.

Within the Communist party, the top functionaries (such as in the Politbureau) have enormous power and are appointed rather than elected—though there are "elections" after the decision is made. There are also powerful officials in the government, such as the Council of Ministers and their deputies. The economic pyramid is ruled by a small group of economic planners at the top (responsible to the government and party leaders) plus some powerful directors of sectors and very large enterprises. The military is, of course, completely hierarchical, with the top generals also being party leaders in some cases. In each of the four hierarchies, orders flow downward, while some information flows upward. At the top are fifty to a hundred people who control all four hierarchies and frequently transfer from one to the other.[70]

This is not the place to consider the possibility that the relative dominance of the economic elite has grown with the "maturing" of Soviet society and that the erosion of Stalinist political structures has largely been due to the increasingly successful struggle of this strata of Soviet society to expand its own political and cultural space most recently via *perestroika* and *glasnost*. The important point to note is that each of the four arenas Sherman describes is governed by a hierarchical organization whose authoritarian dynamics are mutually reinforcing. In these circumstances it should be apparent that the likelihood of a democratic procedure for determining the social welfare function is minimal, as party, state, military, and economic elites seize control of the process of defining society's goals.

In our view, it is only a matter of time before executors in the economy come to recognize that the interests of the various elites have been substituted for society's welfare in the planners' objective function. This creeping realization, combined with increasing apathy, eventually erodes whatever motivation there might have been initially to execute the plan out of feelings of social solidarity. At such time, the only alternative to using increasing repression to elicit people's cooperation and effort is to rely on more material incentives. So in real world scenarios, it is all too likely that even the potential strength of central planning—elimination of competition and promotion of solidarity among the citizenry—will vanish along with self-management.

Under these circumstances we should not be surprised by power struggles over economic "reforms" among the ruling elites—between the coordinator class in the economy, high-ranking party officials, state bureaucrats, and military elites—as well as struggles between managerial and central planning "fractions" of the coordinator class itself. But struggles among the elites must be carefully distinguished from popular challenges to elite rule—which is not to say the latter have not occurred, and will not occur again.[71]

338

10

CONCLUSION

In the introduction we claimed:

1. Traditional welfare theory has, to a great extent, reached the limits of what it can accomplish

2. Further progress in analysis of the labor process, preference development, external effects, and institutional structures requires a new paradigm

3. A welfare theory based on a new paradigm can be elaborated sufficiently to consolidate and integrate current work in these areas, as well as yield substantive new contributions

4. A proper view of the welfare theoretic properties of markets, private enterprise, and central planning is substantially altered in light of the new welfare theory

Part 1 of this volume assessed traditional welfare theory and its weaknesses. Part 2 elaborated a new paradigm and welfare theory including some useful abstract applications. Part 3 reanalyzed familiar economic institutions and models and reached original conclusions. Here we briefly summarize our results and the implications for designing better economic institutions.

10.1 <u>Limits of Traditional Welfare Theory</u>

As we saw in chapter 1 the crowning achievement of traditional welfare theory was the increasingly rigorous demonstration of what are known as the three fundamental theorems of welfare economics. Under appropriate assumptions:[1]

1. Perfectly competitive private enterprise market economies have general equilibria

2. Any general equilibrium of a perfectly competitive private enterprise market economy is a Pareto optimum

3. Any Pareto optimum can be achieved as the equilibrium of a perfectly competitive private enterprise market economy with appropriate initial endowments

The obvious implication drawn from these results was that while real world problems might prevent us from implementing a perfectly competitive, private enterprise economy or might prevent such an economy from reaching its equilibrium, this kind of economic system is socially efficient and completely "flexible" regarding distributive outcomes. No alternative could be superior.

So while neoclassical theory admitted providing no compelling argument for choosing among Pareto optima, neoclassical economists nonetheless confidently placed a "cease search" sign in front of the PrEME exhibit at the "Great Economics Fair." The sign substituted for closure by implying that debates in which contractarians criticize neoclassicists' inability to "close" the "theory of social choice" can be placed on a back burner.

But these conclusions are misleading. First, the neoclassical efficiency and flexibility theorems fail as soon as we correct for the traditional paradigm's inadequate conceptualization of the labor process, external effects, and endogenous preferences. Second, under equally "permissive" (mis)assumptions, the same results obtain with equal plausibility for every other major theoretical economic model. Specifically, existence, efficiency, and flexibility theorems can be proved for public enterprise, competitive market economies of both state-managed and employee-managed varieties, and for public enterprise centrally planned economies. In an even-handed application of traditional theory, placement of the "cease search" sign at the "Great Economics Fair" is completely arbitrary. It depends only on which stall the judge visits first.[2]

Traditional theory consigned the labor process to a "black box" by assuming an exogenous production possibility set that eliminated any need to analyze complexities of the labor process. But when we reviewed the work of economists whose interest in discrimination, labor market structure, and the implications of getting employees to "honor" the wage contract drove them beyond the traditional paradigm, we uncovered good reasons to question the efficiency of private enterprise production as well as the conclusion that competition for profits tends to ameliorate discrimination.

In the case of externalities and public goods, we discovered the traditional paradigm underestimated the problem and failed to provide concepts necessary for treating the problem. By continuing to champion the concept of ordinal, noncomparable preferences over individual commodity spaces the traditional paradigm stalled thinking in the theory of public finance. Labeling nonmarket allocative mechanisms "political" rather than "economic" is hardly an incentive-compatible mechanism for economic theorists! So, not only did the traditional paradigm obstruct research in incentive-compatible mechanisms, it bears primary responsibility for perpetuating the myth that competitive markets yield socially efficient allocations in most situations.

While traditional theory never denied that tastes change, traditional theorists argued that economists need not concern themselves with changing preferences. As a matter of fact, a critical part of the traditional paradigm, the Robbins Principle, served as a methodological injunction prohibiting economists from addressing where preferences come from. In reviewing the work of the few economists who dared to violate this injunction we discovered there was every reason to consider preference development as well as preference fulfillment meaningful and every reason to assume that individual preferences depend on economic institutions as well as cultural, political, and kinship institutions. We also discovered that by ignoring preference development traditional welfare theory systematically misestimates welfare effects of different economic choices. But fundamental disagreements divided those who cared to investigate the implications of endogenous preferences for welfare theory. Gintis claimed endogenous preferences rendered the fundamental welfare theorems false. Pollak disagreed.

Traditional theory certainly does not ask how economic institutions influence preference development. But different preference development effects generate crucial welfare theoretic differences between major economic institutions! Since there is precious little to choose between well-known economic models when viewed in traditional terms, the failure to explore the developmental effects that distinguish different "ideal" economic systems is even more glaring. The traditional paradigm confines comparisons to the "old welfare debate," which is essentially over, and prevents theorists from moving on to the "new welfare debate" over how economic institutions affect incentives and the development of human characteristics and preferences.

10.2 A New Welfare Paradigm and Theory

In chapter 5 we presented a new paradigm stressing the importance of human "natural," "species," and "derived" needs, powers, and characteristics and their mutual interaction with economic roles and institutions. Using this paradigm, in chapter 6 we elaborated a new welfare theory and proved a number of important theorems that enhance the analysis of formal economic models.

The first two theorems established a preliminary case that treating preferences as endogenous has important implications for welfare theory. The first theorem, 6.1, translates a result from Gintis into our terminology.

Theorem 6.1. A neoclassical welfare theory that ignores the fact that present choices of consumption and work activities not only fulfill present preferences or desires but also generate changes in future preferences will consistently misestimate the welfare effects of economic choices.

The second theorem formally establishes a result originally intimated by Gintis, that coincidence between supplies and desires might be indicative of system stability rather than efficiency. If the coincidence is the result of the economy adjusting relative supplies to better accord with people's preferences, it is a sign of the kind of efficiency traditionally called "consumer sovereignty." But if the coincidence results from individuals' rational adjustments of their preferences to better accommodate conditions of supply, it is not "meritorious" but merely "system stabilizing."

Theorem 6.2. In general, not only will rational individuals who recognize their preferences are endogenous adjust to changes in relative terms of supply by changing the relative amounts of those goods they consume, but they will also change their preferences—reducing their preference for relatively more expensive items and increasing their preference for relatively less expensive items—by changing consumption-work choices in earlier periods to change their future human characteristics and the preferences depending on them.

Theorems 6.3, 6.4, and 6.5 reestablish the three fundamental theorems of welfare economics for private enterprise competitive market economies under all the traditional assumptions even if people have perfectly informed endogenous preferences.

Theorem 6.3. Under the usual assumptions, the existence of a general equilibrium in a private enterprise, competitive market economy is assured even if individuals' preferences are endogenous.

Theorem 6.4. Under the usual assumptions, any general equilibrium of a perfectly competitive, private enterprise economy will be a Pareto optimum even if individuals' preferences are endogenous.

Theorem 6.5. Under the usual assumptions, any Pareto optimum can be achieved as the equilibrium of a private enterprise, competitive market economy with the appropriate set of "initial endowments" even if individuals' preferences are endogenous.

These theorems establish that perfectly informed endogenous preferences, in and of themselves, do not disrupt the ability of private enterprise market economies to achieve efficiency and flexibility, Gintis' speculation notwithstanding. Although that settles one debate between Gintis and Pollak, as we discovered, the interpretation of these theorems can be highly misleading.

The possibility of misinterpretation arises because the phrase "under the usual assumptions" not only plays a legitimate technical role in the above theorems, but also hides a "multitude of sins." For Theorem 6.3, the critical technical assumption is that our endogenous well-being functions, WB^i, display the same convexity properties traditionally granted exogenous preference orderings. For Theorem 6.4, the critical assumption is that our endogenous well-being functions, WB^i, do not define any "thick" indifference classes. And for Theorem 6.5, both these technical assumptions are necessary. Since the entire difference between endogenous and exogenous preferences is contained in the difference between our well-being functions, WB^i, and their exogenous counterparts in traditional theory, extending these "usual" assumptions, though not without complications, would legitimately reestablish the fundamental welfare theorems.

But other assumptions are part of the "usual assumptions" granted by traditional theory. While exogenous production possibility sets and absence of externalities have nothing directly to do with endogenous preferences, they are necessary assumptions to establish Theorems 6.4 and 6.5. Those assumptions amount to assuming that nothing inherent in the functioning of the institutions of private enterprise and competitive markets prevents them from organizing production efficiently and supplying both goods and jobs in accord with people's preferences. In chapters 7 and 8 we presented good reasons for not believing that markets and private enterprise are capable of such behavior, even under the most favorable circumstances. In this context, the phrase "under the usual assumptions" hides the multitude of sins that necessarily prevent private enterprise market economies from achieving the results stated in theorems 6.4 and 6.5. But while private enterprise market economies will not achieve the above results, these failures are not in and of themselves due to endogenous preferences.

As a matter of fact, what the three theorems establish is that endogenous preferences, in and of themselves, cannot affect the efficiency and flexibility properties of any economy that *fully* adjusts to people's preferences. Or put differently, if there is no bias in the conditions upon which an economy makes different activities available, the fact that people have perfectly informed endogenous preferences will not prevent the system from having equilibria, or deter the system's efficiency or flexibility.[3] But this does not mean that endogenous preferences don't affect the results of welfare theory.

Theorems 6.6, 6.7, and 6.8 establish the most important formal results of our new welfare theory. In the case of any economy that contains any kind of bias in the terms upon which it makes different activities available, these theorems demonstrate that the extent of the misallocations that will result are far greater, and the nature of those misallocations are far different from what has been traditionally believed by those who treated preferences as exogenous. In other words, these three theorems establish that endogenous preferences do matter to welfare theory, but for reasons different than those previous critics believed.

Theorem 6.6. In an economy that contains a bias in the relative terms of supply of two economic activities: (1) the degree of nonoptimality will be greater than indicated by traditional welfare theory that treats preferences as exogenous; (2) the divergence from optimality will "snowball" or grow over time in a manner that can be precisely defined.

Theorem 6.7. In an economy that contains a bias in the relative terms of supply of two economic activities: (1) individuals' human development patterns will be "warped" in a manner than can be precisely defined; (2) warped human characteristics will "snowball" over time.

Theorem 6.8. The full effects of a bias in the economy will be disguised to analysts who view preferences as exogenous and to participants in the economy who adjust unconsciously and/or forget they have done so after the fact.

In sum, any economy that exhibits no bias in the conditions upon which it makes economic activities available will generate socially efficient outcomes if people's preferences are endogenous, just as it would if people's preferences were exogenous (Theorems 6.3 and 6.4). Likewise, if an economy without biases was "flexible" regarding equity assuming exogenous preferences, it will remain so assuming endogenous preferences (Theorem 6.5). However, to the extent that preferences are endogenous, any economy that contains a bias will generate more inefficiency than would have been anticipated assuming exogenous preferences, and the inefficiency will snowball over time (Theorem 6.6) so that rational individual adjustment to bias aggravates the bias and results in ever-increasing losses of potential well-being. Thus we can legitimately label the behavior "self-warping" (Theorem 6.7) and point out that it is an important example of how individual rationality can be socially counterproductive. Ironically, the process of individual rational adjustment—or self-warping—may prove socially stabilizing if its inhabitants adjust unconsciously or forget they have done so and come only to see themselves as getting what they seek (Theorem 6.8).

While these formal results presumed nothing whatsoever about what kinds of preferences people may have, beyond the fact that those preferences are, to some extent, endogenous, we also presented arguments in favor of human development trajectories characterized by self-management, solidarity, and variety. We outlined four different justifications for these welfare goals: one justification centered on fulfilling particular aspects of human nature; the second applied a modified contractarian methodology; the third was based on the criterion of species survival; and the fourth interpreted our welfare criteria as expressive of the values of the "humanist" heritage.

10.3 New Results

In part 3 we used our new welfare theory to analyze the major economic institutions used today to organize production (private and public enterprise) and allocate goods and resources (markets and central planning). In every case we came to a number of conclusions at odds with traditional beliefs.

10.3.1 Markets

Proponents of markets have silenced their opponents in ingenious ways. External effects are so pervasive that open debate was unthinkable. Yet failure to finesse the issue threatened over two hundred years of economic theory. The solution was to bury the problem of external effects within a traditional paradigm regarded as necessary for generating *any* welfare theoretic conclusions whatsoever. The message was: those who ask just how "exceptional" external effects really are had best be prepared for early retirement.

Those with other employment opportunities who argued that the emperor had no clothes, such as E. K. Hunt, were simply ignored. Pure theoreticians, who tackled problems as they proved susceptible to new theoretical toys, such as Theodore Groves and Co., were potentially more dangerous since they have special status within the establishment. But theorists are seldom politicians. They do not devote much time to debating the importance of the mind games they play and are easily distracted by new toys that appear with a new holiday season which lend themselves to a different set of gedanken experiments.[4]

There are other reasons why market failures have gone so remarkably undernoticed. Losses due to "market failure" have, until very recently, been much less visible than other kinds of waste. Market failure does not appear in the form of 1,000 lb. nails or people working one hour out of eight on the job, which provide vivid images of the inefficiency of central planning. And it is the inefficiency of market disequilibria, not market failure, that is stamped in people's minds by unemployment lines coincident with stockpiles of unsellable goods. Market failure does not even show up as slow economic growth rates, which current Soviet developments demonstrate can shake even long-established economic orders. Losses due to market failure are not subtracted from GNP estimates. Vivid reminders such as Three Mile Island, Chernobyl, and Valdez, Alaska, are still recent, and the ecology movement that seeks to publicize the most heinous examples is still in its political infancy. But irrespective of its relative lack of notoriety, the fact remains that in postfeudal history a plausible case can be made that no economic failure has contributed more to the waste of productive resources than misallocations of markets uncorrected for external effects.

Our formal contribution to a critical reevaluation of markets is contained in Theorems 7.1 and 7.2.

Theorem 7.1. Markets overcharge purchasers of goods with greater than average positive external effects.

Theorem 7.2. Not only will markets misallocate resources initially—undersupplying goods with greater than average positive external effects—but there will be a cumulative divergence away from optimal allocations over time as individuals "rationally" adjust their personal characteristics to diminish their needs for goods with greater than average positive external effects.

In verbal argument we detailed the reasons for expecting most activities to diverge from the average degree of external effects, thereby establishing the prevalence, rather than exceptionality, of the problem. We also explained how the cybernetic and incentive characteristics of market institutions aggravate the allocative bias and how individually rational adjustment compounds the social irrationality.

We also clarified how an elementary confusion between "Pareto optimal" and "Pareto improvement" had blinded public finance theorists about "solutions" to the "free rider" problem. We pointed out that simple proportional taxation is as likely to yield truthful reporting and efficient outcomes as the more complicated taxing schemes discussed in the "incentive-compatible" literature. Although the traditional objection to proportional taxation was really on the grounds of equity rather than efficiency, we explained why the "incentive-compatible" literature is, nonetheless, important as well as innovative. Besides efficiency and alternative notions of equity at stake in the choice of taxation schemes is what kind of incentives will be established for individual preference development. We argued that, in the end, the prospects for diversity or conformity in people's tastes are at stake. And we showed how external effects may imply a fundamental trade-off between short-run efficiency and diversity of tastes.

In sum, we presented a number of criticisms of markets not usually emphasized and suggested a novel interpretation of the "incentive-compatible" literature. We also provided a rigorous explanation of why commonly expressed fears among noneconomists that markets are "socially alienating" are well founded despite disclaimers from "professional economists" that markets are ideal allocative institutions.

10.3.2 Private Enterprise

Our major goal in chapter 8 was to solidify the claim of the "conflict school" that private enterprise production will be inefficient and aggravate economic discrimination and to make clear this conclusion obtains even in conditions of perfect knowledge and competitive labor markets. But before treating this debate we clarified the conditions under which the distributional flexibility theorem holds in both private and public enterprise environments.

First, we pointed out that the flexibility theorem only holds in either setting in a Debreuvian world of perfect foresight where taxing authorities are free to enact any handicaps they may choose, in all time periods, once, and only once, before any races begin. Second, we pointed out that for both political and ideological reasons different kinds of economies will gravitate toward particular distributional "maxims." We showed that while flexible in theory, PrEMEs have practical tendencies to distribute according to the market (mis)judged productivities of individuals' human and nonhuman capital. And that while equally flexible in theory, PuEMEs will tend to distribute according to the market (mis)judged productivities of individuals' human capital. After pointing out that neither principle is the equivalent of distribution according to effort and sacrifice, we proceeded to clarify the most important insights of the conflict school of private employment. Formally our summary of the logic of the conflict school is contained in Theorem 8.1.

Theorem 8.1. Unless there is 100 percent labor turnover each time period, profit maximization under competitive conditions with perfect knowledge implies that any kind of laboring activity that generates employee empowering traits will have an actual market wage that is less than the socially optimal wage and be undersupplied. And any kind of labor activity that weakens employee empowering traits will be paid more than the socially optimal wage and oversupplied.

347

Various writers in the conflict school have argued that work opportunities under participatory, cooperative, and fair conditions constitute laboring activities of the first kind—which will be undersupplied according to Theorem 8.1—whereas work opportunities under discriminatory conditions or in situations with artificial hierarchies constitute laboring activities of the second kind—and will, therefore, be oversupplied. So the common thread running through the conflict school is that socially counterproductive practices such as wage and employment discrimination, exaggerated hierarchies, and de-skilling are part of profit maximization.

Theorem 8.1 clarifies the basis for such behavior and its implications for social efficiency. These practices are all cases of working conditions that tend to erode employee bargaining strength. The primary mechanism through which this occurs is that working under such conditions affects both the individual and group characteristics of employees in future time periods. But while it would be irrational for profit-maximizing employers to ignore these effects when considering technologies and reward structures, by doing so they establish wage rates that diverge from "efficiency prices" for labor services and misallocate productive resources. The social inefficiency is transparent once the divergence between private benefits and social benefits is spelled out.

Theorem 8.2 demonstrates that the fact that people's preferences are endogenous will compound the problem.

Theorem 8.2. Not only will production under private enterprise fail to deliver optimal job mixes in some initial time period—oversupplying work conditions that empower employers vis-a-vis employees—but there will be a cumulative divergence away from optimal allocations in future time periods as individuals "rationally" adjust their personal characteristics to diminish their preferences for work opportunities that are underpaid and enhance their preferences for work opportunities that are overpaid.

In this case, individual rationality by employees proves socially counterproductive by causing inefficiencies generated by employer rationality to grow over time. In conclusion, we pointed out that according to our analysis the traditional model of "perfectly competitive capitalism," or what we prefer to call PrEMEs, is "doubly" flawed and can be expected to increasingly diverge from socially efficient allocations for two separate reasons—one associated with each of its defining institutions.

10.3.3 Central Planning

The "old debate" on central planning should have been closed long ago. We demonstrated that under traditional assumptions public enterprise, centrally planned economies have as much claim to social efficiency and distributional flexibility as their major competitors, and this remains true under the assumption of endogenous preferences as well. We also argued that central planning fares better in the "modern debate" than usually admitted. When information and incentive problems are taken seriously, rather than assumed away by traditional assumptions, we showed how proponents of central planning might still claim efficiency properties for their system. Ironically, their ability to do so is largely due to work on "iterative planning mechanisms" by Western economic theorists, who are by no means proponents of central planning, but who nonetheless developed credible procedures central planners could use to gather information about the technological capabilities of production units. Unfortunately, these information gathering procedures are not "incentive-compatible." But is it naive to think Western theorists, armed with principal-agent models who began work on incentive-compatible mechanisms only recently, may come up with procedures to ameliorate this problem as well? In any case, proponents of PuECPEs can already point out that the same "material incentives" that private enterprise and market economies rely on can be deployed to ensure that the plan calculated is carried out. In sum, a plausible case can be made that, even in terms of the "modern debate," central planning can lay claims to efficiency and flexibility just as a variety of market systems have done.

Yet our major purpose in chapter 9 was not "to praise Caesar." We proposed a "new debate" over the welfare theoretic properties of central planning, highlighting the fundamental flaw in this allocative mechanism even under the most favorable assumptions. Our formal argument is summarized in our third imperfection theorem, Theorem 9.1, and our last snowballing theorem, Theorem 9.2.

> Theorem 9.1. Centrally planned economies will "charge" individual job seekers (in the form of lower wage rates) more for self-managed work activities compared to other activities than is socially optimal resulting in less self-managed work being performed than is socially optimal.

Theorem 9.1 holds because even the most democratic system of central planning is not capable of providing greater than average decisionmaking authority to those working in a particular production unit concerning the fundamental choices about how work will be done in their unit. Instead, "democratic" central planning gives everyone equal say in determining the social welfare function and then mechanically translates that social welfare function into specific production plans for each unit in the economy. This implies that workers in other plants have as much say in determining how work will be done in my work place as I have, and vice versa. Since the effects on those who work someplace and on those who do not are unequal, equal decision-making input fails to approximate self-management.

This is a more fundamental criticism of central planning than those voiced by opponents in the "old" and the "modern" debates. We have shown that even if a Central Planning Board had complete knowledge of the production possibilities of all individual units, and knew all primary resource availabilities and initial stocks of capital goods, even if the social welfare function were determined by democratic "point" voting and voters made no mistakes in evaluating both the fulfillment and development effects of different goods and activities, and even if incentives guaranteed that the plan would be carried out perfectly, central planning would still have a bias against provision of self-managed work activities. Moreover, our new welfare theory demonstrates that when we combine the inherent bias of central planning against self-managed work with recognition of endogenous preferences, the inefficient organization of work "snowballs":

Theorem 9.2. In a centrally planned economy not only will self-managed laboring activities be underpaid and undersupplied at some initial point in time, but the degree of divergence from optimality will be greater than indicated by traditional welfare theory and grow, or "snowball," over time. Accompanying the snowballing nonoptimal allocations will be a "snowballing" apathy consisting of "warped" human characteristics which undervalue self-managed work activity.

But workers' individually rational adjustments are not only socially irrational in that they increase social inefficiency, their adjustments reinforce the authoritarian characteristics of central planning. In general terms, the problem with central planning as seen from every vantage point of our new welfare theory is that it generates authoritarian dynamics. Central planning minimizes producers' knowledge of how they fit into the rest of the economy and generates a monopoly of technical information in the hands of central planners. Central planning embodies command relationships between the planners and production units, which, in turn, promote similar command relationships within production units. And no matter how democratic the process of choosing the social welfare function may be, inherent bias against provision of self-managed work activity "snowballs" as people "rationally" lower their desires for self-managed work.

So, unlike traditional welfare theory that should find central planning equally as "efficient" and "flexible" as public and private enterprise market systems, our evaluation provided a critique of central planning on theoretical as well as practical grounds.

10.3.4 Summary

Until very recently only a small number of abstract economies had been seriously analyzed by welfare theorists. The traditional names for these economies are Perfectly Competitive Capitalism (PCC), Centrally Planned Socialism (CPS), and two versions of Market Socialism (MS). Since each of these economies is simply a combination of particular institutions for organizing production and allocation, we proposed naming them according to their defining institutions. This not only had the advantage of not prejudging what was and what was not a "socialist" economy, but might defuse prejudice and improve the quality of debate. In any case, we simply called the economies: private enterprise market economies (PrEMEs), public enterprise, centrally planned economies (PuECPEs), public enterprise, employee-managed, market economies (PuEEMMEs), and public enterprise, state-managed, market economies (PuESMMEs).

We argued that under traditional assumptions the "old debate" about the welfare theoretic properties of these different economies has been laid to rest. According to the norms of traditional welfare theory, provided they are not clouded by ideological prejudice, each of the above economies can be shown to be socially efficient and flexible. Under the usual assumptions, an appropriate existence, efficiency, and flexibility theorem holds for each of the above systems even when we allow that people's preferences are endogenous.

However, this means traditional welfare theory cannot distinguish between these models in terms of their welfare theoretic properties—a small return for a not inconsiderable investment in technique. Recently, what we called the "modern debate" has relaxed the traditional assumption of perfect information. How central planners might gather information about productive unit capabilities and the quality of such information has been examined. The effects of different kinds of contracts in light of asymmetric information between private employers and their employees has also received attention. As a result, to some extent the modern debate is better able to distinguish between the different systems, which do have different information and incentive properties and, therefore, different problems in these regards.

Moreover, we completely support such efforts. A more realistic treatment of information is long overdue, and this means relaxing the "perfect information" assumption of the traditional paradigm. But in our view important welfare theoretic differences can be noted without dropping the traditional perfect knowledge assumption. In what we called the "new debate," the project of analyzing the relation between fully informed individual rationality and social rationality in different institutional contexts does not fail to draw important distinctions between the major economic systems of the day. Thus before relaxing the perfect knowledge assumption, we recommend clarifying the important welfare theoretic differences between economic systems assuming decision makers are fully informed. As we summarized previously, those differences can best be

351

understood as the inherent biases different institutions display regarding the terms of availability of different activities and the developmental consequences of individually rational adaptation to those circumstances.

10.4 Toward a New Economic System

Traditional welfare theory disguises, rather than clarifies, the fundamental flaws of well-known economic models. The same new paradigm and welfare theory that highlights the deficiencies of traditional economic models, be they private enterprise or public enterprise, market or centrally planned, can also indicate the necessary characteristics of an economic system that improves upon known alternatives.

One step toward elaborating a new model is to clarify the reasons existing models are deficient, as we have attempted to do in this book. Another step is to conceive ways to organize production and consumption that avoid the production inefficiencies caused by "conflicts" over payments and effort and the consumption inefficiencies caused by incentives for individuals to "ride for free." But the implication of the foregoing analysis of allocative relations is that improved organization of production and consumption will only be subverted by market or centrally planned allocations. So, in addition to elaborating new ways to organize production and consumption, we must define compatible new means of allocation that promote solidarity, self-management, and variety. In other words, we must continue the search for allocative mechanisms that allow informed individual rationality to be fully consistent with social rationality.

Adam Smith thought he had detected in competitive markets a shortcut, but he was wrong—the answer is not so easy. Marxists thought the answer lay in public ownership and central planning—translation of the principles of individual goal maximization subject to constraints to social goal maximization subject to constraints. But collective self-management is not so simple, and it is now abundantly clear that this, also, is not the solution. The failures of central planning arise not only from poor implementation; the model is flawed.

But the answer is not to deny the simple truth that for a social species whose individual members are blessed with consciousness, the ultimate interest of each individual lies in consciously attempting to promote the interests of all others as well as his or her own. Instead, we economists should admit we have not yet done our job. We have not yet fashioned allocative mechanisms that allow individuals to behave in a manner consistent with this simple truth. Once we see clearly what must be done and get down to the task, there is every reason to believe better allocative models will be forthcoming. Implementation is another matter, since material interests and not just intellectual obstacles must be overcome.[5]

NOTES

INTRODUCTION

Lionel Robbins, *An Essay on the Nature and Significance of Economic Science*, 2nd ed. (London: Macmillan, 1952).

1. John Stuart Mill, "Of the Liberty of Thought and Discussion," in *The Philosophy of John Stuart Mill*, Marshall Cohen, ed. (New York: Modern Library, 1961), 204-206.

2. See Donald E. Campbell, *Resource Allocation Mechanisms* (Cambridge: Cambridge University Press, 1987) chap. 4, for a concise, self-contained presentation of recent successes in extending welfare theory to an uncertain world. In his words on page 65, "Supposing that individual preferences do not change as random events are realized...the Arrow-Debreu interpretation of the market mechanism is easily extended to accommodate uncertainty. All that is required is a reinterpretation of the notion of a commodity. Just as we distinguish an automobile delivered at one date from the same physical object at another date, insisting that they be identified as two different goods, so we also distinguish between an automobile delivered at one date when one specific random event is realized and the same automobile available at the same date under a different realization. There will be two different commodities and usually two different prices. Under this reinterpretation, an equilibrium of the market mechanism is Pareto optimal provided that a market exists for each of the newly defined goods."

Campbell goes on to explain on pages 65-66 that while the "contingent contract" extension of the Arrow-Debreu model "would require an intolerably large number of markets in practice," and that "an individual would spend all his time negotiating contracts in an astronomical number of markets," a "new mechanism" that includes "markets for securities, one for each possible random event," guarantees that "Pareto-optimal allocations once again emerge at equilibrium," although "the completeness of markets condition is still suspect."

We quote at such length because we are well aware that much recent work in welfare economics has been concerned with the implications of uncertainty, yet we ignore this issue and literature completely. We feel justified in doing so because the "formal solution" of expanding the list of goods for which contingent contracts are written, and the "practical solution" of competitive insurance markets, resolve the issue at the theoretical level with few surprises, as Campbell explains, provided one abstracts from the complications of preference change and incentive compatibility—two issues we treat in great depth.

3. For example, K. Arrow, "General Economic Equilibrium: Purpose, Analytic Techniques, Collective Choice," *American Economic Review* 64, no. 3 (June 1974): 253-72; and J. Hirshleifer and John G. Riley, "The Analytics of Uncertainty and Information—An Expository Survey," *Journal of Economic Literature* 17 (December 1979): 1375-1421.

4. For example, K. Arrow and F. Hahn, *General Competitive Analysis* (San Francisco: Holden-Day, 1971); Peter Diamond and Michael Rothschild, eds., *Uncertainty in Economics: Readings and Exercises* (New York: Academic Press, 1978); and Jean Tirole, *The Theory of Industrial Organization* (Cambridge, Mass.: MIT Press, 1988).

5. For example, Robert Pollak, "Changes in Consumer Preferences: Endogenous Tastes in Demand and Welfare Analysis," *American Economic Review* 68, no. 2 (May 1978): 374-79.

6. It was Adam Smith's genius to know where to locate the fence without a map showing oil deposits and without knowing what "traditional" technology would become.

7. Leonid Hurwicz, "The Design of Mechanisms for Resource Allocation," in *Frontiers of Quantitative Economics*, Michael D. Intriligator and D. A. Kendrick, eds. (Amsterdam: North Holland Publishing, 1974).

CHAPTER 1. TRADITIONAL WELFARE THEORY

1. H. Sidgwick, *The Methods of Ethics*, 7th ed. (London: Macmillan, 1907), as excerpted in *Economic Justice*, E. S. Phelps, ed. (Baltimore: Penguin, 1973), 227.

2. Ibid.

3. John Rawls, *A Theory of Justice* (Cambridge, Mass.: Harvard University Press, 1971), 26.

4. John Stuart Mill, *On Bentham and Coleridge* (New York: Harper Torchbook, 1962), 94.

5. Jacob Viner, quoted in Herb Gintis, "Alienation and Power: Towards a Radical Welfare Economics" (Ph.D. diss., Harvard University, May 1969), 151.

6. I. M. D. Little, *A Critique of Welfare Economics,* 2nd ed. (Glasgow: Oxford University Press, 1950), 258.

7. Lionel Robbins, *The Nature and Significance of Economic Science* (London: Macmillan,1932), 24.

8. Gintis, "Alienation and Power," 110.

9. Little, *Critique,* 276.

10. K. Arrow, "General Economic Equilibrium: Purpose, Analytic Techniques, Collective Choice," *American Economic Review* 64, no. 3 (June 1974): 253-72.

11. Since a careful analysis and criticism of "traditional assumptions" is a primary subject of the remaining chapters in part 1, we will not dwell on them here. But we wish to note that "traditional assumptions" might prove little more than a euphemism for "whatever assumptions are necessary to render the desired conclusions."

12. T. C. Koopmans, *Three Essays on the State of Economic Science* (New York: McGraw Hill, 1957), 54.

13. K. Arrow, "Political and Economic Evaluation of Social Effects and Externalities," in *Frontiers of Quantitative Economics*, Michael D. Intrilligator and D. A. Kendrick, eds. (Amsterdam: North Holland Publishing, 1974), 6.

14. All references will be to John Rawls, *A Theory of Justice* (Cambridge, Mass.: Harvard University Press, 1971); and Robert Nozick, *Anarchy, State, and Utopia* (New York: Basic Books, 1974).

15. Rawls, *Theory of Justice*, 27-30.

16. Nozick, *Anarchy, State, and Utopia*, 32.

17. Ibid., 33.

18. See Nozick, *Anarchy, State, and Utopia*, 150-53, for an exposition of the entitlement approach to distribution, as opposed to the difference principle; and Rex Martin, *Rawls and Rights* (Lawrence, Kan.: University of Kansas Press, 1985), chap. 8. We do not treat this disagreement in depth because it is peripheral to our concerns. But it is worth noting that the difference basically divides the politically liberal new contractarians (Rawlsians) from the politically conservative new contractarians (Nozickians), the latter group dominating among adherents to the contractarian banners in the economics profession.

19. In private communication Rawls has indicated he does not exclude the possibility that public enterprise, competitive market institutions might also be compatible with his liberty and maximin principles.

20. These developments are presented in a variety of advanced microeconomic theory texts, but Gerard Debreu, *Theory of Value* (New York: John Wiley and Sons, 1959), is the original culmination of the modern, choice theoretic version of neoclassical welfare theory.

21. The "principle" of Occam's razor is, of course, that if the same set of conclusions can be deduced from a reduced set of assumptions, the reduction is to be preferred. The loss of the "bliss point" from the set of conclusions nullifies the application of the principle in this case.

22. Rawls, *Theory of Justice*, 23, 24, 27, 29, 30.

23. D. M. Winch, *Analytical Foundations of Welfare Economics* (Baltimore: Penguin, 1973), 144.

24. See Winch, *Ibid., 135-50;* or Yew-Kwang Ng, *Welfare Economics*, rev. ed. (London: Macmillan, 1983), chap. 3, for a concise presentation of the different forms of compensation tests and their contradictoriness.

25. See Milton Friedman, "The Distribution of Income," in *Economics: Mainstream Readings and Radical Critiques*, 3rd ed., David Mermelstein, ed. (New York: Random House, 1976), for an essay that presents this argument concisely.

26. Rawls, *Theory of Justice*, 27.

27. Ibid., 28-29.

28. Nozick, *Anarchy, State, and Utopia*, 31.

29. Rawls, *Theory of Justice*, 27-28.

30. Ibid., 29.

31. Ibid., 27.

32. Ibid., 23.

33. While the ability of centrally planned and market public enterprise economies to achieve a full range of Pareto optimal outcomes, in theory, under assumptions no more generous than those granted private enterprise market economies, is not unknown, it forms a large part of what we call the "old debate," and many still challenge this conclusion. For this reason we begin our treatments of markets, ownership, and central planning in part 3 by clarifying the "old debate" before proceeding to more important concerns.

34. Rawls, *Theory of Justice*, 29.

35. Ibid.

36. While it is obvious we feel a contractarian framework best expresses the traditional welfare paradigm, this is a peripheral point and irrelevant to

the rest of our argument. For our principal quarrel is with the traditional paradigm itself, not with its form of expression.

37. John Stuart Mill, in *The Philosophy of John Stuart Mill*, Marshall Cohen, ed. (New York: Modern Library, 1961).

38. It is of interest that in all three cases the ways in which each variant of traditional welfare theory seeks to protect the sanctity of the individual produce as a by-product an implicit denial of the endogeneity of preferences. In chapter 4 we will review Mill's discussion of how classical utilitarians' denial of a hierarchy of pleasures prevented them from analyzing the phenomenon of preference development, and Gintis' argument for how the Robbins Principle blinds neoclassical theorists to the welfare effects of endogenous preferences. Our own argument that the new contractarian treatment of the original position entails an implicit denial of the endogeneity of preferences as well is presented in chapter 6.

39. Nozick, *Anarchy, State, and Utopia*, 32-33.

40. Rawls, *Theory of Justice*, 29.

CHAPTER 2. THE LABOR PROCESS

1. See Paul A. Samuelson, *Foundations of Economic Analysis* (Cambridge, Mass.: Harvard University Press, 1947), 57; or C. E. Ferguson, *The Neoclassical Theory of Production* (Cambridge: Cambridge University Press, 1971), 7.

2. See Gerard Debreu, *Theory of Value* (New York: Wiley, 1959); or K. Arrow and F. H. Hahn, *General Competitive Analysis* (San Francisco: Holden-Day, 1971), chap. 3.

3. While abstracting from the production process no doubt permitted sharper focus on many aspects of the logic of exchange relations, it always ran the risk of misunderstanding phenomena that are the product of interrelations between the logics of exchange and production processes. While this may appear obvious, once the "abstraction" was embodied in the traditional paradigm most economists lost track of it.

4. See: Harry Braverman, *Labor and Monopoly Capital* (New York: Monthly Review Press, 1974); Michael Burawoy, *Manufacturing Consent* (Chicago: University of Chicago Press, 1979); Richard Edwards, *Contested Terrain* (New York: Basic Books, 1979); David Gordon, Richard Edwards, and Michael Reich, *Segmented Work, Divided Workers* (Cambridge: Cambridge University Press, 1982); David Noble, *America By Design* (New York: Knopf, 1977); Andrew Zimbalist, *Case Studies in the Labor Process* (New York: Monthly Review Press, 1979); Stephen Marglin, "What Do Bosses Do?," *Review of Radical Political Economics*

6, no. 2 (Summer 1974); William Lazonick, "The Subjugation of Labor to Capital: The Rise of the Capitalist System," *Review of Radical Political Economics* 10, no. 1 (Spring 1978); Michael Reich and James Devine, "The Microeconomics of Conflict and Hierarchy in Capitalist Production," *Review of Radical Political Economics* 12, no. 4 (Winter 1981); Kathy Stone, "The Origins of Job Structures in the Steel Industry," *Review of Radical Political Economics* 6, no. 2 (Summer 1974); Michele Naples, "The Structure of Industrial Relations, Labor Militancy and the Rate of Growth of Productivity: The Case of U.S. Mining and Manufacturing, 1953-1977" (Ph.D. diss., University of Massachusetts at Amherst, 1982); Herb Gintis, "The Nature of the Labor Exchange," *Review of Radical Political Economics* 8, no. 2 (Summer 1976); Samuel Bowles, "The Production Process in a Competitive Economy: Walrasian, Neo-Hobbesian, and Marxian Models," *American Economic Review* 75, no. 1 (March 1985).

5. P. Doeringer and M. Piore, *Internal Labor Markets and Manpower Analysis* (Lexington, Mass.: D. C. Heath, 1971).

6. Armen Alchian and Harold Demsetz, "Production Information Costs and Economic Organization," *American Economic Review* 62, no. 5 (1972); Guillermo Calvo, "Quasi Walrasian Theories of Unemployment," *American Economic Review* 69, no. 2 (May 1979); Edward Lazear, "Agency, Earnings Profiles, Productivity, and Hours Restrictions," *American Economic Review* 71, no. 4 (September 1981); Oliver Williamson, "The Organization of Work," *Journal of Economic Behavior and Organization*, no. 1 (1980).

7. See our discussion in chapters 2 and 4 of *Unorthodox Marxism* (Boston: South End Press, 1978) to the effect that Marx's Labor Theory of Value is not only unnecessary to explain the origins of profits, but confuses matters considerably. For a cogent, albeit polemical, argument for a Sraffian theory of prices, wages, and profits as opposed to a Marxian theory see Ian Steedman, *Marx After Sraffa* (London: New Left Books, 1977). For a more rigorous demonstration of the sufficiency of a Sraffian theory of prices, wages, rents, and profits in the more general context of joint production, fixed capital, land, and natural resources see Gilbert Abraham-Frois and Edmond Berrebi, *Theory of Value, Prices, and Accumulation* (Cambridge: Cambridge University Press, 1979), chap. 3. For a demonstration that generalizing the production environment from linear technologies to convex production sets still permits an explanation of profits as due to "exploitation" in terms other than labor values, but renders an explanation of exploitation and profits via the Labor Theory of Value impossible, see John Roemer, *Analytical Foundations of Marxian Economic Theory* (Cambridge: Cambridge University Press, 1981), chap. 2. Finally, for a highly provocative and ingenious treatment of exploitation in general and

misconceptions in the Marxist theory of exploitation, see John Roemer, *A General Theory of Exploitation and Class* (Cambridge, Mass.: Harvard University Press, 1981); and John Roemer, *Free to Lose* (Cambridge, Mass.: Harvard University Press, 1988).

8. Prior to the publication of Cornelius Castoriadis, *Political and Social Writings*, edited and translated by David Ames Curtis (Minneapolis: University of Minnesota Press, 1988), only a few pamphlets published under the pseudonym of Paul Cardan in the 1960s and some essays in *Telos* in the 1970s were available in English. For an excellent review of Castoriadis' work on the occasion of its long overdue printing in the U.S. see Carl Boggs' review in *Z Magazine* (January 1989): 75-77.

9. The essay was finally published long after stirring up a more significant controversy than most published articles in the *Review of Radical Political Economics* 6, no. 2 (Summer 1974).

10. Stone, "Job Structures in the Steel Industry."

11. For a sample of work responding to Braverman's efforts see *Politics and Society* 8, nos. 3, 4 (1978) devoted exclusively to consideration of his work.

12. Herb Gintis, "The Nature of the Labor Exchange and the Theory of Capitalist Production," *Review of Radical Political Economics* 8, no. 2 (Summer 1976).

13. Herb Gintis, "The Nature of the Labor Exchange: Toward a Radical Theory of the Firm," Harvard Institute of Economic Research, discussion paper no. 328 (October 1973): 1-2.

14. Herb Gintis and Donald Katzner, "Profits, Optimality, and the Social Division of Labor in the Firm," in *Sociological Economics*, M. Levy-Garboua, ed. (London: Sage, 1978), chap. 9.

15. R. Coase, "The Nature of the Firm," *Economica* 4 (November 1937).

16. Herbert Simon, *Models of Man* (New York: Wiley, 1957).

17. Coase, "Nature of the Firm," 333.

18. Simon, *Models of Man*, chap. 11.

19. Gintis and Katzner, "Profits," 270.

20. Ibid.

21. Gintis, "Labor Exchange: Toward a Radical Theory," 18.

22. Gintis and Katzner, "Profits," 289.

23. Samuel Bowles, "The Production Process in a Competitive Economy: Walrasian, Neo-Hobbesian, and Marxian Models," *American Economic Review* 75, no. 1 (March 1985): 16-36. For related work which draws less "radical" conclusions see B. Eaton and W. White, "Agent Compensation

and the Limits of Bonding," *Economic Inquiry* 20, no. 3 (July 1982): 330-42; J. Malcomson, "Unemployment and the Efficiency Wage Hypothesis," *Economic Journal* 91 (December 1981): 848-66; C. Shapiro and J. Stiglitz, "Equilibrium Unemployment as a Worker Discipline Device," *American Economic Review* 74, no. 3 (June 1984): 433-44; and R. Sparks, "A Model of Involuntary Unemployment and Wage Rigidity: Worker Incentive and the Threat of Dismissal," *Journal of Labor Economics* 4, no. 4 (1986): 560-81. A useful summary of treatments along traditional lines can be found in J. Yellen, "Efficiency Wage Models of Unemployment," *American Economic Review* 74, no. 2 (1984): 200-205.

24. Bowles, "Production Process," 22.

25. Ibid., 32.

26. Ibid., 33.

27. Ibid., 31.

28. For Bowles' views on this subject see Samuel Bowles, David Gordon, and Thomas Weisscopf, *Beyond the Wasteland* (Garden City, N.Y.: Anchor Doubleday, 1983).

29. Gil Skillman, "Microfoundations of the Conflict Theory of the Firm" (Ph.D. diss., University of Michigan, 1985).

30. S. Ross, "The Economic Theory of Agency: The Principal's Problem," *American Economic Review* 63, no. 2 (May 1973); idem, "On the Economic Theory of Agency and the Principal of Similarity," in *Essays on Economic Behavior Under Uncertainty*, M. Balch, D. McFadden, and S. Wu, eds. (Amsterdam: North Holland Publishing, 1974); J. A. Mirrlees, "Notes on Welfare Economics, Information, and Uncertainty," in Balch, McFadden, and Wu, eds.; idem, "The Optimal Structure of Incentives and Authority within an Organization," *Bell Journal of Economics* 7, no. 1 (Spring 1976); M. Harris and A. Raviv, "Some Results on Incentive Contracts with Applications to Education and Employment, Health Insurance, and Law Enforcement," *American Economic Review* 68, no. 1 (March 1978); S. Shavell, "Risk Sharing and Incentives in the Principal and Agent Relationship," *Bell Journal of Economics* (Spring 1979); M. Harris and R. Townsend, "Resource Allocation Under Asymmetric Information," *Econometrica* 40, no. 1 (January 1981); and S. Grossman and O. Hart, "An Analysis of the Principal-Agent Problem," *Econometrica* 51, no. 1 (January 1983).

31. D. Sappington, "Limited Liability Contracts Between Principal and Agent," *Journal of Economic Theory* 29, no. 1 (Feb 1983).

32. J. Stiglitz, "Incentives, Risk, and Information: Notes Towards a Theory of Hierarchy," *Bell Journal of Economics* 6, no. 2 (Autumn 1975).

33. B. Holmstrom, "Moral Hazard and Observability," *Bell Journal of Economics* (Spring 1979); D. Sappington, "Incentive Contracting with

Asymmetric and Imperfect Contractual Knowledge," *Journal of Economic Theory* 34. no. 1 (October 1984); M. Harris and A. Raviv, "Optimal Incentive Contracts with Imperfect Information," *Journal of Economic Theory* 20. no. 2 (April 1979); J. Christensen, "Communication in Agencies," *Bell Journal of Economics* 12, no. 2 (Autumn 1981); and G. Skillman and H. Ryder, "Bargaining with Costly Unilateral Replacement," Department of Economics, Brown University, working paper no. 88-17 (June 1988).

34. For example: B. Holmstrom, "Moral Hazard in Teams," *Bell Journal of Economics* 13, no. 2 (Autumn 1982); E. Lazear and S. Rosen, "Rank Order Tournaments as Optimum Labor Contracts," *Journal of Political Economy* 89, no. 5 (1981); R. Radner, "Optimal Equilibrium in some Repeated Games with Imperfect Monitoring," Bell Laboratories discussion paper, May 1981; idem, "Monitoring Cooperative Agreements in a Repeated Principal-Agent Relationship," Bell Laboratories economic discussion paper no. 184 (March 1981); and G. Skillman, "Sequential Bargaining in Capitalist Firms," Department of Economics, Brown University, working paper no. 88-28 (November 1988).

35. For recent overviews of empirical work see F. Blau and M. Ferber, "Discrimination: Empirical Evidence for the U.S.," *American Economic Review* 77, no. 2 (1987): 316-20; J. Cotton, "On the Composition of Wage Differentials," *Review of Economics and Statistics* 70, no. 2 (1988): 236-43; G. Cain, "The Economic Analysis of Labor Market Discrimination: A Survey," in *Handbook of Labor Economics*, O. Ashenfelter and R. Layard, eds. (New York: Elsevier Science Publications, 1986); and D. Neumark, "Employers' Discriminatory Behavior and the Estimation of Wage Discrimination," *Journal of Human Resources* 23, no. 3 (1988): 279-95.

36. Michael Reich, appendix to chap. 5, "Models of Class Conflict and Racial Inequality Within the Firm," *Racial Inequality* (Princeton, N.J.: Princeton University Press, 1981), 204-15. For similar theoretical treatments see also: Michael Reich and James Devine, "The Microeconomics of Conflict and Hierarchy in Capitalist Production," *Review of Radical Political Economics* 14, no. 4 (Winter 1981); John Roemer, "Divide and Conquer: Microfoundations of the Marxian Theory of Wage Discrimination," *Bell Journal of Economics* 10, no. 2 (Autumn 1979); and Joel Kaplan, "The Divide and Conquer Hypothesis: An Analysis of Internal Labor Markets and Racial Inequality Among Men in the U.S." (Ph.D. diss., American University, 1985).

37. K. Arrow, "Models of Job Discrimination," in *Racial Discrimination in Economic Life*, A. Pascal, ed. (Lexington, Mass.: Lexington Books, 1972).

38. All quotations in this section are from Arrow, "Models of Job Discrimination," 83-99.

39. Since Arrow does not spell out all his assumptions, we cannot know whether or not he assumes employee immortality or the necessity of a continuous replacement process. In the case of mortals, it would appear the word "always" here may be too strong. And if employers' need to replace mortal workers eventually could be accomplished by infrequent but large scale replacements, the wage differentials should tend to disappear in what we might call the long, long run too. Perhaps more telling is the crucial role played by the assumption "there is only one kind of utility function expressing a trade-off between wages and the proportion of white workers." Just as "competition" only drove out employers' racism when we abandoned the assumption of uniform employer tastes for discrimination, if we allow that white employees are racist to different degrees, it seems wage differentials would eventually vanish as well.

40. The parallel to the Marxist theory of the tendency of the rate of profit to fall due to the introduction of "capital intensive" techniques of production is too striking to go without mention. Marx offered the theory with a list of similarly "counteracting tendencies." However, Okishio proved conclusively there is no need to consider counteracting tendencies since the rate of profit does not tend to fall for the reason Marx originally supposed. Or, for those who (erroneously) insist on continuing to think in terms of "the tendency" and "counteracting tendencies," the "counteracting tendencies" always outweigh the "tendency." Latter-day defenders of the Marxist faith tried to rescue the theory of the tendency for the rate of profit to fall by suggesting that it can still operate in models with fixed capital, or by modifying the usual investment criterion. All was to no avail except in the eyes of those who refuse to abandon a cherished part of their paradigm regardless of, in this case, proven theoretical internal inconsistencies. See John Roemer, *Analytical Foundations of Marxian Economic Theory* (Cambridge: Cambridge University Press, 1981), chaps. 4 and 5 for a rigorous treatment. The latest tack in the rescue attempt is strikingly similar to Arrow's departure from the standard assumption of the traditional debate. Where Arrow proposes "that we look more closely at the long run adjustment process" in context of nonconvexities rather than search for an alternative explanation that works under traditional neoclassical assumptions, Marxist diehards have tried to rescue one of their favorite convictions by abandoning comparative statics adjustment assumptions. Once one enters the murky waters of disequilibrium adjustment dynamics [uneven development] almost nothing can be established with certainty—which in this case proves convenient for diehard believers in the Marxist tendency for the rate of profit to fall.

41. This is the assumption that contains the critical error. But without a paradigm and theory that analyzes the social dynamics that occur within

the production process, the assumption appears perfectly logical. When we look closely inside the black box of private enterprise production in chapter 8 we will see that this is not the case.

42. We do not mean to imply nothing is to be learned about economic discrimination from the neoclassical treatment. No doubt some of what Arrow has analyzed is going on. A full treatment of discrimination must encompass both possibilities—that white workers gain and that employers gain from discrimination against minorities—and analyze the circumstances that would or would not permit each from doing so. Our point is only that the traditional paradigm has blinded neoclassical theorists to a most important aspect of discrimination—the motivation for employers in competitive circumstances to discriminate.

43. Roemer, "Divide and Conquer"; and Reich and Devine, "Microeconomics of Conflict and Hierarchy."

44. Reich, "Models of Class Conflict and Racial Inequality Within the Firm," in *Racial Inequality*, 204-15 appendix to Chapter 5. We do not present Reich's model here because we develop a more general model that incorporates Reich's as a special case in chapter 8.

45. Joan Robinson, *The Economics of Imperfect Competition* (London: Macmillan, 1933), 301-304. For a contemporary application of the Robinson model to wage differences by sex see Janice Madden, "Discrimination: Manifestation of Male Market Power?," in *Sex, Discrimination, and the Division of Labor*, Cynthia Lloyd, ed. (New York: Columbia University Press, 1975), 146-74.

46. Doeringer and Piore, *Internal Labor Markets*. For Piore's methodological characterization of this work see M. Piore, "Labor Market Segmentation: To What Paradigm Does It Belong?," *American Economic Review* 73, no. 2 (May 1983): 249-53. For other recent contributions along institutionalist lines see G. Akerlof, "Gift Exchange and Efficiency Wage Theory: Four Views," *American Economic Review* 74, no. 2 (1984): 79-83; C. Fisher, "Towards a More Complete Understanding of Occupational Sex Discrimination," *Journal of Economic Issues* 21, no. 1 (1987): 113-38; and S. Woodbury, "Power in the Labor Market: Institutionalist Approaches to Labor Problems," *Journal of Economic Issues* 21, no. 4 (1987): 1781-1807.

47. Glen Cain and Harold Watts, eds., *Income Maintenance and Labor Supply: Econometric Studies* (Chicago: Rand McNally College Publication, 1973), chap. 9.

48. One would have to examine what circumstances would generate such a condition. But seniority rules, firm-specific skills, and pension contribution/benefit structures are among a number of possibilities that have been explored.

49. Beyond blinding traditional theorists, the traditional paradigm has affected those who dared to hunt inside the forbidden demesne of the black box as well. While these poachers deserve credit for fearlessly pursuing their intuitions, the traditional paradigm tends to channel their hunting into the unequal information/uncertainty preserve that, if we are correct, is stocked with smaller game. This may even hold for principal-agent theory in its original domain of moral hazard and adverse selection, where future work may bag bigger game by moving to a multiperiod, game-theoretic approach where the human outputs of previous periods are known with ever greater accuracy by all parties and recognized as the human conditions that form the structure of comparative advantages in future conflicts—all of which should be taken into account in a theory of "rational choice."

50. Abba Lerner, "The Economics and Politics of Consumer Sovereignty," *American Economic Review* 62, no. 2 (May 1972): 259.

CHAPTER 3. EXTERNALITIES AND PUBLIC GOODS

1. Richard Musgrave, *The Theory of Public Finance* (New York: McGraw Hill, 1959), 6, 8.

2. Ibid., 10-11.

3. P. A. Samuelson, "The Pure Theory of Public Expenditures," *Review of Economics and Statistics* 36, no. 4 (November 1954); idem, "Diagrammatic Exposition of a Theory of Public Expenditure," *Review of Economics and Statistics* 37, no. 4 (November 1955).

4. Musgrave, *Theory of Public Finance*, 8.

5. Ibid., 134.

6. Ibid.

7. Ibid., 135.

8. C. M. Tiebout, "A Pure Theory of Local Expenditures," *Journal of Political Economy* 64, no. 5 (October 1956): 416-23.

9. Musgrave, *Theory of Public Finance,* 132.

10. Ibid., 7-8.

11. See R. C. D'Arge and E. K. Hunt, "Environmental Pollution, Externalities and Conventional Economic Wisdom: A Critique," *Environmental Affairs* no. 1 (1971): 266-86. E. K. Hunt and R. C. D'Arge, "On Lemmings and Other Acquisitive Animals: Propositions on Consumption," *Journal of Economic Issues* 7, no. 2 (June 1973): 337-53; and E. K. Hunt, "A Radical Critique of Welfare Economics," in *Growth, Profits, and Property,* Ed Nell, ed. (Cambridge: Cambridge University Press, 1980), 239-49. James Campen, "Public Expenditure Analysis" (Ph.D. diss., Harvard

University Press, October 1976); idem, *Benefit, Cost and Beyond* (Cambridge, Mass.: Ballinger, 1986) to some extent echoes elements of Hunt's criticism in his own critique of traditional benefit cost analysis.

12. Hunt, "Radical Critique."

13. Ibid., 246.

14. Ibid., 245. Examination of determinants of the reproduction and transformation of the human and social characteristics that traditional welfare theory takes as "givens" is a constant theme in the alternative approach we favor. Here we find Hunt criticizing traditional theory for accepting "as somehow metaphysically given" the state of social interrelations that define the degree of external effects in the economy. In what follows Hunt outlines the incentives market systems establish for individuals to transform and manipulate what are traditionally taken as "givens."

15. Ibid., 245-46. Hunt goes on to point out that a symmetrical mechanism regarding positive external economies is precisely what is lacking in a free market system. "External economies also offer incentives for individual gain, but the incentive structure here is basically different than for external diseconomies. Without liability or nuisance rules that establish social responsibility, it is in the interest of both generator and recipient to negotiate on external diseconomies. However, with external economies the recipient gains more by attempting to be a free rider except, perhaps, at the margin. Consequently, the incentive for creating or producing external economies is less than that for external diseconomies, except perhaps for altruists" (246).

16. Ibid., 241.

17. In other words, if it were the case that a set of economic institutions yielded Pareto optimal outcomes, we would call those institutions socially efficient. In part 3 we go to great lengths to show this is less likely to be the case for private enterprise, competitive market institutions than commonly assumed. Nor is it the case for public enterprise market economies, nor centrally planned economies, although for reasons not usually emphasized. But our quarrel is with the particular institutions that number among their deficiencies the generation of socially inefficient outcomes. Our quarrel is not with the formalization of the notion of social efficiency known as the Pareto criterion.

18. Whether the notion of social efficiency formalized as Pareto optimality deserves as prominent a role in welfare theory as it has been accorded traditionally, is a different matter, as is the question of whether additional formalizations of social efficiency are needed because the Pareto criterion is insufficient in public choice environments. We might add that it is not clear to us that Hunt really means to challenge Pareto optimality as a useful formalization of the notion of social efficiency as he clearly appears to do

in the passage quoted above. But regardless of Hunt's view, there is a regrettable tendency among not a few radical economists to reject the concept of Pareto optimality altogether.

19. Hunt, "Radical Critique," 241.

20. Ibid., 243.

21. Ibid., 242.

22. Ibid., 243.

23. R. Lipsey and K. Lancaster, "The General Theory of the Second Best," *Review of Economic Studies* 24, no. 1 (1956-57): 11-32.

24. Hunt, "Radical Critique," 243.

25. One must take this statement in the spirit it is offered. It is no doubt possible to choose combinations of economic institutions and welfare criteria in which the theory of the second best would not hold. We mean to suggest that for any reasonably interesting welfare theory and any reasonably interesting economy the theory of the second best will likely apply. Certainly if we insist that our welfare theory include the Pareto criterion, the applicability of the theory of the second best cannot be sensitive to modifications in welfare approach.

26. We regret ending our treatment of Hunt's criticisms of neoclassical welfare theory on a critical note. In our view he is one of the most insightful, modern critics of neoclassical welfare theory. It is most regrettable that his analysis of externalities is known to so few mainstream and nonmainstream economists alike.

27. Jean-Claude Milleron, "Theory of Value with Public Goods: A Survey Article," *Journal of Economic Theory* 5, no. 3 (December 1972): 419-77.

28. Peter Hammond, "Symposium on Incentive Compatibility: Introduction," *Review of Economic Studies* 46, no. 2 (1979): 181.

29. Theodore Groves, "Efficient Collective Choice when Compensation Is Possible," *Review of Economic Studies* 46, no. 2 (1979).

30. W. Vickrey, "Counterspeculation, Auctions, and Competitive Sealed Tender," *Journal of Finance* 16, no. 1 (March 1961): 8-37.

31. Theodore Groves, "The Allocation of Resources under Uncertainty," (Ph.D. diss., University of California at Berkeley, 1970).

32. E. Clarke, "Multipart Pricing of Public Goods," *Public Choice*, 11 (1971): 17-33.

33. L. Hurwicz, "On Informationally Decentralized Systems," in *Decision and Organization*, McGuire and Radner, eds., (Amsterdam: North Holland Publishing, 1972); and idem, "The Design of Mechanisms for Resource Allocation," *American Economic Review* 63 no. 2 (May 1973): 1-30.

34. J. H. Dreze and D. de la Vallee Poussin, "A Tatonnement Process for Public Goods," *Review of Economic Studies* 38 (1971): 133-50.

35. Ibid., 147.

36. Clark, "Multipart Pricing."

37. T. Groves and E. Loeb, "Incentives and Public Inputs," *Journal of Public Economics*, no. 4 (1975): 211-26.

38. T. Groves and J. Ledyard, "Optimal Allocation of Public Goods: A Solution to the 'Free Rider' Problem," *Econometrica* 45, no. 4 (May 1977): 791-92.

39. Taking the two possible ways of lying in turn: if I understate my benefits I will have no direct effect on my own assessment and only very marginally increase the tax bills of all others. If I overstate my benefits I will, again, have no direct effect on my own assessment, and only very marginally decrease the tax bills of others. Since a budget balancing constraint implies that higher assessments for others will eventually yield a downward adjustment in my own assessment, a lingering incentive to understate one's benefits might appear to remain. But this effect is extremely secondary. It is like the effect that implies that a very aware participant in even a competitive market can improve upon "competitive" behavior by taking into account his or her minimal effect on market price—a point well known to traditional theorists.

40. Obviously, among millions of citizens I cannot expect to affect the outcome greatly. So for those who don't bother to vote in presidential elections because the probability of their affecting the outcome is insignificant, there may be no answer to the question why they should study options and report their marginal willingness to pay for public goods carefully. But the point is, there is no incentive to dissimulate. On the other hand, if I have information about the likely differences between my preferences for public goods and the preferences of the rest of my compatriots, there may be strong incentives to overexaggerate those differences when reporting to enhance my (limited) expected impact. But this is a problem that occurs in many contexts for which no "solution" has been found. We might note that as significant as incentive-compatible mechanisms certainly are, they shouldn't be expected to work miracles!

41. A. Gibbard, "Manipulation of Voting Schemes: A General Result," *Econometrica* 41, no. 4 (July 1973): 587-601; and M. Shatterthwaite, "Strategy-Proofness and Arrow's Conditions: Existence and Correspondence Theorems for Voting Procedures and Social Welfare Functions," *Journal of Economic Theory* 10, no. 2 (April 1975): 187-217.

42. J. Green and J. Laffont, "Revelation des Preferences pour les Biens Publics," Cahiers du Seminaire d'Econometrie (C.R.N.S., Paris); and L.

Hurwicz, "On the Existence of Allocation Systems Whose Manipulative Nash Equilibria Are Pareto-Optimal" (Unpublished paper presented at 3rd World Congress of the Econometric Society, Toronto, 1975).

43. See Groves and Ledyard's "Quadratic Mechanism" in "Optimal Allocation," section 4; M. Walker's "Paired Difference Mechanism" in "An Informationally Efficient Auctioneerless Mechanism for Attaining Lindahl Allocations" (Unpublished paper); L. Hurwicz, "Shared Cost Mechanism" in "An Outcome Function with Lindahl Allocation at Nash Equilibria without an Auctioneer" (Unpublished paper); and idem, "Smooth Outcome Functions Yielding Walrasian Allocation at Nash Equilibria without an Auctioneer" (Unpublished notes).

44. Hunt, "Radical Critique," 246.

CHAPTER 4. ENDOGENOUS PREFERENCES AND INSTITUTIONS

1. Milton Friedman, *Price Theory* (Chicago: Aldine Press, 1962), 13.

2. W. M. Gorman, "Tastes, Habits, and Choices," *International Economic Review* 8 no. 2 (June 1967): 218.

3. Jon Elster, *Logic and Society* (New York: Wiley, 1978), 39-40.

4. This theme will be further developed in chapter 8.

5. John Stuart Mill, "On Liberty," sec. 1, paragraph 11, in *The Philosophy of John Stuart Mill*, Marshall Cohen, ed. (New York: Modern Library, 1966).

6. Bertrand Russell, *Philosophical Essays*, rev. (London: Allen and Unwin, 1966), 21.

7. John Stuart Mill, in *The Philosophy of John Stuart Mill*, Cohen, ed., 331-32.

8. See Sidgwick as quoted in chap. 1, footnote 1.

9. Quoted in Herb Gintis, "Alienation and Power: Towards a Radical Welfare Economics" (Ph.D. diss., Harvard University, May 1969),153.

10. Gintis, "Alienation and Power," 137.

11. Ibid., 137-38, 187.

12. Ibid., 184.

13. Ibid., 185-87.

14. Cited in Elster, *Logic and Society*, 40.

15. N. Georgescu-Roegen, "The Theory of Choice and the Constancy of Economic Laws," *Quarterly Journal of Economics* 64, no. 1 (February 1950): 125-38; R. Strotz, "Myopia and Inconsistency in Dynamic Utility

Maximization," *Review of Economic Studies* 23 (1955-56): 165-80; and J. Hasanyi, "Welfare Economics of Variable Tastes," *Review of Economic Studies* 21 (1954): 204-13.

16. C. C. von Weizsacker, "Notes on Endogenous Change of Tastes," *Journal of Economic Theory* 3 no. 4 (December 1971): 345-72.

17. Peter Hammond, "Endogenous Tastes and Stable Long-Run Choice," *Journal of Economic Theory* 13 no. 2 (October 1976): 329-40; C. Lluch, "Expenditure, Savings and Habit Formation," *International Economic Review* 15 no. 3 (October 1974): 786-97; and Marcel Boyer, "A Habit Forming Optimal Growth Model," *International Economic Review* 19 no. 3 (October 1978): 585-609.

18. Robert Pollak: "Habit Formation and Dynamic Demand Functions," *Journal of Political Economy* 78 (July/August 1970): 745-63; idem, "Additive Utility Functions and Linear Engel Curves," *Review of Economic Studies* 38 (1971): 401-14; idem, "Habit Formation and Long-Run Utility Functions," *Journal of Economic Theory* 13 no. 2 (October 1976): 272-97; idem, "Changes in Consumer Preferences: Endogenous Tastes in Demand and Welfare Analysis," *American Economic Review* 68, no. 2 (May 1978): 374-79; idem, "Welfare Evaluation and the Cost of Living Index in the Household Production Model," *American Economic Review* 68 no. 3 (June 1978): 285-99; Robert Pollak and Terence Wales, "Estimation of Complete Demand Systems from Household Budget Data: The Linear and Quadratic Expenditure Systems," *American Economic Review* 68 no. 3 (June 1978): 348-59; and idem, "Equity: The Individual vs. the Family: Welfare Comparisons and Equivalence Scales," *American Economic Review* 69 no. 2 (May 1979): 216-21.

19. Von Weizsacker, "Endogenous Change of Tastes," 345.

20. Ibid., 346.

21. Ibid.

22. Ibid., 347.

23. A. El-Safty, "Adaptive Behavior, Demand and Preferences," *Journal of Economic Theory* 13 no. 2 (October 1976): 298-318.

24. Ibid., 298.

25. Pollak, "Habit Formation," 296.

26. We say of little additional concern to welfare theory because the problems of nonconvexity of preferences have long been recognized. As von Weizsacker admits, his model was specifically excluded by Marshall in his formulations of the usual optimality conclusions of traditional welfare theory under what Marshall formulated as the assumption of decreasing marginal utility: "There is, however, an implicit condition in this law which should be made clear. It is that we do not suppose time to

369

be allowed for any alteration in the character or tastes of the man himself. It is, therefore, no exception to the law that the more good music a man hears, the stronger is his taste for it likely to become; that avarice and ambition are often insatiable; or that the virtue of cleanliness and the vice of drunkenness alike grow on what they feed upon. For in such cases our observations range over some period of time; and the man is not the same at the beginning as at the end of it." (Alfred Marshall, *Principles of Economics*, 8th ed. [London: Macmillan, 1962], 79.)

27. In his *Ulysses and the Sirens* (Cambridge: Cambridge University Press, 1979), Jon Elster's discussion of "The Locally Maximizing Machine" is similar to "myopic habit formation," and "The Globally Maximizing Machine" is akin to "purposeful preference molding." In his *Sour Grapes* (Cambridge: Cambridge University Press, 1983), Elster's "thin theory of individual rationality" considers only our "preference fulfillment effect" while his "broad theory of individual rationality" considers our "preference fulfillment effect" as well.

28. Von Weizsacker, "Endogenous Change of Tastes," 371.

29. Ibid.

30. Ibid.

31. Pollak, "Changes in Consumer Preferences," 374.

32. Pollak, "Habit Formation," 292.

33. The "impossibility" result derived independently by Pollak and El-Safty in the case of myopic habit formation stems from two considerations we will be careful to exclude in our treatment in chapter 6. (1) Habit formation makes nonconvexities highly likely. While true, we will waive the objection since it is well known that nonconvexities create problems for existence proofs. (2) Myopic adaptive behavior allows for the possibility that individuals will become "mired" in local optima that are not global optima. This is the principal focus of Pollak and El-Safty in their 1976 papers discussed previously. They demonstrate that a "local maximizing machine"—in Elster's words—will only succeed in global maximizing under highly restrictive assumptions about the nature of the local maximization process, namely the "separability" or "additivity" of the short-run utility functions. Since we will stipulate perfect foresight, we bypass this problem that has been the principal focus of the technical literature.

34. Pollak, "Habit Formation," 295.

35. Ibid., 294.

36. Ibid., 296.

37. Ibid.

38. We will leave to Pollak and others specializing in the field of empirical demand estimation to decide if myopic habit formation is more important, even if less tractable, to analyze than conscious preference molding when studying actual human behavior.

39. Thorstein Veblen and economists of the institutionalist school have long argued that actual consumer behavior can be better understood through the concepts of "invidious comparison," "conspicuous consumption," and "habit" or "inertia" than through the axioms of rationality. Let us assume for the moment that they are largely correct in this judgment. This would still not provide a cogent argument for abandoning an analysis of how an economy would function if people behaved in accordance with the axioms of rationality since this is the only way to determine the "welfare effects" of the economic institutions that "define" the economy. In a sense, Pollak is making the same error that many institutionalist economists have made in presuming a conflict of interest here.

40. Pollak, "Changes in Consumer Preferences," 377.

41. Ibid.

42. While Pollak is correct that unconditional preferences are the relevant preferences for welfare analysis and that such preferences cannot be inferred from market behavior—they are not the same as "revealed preferences"—he is incorrect that little can be concluded regarding welfare in the context of endogenous preferences, as we will see.

43. Pollak, "Changes in Consumer Preferences," 374. We must point out that while Pollak admits to this problem in 1978, the insight was not his own. Gintis explained this very problem in just such language in numerous publications between 1969 and 1974 of which Pollak acknowledges being aware. But as we will see in chapter 6, both Pollak's and Gintis' intuitions were wrong in important respects regarding the relation between endogenous preferences and the fundamental theorems of welfare economics.

44. Ibid., 377.

45. Gintis is not the only author to conceptualize "purposeful preference molding" and grapple with the dilemmas they pose. Whereas Georgescu-Roegen and Strotz discussed the implications of endogenous preferences for "irreversible" demands in the 1950s, Harsanyi was the first, to our knowledge, to examine the welfare implications of what we call purposeful preference molding. Gintis' focus is very much in the tradition pioneered by Harsanyi in "Welfare Economics of Variable Tastes." More recently, Jon Elster has done much to bring the importance of this issue to the attention of a wider audience in a brief section on "Endogenous Change of Tastes" in chapter 2 of *Logic and Society*, in sections 5 and 6 of chapter 2 of *Ulysses and the Sirens*, in chapters 1 and 4 of *Sour Grapes*, and in his

own contribution in *The Multiple Self*, Jon Elster, ed. (Cambridge: Cambridge University Press, 1986).

We focus our attention here on Gintis because his work preceded Elster's, because our own intellectual debt is to Gintis rather than Elster whose work we only became aware of after formulating our own views on these matters, and because Gintis, as an economist, speaks the "language" of economists more consistently than Elster. But this choice is partly idiosyncratic on our part and we find ourselves very much in agreement with many of Elster's early views on these matters. We are less taken with the notion of "multiple selves," but this concept is admittedly aimed at a different set of problems than those we have found most intriguing.

46. Gintis, "Alienation and Power," 102-105.

47. Ibid., 105-106.

48. Ibid., 106.

49. Consistency requires that if bundle A is preferred to bundle B, then bundle B cannot be preferred to bundle A. This assumption is justified by traditional welfare theory by appealing to the intuitive notion of simple rationality. We agree that consistency is implied by rationality under the assumption of exogenous preferences. But under the assumption of endogenous preferences lack of "consistency" may be perfectly rational. If bundle A consists of an AM radio and an adult education course in the appreciation of classical music, and bundle B contains an FM radio and an adult education course in the appreciation of classical music, I might very well "reveal" a preference for bundle A in the first time period and for bundle B in a later time period when the AM radio has worn out and the music appreciation course has had a chance to affect my auricular preferences.

Elster treats this issue in *Ulysses and the Sirens*, chapter 2, section 5 on "inconsistent time preferences." And possibilities such as this caught the attention of Georgescu-Roegen, "The Theory of Choice and the Constancy of Economic Laws," and Farrel, "Irreversible Demand Functions," *Econometrica* 20 no. 2 (April 1952): 171-86.

If it is admitted that this is perfectly reasonable or "rational" behavior that an adequate theory should be able to explain, the only way to salvage the axiom of consistency (much less transitivity) is to employ the artifice of telescoping a dynamic human world that moves unidirectionally through time into a static world of homo-economi making one single choice, in what could hardly be called their "lives," of all consumption and work bundles for every time period of their existence in the single choice period of the present. As we make clear later in this chapter, we agree with Gintis that to do this is to adopt a model that grossly violates important aspects of our actual human condition. On the other hand, we also believe that adopting just such a model of endogenous preferences permits us to shed a great deal of light on the most important welfare theoretic questions concerning the important economic systems of our day. But all this is yet to come.

50. Gintis, "Alienation and Power," 118. In previous citations Pollak indicated that he also appreciated this complication.

51. Gintis, "Alienation and Power," 107-108.

52. As best we can ascertain, the first economist to elaborate the notion of utility depending on price was Thorstein Veblen in his famous notion of conspicuous consumption. To the extent people attempt to consume *relatively* more than others to achieve social status through "invidious comparison," traditional welfare theoretic conclusions are obviously misplaced. While the usual reaction has been to assume that goods consumed for status are relatively few and exceptions to the rule, some neoclassical economists have grappled with the complications they pose.

See Oscar Morgenstern, "Demand Theory Reconsidered," *Quarterly Journal of Economics* 62 (1948): 165-201; H. Leibenstein, "Bandwagon, Snob, and Veblen Effects in the Theory of Consumer Demand," *Quarterly Journal of Economics* 64 (1950): 183-207; R. Kalman, "A Theory of Consumer Behavior When Prices Enter the Utility Function," *Econometrica* 36 no. 3-4 (1968): 497-510; H. Hayakawa and Y. Venerias, "Consumer Interdependence via Reference Groups," *Journal of Political Economy* 85 (1977): 565-99; and Robert Pollak, "Price Dependent Preferences," *American Economic Review* 67 no. 2 (March 1977): 64-75. Of course James Duesenberry's famous "relative income hypothesis" is rooted in a Veblenesque view of consumption. *Income, Savings, and the Theory of Consumer Behavior* (Cambridge, Mass.: Harvard University Press, 1949).

53. Gintis, "Alienation and Power," 106.

54. Ibid., 106-107.

55. Although the reason is ultimately of no consequence, perhaps Gintis was overly influenced by his study of Mill, who placed great emphasis on the problem of uncertainty in the analysis of preference development.

56. Gintis, "Alienation and Power," 99.

57. Ibid., 127.

58. Ibid., 100.

59. Ibid., 110.

60. Ibid., 112.

61. Ibid., 113.

62. Ibid., 119, 121, 122, 127.

63. Ibid., 127.

64. Ibid., 262.

65. Gintis, "Welfare Criteria with Endogenous Preferences: The Economics of Education," *International Economic Review* 15, no. 2 (June 1974): 426, Theorem 5.

66. Ibid.

67. Ibid., 427.

68. Ibid., 426.

69. See our treatment of these issues in chapter 9 on central planning.

70. Gintis, "Alienation and Power," 18.

71. Roy Harrod, "Scope and Method of Economics," *Economic Journal* 48, no. 191 (September 1938): 386.

72. Joseph Schumpeter is perhaps the best-known proponent of this view.

73. This contradiction has been treated in a subfield of traditional economic theory regarding patents and copyrights and is not really resolved. Rather, the consequences and best practical course of action are debated. We suspect, however, that the newest technological revolution in microcomputers and software will focus much more attention on the issue. When the "commodity" is knowledge in the form of a program recorded on a diskette that can be almost costlessly transferred from the first buyer to all potential subsequent buyers; when the market is "mass" rather than a small number of business and institutional clients whose subsequent transfers can be reasonably policed; and as long as the U.S. Constitution makes searches of tens of millions of homes legally difficult as well as economically costly; we have the makings of an interesting test of how optimal the effect of private enterprise market institutions on technological progress really is. We hasten to point out that it should not be assumed that the outcome would be the same in a different institutional setting.

It also bears mentioning that French, German, and Japanese "visions" of the role of the state in fomenting technological change and structural transformations in a private enterprise market economy has always differed markedly from Anglo-American laissez-faire conceptions. Obviously, some interesting "success" stories are on the opposite side of the great ideological divide. See Andrew Shonfield, *Modern Capitalism* (London: Oxford University Press, 1974) for an interesting, though dated, comparison of the French and English experiences.

74. See Gintis' discussion of Marshall in "Alienation and Power," 40-41.

75. John Sawyer, "Social Structure and Economic Progress: General Propositions and Some French Examples," *American Economic Review* 41 no. 2 (May 1951): 321-29.

76. Ibid., 321-22.

77. Ibid., 322.

78. Ibid., 323.

79. Ibid., 324.

80. Ibid., 322-23.

81. Of course, to the extent people do not follow the dictates of individual rationality, the social impact of institutions will be less. But the critical word here is "less." The impact will be "less" to the extent actual behavior deviates from "promoted" behavior, but not "different." In the extreme, one might argue that if there were literally no correlation between rational and actual behavior there would be no "scientific" purpose to welfare theory. But in this case there would be no "scientific" purpose in studying any social institutions, or anything else in the "social sciences" for that matter.

82. Oscar Lange and Frederick Taylor, *On the Economic Theory of Socialism* (New York: Monthly Review Press, 1964). An interesting feature of the Lange-Lerner-Taylor model is that optimality properties do not depend on market structures being atomistic or competitive. Their use of a Central Planning Board for making price adjustments in intermediate markets is basically irrelevant from a welfare theoretic point of view if we are only interested in equilibria in any case. Whether their adjustment mechanism is an improvement on the "natural" market mechanism might, however, be of interest to modern, post-Keynesian disequilibrium theory.

83. Traditional theory equates "socialism" with "public enterprise economies." While at one level it is a matter of semantics, we prefer to define "socialism" to mean an economy in which those who carry out economic activities are in a position to conceive and coordinate those activities themselves. But if we use the term this way, neither CPS nor WSMS can be deemed socialist (see Michael Albert and Robin Hahnel, *Socialism Today and Tomorrow* [Boston: South End Press, 1981]). The issue transcends semantics because by attaching the label "socialist" to countries such as the Soviet Union, China, etc., the rulers of those countries attempt to legitimate actions that pursue wealth and power for an elite as "serving the people," and denigrate criticism as "attacks on working people." Attaching the label "socialist" to these countries also permits rulers of capitalist countries to denigrate the label and create a context in which they claim all who criticize capitalism are pro-Gulag. In short, equating "socialism" with existing public enterprise economies is part of the Orwellian process of constricting what can be thought in a world where thought-without-limits would, as always, be a threat to the powers that be.

84. To avoid misinterpretation, when we say all the above systems are equally efficient, we mean each is capable of generating Pareto optimal

375

outcomes under appropriate assumptions. In general, these assumptions concern perfect information for decision makers, faithful execution of all decisions, and, in market systems, ability to achieve a general equilibria. But the decision makers are different in the different systems, and the information they are likely to possess and the incentives they face may be different as well. Therefore, formulation of the assumptions necessary for different systems to achieve Pareto optimality differ. All of which has been the subject of what we call the "modern debate" over the information and incentives properties of economies. But while we recognize that "practical" considerations such as these certainly merit discussion, we find the necessary assumptions for the different systems essentially equivalent.

CHAPTER 5. A NEW WELFARE PARADIGM

1. An interested reader might well begin with Michael Albert, Leslie Cagan, Noam Chomsky, Robin Hahnel, Mel King, Lydia Sargent, and Holly Sklar, *Liberating Theory* (Boston: South End Press, 1986).

2. In our opinion, paradigms in the social sciences should not be judged entirely on the basis of immediate results. Because so many unanswered questions always remain, using this criteria alone is too risky. While a new paradigm may prove fruitful in some areas, internal weaknesses may present roadblocks to progress in other areas later. This is precisely what we claim has happened with the traditional welfare paradigm. So it is important to continuously requestion our underlying assumptions about human beings and society in light of new scientific knowledge—a process that is always controversial and subject to ideological influences. However, in a book proposing a new approach it seems sufficient to present a new paradigm that yields interesting new results—the most important first step in any case. Those who are sufficiently interested will no doubt have to examine the merits of the new paradigm more closely to weed out inaccuracies and add new concepts if the paradigm is to continue to facilitate progress.

3. See Peter Kropotkin, *Mutual Aid: A Factor of Evolution* (New York: New York University Press, 1972).

4. If human society and our environment remained very different from neolithic conditions and persisted for an equally long period, we would have to consider further evolution of "human nature." But more pressing matters are likely to change things first. If increasing understanding of the evolutionary process does not change the nature of our subjection to its "laws," advances in genetic engineering certainly will. But these issues are not important to our present purposes.

376

5. Our view of human nature owes immeasurably to the work of Noam Chomsky. Readers might consult any of his more popular books on linguistics, for example, *Language and Problems of Knowledge, The Managua Lectures* (Boston: MIT Press, 1988).

6. We wish to practice no sleight of hand here. The fact that we do not have wings distinguishes us from pigeons. The fact that we can mate only with other humans distinguishes us from all other species. But these "physical" genetic differences are not what is critical to a human nature-based approach to welfare theory. The key assertion is that part of human nature includes particular intellectual, psychological, emotional attributes, and potentials that have important implications for what social arrangements will prove "stable" and "fulfilling." This is the approach we develop.

7. See David Cohen, ed., *Psychologists on Psychology*, (New York: Tapplinger, 1977) for a critique of Skinnerian approaches to psychology and policy-making.

8. Richard Lichtman, "Marx and Freud: Marx's Theory of Human Nature," part 3, *Socialist Revolution* 7, no. 36 (November-December 1977): 45. To avoid any misrepresentation, we should note that Lichtman argues against this interpretation of Marx's views on the subject. However, he argues that this is, in fact, the interpretation of most Marxists.

9. Karl Marx, *Capital, Vol. 1, The Process of Capitalist Production* (New York: International Publishers, 1967), 178.

10. Even if, as Kelvin Lancaster suggested, one defines utilities as functions of activities rather than commodities, or defines preference orderings on an activity space rather than a commodity space, this problem persists. The question of how a particular activity was selected and how society determined that access to different activities and their consequent enjoyment was to be distributed is of welfare significance for humans.

11. It is worth noting that Jurgen Habermas and many of his disciples consider communicative structures as important as decision-making structures. When they assess the processes as well as results of social decision making, they find the fairness and efficiency of communication systems as important as the rules of decision making. The relevant questions are: Who has access to what information? What means for conveying information and opinions exist? How is the communicative interchange organized? These are some of the interesting questions the "modern" Frankfurt school has focused on. Remarkably, just by setting minimal goals for "humane communication," members of this school have elaborated guiding values for much of society.

12. Peter Marin, "The Human Harvest," *Mother Jones* (December 1976): 38.

13. Bertell Ollman, *Alienation* (Cambridge: Cambridge University Press, 1973), 108.

14. Karl Marx, *Introduction to a Critique of Political Economy* (New York: International Publishers, 1972), 268.

15. Marin, "Human Harvest," 32.

16. As we saw in chapter 4, the unconscious way in which present actions can influence future preferences was the primary concern and focus of economists such as Pollak who focused on myopic habit formation.

17. While traditional welfare theorists have not focused attention on this dynamic, it is not difficult to extend traditional theory in ways that do so. As we will see in chapter 6, once preferences are treated as endogenous, the same analysis applied by traditional welfare theorists in human capital theory facilitates analysis of this trade-off. Moreover, the so-called "wealth effect" used to explain why those with limited means may rationally not insist on as great "compensating wage differentials" for undesirable job characteristics as those who are better-off applies here as well. See Norman Waitzman, "The Occupational Determinants of Health: A Labor Market Segmentation Analysis" (Ph.D. diss., American University, 1988) for an excellent evaluation of this approach to health risks.

18. The rather surprising extent to which this argument can be developed without making specific assumptions concerning the nature of people's preferences is a primary concern of chapter 6. But suffice it to say that the entire argument is totally foreign to traditional welfare theory and beyond the vision of the traditional paradigm.

19. Individuals choose from a limited menu of activities. Choice of menus is a social choice of how social activities will be organized and packaged by major social institutions.

20. It is sufficient for now to indicate how different welfare issues will look from the perspective of our new paradigm. Justifying the merits of our new approach is the subject of the rest of the book.

21. See Joseph Weizenbaum, *Computer Power and Human Reason* (New York: Freeman and Company, 1976); and David Noble, *America By Design* (New York: Knopf, 1977). We emphasize institutions and roles in our discussion of societal boundaries, but artifacts can have considerable importance in their own right. In some circumstances, the "boundary" of "artifacts" is so complex to use or replace or imposes such powerful operational dictates that the objects themselves delimit role possibilities.

22. This point is relevant to some naive interpretations of anarchism. Human social life without institutions is impossible. Consequently, the vision of human liberation as the abolition of social institutions is a deceptive pipe dream. The intuition common to anarchist and existentialist

thought that all social institutions mold, constrain, and limit individual human choice, no matter how gently and subtly, is well founded. But the conclusion that liberation means abolition of these constraints on individual action does not follow once we recognize that this is humanly impossible. See Albert et al., *Liberating Theory* for further discussion of a more useful conception of "liberation" as the informed and democratic choice of social institutions that permit maximum development and fulfillment of human potentials.

23. In our view, Thorstein Veblen, founder of the institutional school of economics, and Talcott Parsons, a giant of modern sociology, both underestimated the potential for applying the human tool of consciousness to the task of analyzing and evaluating the effects of social institutions. This led Veblen to overstate his case against what he termed "teleological" theories of history and rendered Parsonian sociology powerless to explain the process of social change. While many could be cited on this subject, we find the work of Anthony Giddens particularly useful in avoiding the pitfalls of unjustifiable "functionalism" and sterile behavioral sociology. We hope we have applied Giddens' insights in constructing our paradigm and theory.

See Anthony Giddens, *Central Problems in Social Theory: Action, Structure, and Contradiction* (Berkeley: University of California Press, 1979); *Contemporary Critique of Historical Materialism* (Berkeley: University of California Press, 1981); *Social Theory and Modern Sociology* (Cambridge: Polity in association with Blackwell, 1987); and *Social Theory Today* (Cambridge: Polity in association with Blackwell, 1987).

24. See Albert et al., *Liberating Theory.*

25. The distinction between primary and produced inputs is also critical in studying the relation between price determination and income distribution in private enterprise market economies. For an excellent treatment see G. Abraham Frois and E. Berrebi, *Theory of Value, Prices, and Accumulation* (Cambridge: Cambridge University Press, 1979).

26. Of course, human economic efforts are often required to discover and make available natural resources we define as "nonproducible." And in some cases human processes can produce facsimiles of nature's products. With sufficient crushing, shale will become oil, and coal will become diamond. And sometimes it is possible to develop producible "synthetic" substitutes for dwindling resources. In any case, we do not suggest the distinction between produced inputs and resources to ignore these possibilities, but simply to allow the framework to assess properly the impact of economic choices that deplete resources or otherwise alter ecological balances.

27. While it is often not important for welfare theoretic purposes to account for the duration and intensity of efforts carried out in consumption activities, we discuss important exceptions below.

28. There are additional conceptual and practical problems in defining and measuring "services" as outputs, but we have no particular contributions to make on this subject.

29. The levels of fulfillment, which we define as the human outputs of economic activity, are not the only human consequences of economic activity. Indeed a critical difference between an endogenous as opposed to exogenous conception of preferences is the potential transformation (or reinforcement) of human characteristics that results from engaging in an economic activity. But rather than call the transformations of human characteristics human outputs, we will analyze these highly important human consequences as changes in the values of human state variables.

30. "On the job training" is one of the ways this far more general phenomenon has received attention. A transformation deemed to be an improvement in workers' specifically job related skills is focused on as one of the results of organizing and carrying out the activity in a particular manner.

31. We do not mean to imply that all activity of women in the home should be conceptualized through economic metaphors. Quite the contrary, we are highly critical of "economistic" interpretations that presume these activities will only be taken seriously if interpreted as "economic production." Elsewhere we have argued strenuously that many of these activities are best conceptualized as kinship activity—activity oriented primarily toward satisfying sexual, effective, and child-rearing needs organized according to a particular (usually sexist) sex/gender system or division of responsibilities and rewards—and that they are no less important for being so.

But some activities usually assigned to housewives are appropriately conceived as primarily economic. We submit that in most such cases they fit the category of "consumption activity" better than "production," and that our paradigm provides for a serious treatment of those efforts just as it does "productive" efforts. To put it differently, the traditional paradigm, and some of its better-known competitors generate a biased attitude toward economic as opposed to noneconomic activity, and toward production as opposed to consumption activity. Only if one denigrates the importance of kinship and consumption activity is there a problem with applying these labels to activity in the home primarily carried out by women.

The paradigm presented in this chapter attempts to overcome both these biases. In our view many treatments of "housework" by Marxist and Marxist/Feminist authors in the 1970s incorporated the biases and resulted in skewed analyses. For one example by an author with whom we are in agreement on most matters, see Ann Ferguson, "Women as a New Revolutionary Class," in *Between Labor and Capital*, Pat Walker, ed. (Boston:

South End Press, 1979). In Michael Albert and Robin Hahnel, *Marxism and Socialist Theory* (Boston: South End Press, 1981), we elaborate our criticism of this literature.

32. In this regard economists have adopted the approach of philosophers rather than psychologists. For most of us this is an unconscious choice. In our view it is far more justifiable for welfare theory than the so-called "analytical" theory of consumer behavior. But in any case, it is interesting to note that the "basic needs" school of development theory is perhaps the only area in which economists adopt a psychological paradigm rather than a philosophical one. Abraham Maslow's hierarchy of needs is an admirable paradigm for economists working in this genre.

33. Readers might inquire about the relationship between our concept of an "activity possibility set" and the traditional concept of a firm's "production possibility set." The traditional concept is aptly described as a book of blueprints in which each page represents a way to turn a vector of inputs into a vector of outputs known to a particular firm. Since in the traditional conception no particular people inhabit firms, it is a little difficult to know "to whom" these technologies must be known, or why the book of blueprints would not be the same for all firms. In any case, in its usual variant, the production possibility set is limited only by technologies known to a firm at a particular time. In contrast, $A(i,t)$ is limited not only by technologies known to the members of a particular group i, at time t, but by individual and group human characteristics of group i at time t. For example, suppose a particular activity of which group i was fully aware required behavior members of group i were either individually or collectively incapable of carrying out. The activity could not be undertaken.

CHAPTER 6. A NEW WELFARE THEORY

1. Truly individual activities are incorporated in this formalization as activities carried out by a group, i, with a single member.

2. Differences in intensity can be handled in either of two ways. Hours of indoor carpentry at intensity A and hours of indoor carpentry at intensity B can be defined as two different elements in "work space." Alternatively, we can define hours of indoor carpentry as a single element of work space and attach the appropriate intensity rating to that element before applying our instantaneous preference ordering to evaluate the welfare effects of the work activity, as was explained in chapter 5.

3. Insisting that expenditures be covered out of current income introduces the complication that an individual's marginal utility of income will probably differ in different time periods. While this is somewhat bother-

some, the additional complexities of permitting individuals to borrow and lend are more burdensome still, and in no way affect any of our results.

4. Readers familiar with the neoclassical literature on endogenous preferences will no doubt be struck by the difference between the conclusions we derive and the conclusions published by Pollak, El-Safty, Hammond, and Gintis. In most cases this is not because their conclusions do not follow from their premises, as we hope is the case for us as well. Pollak, El-Safty, and Hammond found that only in very restricted cases would individual optimization yield anything we should consider a welfare optimum, because they assumed *myopic* adaptive behavior in which individuals optimize at each moment according to their instantaneous preference ordering *ignoring* the preference development effects of these choices. Moreover, by concentrating on *habit* as the kind of endogeneity, they (correctly in their case) envisioned serious existence problems due to nonconvexities. Gintis did err in concluding that many of the multiple equilibria he envisioned would be nonoptimal because, while he conceded a perfect knowledge counterpart to the CPS, he lapsed into thinking in the same terms as Pollak, El-Safty, and Hammond—namely of myopic, local, maximizing machines. Our conclusions follow rather directly from our model of endogenous preferences *with perfect knowledge* since these effectively create global maximizing machines insightful enough to scan all individual local maxima and select only individually global maxima.

5. This proposition was first demonstrated by Herb Gintis, "Welfare Criteria with Endogenous Preferences: The Economics of Education," *International Economics Review* 15, no. 2 (June 1974): 422, Theorem 3.

6. If some of the budget constraints were nonbinding, or if the solution point were not interior, we could model the individual's maximization problem as a general nonlinear programming problem and analyze the full set of Kuhn-Tucker conditions. However, since nothing relevant to the discussion is lost by considering the simpler case, for convenience we will do so.

7. We ignore the complication of discrepancies between private and social cost and individual and social benefit for now.

8. While this assumption may appear more restrictive than modern traditional treatments, we do not believe this objection is consequential. We have chosen to present this part of our argument using the admittedly outdated concepts of utility functions and marginal utilities simply because the exposition is easier. But none of our results depend on this simplification. In this context, our assumption of diminishing marginal utilities is merely the analogue of the assumptions of diminishing rates of substitution in consumption or convex sets of at-least-as-preferred-as consumption bundles—common assumptions in modern traditional treatments necessary for deriving well-known results.

9. K. Arrow and F. Hahn, *General Competitive Analysis* (San Francisco, Holden-Day, 1971), chap. 6, briefly treats the case where prices affect utilities in the sense of conspicuous consumption. But the sense in which utility depends on price due to our conceptualization of endogenous preferences is entirely different from the cases analyzed in Arrow and Hahn, and their analysis is, therefore, not relevant to our concerns.

10. Quite to the contrary, we will argue in chapters 7 and 8 that there are major problems with both private enterprise and market institutions, which in combination with endogenous preferences produce a snowballing non-optimality of double proportions in even the most perfectly competitive, private enterprise market economies.

11. However, as we explain below, there is good reason to believe that extending the convexity assumptions to endogenous well-being functions stretches credulity more than under traditional conditions. Put differently, it appears additional reasons to fear nonconvexities when preferences are recognized to be endogenous make the usual convexity assumptions less plausible.

12. Gerard Debreu, *Theory of Value* (New York: Wiley, 1959), chap. 5; or K. Arrow, "General Economic Equilibrium: Purpose, Analytic Techniques, Collective Choice," *American Economic Review* 64, no. 3 (June 1974): 253-72.

13. See Debreu, *Theory of Value*, chap. 4, sec. 4.8 for treatment of these technical complications.

14. Ibid., sec. 4.9.

15. Arrow and Hahn, *General Competitive Analysis*, chap. 7.

16. Peter Dorman is a notable exception who has developed this theme recently in a number of working papers soon to be published.

17. See Emile Durkheim, *The Rules of Sociological Method*, 8th ed. (Chicago: University of Chicago Press, 1938); and Max Weber, *The Theory of Social and Economic Organization* (New York: Oxford University Press, 1947) for compelling arguments from two founders of modern interactive social theory .

18. Arrow and Hahn, *General Competitive Analysis*, chap. 7; and R. N. Anderson, M. A. Khan, and S. Rashid, "Approximate Equilibrium with Bounds Independent of Preferences," *Review of Economic Studies* 44 (1982): 473-75.

19. Debreu, *Theory of Value*, sec. 6.3.

20. Ibid., sec. 6.4; and Arrow, "General Economic Equilibrium," 263-64.

21. Readers still plagued by visions of "multiple self-fulfilling equilibria," many of which are socially inefficient, should recall the assumptions

inherent in Debreuvian models of perfect foresight and a single choice for all time periods, which was the model Gintis finally agreed to use when drawing welfare conclusions, i.e., his "complete knowledge counterpart to the individual's CPO." Gintis' socially inefficient nightmares are effectively ruled out by individuals who would reject them as individually nonoptimal when scanning all possible trajectories prior to making their choices for each and every time period before beginning. Pollak, El-Safty, and Hammond's conclusions that "long-run demand functions can only be rationalized by a utility function if and only if the short-run utility function is such that any good that experiences learning or taste change is separable from all other goods" (A. El-Safty, "Adaptive Behavior, Demand and Preferences," *Journal of Economic Theory*, no. 13 [1976]: 298) also stems from their decision not to grant individuals perfect knowledge of their "meta" utility function so they can maximize using this information, but instead must maximize "myopically" with their short-run utility functions incognizant of preference development effects.

22. When we say the economy was a marshmallow influenced only by people's "economic wills" we do not mean it could furnish any technology, supply of natural resources, or initial human characteristics people might want. We mean with what traditional economic theory calls a particular set of "givens," the economy was a marshmallow to be molded entirely by people's wills.

23. It should be clear that endogenous preferences have nothing to do with the economic system. They are a property that people can be presumed to have or not have. If private enterprise market economies generated no inefficiencies, recognizing that their inhabitants are imbued with this capacity could not make them do so!

24. We also assume no exchange of goods between firms and consumers can increase a consumer's satisfaction without decreasing a firm's output or increase a firm's output without decreasing some consumer's satisfaction. In other words, we assume no misallocation of goods between use in production and consumption.

25. Clarification is in order because "net marginal social costs" would be redundant in some conceptualizations. We define the "marginal social cost" of supplying an activity to be all additional costs to society of making an additional unit available irrespective of who consumes it. These costs would include not only the increase in costs to the supplier, but any additional costs to society that the economic system, for whatever reason, fails to charge the supplier, e.g., the costs of pollution as well as inputs that must be paid for. Marginal social costs and marginal private costs would be equal if and only if there were no externalities in production activities. We define "net marginal social cost" as the marginal social cost minus the

benefits all others enjoy as a result of the fact that the good has been made available to a particular individual. In "private" activities the two are the same. But in "consumption" activities with "external" or "public" effects, marginal social costs and net marginal social costs will differ. In other words, net marginal social costs and marginal social costs would be equal if and only if there were no externalities in consumption activities. So while marginal social cost is determined entirely by conditions within the production sector, net marginal social cost depends on the nature of consumption activity and consumers' preferences as well. Moreover, the net marginal social cost of something will, in general, vary depending on who "consumes" it. The net marginal social cost of supplying person i with another unit of activity b will be different from the net marginal social cost of supplying person j with another unit of activity b if i and j do not benefit equally from the *other* person's consumption of b.

26. Note that definitions (M 3.3) could have been stated in terms of enhancing appreciation of one activity relative to the other and developing one characteristic relative to the other since it is perfectly possible an action might have developmental or appreciation consequences on more than one characteristic or good. In this case (M 3.3) would specify: engaging in activity y increases characteristic S more than P as compared to engaging in activity x; engaging in activity x increases characteristic P more than S as compared to engaging in activity y; characteristic S enhances appreciation of activity a relative to activity z as compared to characteristic P; and characteristic P enhances appreciation of activity z relative to activity a as compared to activity S. But formulating the model in this way only complicates matters without enriching results.

27. This is a further simplification. In our model of an individual with endogenous preferences, we assumed the overall individual welfare function was a linear weighted sum of utility in each time period where the weights represented the individual's subjective rates of time discount. Here we specify weights of one, thereby assuming a zero rate of time discount. While such an assumption might not be farfetched for the immortals we have created, the real point is that none of our results are affected by the additional simplification.

28. Of course if providing i with a unit of b or c to consume does not affect the utilities of others, the ratio of net marginal social costs reduces to the ratio of marginal social costs. Some might object that in this formulation of net marginal social costs we have only included the immediate preference fulfillment effects on well-being for $j \neq i$, and not incorporated the future preference development effects on well-being. While true, the additional complication does not affect our results. Moreover, since our proof considers the production of goods a and z, neither of which have developmental effects, the formulation is accurate for the case we will treat.

29. If, and only if, all individuals are charged the net marginal social costs of providing them with activities will the sum of individual demands that yields the market demand be such that marginal social costs will be equal to marginal social benefits. To see this, if i is charged an amount equal to the net marginal social cost of providing him or her another unit of an activity, under competitive conditions i will demand that activity up to the point where the marginal private benefit is equal to the net marginal social benefit thereby establishing: {Marginal Benefit to i = Marginal Social Cost - Marginal Benefit to all others}. But in this case: {Marginal Social Cost = Marginal Benefit to i + Marginal Benefit to all others} = {Marginal Benefit to all}, or Marginal Social Benefit. And clearly, charging i anything different than the net marginal social cost of the activity will leave Marginal Social Cost not equal to Marginal Social Benefit.

30. We make the additional assumption of no corner solutions here to simplify the argument, but note that all our conclusions are valid without this assumption as well.

31. As explained above, the "optimal" prices to charge individual purchasers are the net marginal social cost of supplying the individual with another unit of the activity.

32. When we say neoclassical theory here, we mean traditional welfare theory, which treats preferences as if they were exogenous.

33. The logic of this adjustment is, of course, a primary subject of traditional price theory, and the conclusion is warranted except in the case of "Giffen" goods.

34. In part we did not assume this because it was not necessary for our conclusions. In part we did not assume this in order to distinguish our analysis from any kind of habit formation, be it myopic or not.

35. Excluding technical concerns, the assumption of endogenous preferences does not affect theorems guaranteeing the existence of general equilibria in market systems, or the ability of a procedure to generate feasible plans in planning systems. We proved this result for market systems as Theorem 6.3 and will prove it for centrally planned systems in chapter 9. We relegate this part of our summary to a footnote because when we speak of "any economy," as we did previously in the text, this presupposes a system that has a general equilibrium or can produce a feasible plan. Any model we theorized that did not have a general equilibrium or generate a feasible plan could not "be" an economy and should be discarded as an internally inconsistent model that cannot represent "an economy"— even in theory.

36. Rawls stated this qualification as follows: "Each person is to have an equal right to the most extensive basic liberty compatible with a similar

liberty for others." (John Rawls, *A Theory of Justice* [Cambridge, Mass.: Harvard University Press, 1971], 60.)

37. We do not mean to imply that this issue could be easily resolved by empirical studies. In our view paradigms do have a legitimate role to play in just such situations.

38. In a slightly different conception—more applicable to artisans than farmers—each actor is seen as being capable of producing the tools required before going on to use them to produce whatever products he or she will eventually consume or trade. This reduces the concept of "wherewithal" entirely to personal capacities since now no specific tools are required to engage in an activity; they can be self-produced prior to the activity—or essentially as part of a larger redefined activity. Once this is accomplished, all that is necessary to permit individuals to switch from one "choice activity set" to another should they so desire is to grant all the capability to learn how to make the tools required to produce any product. In other words, in its most operational form the classical liberal paradigm renders individual economic choice activity sets not only independent but identical. That neoclassical theory tells us the outcome of an exchange economy with identical production possibility sets is indeterminate has seldom been seen as contradictory.

39. In terms of our qualitative model, the more "input flows" an activity requires to be supplied from other activities, the less "self-sufficient" it is. Or, put differently, the greater "division of labor" it presumes.

40. B is in no position to infringe upon the liberty of A if we assume that B cannot make A do what would enable B to do what B would like to do as B's part of the division of labor. Of course, if B can compel A to carry out A's part in the division of labor that B prefers to mutual autarchy, then B is infringing on A's liberty in an obvious way. We wished to point out the less obvious way in which A infringes upon B's liberty by choosing to act "independently."

41. This is commonly referred to as "left adventurism."

42. This "error" is commonly referred to as "right opportunism."

43. At the risk of sounding ridiculous to those outside the profession, an economists' explanation of the well-being generated by closely knit families would be that family solidarity creates powerful positive externalities that multiply the overall well-being that results from the good fortunes of individual members—and we are not referring to prolonged visits of poor relations and zero interest rate loans between kin.

44. See the chapters on "community" in Michael Albert and Robin Hahnel, *Marxism and Socialist Theory* (Boston: South End Press, 1981); and Michael Albert et al., *Liberating Theory* (Boston: South End Press, 1986).

45. See our treatment in chapter 1.

46. It is interesting to note that according to Rawls any objection to an increase in inequality that improved the position of the worst-off could only be the result of envy. On these grounds Rawls refuses to sustain any objections to increases in inequality that have the effect of improving the "objective" position of the worst-off. Our inclination is to be unable to accept great deviations from material equality as anything other than evidence of failure to apply equality of consideration sincerely. After all, "super people"—somehow deserving of much greater material reward for their participation in joint social endeavors—only exist in the context of a particular set of social conditions, values, and reward structures. Ultimately the development of solidarity requires eliminating any circumstances that translate differences in talents or skills, that most certainly do, will, and *should* exist, into differences in material well-being and power. In other words, there *would* be Magic Johnsons and Albert Einsteins whose talents are appreciated. But they would not be paid millions. In our view, since failure to rectify the circumstances that result in inequalities—even should they improve the material well-being of the worst-off—"objectively" limits solidarity, we have an "efficiency" reason for possibly sustaining objections to such inequalities. But perhaps the difference is only one of semantics: what we see as "refusal of the disadvantaged to have solidarity with those who don't put their money where their mouth is," Rawls calls "envy."

47. Robert Nozick, *Anarchy, State, and Utopia* (New York: Basic Books, 1974), 310.

48. One of the authors is a parent of identical twins. Besides sharing the same genes they have been each other's most important "environment" both inside the womb and since birth as well. They could have developed similar characteristics, but instead they have developed quite differently (which should come as no surprise to anyone who has known genetically identical siblings). The claim here is that by developing very different characteristics, and thereby providing one another with very different "environments," they have "optimized." Not that things have turned out perfectly! But identical developmental trajectories would have been a nightmare. More seriously, the psychological literature on twins affirms the importance of different development trajectories.

49. One does not have to assume "risk aversion" on people's part to deduce that it is rational to minimize risk in this way!

50. For example, Veblen clearly saw an inherent contradiction between what he called the human instinct to workmanship and the acquisitive instinct. In our human nature-based approach we postulated no such "acquisitive instinct," nor did we postulate any "aggressive" instinct or

innate need to dominate. We find institutional explanations more compelling explanations for the ubiquity of acquisitive, aggressive, power-seeking behavior and think these kinds of behavior are best explained as the outgrowth of desires to satisfy "natural" needs for security, social esteem, and self-management under particular "contradictory" social conditions. But others may disagree.

51. By "antisocial behavior" we mean behavior that is contrary to the interests of species survival, not behavior in opposition to established social norms and institutions which, depending on the "social rationality" of the norms, may or may not be contrary to the interests of species survival.

52. Evidence in favor of this view will be presented in part 3.

53. When we say "believe" we understand that belief may be unconscious or implicit. Indeed one of our major contentions is that very often the most important "beliefs" of theorists are unconscious and implicit.

54. By our treatments of classical utilitarianism, modern neoclassical theory, and modern contractarianism in chapter 1, it must have been obvious we recognized differences between them. As we were careful to explain, the entire philosophical basis of modern contractarianism is different from utilitarian and neoclassical theory. Why then did we lump them together under the label "traditional welfare theory"? The full reason can only now be apparent. What we have just explained is that their implicit conception of preference formation is the same. In other words, in this respect they are based on the same paradigm—the traditional paradigm we have criticized and proposed replacing. We believe that those who have used modern contractarian concepts have also accepted other aspects of the traditional paradigm such as the presumption that private effects are pervasive and external effects exceptional. Classification of modern contractarianism as part of traditional welfare theory does not rest on its treatment of preferences (or "individual's conceptions of the good") as exogenous alone. The criterion we used for classification purposes was the paradigm accepted by those using the approach, which they sought to express in different theoretical form. The philosophical form the theory takes was not our criterion for classification purposes, although it might well be for other purposes.

55. If the joys of conspicuous wealth, aggression, and domination are so attractive that people are loath to choose paths that do not afford them even small probabilities of enjoying these joys, why not consider "slave for a day" type solutions? Take the presumed aggregate benefits of enhancing dominating tendencies and instead of permitting people to "win" or "lose" individual benefits permanently, we could insist on temporary rich (and poor), temporary mugger (and muggee), and temporary boss (and worker) outcomes. It is curious this has seldom occurred to those who claim to

prefer a rugged, roll-the-dice, Horatio Alger, John Wayne world. But then many argue for this from the heights of power and with the benefit of hindsight, rather than from the original position behind the veil of ignorance.

56. There is a difference between the debate over the maximin principle versus maximizing expected benefits and what we consider here worth noting. The maximin principle justifies any change that improves the position of the worst-off. Maximizing expected benefits justifies any change that generates positive aggregate benefits. The maximin principle could fail to approve a change that had positive aggregate benefits, just as maximizing expected benefits could fail to approve a change that would improve the position of the worst-off. But the cases we discuss here all generate aggregate benefits by assumption. What we are comparing are on the one hand development trajectories that not only generate aggregate benefits (and, therefore, increase expected individual benefits) but are Pareto improvements as well (greater self-management and solidarity), as compared to trajectories that increase expected individual benefits (by assumption) but are not Pareto improvements because some will become worse off (greater acquisitiveness and aggression). It is still possible that people who are not "risk-averse" would choose the latter over the former, but in our view this "counterargument" is weaker in our context than in the well-known debate over Rawls' maximin principle.

57. See Jon Wisman, "Economic Reform for Humanity's Greatest Struggle" (the prize-winning essay for the $10,000, 1987 Speiser Essay Contest), for a highly persuasive argument for self-management on precisely these grounds. A slightly adapted version was published as Jon Wisman, "An Economic Response to the Threat of Nuclear War" Forum for Social Economics, Villanova University College of Commerce and Finance and Temple University School of Business and Management, 1987.

CHAPTER 7. MARKETS

1. Ernest Mandel, "In Defense of Socialist Planning," *New Left Review*, no. 159 (September-October 1986): 5-38; and Alec Nove, *The Economics of Feasible Socialism* (London: George Allen and Unwin, 1983). Lest there be any doubt about which way the wind blows still, see Diane Elson, "Socialization of the Market," *New Left Review*, no. 172 (November-December 1988): 3-44.

2. See C. J. Bliss, "Prices, Markets, and Planning," *Economic Journal* 82 (March 1972): 87-100, for an excellent example of the terms of the debate from the perspective of a traditional critic of markets. See Allan Buchanan, *Ethics, Efficiency, and the Market* (Totowa, N.J.: Roman and Littlefield,

1985), chap. 2, for an excellent summary of "Efficiency Arguments For and Against the Market," 14-46, from the traditional perspective. Charles E. Lindblom, *Politics and Markets* (New York: Basic Books, 1977) is another well-known treatment.

3. In this case, as in many others, "new" ideas are seldom completely new. The market perfection theorem was very much a theme of the Austrian School, which had long objected to the traditional neoclassical truce regarding markets. See Don Lavoie, "A Critique of the Standard Account of the Socialist Calculation Debate," *The Journal of Libertarian Studies* 5, no. 1 (Winter 1981); and idem, *Rivalry and Central Planning: The Socialist Calculation Debate Reconsidered* (Cambridge: Cambridge University Press, 1985) for a modern discussion of themes emphasized by von Mises and Hayek.

4. Oscar Lange and Frederick Taylor, *On the Economic Theory of Socialism* (New York: Monthly Review Press, 1964).

5. To contrast PuEEMMEs with more familiar private enterprise market systems: in PrEMEs buying shares of stock gains entrance to stockholders' meetings where one can cast as many votes as one's shares of stock on any proposition. But in employee-managed enterprises, simply being an employee gives you the same number of votes in the workers' council as every other employee—and there are no other voters.

6. The same critics also claim that equilibria of employee-managed market economies are less stable than equilibria of their private enterprise counterparts and that adjustment dynamics are perverse. In our opinion, this conclusion is also more a product of inappropriate choice of model than of any actual tendencies of PuEEMMEs. But we do not treat this issue here. In models where labor is the only input in production, and no entry and exit of new firms is permitted, adjustment in PuEEMMEs is certainly more problematical than in PrEMEs. But we have chosen to ignore all problems of dynamic adjustment of market systems in an effort to give market economies every benefit of the doubt and focus on other concerns. In this spirit we ignore a major component of the literature critical of PuEEMMEs.

7. Benjamin Ward, "The Firm in Illyria, Market Syndicalism," *American Economic Review* 48 no. 4 (September 1958): 566-89; idem, *The Socialist Economy: A Study of Organizational Alternatives* (New York: Random House, 1967), chap. 8; Evsey Domar, "The Socialist Collective Farm as a Producer Cooperative," *American Economic Review* 56 (1966). For more recent literature parting from the view that PuEEMME enterprises seek to maximize profits per employee see: John Bonin, "The Theory of the Labor Managed Firm from the Membership's Perspective with Implications for Marshallian Industry Supply," *Journal of Comparative Economics* 5, no. 4 (December 1981): 337-51; John Bonin and Luis Putterman, "Economies

of Cooperation and the Labor Managed Economy," in *Fundamentals of Pure and Applied Economics* and the *Encyclopedia of Economics*, J. Lesourne and H. Sonnenschein, eds. (1985); Norman Ireland and Peter Law, *The Economics of Labor-Managed Enterprises* (New York: St. Martins Press, 1982); and J. M. Montias, "On the Labor-Managed Firm in a Competitive Environment," *Journal of Comparative Economics* 10, no. 1 (1986): 2-8.

8. Again, we note that critics also charge that PuEEMMEs are less able than PrEMEs to adjust to new general equilibria when technologies and preferences change. But since we have focused on the properties of market equilibria and deliberately left issues of dynamic adjustment aside, we will not concern ourselves with this side of the debate.

9. This is true for the same reason enterprises in Debreuvian models of competitive PrEMEs cannot be expected to achieve equal rates of profit on "capital advanced." What Debreu calls "profits" are actually rents or "quasi rents" that are the result of the unique technological capabilities of a particular enterprise, which are not competed away because each firm is distinguished by its unique production possibility set and the number of firms is fixed in his model.

10. Gerard Debreu, *Theory of Value* (New York: Wiley, 1959), chap. 6. More precisely in his model and analysis

1. For PuEEMME the definition of an equilibrium (Debreu, sec. 6.2) must be changed to read: "y_j* maximizes py_j/y_h on Y_j, for every j where h is the input labor" instead of "y_j* maximizes py_j on Y_j for every j" (p. 93).

2. In the proof that an equilibrium is an optimum (Debreu, sec. 6.3), although it is still true in PuEEMME that "x_i* minimizes p_a on X_i," it is no longer the case that "$-y_j*$ minimizes p_a on $-Y_j$" so the conclusion that "$\sum x_i* - \sum y_j*$, which is equal to ω, minimizes p_a on $G = \sum X_i - \sum Y_j$"—which is necessary to show that $[(x_i*), (y_j*)]$ is an optimum (Debreu, 94)—no longer follows.

3. In the proof that an optimum is an equilibrium (Debreu, sec. 6.4), an optimum allocation still requires that $\hat{y}_j$ is such that "$-\hat{y}_j$ minimizes p_a on $-Y_j$ for every j." But it is not true that $-\hat{y}_j$ is the same as $-y_j*$ the equilibrium production such that y_j* maximizes $py_j \neq y_h$ on Y_j.

11. Branko Horvat, *Towards a Theory of Planned Economy* (Belgrade: Yugoslav Institute of Economic Research, 1964); idem, "Critical Notes on the Theory of the Labor Managed Firm and Some Macroeconomic Implications," *Komunikacije* (1972); and Jan Vanek, *The Economics of Workers' Management: A Yugoslav Case Study* (London: Allen and Unwin, 1972).

12. Horvat, "Critical Notes," 290.

13. Vanek, *Economics of Workers' Management*, 174-76.

14. Branko Horvat, "The Theory of the Worker Managed Firm Revisited," *Journal of Comparative Economics* 10, no. 1 (1986): 12.

15. Jaroslav Vanek, *The General Theory of Labor Self-Managed Economies* (Ithaca, N.Y.: Cornell University Press, 1970), 135.

16. Dilip Madan, "Long-run Competitive Equilibrium and the Capital Controversy," Economics Discussion Paper no. 3/74, (Bundoora Victoria, Australia: Department of Economics, La Trobe University, April 1974). William Novshek and Hugo Sonnenschein, "General Equilibrium with Free Entry: A Synthetic Approach to the Theory of Perfect Competition," *Journal of Economic Literature* 25, no. 3 (September 1987): 1281-1306, published a similar model.

17. Of course, in perfectly competitive PrEMEs there are no monopsonistic input markets. But if any such markets should become less than perfectly competitive, it is well known that a private enterprise market economy fails to produce socially efficient outcomes. PuESMMEs of the Lange-Lerner-Taylor variety are not subject to this problem even should input market structures be monopsonistic.

18. Again, perfectly competitive PrEMEs do not have monopolistic product markets. But should a market become monopolistic in private enterprise market economies inefficiency results, whereas in PuESMMEs it would not.

19. In any case, the "pseudomarket" adjustment mechanism, which was inexplicably proposed only for intermediate goods, is not a necessary feature of PuESMMEs. One could postulate a PuESMME with "free-market" adjustments everywhere, or with pseudomarket adjustments everywhere, for that matter. In any case, this issue affects dynamic adjustment and stability of equilibria, but does not affect the optimality properties of equilibria once they are achieved.

20. It should be noted that losses are not necessarily a sign of lack of effort or inefficiency in Lange-Lerner-Taylor enterprises. It is possible that losses are precisely the result of obeying the managerial rules that are substituted for the criterion of profit maximization.

21. Under Lange's bonus distribution rule, all workers would be induced to work too much and take too little leisure time given their actual preferences for income versus leisure.

22. PuESMMEs do not fare nearly so well in the eyes of our new approach. PuESMMEs share with PrEMEs the dubious distinction of being doubly inefficient according to our analysis, whereas PuEEMMEs and PuECPEs display snowballing inefficiency along only a single axis. But this argument is yet to come.

393

23. As the reader likely suspects, there are reasons for expecting such biases in both PuEEMME and PuESMME according to our new welfare paradigm, as we will see shortly.

24. Marx's famous "general law of capitalist accumulation" is the best known of such theories. But there has been a resurgence of interest among modern political economists in "the political economy of the business cycle." For example, see: Rayford Boddy and James Crotty, "Class Conflict and Macro-Policy," *Review of Radical Political Economics* 7 no. 1 (Spring 1975): 1-17; Thomas Weisskopf, "Marxist Crisis Theory and the Rate of Profit in the Postwar U.S. Economy," *Cambridge Journal of Economics* 3 no. 4 (December 1979): 341-78; Robin Hahnel and Howard Sherman, "Income Distribution Over the Business Cycle," *Journal of Economic Issues* 13 (March 1982): 49-73; Samuel Bowles and Herb Gintis, "The Crisis of Liberal Democratic Capitalism," *Politics and Society* 11 no. 1 (1982): 69-79; and Howard Sherman, "Changes in the Character of the U.S. Business Cycle," *Review of Radical Political Economics* 18, nos. 1 and 2 (Summer 1986): 190-204.

25. The development of post-Keynesian disequilibrium theory is one example. See Axel Leijonhufvud, *On Keynesian Economics and the Economics of Keynes* (New York: Oxford University Press, 1968); and Robert Clower, *Monetary Theory: Selected Readings* (Harmondsworth: Penguin, 1969). For a brief, but excellent summary presentation see Laurence Harris, *Monetary Theory* (New York: McGraw Hill, 1981), chap. 13.

26. One of the foremost scholars of PuEEMMEs published a whole book on the subject. Branko Horvat, *Business Cycles in Yugoslavia* (White Plains: International Arts and Sciences Press, 1971).

27. Such is the case for Lange, Taylor, and Lerner's version of PuESMME, as we pointed out above.

28. See Paul Blumberg, *Industrial Democracy: The Sociology of Participation* (New York: Schocken Books, 1969).

29. See Maurice Dobb, *Soviet Economic Development Since 1917* (New York: International Publishers, 1968).

30. In a similar vein, the ability of producers in a single unit to make sensible choices about their activity depends on their knowledge of their productive possibilities. But if one does not envision workers deciding how to organize their own activities, but instead obeying instructions from an owner or manager, then, obviously, it is the owner or manager who must be aware of the possibilities in order to make informed decisions.

31. We have obviously arrived at the traditional view of markets as cybernetic miracles that dates back at least as far as Adam Smith. Markets

eliminate the need for anyone to receive information about what is, without doubt, very extensive and complicated interrelations. As long as actors understand their individual goals and possibilities they need not know anything about others' situations for a market system to function effectively. The miracle is not so much the information that markets supply since they supply precious little information at all. The miracle is rather that actors need not know anything about others to make their choices in market economies. As a matter of fact, providing everyone with as much information about others as they have about themselves would presumedly not change the decisions they make one iota in a competitive market economy.

32. Although there are important differences between barter and monetized exchange systems, they are irrelevant to our purposes and we can safely ignore the issue.

33. Paul Sweezy provides a typical Marxist formulation of this information-disguising property of markets: "The quantitative relation between things… is in reality only an outward form of the social relation between the commodity owners…. The exchange relation as such apart from any consideration of the quantities involved, is an expression of the fact that individual producers, each working in isolation, are in fact working for each other. Their labor, whatever they may think of the matter, has a social character, which is impressed upon it by the fact of exchange." Quoted in R. Edwards, M. Reich, and T. Weisskopf, eds., *The Capitalist System*, 1st ed. (Englewood Cliffs, N.J.: Prentice Hall, 1972), 112.

34. Indeed, as we will see shortly, Arthur DiQuattro suggests something along these lines as a way of avoiding "commodity fetishism" in PuEMEs.

35. Deleting such information when decisions are to be made by profit-maximizing owners or managers who can have no use for such details is obviously economizing.

36. Arthur DiQuattro, "Alienation and Justice in the Market," *American Political Science Review* 72, no. 3 (September, 1978): 885-86.

37. To his credit DiQuattro notes that Karl Marx did not subscribe to his view. DiQuattro quotes Marx: "Goods produced for exchange by workers who do not come into social contact with each other until they exchange their products are bound to assume a fetishistic quality in the experience of the producers" and "Fetishism… attaches itself to the products of labor as soon as they are produced as commodities, and which is therefore inseparable from the production of commodities" (DiQuattro, "Alienation and Justice in the Market," 885).

38. Karl Marx, *Economic and Philosophical Manuscripts of 1844* (New York: International Publishers, 1964), 148.

39. Adam Smith, *The Wealth of Nations* (New York: Random House, 1937), 14.

40. Letter from Karl Marx to P. V. Annekov, December 28, 1846, in Karl Marx, *Collected Writings* (New York: International Publishers, 1940).

41. Gar Alperowitz, "Socialism and a Pluralist Commonwealth," in *The Capitalist System*, Edwards et al., eds., 527.

42. Frank Roosevelt, "Market Socialism: A Humane Economy?" *Journal of Economic Issues* 3, no. 4 (December 1969): 18.

43. Different forms of taxation and expenditure policies as well as voluntary associations are included here under the title "makeshift social structures."

44. E. K. Hunt, "A Radical Critique of Welfare Economics," in *Growth, Profits, and Property,* E. Nell, ed. (Cambridge: Cambridge University Press, 1980), 244.

45. The increasingly prevalent belief among defenders of market systems that external effects can be adequately handled by an appropriate (re)definition of individual property rights completely misses the point. All that is accomplished by a redefinition of individual property rights is a swapping of who has the right to generate external effects for whom. No redefinition of individual property rights can ever move us from a situation with external effects to a system without them.

46. We defined utility functions on individual consumption and work space in chapter 6, only because the points we wished to demonstrate in that chapter—the implications of endogenous preferences—could be proved under the traditional assumption of external effect exceptionality. However, as the paradigm developed in chapter 5 made clear, we believe individual well-being functions should be defined on all human activity space.

47. K. J. Arrow, "Political and Economic Evaluation of Social Effects and Externalities," in *Frontiers of Quantitative Economics*, Michael D. Intriligator and D. A. Kendrick, eds. (Amsterdam: North Holland Publishing, 1974), 18.

48. Notice that "guide" is not the same as "solution." While the concept of self-management may help clarify the nature of what we strive for, it does not tell us how best to achieve such a decision-making arrangement. There is not even any guarantee that such an arrangement is possible.

49. There is no clear-cut goal in terms of the traditional paradigm for two reasons. When one person's individual freedom conflicts with another's in the sense that its exercise would violate the individual freedom of another, there is no guide to action. While some might claim that this is precisely the role played by property rights in the traditional paradigm, property rights only establish a clear guide if there are justifications for one system of property rights over another. But the second ambiguity arises from the

conflict between the imperative of free exercise of individual freedom with the imperative of social efficiency, which is how Arrow sees the dilemma in the quote above.

50. Again, the important "dilemma" of finding a system of economic decision making that accomplishes this aim is not a dilemma of criteria—that is of our welfare theory—but a dilemma of economic system design.

51. Hunt, "Radical Critique," 241.

52. Ibid., 245.

53. Richard Musgrave, *The Theory of Public Finance* (New York: McGraw Hill, 1959), 134.

54. Arrow, "Political and Economic Evaluation."

55. Ibid., 16.

56. Ibid., 17.

57. As a matter of fact, there is no way for the coalition of affected partners to effectively challenge claims regarding coalition membership. If the coalition is negotiating a bribe to be paid to the actor creating the external effect, it is in everyone's interest to decline membership even if they are affected. If the coalition is negotiating a bribe to be received from an actor who must obtain coalition approval to do what he or she wishes, it is in everyone's interest to claim membership even if they are unaffected.

58. Note that the only role "property rights" plays is in determining whether or not it is the coalition of affected parties that must bribe the economic actors whose activity affects them, or the economic actors who must pay the affected coalition for infringing on their "right" to be unaffected. Property rights merely establish whose "individual freedom" takes precedent over whose. If actors have the legal right to do as they please, it is the coalition of affected parties who must bribe in order to influence the decision. If the affected parties have the legal right not to be affected, actors must bribe the coalition in order to obtain their permission to do what the actors please. In either case, the dilemma we are explaining is the same. Coalition members have an incentive to misrepresent the degree to which they are affected to minimize their share of the assessment or maximize their share of the payment received, and there is no effective means for the coalition to challenge such misrepresentations without cutting off their noses to spite their faces.

59. In Arrow's opinion the argument that unrestricted bargaining will lead to Pareto efficient outcomes "is not easy to evaluate in the absence of a generally accepted concept of solution for game theory," despite arguments to the contrary by those such as Zeuthen, Harsanyi, Shapley, and Selten. And since Von Neumann and Morgenstern generalized Edgeworth's nineteenth-century conclusion that the results of such bargaining are in-

determinate, it is not difficult to foresee nonoptimal outcomes. In Arrow's words, "it is certainly a matter of common observation, perhaps especially in the field of international relations, that mutually advantageous agreements are not arrived at because each party is seeking to engross as much as possible of the common gain for itself." In a similar vein Arrow observes that "each owner of a small parcel whose acquisition is essential to the execution of the enterprise can demand the entire net benefit [in which case] an agreement may never be reached or may be long delayed. At positive discount rates even the latter outcome is not Pareto efficient. It is to avoid such losses that the coercive powers of the state are invoked by condemnation proceedings" (Arrow, "Political and Economic Evaluation," 10).

60. To keep matters tidy we would have to assume that no individual's use of the park or bridge diminishes its usefulness to others and that ships pass by the lighthouse one at a time.

61. Arrow, "Political and Economic Evaluation," 17.

62. Note that this conception already assumes interpersonal utility comparisons. Each individual reports marginal willingness to pay in terms of some moneylike good.

63. Musgrave, *Theory of Public Finance,* 134.

64. It would not matter whether taxes were proportional share, based on income, wealth, or any other criterion. As long as citizens who truly care little for the public goods are "compelled" to pay a positive tax, they would be worse off than under a market/voluntary association allocation.

65. Note that a citizen who benefits from the public goods would be made worse off by a move from a system with government back to free-market anarchy, implying that this move cannot be a Pareto improvement either. But this does not mean there is no difference between the government that collects taxes unrelated to benefits and free-market anarchy with regard to efficiency. If the government provides public goods to equate marginal social benefits and costs, it will achieve Pareto optimality irrespective of how it decides to tax people. The taxes are simply lump-sum redistributive transfers affecting equity. Free-market anarchy, on the other hand, cannot achieve Pareto optimality if there are external effects.

66. Musgrave, *Theory of Public Finance,* 133-34.

67. P. A. Samuelson, "The Pure Theory of Public Expenditures," *Review of Economic Statistics* 36 (November 1954): 387-89.

68. C. M. Tiebout, "A Pure Theory of Local Expenditures," *Journal of Political Economics* 64, no. 5 (October 1956): 416-23.

69. We interpret property, wealth, or income taxes here as an indication of "ability to pay" rather than as an indication of the degree to which one is

benefited by the maintenance of public order responsible for preserving the integrity of one's property, wealth, or income.

70. This need not be the case if the government chooses to ignore citizens' preferences in deciding how much and what kind of public goods to provide. But we would think in any system with claims to efficiency and equity citizens' preferences would be taken into consideration and individuals' preferences given more or less equal weight.

71. We emphasize that we are concerned here with issues of central finance, so that providing minorities with different packages, implementing more than one solution, and "voting with one's feet" are ruled out. In central finance, satisfying minority preferences implies denial of majority sentiments.

72. Again, we assume individuals' preferences have more or less equal weight in determining what public goods will be provided.

73. See Samuelson, "Pure Theory of Public Expenditures," 387.

74. We should note that the snowballing nonoptimality will be all the worse to the extent there is a correlation between the sign and degree of public characteristics themselves and the developmental effects of consuming such goods on future preferences. In other words, while there will be snowballing nonoptimality in any event, if engaging in social and/or private activities is "habit forming" in Pollak's sense, the snowballing nonoptimality will be all the worse.

CHAPTER 8. PRIVATE ENTERPRISE

1. It is of course skepticism regarding the likelihood of such repeated successful applications of political will that leads egalitarian critics of PrEMEs to challenge its practical claim to fairness.

2. In a Debreuvian treatment of time this is not an issue because all choices for all periods are made at once with perfect foresight—before anything starts happening. That is why "lump-sum redistribution" does not pose incentive problems in a Debreuvian world. It only happens once, and before people begin to act at that. The third fundamental welfare theorem says any Pareto optimum can result from a private enterprise market economy under the appropriate redistribution. It should be understood that Debreuvian "redistributions" reshuffle endowments for all actors in all time periods— once, before the economy begins to operate. And in Debreuvian models there are no unforeseen inequalities that accumulate and need to be ironed out over and over again along the way. All eventualities were accounted for in that single, all-seeing redistribution before things got started. But while this could happen in a Debreuvian world without influencing incen-

tives, the third fundamental welfare theorem does not tell us a particular Pareto optimum can be achieved by repeatedly redistributing along a trajectory through real time. Conservatives are correct to point out this is a misconception of the flexibility theorem that ignores the obvious incentive implications of such a policy.

3. There are always exceptions. The stability of egalitarian redistribution in Sweden, for example, is impressive. But we suspect that comparison of the degree of inequality in private and public enterprise economies on average would bear out the view that expecting egalitarian distributions from private enterprise systems is like swimming against the current: possible, but not the easiest way to cover distance through water.

4. This is not the case for human capital theory, but then human capital theory had to overcome the myopia of the traditional paradigm to which we refer before being accepted as part of traditional theory.

5. Even here there are subtleties to be considered. To the extent that human productive assets are generated through training or education, while not exactly "transferable," at least individuals that begin without them can acquire them if we are willing to wait the necessary time. Cognizance of the time that may be necessary certainly affects the "meaning" one attaches to the third fundamental theorem. But more importantly, there are presumably some human productive assets which are not the product of training or education, but due to genetic endowment. To the extent that human assets that the combination of preferences, income distribution, technology, and institutional influences render "productive" to differing extent are of this nature, there is no meaningful sense in which they could be considered transferable short of a tampered rerun of the genetic lottery!

6. Again, we are not speaking of repeated assessments that would necessarily affect incentives, but of a one-time-only assessment for all periods of time that occurs with perfect foresight prior to the first period.

7. Indeed, the very same "practical" considerations that lead opponents of PrEMEs to be unswayed by the theoretical income flexibility of PrEMEs, and insist that PrEMEs will display what they view as income distribution "problems," operate in PuEMEs to militate against redistributions those who favor PuEMEs would find objectionable.

8. Alternatively we could pay people their salary whether they are working, in training, or in formal educational programs.

9. If asked we expect most would testify that their "school" time had been more enjoyable than their "work" time. But those who receive a greater than average share of education are usually as quick to forget this fact as they were happy to benefit from it. In any case, in public enterprise economies the fiscal assumptions are largely fulfilled, and education is "public" to a great extent in many private enterprise economies as well.

10. No doubt Nozick and others attracted to this maxim would object to our formulation. They would probably insist on something like: from each according to his or her genetic and property inheritance, to each according to his or her genetic and property inheritance; or better still, from each according to his or her productive assets, to each according to the full contribution of his or her productive assets. And by their assets Nozick and followers would mean both their personal abilities and the potential contribution of the nonhuman assets they own. We do not wish to quibble, but think there is a meaningful sense in which the use of someone's human capabilities must come "from" that person, whereas the use of physical objects requires that nothing come "from" those deemed their owners.

11. Of course, the more usual phrasing is: (3') from each according to ability, to each according to work, and (4') from each according to ability, to each according to need. But the interpretation of 3' has been the subject of great controversy among Marxists and all concerned with "postcapitalist" economies. If one means by "work" what we call loosely "effort," meaning some appropriate combination of time and intensity of labor along with degree of disagreeableness—then 3' is merely another wording of 3. But if one means by "work" "the productivity of one's efforts as determined by the conditions of the economy and one's genetic and accumulated human assets," as those we have described elsewhere as "coordinator apologists" interpret 3', then 3' is another wording of maxim 2, and should be relabeled 2'. While there has never been much doubt about the meaning of 4', traditionally Marxism has viewed increases in economic productivity to the point of nonscarcity as the key to its implementation. We regard this self-delusion at best, and at worst an attempt to deflect rightful impatience and resentment on the part of those disadvantaged during the supposed "transition." For both ecological and sociological reasons the traditional Marxist vision of how economies might arrive at 4 is misleading. In our view, the key to a "transition" to 4 is a lengthy period of solidarity building in 3.

12. Which is not to say powerful political pressure may not be mounted by those with greater "human capital" in PuEMEs to reprivatize payments to nonhuman productive assets, as can be observed in China and the Soviet Union today. After all, the fact that PuEMEs place limits on individuals' accumulation of wealth and their ability to pass on wealth to their heirs will not go unchallenged by those who deem themselves "fettered."

13. In John Roemer, *A General Theory of Exploitation and Class* (Cambridge, Mass.: Harvard University Press, 1982), he effectively defines "capitalist" exploitation as income distributions that express Maxim 1, and "socialist" exploitation as income distributions that express Maxim 2. In his terms we find "socialist" exploitation no more justifiable than "capitalist" exploitation. In fact, in societies created by movements

seeking social justice, the historical rather than purely ethical imperative to eliminate inequalities is even stronger in our view! But because socialist movements have historically sought economic justice as one of their principal goals, we reject Roemer's terminology as inappropriate. For us Maxim 3 corresponds to economic justice, fairness, or the absence of economic exploitation—one of the principal historical goals of socialist movements. And income distributions expressive of Maxim 3 would not contain what Roemer calls "socialist" exploitation. The undeniable fact that such exploitation exists in societies that are commonly called "socialist" is simply evidence that they fail to correspond to the societies envisioned by the socialist movements that may have inspired them, and that such societies are labeled inappropriately. We would remind those tempted to accuse us of confusing socialism with communism that Maxim 3 is quite different from Maxim 4, which corresponds to human solidarity—a social relation beyond fairness. Which is not to say that the trust created by a lengthy history of fairness is not the most likely "transition" to solidarity. We might add that recently John Roemer has offered a persuasive argument against the morality of what he terms "socialist exploitation" as well as "capitalist exploitation." See John Roemer, *Free to Lose* (Cambridge, Mass.: Harvard University Press, 1988), chaps. 5, 9, and 10; idem, "Equality of Talent," *Economics and Philosophy* 1 (Fall 1986); and idem, "Equality of Resources Implies Equality of Welfare," *Quarterly Journal of Economics* 101 no. 4 (November 1986): 751-84.

14. Ariel Rubinstein, "Perfect Equilibrium in a Bargaining Model," *Econometrica* 50 (1982): 97-110; and Gil Skillman, Jr., "Sequential Bargaining in Capitalist Firms," working paper no. 88-28, Department of Economics, Brown University (November 1988).

15. For example, in the 1970s it was well known in the Washington, D.C., area that private consulting firms working on defense projects had to pay a "wage premium" for professional workers in comparison to firms that consulted only on civilian contracts.

16. Until the recent work of John Roemer in *A General Theory of Exploitation and Class*, who would be employers and who would be employees was determined exogenously in Marxist analyses. In most cases it was simply assumed that some small group of individuals owned all the means of production and everyone else was free only in the sense that they were free to work for whichever of these employers would have them. Roemer's endogenous determination of "class" position based only on the assumption of an unequal initial distribution of wealth is unique in the Marxist approach to this matter. Roemer's work in this regard is provocative and illuminating, the frenzied rejection from Marxist officialdom notwithstanding.

17. After all, theories of capitalist "crisis," such as the theory of the "tendency for the rate of profit to fall" and "under consumption" theories, which have long enamored Marxists, would merit no attention if individual capitalists could always be counted on to behave in their class' best interests. We say this without implying that after careful consideration most of these theories merit much attention in any case. Our point is simply that if capitalists were assumed to be capable of conspiring to always act in their class' interests, such crises would be prima facie impossible.

18. We do not reproduce Reich's formal demonstration of this result since we will re-derive this result and others in a more general model below. See Michael Reich, "Models of Class Conflict and Racial Inequality Within the Firm" in *Racial Inequality* (Princeton, N.J.: Princeton University Press, 1981), 204-15, appendix to chap. 5, for Reich's demonstration.

19. We are suggesting here that traditional theorists might "certify" Reich's criticism as theoretically unassailable, but dismiss it as insignificant in practical terms. This would be similar to the rebuttal Keynesians offered to Pigou's argument that falling prices would raise real assets and, thereby, raise private consumption, eventually lifting economies out of "liquidity traps." Keynesians "certified" Pigou's logic, but challenged the empirical significance of the "Pigou Effect," arguing that there would be many red faces if we all held our breath and waited for the "Pigou Effect" to save the day.

20. When we use the term "real wage," we mean payment per unit of work effort, so the "real wage" incorporates both payment and "extraction." For example, the real wage would fall if payment declined or extraction increased. Since inflation is not a phenomenon we treat, there should be no confusion with the other (more common) sense in which "real wage" is used.

21. None of which would be any surprise to previous contributors to the conflict theory, nor to most traditional theorists.

22. We do not mean to rule out the possibility implicit in Reich's analysis that present work activity can affect present characteristics. But in our view, it is far more plausible that important effects would be felt in the future. In any case there are many more periods in the future than in the present, so the total future effects are likely to be greater than the present effects.

23. In another sense the human characteristic transforming effects of work activity matter to employees. Since characteristics "parameterize" preferences, work activity has a preference-developing effect as well as a preference-fulfilling affect. While traditional theory is blind to the preference-developing effects of economic activities in general, we can easily lump these effects together with the preference-fulfilling effects commonly discussed as job satisfaction—or lack thereof. We do not

emphasize this aspect of the situation here because, as with preference fulfillment effects, employers have no reason to care one way or another about these effects. Except for the fact that workers may be willing to accept lower wages for greater preference-developing effects, employers have no interest in the matter. The assumption of competitive labor markets can be interpreted as guaranteeing compensating market wage differentials for these effects, but in any case employers have no "axes" of their own "to grind."

24. The reader should not confuse a degree of endogeneity with a degree of indeterminacy. As we will see, perfect information, competitive models permit no indeterminacy in wage or effort determination. But part of the "determinate" outcome is an endogenously determined wage-effort effect that derives from employer manipulation of conditions he or she controls in the production process. Moreover, we demonstrate that this "determinate" outcome is socially inefficient.

25. So far these are rebuttals to other's formulation of the "conflict theory" of the labor process under private ownership.

26. In many, if not all, actual, historical, private enterprise settings there are a number of deficiencies that our generous assumptions have permitted to pass unchallenged. We had every intention of organizing the "debate" in this way, but take this opportunity to remind the reader of the rarified theoretical world we are traveling in!

27. Traditional theory confirms this interpretation in the form of the zero profit assumption in competitive, steady state models.

28. Again, this is consistent with traditional assertions to the same effect. Interestingly enough, Marxist authors such as John Roemer who abstract from the difference between labor power and labor and stipulate competitive labor markets come to the same conclusion. The isomorphism between Roemer's "Labor Market Island," in which those with financial capital hire wage labor, and "Credit Market Island," in which those with financial capital lend it to those without, is an excellent example of the effect of abstracting from one of the two distinguishing features of what most call capitalism—namely the institution of private ownership and management of the means of production. See Roemer's *General Theory of Exploitation and Class.*

29. While it is not relevant to the present argument, we seriously doubt that if employees ever even approximated this degree of power over employers they would "choose" to maintain private enterprise market institutions. At a minimum there would be every incentive to opt for an employee-managed, public enterprise market economy of the kind we discussed in the preceding chapter. And, in our opinion, once they understood the deficiencies of market institutions they would opt for some system of participatory planning in conjunction with public enterprise.

30. Whether we have "homogeneous" labor of a single category and productivity or "heterogeneous" labor of different categories and/or productivities is irrelevant. When we talk of "net product" that under one set of conditions would go entirely to employees and under another set of conditions would go entirely to employers, this "net product" could be divided up among one, or more than one, category of employees, who could receive the same or quite different wage rates.

31. Admittedly, this is not a particularly "traditional" view of financial capital. Ultimately financial capital is simply credit—the willingness of some agents in the economy to trust other agents' promises of repayment. In this light the "supply" of financial capital is not a fixed number but a supply schedule with a degree of elasticity. Put this way, our proposition becomes that competitive credit markets (which are merely the "flip side" of competitive labor markets) do not guarantee an infinitely elastic supply of credit at a rate of interest that is only infinitesimally positive. Traditional theorists no doubt would object there is no reason to believe credit would not be infinitely elastic at an infinitesimal interest rate in a steady-state world inhabited by immortals rendered risk free by the full knowledge assumption. Perhaps, but can't we then be excused for considering a world in which some put others to work without expectation of any return for themselves somewhat "rarified"? Notice that whether the credit derives from employers' own wherewithal or from others who finance "entrepreneurs" seeking to expand activities with positive returns beyond the limits of their own wherewithal is of no consequence. It is still a matter of whether some agents in the economy are willing to put others to work with no expectation of return for themselves.

32. Admittedly, it is possible to rephrase this conclusion in a way that appears to preserve the conclusions of traditional theory. If the zero rate of profit assumption is taken as a proxy for complete domination of employee over employer with regard to the conflicts of interest between them, it is possible to continue to insist that under traditional assumptions, which include a zero long-run rate of profit, private employers' choice of technology and reward structures will be Pareto optimal and nondiscriminatory. But the conclusion can now be seen for the trivial tautology it is. Once a zero rate of profit is seen to stand for complete labor dominance, it is trivial that employers cannot do anything other than what their employees would wish them to do! Of course we have "producer sovereignty"—all powerful employees would be irrational to permit anything less. Similarly, it would be irrational of all-powerful and all-knowing employees to permit themselves to be manipulated by discriminatory ploys into a situation in which they have less than complete control.

33. To see this, imagine an economy in which there are millions of employees and millions of employers, complete mobility of both labor and

capital, and job information available to all at electronic speeds—i.e., indisputably competitive labor markets. If employees everywhere were characterized by complete knowledge of production procedures, full solidarity with one another, a strong conviction that only those who actually work deserve reward, and a great amount of energy and militancy for pursuing their convictions, the normal rate of profit might well approach zero. On the other hand, if employees are largely ignorant of how to carry out production without direction and supervision, suspicious and antagonistic toward one another, receptive to employers' claims to substantial rewards, and totally devoid of militancy, it is inconceivable that the normal rate of profit in the economy would not be significantly positive.

34. The choice of material input and output mixes, a principal concern of traditional theory, is one obvious example where nothing is lost by abstracting from the strength of employers' bargaining positions vis-a-vis their employees.

35. Presumably, few would argue this assumption is without interest given the history of "real world" private enterprise economies!

36. One might conclude from this that traditional theorists interested in preserving the accuracy of their conclusions would be honor-bound to root for employees to consolidate their power over employers, for otherwise "producer sovereignty" and "productivity-based wages" will not obtain. At a minimum, they should point out the illogic of highly prominent claims to the contrary, namely that reducing labor's bargaining strength will improve the "efficiency" of the U.S. economy!

37. It does not concern us if it is the "immediate" employer who earns positive profits or an "indirect employer" in the form of a financial backer who receives the positive profits as interest payments from the "immediate" employer.

38. Which is not to say we believe employees would be best off doing nothing, if they could get away with it, or that employees could not gain positive satisfaction from work efforts they knew to be socially productive and fairly distributed.

39. We are not speaking of Gintis and Katzner here, since their point was precisely the implausibility of their sufficient conditions.

40. Not all public enterprise, employee-managed economies are the same. For present purposes the important features are: (1) The employees are empowered to manage the enterprise either directly or through delegates of their choosing, and (2) the well-being of every employee is directly affected by the performance of his or her fellow employees. The latter might be because the performance of fellow employees affects one's income or because it affects the burdensomeness of one's work assignments. Both public enterprise, employee-managed, market economies

(PuEEMMEs), and public enterprise, employee-managed, decentrally planned economies (PuEMDPEs) meet these conditions. While Bowles favors the former and we favor the latter, the differences are not important to the issue at hand.

41. Fellow productive employees might also be in a better position to detect malfeasance than supervisory employees who are not engaged in productive activity. But this effect implies asymmetric knowledge about productive possibilities on the part of employers (or their supervisors) and employees. And while we believe this assumption is frequently reasonable, we also believe, as did Bowles, that there is an argument for inefficiency independent of asymmetric knowledge of production. Therefore, we waive the point for the same methodological reasons Bowles did.

42. By "strictly welfare theoretic terms," we mean explanations resting entirely on the assumption of pursuit of rational, individual self-interest under particular circumstances, without implying that actual human behavior is not considerably more complex.

43. Translated into traditional terms, empathetic preferences are characterized by positive direct externalities—I am happier if you are happier.

44. Presumably most would agree it is not irrational, for instance, to neglect the interests of one's employer more than the interests of one's family and friends even if there is greater opportunity to shirk in the latter case. Our paradigm and concepts help explain why this is the case. For a formal demonstration of the argument in terms of the new paradigm see the last two sections of this chapter.

45. For a fuller discussion of these issues see Michael Albert et al., *Liberating Theory* (Boston: South End Press, 1986).

46. To his credit Reich notes that both possibilities exist within his model. But Reich takes a strong stand that in the United States, white workers have lost more than they have gained from racial discrimination. For someone who argues the opposite case, see Michael J. Carter, "Competition and Segmentation in Internal Labor Markets," *Journal of Economic Issues* 15 (December 1982): 1063-1077. Unlike Reich, Carter errs in thinking the case for net gains to white employees can be proved theoretically. On the other hand, we do not find Reich's empirical evidence to the contrary conclusive and retain an open mind on the balance of effects in the U.S. case. But the actual outcome during a particular period in the U.S. is neither here nor there as far as the general theory of such relations is concerned.

47. For an excellent assessment of the evidence with respect to economic discrimination against women in the U.S., see the series published by National Academy of the Sciences Press, Washington, D.C.: Donald Trieman and Heidi Hartman, eds., *Women, Work, and Wages* (1981); Barbara Reskin, ed., *Sex Segregation in the Workplace: Trends, Explana-*

tions, Remedies (1984); Heidi Hartman, ed., *Comparable Worth: New Directions for Research* (1985); and Barbara Reskin and Heidi Hartman, eds., *Women's Work, Men's Work: Sex Segregation on the Job* (1986).

48. There are additional reasons, in the real world, why racial and sexual discrimination rooted in spheres of social life outside the economy will necessarily bias economic relations as well. See Albert et al., *Liberating Theory* for discussion and references.

49. If those released remain unemployed, and the quantity or quality of outputs resulting from less skill-intensive or less skill-dispersed technologies declines, there is, of course, a loss from society's point of view.

50. For private employer "economizing" of scarce productive skills to be fully consistent with the social interest, the relative wages of different categories of labor must obviously be accurate measures of relative scarcities and job satisfactions. While in the argument that follows we waive the point, there is no reason to believe the kinds of biases we have described in market prices do not apply to wages as well. At a minimum, wages must be indirectly affected by biases in other prices. And the discussion to come will make clear that in private enterprise economies there is every reason to expect factors other than productivities and desirabilities enter into wage determination in any case.

51. In this light, the incentive for employers to engage in non-job-specific, on-the-job training resides in the absence of labor markets sufficiently competitive and "tight" to generate full compensating wage differentials for more skilled employees who remain with the employer who "trained" them. Alternatively, such programs are means of attracting better employees, but in this status they are simply one among many "come-ons."

52. It is possible for excessive fragmentation to diminish productivity, as many studies of quality control problems indicate. This does not negate our point in the least. It simply means that in some situations a profit-maximizing employer may have to weigh the trade-off between the profit-increasing "bargaining power" effect and the profit-decreasing "productivity" effect of increased fragmentation.

53. One would have to examine what circumstances would generate such a condition. But seniority rules, firm-specific skills, and pension contribution/benefit structures are among a number of possibilities that have been explored.

54. This latter effect was ignored in Reich's model, but as we explained, employer bargaining power is just as likely to affect wages as effort extracted. We remind those who might think we have contradicted our assumption of a competitively determined wage rate by making wages partially dependent on employer bargaining power of our previous argument that the assumption of "competitive labor markets" does not settle

the issue of wage and effort determination. The entire discussion is premised on the assumption of some degree of endogeneity in the determination of those issues over which employers and employees have conflicting interests. If there is any endogeneity—if the competitive labor market only establishes limits on the wage/effort package that results—it is just as appropriate to recognize the potential effects of employer bargaining power on wages paid as on effort contracted. After all, if there is no degree of endogeneity, there is no possibility of employer bargaining power affecting effort since in this case the competitive labor market would presumably determine not only the wage rate, W_k, but the degree of effort that would expended per hour as well. It is simply that we are not used to writing down that part in traditional notation. Put differently, any who would object to stipulating the wage rate as a partial function of employer bargaining power should object to writing effort as a function of bargaining power as well.

55. It is clear that the nontraditional future wage effect (wage enhancing for work type-1, wage reducing for work type-2) has only a distributional impact. Nothing more is produced and no additional effort or time is expended. But the nontraditional effort effect does affect future output. However, this is not a "social benefit" because the increased output from additional effort is the result of increased effort from employees. While increased effort is of no consequence to employers who do not have to pay for it, it must be added to social costs. If we can assume that competitive labor markets have succeeded in equating the marginal disutility of work done with the wage paid, the increased future output is exactly canceled by the increased future disutility of the extra effort to be expended.

56. Since the rate of labor turnover varies dramatically in different private enterprise economies around the world and between different industries within those economies, there are obvious possibilities for empirically testing the strength of this effect.

57. "Among employees" is important here, since the argument is that perceptions of fair treatment of employees vis-a-vis one another, or the absence of unfair "privileges" among employees, contributes to employee solidarity. This is not inconsistent with the claim that employee perceptions of unfair distribution of duties and rewards between owners and employees contributes to employee solidarity as well.

58. The discrimination may be on the basis of race, gender, sexual preference, or any other social characteristic that generates suspicion, mistrust, and hostility.

59. The phrasing in parentheses is the more common terminology of those who think in terms of the conflict school. We supply the translation for those unfamiliar with either semantic.

60. The sum of terms in the second line of expressions (8.1) and (8.2), the nontraditional effects, are precisely what summarizes the effects of such practices on employer profits.

61. The proof is immediate applying Theorem 6.6 to Theorem 8.1 written for period $(t+k)$.

62. Obviously these are not exactly the "most favorable institutional conditions imaginable," since we do not conclude that PrEMEs are cybernetic miracles and efficiency machines.

CHAPTER 9. CENTRAL PLANNING

1. Enrico Barone, "Ministry of Production," in *Collectivist Economic Planning,* F. A. Hayek, ed. (London: Routledge Press, 1935).

2 Later, we will analyze procedures by which planners might accumulate such information.

3. A number of texts elaborate the theory and various solution algorithms of different kinds of mathematical programming problems. See G. Hadley, *Linear Programming* (Reading, Mass.: Addison Wesley, 1962); idem, *Nonlinear and Dynamic Programming* (Reading, Mass.: Addison Wesley, 1964); Willard Zanguil, *Nonlinear Programming: A United Approach* (Englewood Cliffs, N.J.: Prentice Hall, 1969); and Michael Intriligator, *Mathematical Optimization and Economic Theory* (Englewood Cliffs, N.J.: Prentice Hall, 1971).

4. Perhaps it bears pointing out that only final consumers use savings and loans in such a system. Production units do not borrow the "savings" of the "household sector" to "invest." The S&L's are simply clearinghouses for final consumers who wish to contract with one another concerning transfers of purchasing power through time.

5. Obviously, if wages affect work effort or if wage rates affect the educational and training preferences of individuals, which in turn affect the number of people who become qualified in different categories, the Central Planning Board cannot ignore efficiency effects when setting wage rates. But traditional welfare theory equates labor hired with labor done, and in Model 4 the availabilities of different kinds of labor in different time periods are givens. Alternatively, in some versions of central planning the supplies of different kinds of labor are "planned," just as the economy is planned, according to relative productivities and educational production coefficients. In either of these cases wages can be set without affecting the supplies of different kinds of labor.

6. This illustrates an interesting contrast between "individual" flexibility— the freedom of individual personnel departments and employees to

negotiate—and "social" flexibility—the range of labor income distributions the system can generate. Of course, even under labor market system 3b, a system of one-time-only, positive and negative lump-sum taxes for all individuals in all periods that does not affect the "speed of the steeds" preserves the validity of the third fundamental welfare theorem for PuECPEs.

7. If the $v_i(t)$'s and $w_l(t)$'s in the social welfare function are determined independently of any prices and wage rates that may develop under any of the goods and labor market systems discussed previously, then those markets, prices, and wages have no effect on the production plan. That is, they have no effect on how much of each final good will be produced and how much of each kind of labor service will be used.

8. We mentioned in chapter 4 that Gintis proved Pareto optimality could be achieved in the general equilibrium of a particular type of economy even if people's preferences were endogenous. (Herb Gintis, "Alienation and Power: Towards a Radical Welfare Economics" [Ph.D. diss., Harvard University, May 1969], 282, Theorem 5). His model stipulated a production sector of the economy that adjusted efficiently to changing price signals for final goods and "primary" factors and a Central Planning Board that announced a particular equilibrium price path for final goods and primary factors that the production sector and individuals with endogenous preferences would react to. This model is very close to our own model of a centrally planned economy with free markets in labor services and final goods, where the weights for different arguments in the social welfare function are taken from their respective market prices. Rather than reproduce Gintis' proof under essentially similar assumptions, we refer the reader to his efforts for a demonstration that a centrally planned economy with free markets in labor and final goods can achieve optimality if individuals have perfect knowledge of their own endogenous preferences, even if the Central Planning Board does not.

9. E. Malinvaud, "Decentralized Procedures for Planning," in *Activity Analysis in the Theory of Growth and Planning,* E. Malinvaud and M. Bacharach, eds. (London: Macmillan, 1967), 170.

10. While dealing more "realistically" with information problems, it can be argued that all the procedures we review next are still "naive" regarding "incentive" problems. Specifically, all the procedures implicitly assume that local management responds truthfully to CPB queries. We discuss the "naivite" of this assumption later.

11. Benjamin Ward, *The Socialist Economy: A Study of Organizational Alternatives* (New York: Random House, 1967), 45.

12. Ibid. If c is our column vector of final demands, or net output, the Central Planning Board will have succeeded in finding the vector of gross outputs, $\mathbf{x}$, as: $c + Ac + AAc + \ldots = \mathbf{x}$.

13. Ibid., 45-56.

14. J. M. Montias, "Planning with Material Balances in Soviet-Type Economies," *American Economic Review* 49 no. 5 (December 1959): 963-85.

15. There are ways to ameliorate the deficiencies of material balances Ward does not discuss. (1) Planners need not wait until the final iteration to check if the planned gross outputs are feasible. After each iteration resource feasibility could be checked, since there is no point in further iterations once feasibility is violated. (2) After the first response from all sectors the central planners can calculate the input-output matrix for the economy by dividing each sector's input requests by the final demand for the sector. If they asked each sector to respond with primary as well as intermediate input needs to meet the final demand, they could similarly calculate the economy's primary input coefficient matrix. If the central planners knew the social welfare function, they could then use the input-output matrix and primary input coefficient matrix to solve the "social optimization problem." This would allow substitution between different goods in the vector of final demands in light of productive possibilities. But this procedure would still be inefficient in the case of multiple processes. And it resembles some aspects of more efficient procedures we discuss below more than it resembles the traditional practice of material balances in any case.

16. George Danzig and Philip Wolfe, "The Decomposition Algorithm for Linear Programs," *Econometrica* 29, no. 4 (October 1961): 767-78.

17. Leonid Hurwicz, "The Design of Mechanisms for Resource Allocation," in *Frontiers of Quantitative Economics*, Vol. 2, Michael D. Intriligator and D. A. Kendrick, eds. (Amsterdam: North Holland Publishing, 1974), 10.

18. Ibid.

19. William J. Baumol and Tibor Fabian, "Decomposition, Pricing for Decentralization and External Economies," *Management Science* 11 (September 1964): 1-32.

20. Hurwicz, "Design of Mechanisms," 11.

21. Malinvaud, "Decentralized Procedures," 170-208.

22. Hurwicz, "Design of Mechanisms," 15.

23. Malinvaud, "Decentralized Procedures," 174-75. Malinvaud's "utility function," $u(x)$ is our social welfare function. His "set of acceptable final consumption, X" is a feasibility constraint beyond what we posed in our model stipulating minimal quantities of food, shelter, clothing, etc. The rationale for such a feasibility constraint derives from requirements of work force survival.

24. Ibid., 177.

25. Ibid., 178.

26. J. Kornai and T. Liptak, "Two-Level Planning," *Econometrica* 33 no. 1 (January 1965): 141-69.

27. Hurwicz, "Design of Mechanisms," 11.

28. Ibid.

29. S. A. Marglin, "Information in Price and Command Systems of Planning," in *Public Economics*, J. Margolis and H. Guitton, eds. (London: Macmillan, 1969), 54-77.

30. Hurwicz, "Design of Mechanisms," 12.

31. G. M. Heal, "Planning Without Prices," *Review of Economic Studies* 36 (1969): 347-48.

32. J. H. Dreze and D. de la Vallee Poussin, "A Tatonnement Process for Guiding and Financing an Efficient Production of Public Goods," Core Discussion Papers No. 6922 (Belgium: Universite Catholique de Lourain, 1969).

33. E. Malinvaud, "The Theory of Planning for Individual and Collective Consumption," paper presented at the Symposium on the Problem of National Economy Modeling, Novosibirsk, 1970).

34. Hurwicz, "Design of Mechanisms," 17-18.

35. G. M. Heal, "Planning, Prices, and Increasing Returns," *Review of Economic Studies* 38 (1971): 281.

36. Hurwicz, "Design of Mechanisms," 12.

37. Heal, "Planning, Prices, and Increasing Returns," 281.

38. M. Aoki, "Two Planning Processes for an Economy with Production Externalities," Harvard Institute for Economic Research, discussion papers, no. 157 (Cambridge, Mass.: 1970).

39. Hurwicz, "Design of Mechanisms," 13.

40. T. C. Koopmans, "Analysis of Production as an Efficient Combination of Activities," in *Activity Analysis of Production and Allocation,* T. C. Koopmans, ed., Cowles Commission Monographs, no. 13, (New York 1951), 33-97.

41. Hurwicz, "Design of Mechanisms," 14.

42. P. A. Samuelson, "Market Mechanisms and Maximization," in *Collected Scientific Papers of Paul A. Samuelson,* vol. 1, J. E. Stiglitz, ed. (Cambridge, Mass.: MIT Press, 1966), 425-92.

43. K. J. Arrow and L. Hurwicz, "Decentralization and Computation in Resource Allocation," in *Essays in Economics and Econometrics*, R. W. Pfouts, ed. (Chapel Hill, N.C.: 1960), 34-104.

44. Hurwicz, "Design of Mechanisms," 14.

45. H. Uzawa, "Iterative Methods for Concave Programming," in *Studies in Linear and Nonlinear Programming*, K. Arrow, L. Hurwicz, and H. Uzawa, eds. (Stanford, Calif.: Stanford University Press, 1958), chap. 10.

46. Abram Bergson seems to be the first to have posed the relationship between central planners and plant managers as a principal-agent relationship. Abram Bergson, "Managerial Risks and Rewards in Public Enterprises," *Journal of Comparative Economics* 2, no. 3 (September 1978): 211-25. But Bergson did not work out the implications of moral hazard in this setting. However, Pak-Wai Liu, Kent Osband, Pamela Brown, Jeffrey Miller, and James Thornton have recently gone a long way toward doing so. See Pak-Wai Liu, "Moral Hazard and Incentives in a Decentralized Planning Environment," *Journal of Comparative Economics* 10, no. 2 (June 1986): 91-105; Kent Osband, "Speak Softly, but Carry a Big Stick: On Optimal Targets under Moral Hazard," *Journal of Comparative Economics* 11, no. 4 (December 1987): 584-95; P. C. Brown, J. Miller, and J. Thornton, "An Optimal Incentive Scheme for Planning with Targets," *Journal of Comparative Economics* 11, no. 4 (December 1987): 596-600; and Pak-Wai Liu, "Optimal Incentive Schemes with Targets: First Best or Second Best," *Journal of Comparative Economics* 11, no. 4 (December 1987): 601-602.

47. See M. Keren, "On the Tautness of Plans," *Review of Economic Studies* 39 (December 1972): 469-86; M. L. Weitzman, "The New Soviet Incentive Model," *Bell Journal of Economics* 7, no. 1 (Spring 1976): 251-57; J. P. Bonin, "On the Design of Managerial Incentive Structures in a Decentralized Planning Environment," *American Economic Review* 66, no. 4 (September 1976): 682-87; J. Bonin and A. Marcus, "Information, Motivation, and Control in Decentralized Planning: The Case of Discretionary Managerial Behavior," *Journal of Comparative Economics* 3, no. 3 (September 1979): 235-53; M. L. Weitzman, "The 'Ratchet Principle' and Performance Incentives," *Bell Journal of Economics* 11, no. 1 (Spring 1980): 302-308; B. Holmstrom, "Design of Incentive Schemes and the New Soviet Incentive Model," *European Economic Review* 17, no. 2 (February 1982): 127-48; and David Granick, "Institutional Innovation and Economic Management: The Soviet Incentive System, 1921 to the Present," in *Entrepreneurship in Imperial Russia and the Soviet Union*, G. Guroff, ed. (Princeton, N.J.: Princeton University Press, 1983), 223-57.

48. Liu, "Moral Hazard," 91.

49. Malinvaud, "Decentralized Procedures," 171.

50. According to our work in chapter 7, public enterprise market economies have been as deserving as private enterprise market economies of such status, even though they have been accorded it less often. In any case, the important conclusion here is that public enterprise, centrally planned economies merit such status as well under the rules of the "old debate."

51. If laboring activities, and "bads" as well as "goods" are included in the social welfare function—as they should be—each person would assign a positive or negative sign to each argument before assigning whatever number of personal points he or she wished to that argument. The important thing is simply that the sum of the absolute values of all votes cast by an individual would be equal to the number of points he or she were permitted to vote.

52. Recent discussions and "reforms" in the Soviet Union and elsewhere have made this point more than academic.

53. Hurwicz, "Design Mechanisms," 38-39.

54. Ibid., 22.

55. Ibid., 16.

56. This includes all the gradient methods discussed earlier.

57. M. L. Weitzman, "Iterative Multi-level Planning with Production Targets," *Econometrica* 38, no. 1 (1970): 54.

58. Ward, *Socialist Economy*, 64.

59. Industry Ministries and provincial planning boards form intervening layers between production units and the CPB, but do not change the essential characteristic Ward identifies as the defining trait of hierarchic organizations: "no participant, directly or indirectly, is both superior to and subordinate to another."

60. Ward, *Socialist Economy*, 102.

61. While we may be less daunted than some by the formidable literature detailing conceivable difficulties with majority rule, we by no means deny these problems. For an excellent interpretation of the technical literature the interested reader should consult Alfred F. MacKay, *Arrow's Theorem: The Paradox of Social Choice* (New Haven: Yale University Press, 1980). But for now we waive all such objections because we wish to focus on a different problem with voting specific to central planning.

62. This last assumption might be more justified for a voting procedure in which everyone has the same number of points to vote and must use them to vote for public and private goods at the same time, than for market institutions. But "gamesmanship," "voting paradoxes," and "external effects" are admittedly difficult problems for any allocative mechanism to deal with successfully. While we allude to our belief that ideas from the literature on incentive-compatible mechanisms can be incorporated into a decentralized planning procedure that has more desirable properties than markets and central planning in our conclusion, we abstract from these problems here as irrelevant to our critique of central planning.

63. To argue that central planning is socially inefficient in this regard it is actually necessary to show that work in centrally planned economies,

regardless of occupation, will be characterized by less self-management than is possible under some alternative decision-making structure. The situation is completely analogous to the one we treated in chapter 8 regarding Bowles' claim that PrEMEs are inefficient because they aggravate malfeasance. The charge of social inefficiency always implies that there is some way of avoiding the problem—a feasible alternative that, at least, ameliorates the problem. We do not spell out the feasible alternative we prefer here, because in fact, demonstrating that our alternative model of participatory, decentralized planning is both feasible and optimal entails a complicated argument that we are still in the process of formalizing. But for now PuEEMMEs are sufficient as an alternative decision-making structure that provides work characterized by more self-management than PuECPEs. So the alternative of PuEEMMEs renders the charge that PuECPEs are inefficient in this regard complete.

64. If actual centrally planned economies provide no self-managed work opportunities, on any terms, for the vast majority of citizens, then the bias is even more extreme than we have assumed, and our case is all the stronger.

65. This would be the finding of traditional welfare theory if it were not encumbered by ideological biases, or if it were applied by the likes of a Leonid Hurwicz or Kenneth Arrow.

66. For our own thoughts on these subjects see Michael Albert and Robin Hahnel, "Ticket to Ride: New Locations on the Class Map" in *Between Labor and Capital*, Pat Walker, ed. (Boston: South End Press, 1979). Besides other essays in Walker's collection, and particularly the lead essay by John and Barbara Ehrenreich, see also Donald Stabile, *Prophets of Order* (Boston, South End Press, 1984), for an analysis of the development of the coordinator class in the U.S.

67. For full treatment see: Michael Albert and Robin Hahnel, *Marxism and Socialist Theory* (Boston: South End Press, 1981); idem, *Socialism Today and Tomorrow* (Boston: South End Press, 1981); and idem, *Political Economy of Participatory Economics*, (Princeton, N.J.: Princeton University Press, forthcoming, 1990).

68. This has been the dominant view of international Trotskyism and Social Democracy over the years. See the writings of E. H. Carr, Alec Nove, and Isaac Deutscher for high-quality examples.

69. See the more recent writings of Paul Sweezy and Daniel Singer for high-quality examples of this interpretation of the Soviet Union.

70. Howard Sherman, *Foundations of Radical Political Economics* (Armonk, N.Y.: M. E. Sharpe, 1987), 286-87.

71. See Albert and Hahnel, *Socialism Today and Tomorrow*.

CHAPTER 10. CONCLUSION

1. As our analysis in part 3 indicates, "inappropriate assumptions" would be a more accurate qualification here. But regardless of their relevance, they are the assumptions typical of the traditional paradigm.

2. We are speaking here of properties of different theoretical models studied at the "highest" level of abstraction, that is, abstracting from information and incentive problems. As we discussed in chapter 9, the "modern" debate among traditional theorists is largely concerned with differences of this kind between economic systems. That is, the "modern" debate is conducted at a lower level of abstraction than the "old" debate. As we indicated, one reason for this shift might well be because at the highest theoretical levels traditional theory cannot meaningfully distinguish among any of the theoretical models studied.

3. We hasten to reiterate that under the usual assumptions not only will PrEMEs be (mis)perceived as containing no such biases, but PuEMEs and PuECPEs will be (mis)perceived as having no such biases as well.

4. We do not intend this as a criticism of Groves et al. We see no reason why societies heavily endowed with graduates of higher education should not enjoy the luxury of a division of intellectual labor that includes a role for those with a special talent for formal, abstract theorizing. We merely point out that there was no rush of economists with a more political "bent" to promote the theorists of incentive-compatible mechanisms for Nobel consideration!

5. For our technical formulation of a new economic model see Michael Albert and Robin Hahnel, *Political Economy of Participatory Economics*, (Princeton, N.J.: Princeton University Press, forthcoming, 1990). For a detailed account of the social relations of the new type economy we propose as it might look when implemented in the U.S., see Michael Albert and Robin Hahnel, *Looking Forward: Humane Economics in our Lifetimes*, (Boston, Mass.: South End Press, forthcoming, 1990).

INDEX

Absolute collective, 122
accommodation, between social spheres, 132
acquisitive instinct, 199-200
activity possibility set, 381n.33
activity space: consciousness and, 124-25; endogenous preference model, 143-44, 381n.2
additive separability, in centrally planned economies, 312-14
adjustment dynamics, markets and, 206
aggregate market expansions and contractions, 217, 394nn.24-25
"alienated labor," 35, 223
allocative mechanism, 219-20
Alperowitz, Gar, 225
American Economic Review, 5, 42-44, 104-105
anarchy, economic institutions and, 129, 378n.22
antisocial behavior, 196, 389n.51
Aoki's quantity-guided procedure, 316
Arrow, Kenneth, 234-35; on economic discrimination, 46-53; on employment discrimination, 265-66; on impossibility theorem, 25-26; on unrestricted bargaining, 397n.59
Arrow-Debreu economic model, 353n.2
artifacts in social institutions, 127, 378n.21
asymmetrical information: malfeasance in PuEEMEs, 278, 407n.41; in private enterprise market economies (PrEMEs), 261-63
"at least as preferred to" consumption set, 158
Austrian School's market perfection theorem, 391n.3
authoritarianism: centrally planned economies and, 319, 326-28, 415n.59; class theory and, 337-38; snowballing of, in centrally planned economy, 333-36
authoritative allocation model, 40-41
availability of commodities, endogenous preferences and, 93-94
axioms of rationality, species needs and potentials, 118

Babbage, Henry, 39, 281
Babbage Principle, 39
bargaining power, of employees, 53-55; wage rates and, 288-93, 408n.54
"bargaining strength" enhancing effect of technology, 283-84, 408n.52
bartering, 395n.32
Becker, Gary, 49
behavior and laws of evolution, 115-16
behaviorist school of psychology, 116-17, 377n.8

419

exchange relations, production function and, 33-34, 357n.3

expectations: consciousness and, 129; income distribution and, 254, 399n.2

exploitation, class and, 402n.16

external effect exceptionality, 4, 7; in centrally planned economies, 329-30, 415n.62; incentives for negative effects, 232-33; public goods and, 62-68, 227-29

external labor markets, 286-88

Externalities and public goods, 7; Groves' theory on, 68-72; Hunt's theory of, 61-68; influence of welfare theory on, 72-73; Pareto optimality and, 235-40; prevalence of, 227-46; social efficiency theorem and, 158; theory of, 59-60

extraction, competitive labor markets and, 271-72

Fixed tastes and Pareto optimality, 81-82

Flexibility Theorem: in centrally planned economies, 308, 410n.6; private enterprise and, 254-57, 347-48, 400n.5

flow variables, in economic sphere, 133-34; formalization of, 135-36

fragmentation of employees, productivity and, 285-86, 408n.52

Frankfurt school of economics, 377n.11

freedom, need for, 119-20

free market mechanism: efficiency in, 240; labor markets, in centrally planned economies, 307-308; state-managed market economies and, 214, 393n.19

"free rider" problem, 4, 7; incentive-compatible mechanism, 70-72; market failure and, 346-47; public finance theory, 60; taxation systems and, 240

Friedman, Milton, 187

functional-structural social analysis, 104

Gedanken experiment in preference structure, 95

general equilibria: centrally planned economies and, 386n.35; endogenous preferences and, 152, 342-43; existence theorem, 153-57, 383n.11; lacking in employee-managed market economies, 209-10, 213, 391n.6; in traditional welfare theory, 339-41

"general law of capitalist accumulation," 394n.24

genetic advantages: flexibility theorem and, 254, 400n.5; human development and, 115-16, 377n.6; income differential and, 258-59, 401n.10

Georgescu-Roegen theory, 81, 371n.45

Giddens, Anthony, 183, 379n.23

Gintis, Herb, 39-42; on employment discrimination, 268; on endogenous preferences, 146-47, 342-43, 382n.4; institutional economics, 102; on Mill's preference theory, 78-79; on multiple equilibria, 159-60, 383n.21; neoclassical welfare theory, 15; preference development, 101; profit maximization and social efficiency, 276-78;

purposeful preference molding, 89-99, 371n.45; taste change and welfare analysis, 371n.43

goods: developmental effects of, 182, 386n.34; distribution of, in centrally planned economic models, 303-305. *See also* Public goods

governments, resource allocation and, 237-38

gradient procedures, in centrally planned economies, 316-17

"greatest happiness" criterion for social good, 14

Groves, Theodore, 68-72

Guttkind, Erich, 122

Haavelmo, Trygve, 81

Habermas, Jurgen, 377n.11

habit formation: endogenous preferences and, 382n.4; preference development and, 182, 386n.34; preference fulfillment, 119. *See also* myopic habit formation

Hammond, Peter, 69, 81, 100; on endogenous preference, 146, 382n.4

happiness, welfare theory and, 120. *See also* well-being

Harrod, Roy, 102

Hasanyi, 81, 371n.45

"hatchet" efficiency theory, 17

"hedonistic calculus," neoclassical welfare theory and, 21-22

Hicks-Kaldor Scitovsky analysis of endogenous preferences, 96

hierarchies: artificial, in homogeneous labor force, 281; authoritarian roles in centrally planned economies, 326-28; control of capitalism and, 37-38;

nonartificial, 285-86; of preferences (pleasures), 14-15, 30-31

Hobbesian hypothesis, laws of evolution and, 115-16

homogeneous labor force, artificial hierarchies in, 281

Horvat, Branko, 211-12

"human capital" in economic institutions, 254-57, 259-60, 400n.4, 401n.12

human center: defined, 127; evolutionary laws and, 144-27; rational preference development and, 183; and snowballing nonoptimality in private enterprise, 294; social spheres and, 130-32

human characteristics, 116-17, 377nn.6, 8; competitive labor market and, 274-75, 405n.30; conflict of interest and, 268-72; conflict theory and, 267-68, 403n.20; dynamic vs. static view of, 189-90; group aggregation, 138; importance of in private enterprise market economies (PrEMEs), 267-68, 403n.20; profit maximization and social efficiency, 277-78; "rational adjustment of," 251-52; social institutions and, 123; variety and, 192-93

human development: alternative approaches to, 194-202; contractarian approach to, 196-201; evaluation of, 184-202; evolutionary laws and, 115-16, 376n.4; human nature and, 185-94; Huxley vs. Kropotkin on, 114-15; self-management and, 185-89; snowballing theorem, 163-65; social organizations and, 113-14; solidarity and, 189-92; species survival and